BECOMING EVIL

BECOMING EVIL

How Ordinary People
Commit Genocide
and Mass Killing

JAMES WALLER

OXFORD
UNIVERSITY PRESS

2002

OXFORD

UNIVERSITY PRESS

Oxford   New York

Auckland   Bangkok   Buenos Aires   Cape Town   Chennai
Dar es Salaam   Delhi   Hong Kong   Istanbul   Karachi   Kolkata
Kuala Lumpur   Madrid   Melbourne   Mexico City   Mumbai   Nairobi
São Paulo   Shanghai   Singapore   Taipei   Tokyo   Toronto

and an associated company in Berlin

Copyright © 2002 by James Waller

Published by Oxford University Press, Inc.
198 Madison Avenue, New York, New York 10016

www.oup.com

Oxford is a registered trademark of Oxford University Press

The excerpt on pp. 51–54 from *Black Dog of Fate*, by Peter Balakian,
© 1997 by Peter Balakian, is reprinted by permission of
Basic Books, a member of Perseus Books, L.L.C.

Library of Congress Cataloging-in-Publication Data
Waller, James, 1961–
Becoming evil: how ordinary people commit genocide and mass killing / James Waller.
p. cm.
Includes bibliographical references (p.) and index.
ISBN 0-19-514868-1
1. Genocide—Psychological aspects.   2. Social psychology.   I. Title.
HV6322.7   W35   2002
364.15'1'019—dc21   2002070404

1   3   5   7   9   8   6   4   2

Printed in the United States of America
on acid-free paper

To the memory
of the more than 100 million
men, women, and children who have met a violent death
at the hands of their fellow human beings
in the past century.

FOREWORD

The Holocaust was a man-made event, as have been the many other acts of genocide and mass killing that stain our history. Indeed, one of the most haunting questions that these acts of mass killing pose to us all is, quite simply, "How were they humanly possible?" When confronting the awesome task of trying to explain the behavior of the genocidal perpetrators, however, scholars have not reached any consensus. One group of answers to that inevitable question has focused on particularities. What culture, society, or nation, what ideology, historical prejudice, or ethnic hatred, what psychological profile or cluster of personality traits, what unusual situation or special circumstance is to be deemed the cause of such aberrant human behavior? The underlying assumption to this approach is that there is a fatal flaw, a major deviation from the norm, that must be discovered to account for it.

Given that most societies do not commit genocide and most people do not become genocidal killers, there is an intuitive common sense to such an approach. If "extraordinary evil" is not the norm either historically or in our everyday experience, then its source must be found in some abnormality particular to those peoples and societies that do perpetrate "extraordinary evil." Such a commonsense assumption is also comforting. We look for flaws in others, not latent potentials within ourselves. For surely "we" and "our" society could not do what the perpetrators and their societies have done.

There is a second approach, the one embraced by James Waller in this book, that takes as its starting point the challenge of understanding how on occasion "ordinary" people have committed "extraordinary evil." What basic aspects of human nature and tendencies of individual behavior, what commonplace mechanisms of social interaction, both within groups and between in-groups and out-groups, have on occasion come together with the fatal consequence that large numbers of ordinary people become genocidal perpetrators? The explanations that result from such an approach are inherently both universalistic and multicausal.

That many of the perpetrators of "extraordinary evil" were not exceptional people is not, of course, a new discovery. More than four decades ago, Raul Hilberg noted that the Holocaust perpetrators were drawn from a cross section of German society. And the crux of Adolf Eichmann's defense strategy was the attempt to disguise his own career as that of a minor cog in the machinery of destruction. Hannah Arendt's concept of the "banality of evil," derived from her observation of the Eichmann trial, has proved more durable than her conclusions about her star example. One decade ago I dubbed the killers of Reserve Police Battalion 101 "ordinary men." However, insofar as I attempted to bolster my empirically based study with conceptions and insights from social psychology, I made use of findings that dated mostly from the 1960s, especially the classic experiments of Stanley Milgram and Philip Zimbardo.

In recent years there has been another surge of interest by social and now evolutionary psychologists in studies relevant to understanding how "ordinary" people commit "extraordinary evil." One of the great merits of James Waller's book is that he provides invaluable summaries of this new research for scholars who wish to make use of such insights but whose own expertise lies elsewhere. Moreover, Waller's synthesis organizes these findings into an overall model that allows others to see just where these different findings fit into the major categories of explanation. Even those of us who have long advocated multicausal interpretations based on multidisciplinary scholarship can quickly see how partial and incomplete our previous attempts have been. James Waller expresses the modest hope that his model will stimulate further discussion. I think it is destined to be one of the foundations upon which further scholarship is based.

Christopher R. Browning
Frank Porter Graham Professor of History
University of North Carolina at Chapel Hill

PREFACE

"I Couldn't Do This to Someone"

June 1999. A small hillside village in southern Kosovo. Its name is Dobrodeljane, and it was home to hundreds of ethnic Albanians. It has been a virtual ghost town since March 25, the day after the NATO air strikes began. Now, nearly a month later, a trickle of families return to claim bodies and possessions. One family claims two bodies—one shot in the head, another with a pitchfork in the gut and a missing leg. Every one of Dobrodeljane's 170 houses has been destroyed or heavily damaged. Most were trashed by police and soldiers, who used them, then looted them and set them ablaze. There is no electricity or water. The shops are empty and stockpiles of food have been burned.

Sadri Sikaqi, sixty-five, and his wife Mihrie, sixty-two, pick over the ruins of their home, which they had rebuilt after their first house was destroyed in a battle between Serbian militiamen and ethnic Albanian guerrillas the previous August. More than a decade of repression has culminated in a three-month killing spree by the Yugoslav army and Serbian security forces. With this has come the expulsion and displacement of more than 855,000 people—most of whom are ethnic Albanians—forced to flee Kosovo in fear of their lives. Today, the immediacy of the threat is over. In its place, though, is the aftertaste of a world gone mad. How do we explain the existence, and persistence, of extraordinary human evil? What type of people could do this? Sikaqi, standing at the living room window with a view of his razed village, the concrete walls burned black, the bodies buried in the rubble, offers his own answer. "Only people who aren't human could do this. I couldn't do this to someone."[1]

Unfortunately, history is littered with examples of people who *could* do this to someone and *did*. According to Jewish-Christian tradition, the first time that death appeared in the world, it was murder: Cain slew Abel. "Two men," says Elie Wiesel, perhaps the most widely read writer on the Holocaust, "and one of them became a killer."[2] The book of Genesis goes on to record that Cain was banished from Eden. He subsequently founded our first city—in the land of Nod, east of Eden—and named it Enoch, after his firstborn son. Through Enoch, Cain's line continued and prospered. Thousands of years later, we all can be considered the children of Cain. At the very least, we bear the taint of the violent legacy he ushered into the world when he killed his brother.

Throughout human history, social conflict is ubiquitous. Wars erupt naturally everywhere humans are present. Since the Napoleonic Wars, we have fought an average of six international wars and six civil wars per *decade*. An average of three high-fatality struggles have been in action somewhere in the world at any moment since 1900. The four decades after the end of World War II saw 150 wars and only 26 days of world peace—and that does not even include the innumerable internal wars and police actions. Buried in the midst of all of our progress in the twentieth century are well over a 100 million persons who met a violent death at the hands of their fellow human beings. That is more than five times the number from the nineteenth century and more than ten times the number from the eighteenth century.[3]

Michael P. Ghiglieri, an anthropologist at the University of Northern Arizona, even contends that war vies with sex for the distinction of being the most significant process in human evolution. "Not only have wars shaped geopolitical boundaries and spread national ideologies," he writes, "but they also have carved the distributions of humanity's religions, cultures, diseases, technologies, and even genetic populations."[4]

There is no sign that we are on an ascendant trajectory out of the shadow of our work of decreation. At the close of the twentieth century, a third of the world's 193 nations were embroiled in conflict—nearly twice the Cold War level. The bipolar Cold War system has disintegrated into a system of "warm wars," with randomized conflicts popping up in all corners of an interdependent world. Army ret. maj. Andy Messing Jr., executive director of the conservative-oriented National Defense Council Foundation, warns that the growing proliferation of weapons of mass destruction and an increasing world population only add to the danger. In his words, "It's going to be a very tough next 20 years."[5] Even more liberal-leaning voices recognize that present-day population growth, land resources, energy consumption, and per capita consumption cannot be sustained without leading to even more catastrophic human conflict.

The greatest catastrophes occur when the distinctions between war and crime fade; when there is dissolution of the boundaries between military and criminal conduct, between civility and barbarity; when political, social, or religious groups embrace collective violence against a defenseless victim group as warfare or, perhaps worse yet, as "progress." Such acts are human evil writ large.

As I worked on the final revisions of this book, I—like the rest of the world—was shocked by the events of September 11, 2001. On that day, around 2,830 defenseless victims were killed by the terrorist attacks now attributed to Osama bin Laden. This is an example of terrorism "from below," that is, violence motivated by grievances against, or ideologies opposed to, an existing state. As we have come to know far too well, such terrorism can cast a debilitating shadow on the human experience. Generally, however, it is terrorism "from above"—state-directed terrorism imposed on its own citizens—that is the larger contributor to human suffering.[6]

Scholars use two terms to classify the collective violence stemming from state-directed terrorism. *Mass killing* means killing members of a group without the intention to eliminate the whole group or killing large numbers of people without a precise definition of group membership. Collective violence becomes *genocide* when a specific group is systematically and intentionally targeted for destruction.

Raphael Lemkin, a Polish Jewish émigré and noted scholar who taught law at Yale and Duke Universities, first coined the term "genocide" in 1944. Since that time, there has been an ongoing debate about how, exactly, genocide ought to be defined. On December 9, 1948, after lengthy discussion and ample political compromise, Article II of the United Nations Convention on the Prevention and Punishment of the Crime of Genocide was adopted and specifically defined genocide as "acts committed with the intent to destroy, in whole or in part, a national, ethnic, racial or religious group" by killing members of the group, causing them serious bodily or mental harm, creating conditions calculated to bring about their physical destruction, preventing births, or forcibly transferring children to another group. For a variety of reasons (most notably the exclusion of political, social, and gender groups) the UN definition of genocide has been less than satisfactory for many scholars and jurists. As a result, it is not surprising that over the years the heat of definitional controversy has only intensified.

Without controversy, however, is the fact that the human reality of mass killing and genocide predated its semantic taxonomy. Aptly dubbed the "Age of Genocide," the past century saw a massive scale of systematic and intentional mass murder coupled with an unprecedented efficiency of the mechanisms and techniques of mass destruction. On the historical heels of the physical and cultural genocide of American Indians during the nineteenth century, the twentieth century writhed from the near-complete annihilation of the Hereros by the Germans in South-West Africa in 1904; to the brutal assault of the Armenian population by the Turks between 1915 and 1923; to the implementation of a Soviet man-made famine in the Ukraine in 1932–1933 that left several million peasants starving to death; to the extermination of two-thirds of Europe's Jews during the Holocaust of 1939–1945; to the massacre of approximately half a million people in Indonesia during 1965–1966; to mass killings and genocide in Bangladesh (1971), Burundi (1972), Cambodia (1975–1979), East Timor (1975–1979), and Rwanda (1994); and, finally, to the conflict that continues to plague the former Yugoslavia. All told, it is estimated that 60 million men, women, and children were victims of mass killing and genocide in the last century alone.[7]

The dawn of the twenty-first century brings little light to the darkness. Sudan, the largest country in Africa, continues its decades-long assault on itself. Of all the wars that have taken place around the world since 1945, the civil war in Sudan and the accompanying genocide against the people of the country's south have claimed more lives than any other single conflict. All told, the war has killed more than 2 million from a population of approximately 30 million people. An additional 4.5 million people have been driven from their homes—more internally displaced persons than anywhere else in the world. The severity of the situation has increased to the point that the United States Holocaust Memorial Museum's Committee on Conscience recently issued a "genocide warning" for Sudan and is engaging in a determined campaign to alert the international conscience to the genocidal practices occurring in that country.

The persistence of inhumanity in human affairs is incontrovertible. I am speaking here not of isolated executions but of wholesale slaughters. As collectives, we engage in acts of extraordinary evil, with apparent moral calm and intensity of supposed purpose, which could only be described as insane were they committed by an individual. How do we explain the extraordinary evil that we perpetrate on each other in the name of our country, race, ethnicity, political party, or god?

Professionally, these questions fall within the realm of what I do. I am a social psychologist. I work in a fascinating field that explores how our thoughts, feelings, and behaviors are influenced by our interactions with other people. Take a course in social psychology and you will study how "social loafing" seduces a group of twelve to produce work equivalent to a group of six; how your choice of the shirt or slacks you wore today was influenced by implicit, and explicit, pressures to conform; how the faulty group decision making that led to the *Challenger* disaster could have been avoided; why you married the person you married and why you may, or may not, regret that choice; why thirty-eight residents stood by and did nothing while a young woman named Kitty Genovese was assaulted, and eventually murdered, outside an apartment building in New York City in 1964.

In this incredibly rich field, I have been most drawn to understanding how we "misrelate" to each other. What are the psychological dynamics of why we hate and exclude others simply because of what they look like, where they come from, or what they believe? This puts me in the arena of "-isms"—sexism, ageism, antisemitism, ableism (prejudice against disabled people), and fatism (prejudice against overweight people). My first two books each dealt with the particular "-ism" of race—*Face to Face: The Changing State of Racism across America* and *Prejudice across America*.[8] The question of how ordinary people come to commit extraordinary evil is an extension of my professional interests in human "misrelation" and has spurred my involvement in the field of Holocaust and genocide studies.

Personally, these questions fall within the deeper realm of *who* I am. At this level, these are not questions that I can distance myself from by objectifying them in someone or something else. Rather, these are questions about *my* fundamental human nature. Who am I and of what am I capable? Rather than dispassionately looking at someone else and asking "How could they?," I am compelled to look at myself and ask "Could I?" Could I be capable of such brutal inhumanity? Could you? If so, what does that say about the nature of human nature and the future of how we should live together? These are the ultimate questions that—as we seek to answer them—make it impossible for us to ever think the same again about societies, other human beings, and ourselves.

How important is the problem of ordinary people committing extraordinary evil? If we use the number of deaths as the basis for assigning importance, it can be argued that there is no more pressing problem facing humans today. Certainly, this problem poses much more than a distant sense of random menace to us. In every corner of the world, it strikes home too closely and far too frequently to be marginalized. The millions of victims of mass killing and genocide do not make a choice to endanger or end their lives. They are "victims" in the truest sense of the word. Understanding their victimization, and the people who perpetrated it, is one of the most central and enthralling issues facing humankind.

Rather than another descriptive catalog of the atrocities we perpetrate on each other, we stand much more in need of explanation and understanding. How do people come to commit extraordinary evil? In the pages that follow, I will outline an explanation of extraordinary human evil that considers the wide range of factors involved in the process of ordinary people coming to commit extraordinary evil. This four-pronged explanatory model, drawing on case studies of perpetrator behavior from an atrocious litany of genocides and mass killings, is not an invocation of a single broad-brush psychological state to explain extraordinary human evil. Rather, it is a detailed analysis of the influences that help shape our responses to authority and unleash our destructive capacities.

To offer a psychological explanation for the atrocities committed by perpetrators is not to forgive, justify, or condone their behaviors. Instead, the explanation simply allows us to understand the conditions under which many of us could be transformed into killing machines. When we understand the ordinariness of extraordinary evil, we will be less surprised by evil, less likely to be unwitting contributors to evil, and perhaps better equipped to forestall evil. Ultimately, being aware of our own capacity for evil—and the dispositional and situational factors that foster it—is the best safeguard we can have against future genocides and mass killings. It is the pursuit of that awareness, and of what we can do to cultivate the moral sensibilities to curb extraordinary human evil, which drives me to write this book.

ACKNOWLEDGMENTS

One of the many joys of finishing a book—in addition to getting on with one's life—is the opportunity to thank the people without whom the book would not have been written. As always, I have benefited from the gracious support of my colleagues in the Department of Psychology at Whitworth College—Noel Wescombe, Adrian Teo, and Noelle Wiersma. Beyond their collegial support, each of them also offered invaluable comments on select chapters. Other friends who gave of their time in shaping the content and voice of the book were Israel Charny, Henry Greenspan, Jennifer Hammer, David Holt, Heather Ann Looy, Michael Peterson, Jack Robinson, Julia Stronks, and John Yoder. A special note of thanks also to Tammy Reid and the academic affairs office at Whitworth College for their financial support in securing the photographs included in this book. My indebtedness to the work of a community of scholars, too numerous to list here, is apparent from the chapter notes.

I also want to thank Bill Robinson for encouraging me to continue to take risks as a teacher-scholar at a time in my career when I had become hesitant to do so. A special note of appreciation is due the outside readers—Stephen Haynes and David Myers—and two anonymous readers from Oxford University Press. Thanks also go to Kathy Fechter, Gail Fielding, Kristie Kopp, Andrea LeGore, and Rebekah Nelson, who helped in a myriad of tasks related to manuscript preparation—including, but not limited to, never-ending photocopying, interlibrary loan requests, and book orders.

The initial stages of my research were supported by a generous fellowship from the Pew Charitable Trusts, granted through the Pew Evangelical Scholars Program at the University of Notre Dame. Several colleagues deserve my warm thanks for assisting me in the preparation and submission of the fellowship proposal; among these are Deborah Abowitz, Jean Bethke-Elshtain, Christopher Browning, Harold Heie, Stanton Jones, Lynn Noland, Dale Soden, and Zev Weiss. I am particularly indebted to Zev Weiss, Christopher Browning, Peter Hayes, and everyone at the Holocaust Educational Foundation for their dedicated support of my development as a teacher-scholar in Holocaust and genocide studies. A very special note of thanks also to my dear friend Eva Lassman, whose life and testimony as a Holocaust survivor has added an immeasurable depth for the hundreds of students with whom she has spoken in my courses over the years.

Throughout the writing of the book, I have benefited from several opportunities to present my work as it was evolving and have it shaped by feedback from colleagues near and far. These included a Faculty Scholarship Forum (December 1999) and Showcase presentation (March 2001) at Whitworth; professional presentations at the Thirtieth Annual Scholars' Conference on the Holocaust and the Churches (March 2000) and the Lessons and Legacies conference sponsored by the Holocaust Educational Foundation (November 2000); local presentations at the Anne Frank Exhibit (May 2000) and as a featured speaker at Yom Hashoa at Spokane's Temple Beth Shalom (April 2001); and an invited presentation at a conference on human nature sponsored by the Weyerhaeuser Center for Christian Faith and Learning at Whitworth College (July 2001).

Two other special learning opportunities deserve mention and thanks. In June 1999, I was a participant in the First Annual Seminar for Faculty Teaching Holocaust Courses, sponsored by the University Programs Division of the Center for Advanced Holocaust Studies at the United States Holocaust Memorial Museum (USHMM) in Washington, D.C. The three-week seminar was taught by the world-renowned Holocaust scholar Raul Hilberg, professor emeritus at the University of Vermont. The precision and rigor he brings to his scholarship was inspiring, as were the commitment and passion evidenced by the other twenty-two participants in the seminar. Also, a special thanks to Ron Kurpiers, librarian at the USHMM, whose gracious spirit made the museum library a wonderful place of reflection as well as research.

In November 1999, with the support of my college president, Bill Robinson, I was able to visit—for the first time—Yad Vashem, the Holocaust Martyrs' and Heroes' Remembrance Authority, on the Mount of Remembrance in Jerusalem, Israel. The overwhelming power of that memorial came at a critical juncture when I needed to have faces brought back to the victims of mass killing and genocide that were beginning to become only dots and lines on the screen of my computer.

Thanks also go to Joan Bossert, Mia McIver, Kim Robinson, Christi Stanforth, and the wonderful staff at Oxford University Press who first saw a vision for my manuscript and worked diligently and professionally to turn it into a book.

Writing about perpetrators of extraordinary human evil was made more deeply personal and even more painful whenever I looked into the eyes of my three children. At the same time, however, their smiles, laughter, and love made me even more grateful and happy to return to their world after I left my keyboard. So, Brennan, Hannah, and Noah, thank you for being a rainbow of realistic hope at the many times when goodness seemed so far away from me as I immersed myself in an impenetrable monotony of cruelties over the past few years.

Finally, my deepest appreciation goes to my wife, Patti, who over the course of our marriage has shown me the best of what love can do to warm the soul. At times, I feel like nothing is ever real until I tell her about it, and far too often she has patiently lent her ear and heart to the innumerable trials and tribulations that go with writing, and selling, a book. Thanks, Patti, for the steadfast support and encouragement over the years!

March 29, 2002   J. W.
Spokane, Washington

CONTENTS

Foreword by Christopher R. Browning   vii

PART I. WHAT ARE THE ORIGINS OF EXTRAORDINARY HUMAN EVIL?

Introduction: A Place Called Mauthausen   3

1. The Nature of Extraordinary Human Evil   9

   "Nits Make Lice"   23

2. Killers of Conviction: Groups, Ideology, and Extraordinary Evil   29

   Dovey's Story   50

3. The "Mad Nazi": Psychopathology, Personality, and Extraordinary Evil   55

   The Massacre at Babi Yar   88

4. The Dead End of Demonization   94

   The Invasion of Dili   124

PART II. BEYOND DEMONIZATION: HOW ORDINARY PEOPLE COMMIT EXTRAORDINARY EVIL

A Model of Extraordinary Human Evil   133

5. What Is the Nature of Human Nature? Our Ancestral Shadow   136

   The Tonle Sap Massacre   169

6. Who Are the Killers? Identities of the Perpetrators   175
    Death of a Guatemalan Village   197

7. What Is the Immediate Social Context? A Culture of Cruelty   202
    The Church of Ntamara   230

8. Who Is the "Other"? Social Death of the Victims   236
    The "Safe Area" of Srebrenica   258

PART III. WHAT HAVE WE LEARNED
AND WHY DOES IT MATTER?

9. Conclusion: Can We Be Delivered from Extraordinary Evil?   267

Notes   281
Selected Bibliography   303
Index   311

I

WHAT ARE THE ORIGINS OF EXTRAORDINARY HUMAN EVIL?

Introduction:
A Place Called Mauthausen

August 1992

While a visiting professor at the Catholic University in Eichstatt, Germany, I took a Saturday train from nearby Munich to the small Austrian town of Mauthausen, an idyllic market community that lies just fourteen miles east of Linz and nuzzles peacefully along the north bank of the Danube. In the evocative description by historian Gordon J. Horwitz, it "sits amid lovely rolling hills whose fields cover the Austrian landscape like the bedspread of a giant."[1]

Less than three miles from the town's center, however, stands a reminder of one of the most brutal chapters in human history. There, in a moral interruption of the Austrian landscape, is the hilltop site of a former Nazi concentration camp. Portions of the thick granite walls of the camp—8 feet high and 462 yards around—are immediately visible. The Mauthausen camp draws relatively few visitors. Although Austrian schoolchildren make a compulsory trip, it remains a place whose story is not widely known.

From 1938 to 1945, Mauthausen was the central Nazi concentration camp for all Austria. Unlike the extermination camps in the former Polish territory—Chelmno, Belzec, Sobibor, Treblinka, Auschwitz, and Majdanek—Mauthausen was not a killing center specifically designed to carry out genocide. Rather, Mauthausen was a labor camp that, early on, was primarily a place in which inmates mined the rich resources of the local granite for the SS, the elite corps of the Nazi Party. Here, in an imposing and frightful pit whose walls rose some 300 feet in height, the inmates worked up to eleven hours per day, shouldering heavy blocks of stone. The Mauthausen quarry birthed hundreds of thousands of such stones for streets, monuments, and buildings throughout Hitler's Germany. After 1943, most

Mauthausen prisoners were reassigned to work for the military industry in the region—principally in the construction of subterranean tunnels to house factories for rocket assembly and production of plane parts. As a result, the Mauthausen complex eventually comprised a network of forty-nine satellite camps extending across the length and breadth of prewar Austrian territory.

In its beginning, Mauthausen was a depository for German and Austrian criminals and "asocial elements." Over time, however, there was a rapid expansion and diversification of the inmate population. Political prisoners (Jews, communists, and intellectuals), prisoners of war from territories occupied by the advancing German armies (Poland, Czechoslovakia, the Soviet Union, the Netherlands, Belgium, Luxembourg, and France), and those in "protective custody" were added to the inmate rolls. In January 1941, Reinhard Heydrich, chief of the Security Police and Security Service, devised a classificatory scheme in which he divided the "non-killing camps" into three categories of ascending severity. Only Mauthausen, and its subsidiary camp of Gusen, was placed in the most severe category. The most dangerous, threatening, and "unreformable" inmates were assigned to Mauthausen.

In truth, though, Mauthausen's severity existed long before Heydrich's official sanction. Beginning with the outbreak of war in the late summer of 1939, Mauthausen developed a reputation as a center for the torture and murder of its inmates. To the raucous cries of "Attention! Parachutists!," for example, SS men stationed around the rim of the stone quarry would hurl prisoners off the edge to their deaths. Others encouraged prisoners to go beyond the wire to pick fruit, shooting these "raspberry picker details" for amusement.

As time went on, the cruelty could be counted in the soaring death rates. In 1939, the camp recorded a death toll of 445. In 1941, Mauthausen reported an inmate mortality rate of 58 percent, compared with 36 percent at Dachau and 19 percent at Buchenwald. In June of that year, 348 Dutch Jews arrived at Mauthausen. Three weeks later, not a single one of them was still alive. In 1942, the death toll had risen to 14,293. In that same year, the camp forwarded to Berlin eleven and a half pounds of dental gold torn from the mouths of its victims. From January to April 1943, 5,147 more perished. The first five months of 1945 saw Mauthausen reach its inmate peak of 84,500 and also saw 52,814 die. In all, it is conservatively estimated that more than 200,000 prisoners passed through Mauthausen. It is believed that at least 119,000 of them died, of whom 38,120 were Jews.

Mauthausen was the last camp to be liberated by the Allies. At its liberation on May 5, 1945, the main camp was a scene of unimaginable horror. Severe overcrowding and reduced food rations had hastened the death of many. In the camp hospital, cases of cannibalism were documented. The crematoria could not burn all the decaying corpses. Shallow mass graves only barely concealed thousands of others. One member of the liberating forces wrote home: "It is really the smell that makes a visit to a death camp stark reality. The smell and the stink of the dead and dying, the smell and the stink of the starving. Yes, it is the smell, the odor of the death camp that makes it burn in the nostrils and memory. I will always smell Mauthausen."[2]

Mauthausen was clearly the harshest of the "non-killing camps." In all, there were fewer than 18,000 survivors on the day of liberation. (One of those was the future Nazi-hunter Simon Wiesenthal.) Since the liberation of Mauthausen came during the same week as the surrender of Germany, however, it was little noticed in the press. It has never become the symbol of human evil that is now synonymous with the names of Dachau, Flossenburg, Bergen-Belsen, and Buchenwald. Yet, for sheer brutality, it may well have matched them all. And Franz Ziereis was its commandant.

June 1999

I sit in the library of the United States Holocaust Memorial Museum in Washington, D.C. In front of me is a picture of Franz Ziereis. I have thought of him often over the past seven years. What type of man was capable of overseeing the atrocity that was Mauthausen? In my mind's eye, I have constructed an image of a monster whose face betrayed the pure evil that lay within him, a monster for whom brutality was as much a part of his being as was the blood that pulsed through his veins.

The picture in front of me, though, contradicts all I have imagined. Ziereis stands comfortably, but not supremely, atop one of the granite walls surrounding Mauthausen. His left hand rests lightly on a stair railing. There is just the hint of a guarded smile on his face. But for the conspicuous SS uniform, he could easily be mistaken as someone's father on a weekend stroll at a local park. His soft features and elegant appearance give a disquieting truth to the nickname those closest to him preferred—"Baby Face Ziereis." The contradiction is disturbing. It would be so much easier if his physical features mirrored the cruelty that I know he oversaw and committed. There is something about his ordinariness that makes those atrocities

Franz Ziereis, commandant of Mauthausen from August 1939 to May 1945. Photo (taken between 1939 and 1945) by Andras Tsagatakis, courtesy of USHMM Photo Archives.

even more unsettling. I am driven to know more about this man, primarily in the hope of discovering something that betrays the violent nature hidden by his innocent exterior.

Born of a working family in Munich on August 13, 1905, Ziereis had two sisters, one older than he, and a younger brother. His father, killed in the First World War when Ziereis was eleven years old, drove a horse-drawn cart. Though Franz Ziereis described himself as a merchant and carpenter by profession, he was, in reality, a career soldier. When just over eighteen years old, he enrolled in the Nineteenth Bavarian Infantry Regiment of the Reichswehr (the regular German army), in which he remained until September 1936. Lacking a high school diploma, he had no real chance of ever becoming an army officer. Shortly after he was discharged, however, he was offered a job as a training officer in the Waffen-SS with the rank of first lieutenant and opportunities for advancement. Ziereis accepted the offer without hesitation and joined the Nazi Party. He won quick praise for his abilities as a training officer and was promoted to Hauptsturmführer (captain). He arrived as commandant of Mauthausen in August 1939. In 1941 he was promoted to Sturmbannführer (major), in 1943 to Obersturmbannführer (lieutenant colonel), and in 1944 to Standartenführer (colonel).

Ziereis's personal and military history does not show that he possessed any particularly outstanding leadership skills or abilities. Nor did he have an above-average intelligence. Even Ziereis himself saw his rapid career advancement as a "payoff" from Heinrich Himmler, head of the SS, for agreeing to remain as camp commandant rather than being transferred to the front lines of the war—a transfer that the would-be hero (or martyr) claimed he requested often (though his personnel file contains no record of such requests). Those who knew him spoke of him as a model husband and a devoted father. In short, he was as ordinary as ordinary gets, with one singular exception: his seemingly boundless capacity for brutality.

How brutal was he? Ziereis, the dutiful father, was reputed to give prisoners to his young son for live target practice. He admitted taking part in the shooting of other prisoners because, in his opinion, "the new SS troops shot bad [*sic*] from the small fire arms."[3] To facilitate his own skill, he would sometimes stand on a convenient vantage point from which to view a newly arrived transport and select random prisoners as targets for his own shooting practice. He admitted to frequently driving the infamous gas vans in which carbon monoxide exhaust fumes were routed back into the cargo area to kill prisoners. He also personally participated in the beating and execution of scores of prisoners. Other commandants at subcamps under his command tanned the tattooed skin from victims' bodies for use as bookbindings, lampshades, and leather satchels. Ziereis refrained only because Berlin quickly forbade the practice. Shortly before liberation, he had planned to follow orders to gather all of the thousands of remaining prisoners at Mauthausen, assemble them in the subterranean tunnels, and blow them up with twenty-four tons of dynamite. Later, on his deathbed, Ziereis would maintain that he refused these orders—primarily under his wife's influence. In reality, though, it was only the arrival of the American forces on May 5, 1945, that prevented Ziereis from enacting this horrendous mass execution.

Several days after the liberation of Mauthausen, an ex-prisoner spotted Ziereis. An American patrol was sent to apprehend him. Ziereis opened fire and in the exchange of gunfire was severely wounded. He was taken to the U.S. Army's 131st Evacuation Hospital, where he was operated on by a former inmate of Mauthausen. His wounds proved fatal, but he lingered on for several days before dying during the night of May 22–23, 1945.

I return to the photograph of Ziereis. The contradiction it raised in my mind earlier is now heightened. Ziereis is just one of the millions of weeds of extraordinary evil that strangle the field of human experience. It is easy to flinch and dismiss him as a monster, too unlike us to be understood. He reminds us, however, that—except for a small number of the architects of the extermination process and a few sadists who enjoyed taking part in it—most of the perpetrators of the Holocaust and other cases of mass killing and genocide were extraordinary only by what they did, not by who they were. They could not be identified, a priori, as having the personalities of killers. Most were not mentally impaired. Nor were they identified as sadists at home or in their social environment. Nor were they victims of an abusive background. They defy easy demographic categorization. Among them we find educated and well-to-do people as well as simple and impoverished people. We find church-affiliated people as well as agnostics and atheists. We find people who were loving parents as well as people who had difficulty initiating and sustaining personal relationships. We find young people and old people. We find people who were not actively involved in the political or social groups responsible for institutionalizing the process of destruction as well as those who were. We find ordinary people who went to school, fought with siblings, celebrated birthdays, listened to music, and played with friends. In short, the majority of perpetrators of extraordinary evil were not distinguished by background, personality, or previous political affiliation or behavior as having been men or women unusually likely or fit to be genocidal executioners.

This reality is unsettling because it counters our general mental tendency to relate extraordinary acts to correspondingly extraordinary people. But we cannot evade this discomforting reality. We are forced to confront the ordinariness of most perpetrators of mass killing and genocide. Franz Ziereis and the countless other perpetrators of extraordinary evil throughout human history bring us face to face with questions that force us to turn a flashlight on the darkest recesses of who and what we are. Is it possible to segregate the perpetration of extraordinary evil as abnormal despite its constant presence within our species? Or is it more accurate to include such evildoing in the "normal" human activity engaged in by ordinary people like you and I? To answer these questions, it is first necessary to define what we mean by the phrase "extraordinary human evil."

1

The Nature of Extraordinary Human Evil

> When we have overcome absence with phone calls, winglessness with airplanes, summer heat with air conditioning—when we have overcome all these and much more besides, then there will abide two things with which we must cope: the evil in our hearts and death.
>
> Nicholas Wolterstorff, *Lament for a Son*

IT IS EASY TO DETACH OURSELVES FROM perpetrators of extraordinary human evil and their victims. Most of us know nothing—in an experiential sense—about the perpetration of extraordinary evil. We have not been through anything in our personal lives that remotely compares to the atrocities inflicted on millions of victims of extraordinary evil across the globe. Each of us is, though, the surviving heir of catastrophes and destruction that we never experienced. As such, we are called to find meaning where there appears to be none.

We have, due to the considerable efforts of scholars in Holocaust and genocide studies, an incredibly exhaustive account of the inhumanity we perpetrate on each other. The opening of archives throughout Eastern Europe, the emergence of primary source materials from Cambodia, Rwanda, and the former Yugoslavia, and the cultivation of oral collections from victims and perpetrators of extraordinary evil around the world continue to yield even more documentation to be translated, sorted, and analyzed.

After all of that, though, we are still left with the "big questions." One of the most urgent is why ordinary people commit extraordinary evil. Historian Saul Friedlander, who divides his time between professorships at Tel Aviv University and at UCLA, suggests that we now need the lens of psychology to bring some focus to the "incomprehensibility" of extraordinary human evil that scholars continue to document.[1] Questions of motive and the social environment in which evil is practiced must be addressed if we hope to shed additional light on the actions of ordinary citizens doing their "jobs" in extraordinary situations.

To their credit, many scholars in the field psychologize about the origins of extraordinary human evil. Most follow the shopworn procedure of harvesting a grain of explanation from undergraduate textbook accounts of Stanley Milgram's research on obedience to authority (see chapter 4) or Philip Zimbardo's Stanford prison simulation (see chapter 7). Often, though, their reading of this research fails to bring out the rich nuances of understanding human behavior. Even more limiting is their relative unawareness of the expansive wealth of equally insightful contemporary psychological research that followed in the decades after these classic works. Despite their good intentions, most nonspecialists simply do not bring the training or experience necessary to fully mine the potential of what contemporary psychology can offer. As a result, the explanations they cull from psychology often seem too trivial and too mundane to offer a thorough understanding of extraordinary human evil.

In our search for an explanation of the origins of extraordinary human evil, it is vital that we recognize our interdependence. Regardless of disciplinary perspective, we are all students in the slow business of understanding what it means to be human and, often, what it means to be inhuman. Only in collaboration will we come to a fuller understanding of our inhumanity to each other. Only by weaving ideas from many disciplines into a cohesive tapestry will we begin to understand extraordinary evil.

The goal of this book is to offer a psychological explanation of how ordinary people commit extraordinary evil. It is an attempt to go beyond the minutiae of thick description ("who," "what," "when," and "where") and look at the bigger questions of explanation and understanding: to know a little less and understand a little more. To begin, we must be clear about the boundaries of the investigation—exactly what do we mean by "evil" and, particularly, "extraordinary evil"?

The Nature of Evil

In virtually every human culture, there has existed some word for "evil," a linguistic acknowledgment of its reality in everyday human affairs. For millennia, the concept of evil was central to religious, and much secular, thought. Despite its universality, however, it is not a construct with a generally accepted definition. Part of this stems from the fact that it is a word that has fallen out of widespread use. Until the events of September 11, we hardly used the word "evil" in everyday conversation. Even now, for many, it seems redundant with other more often used terms. In general conversation, we easily substitute "moral wrongness" or "bad" for the term "evil" without any loss of meaning. Some see "evil" as grandiose and others find it esoteric, mystical, or supernatural. For most of us, "evil" is simply an antiquated concept. It is a relic heavy with archaic baggage (for example, the notion of sin). In short, though we know it from fairy tales, children's books, comic books, horror films, and Sunday school class, "evil" is a word modern folk do not often hear or use.

Until recently, the concept of evil also had almost completely disappeared from the vocabulary of the social sciences that seek to understand the human situation. In 1969, the eminent sociologist Kurt Wolff of Brandeis University wrote, "To my knowledge, no social scientist, as a social scientist, has asked what evil is. 'What is evil?' is a question that rather has been raised (both in the West and in the East) by philosophers and theologians, as well as by uncounted, unclassified, unrecorded people since time immemorial."[2] More than three decades later, it appeared that little had changed: a survey of psychology articles written in the past ten years found only *nine* that were pertinent to the concept of evil.[3] The prevailing normative picture of humankind held up by the social sciences still portrayed, for the most part, rational creatures who could be expected to relate to and treat fellow humans with basic empathy, kindness, respect, and decency. Most recently, however, there are signs that the social scientific neglect of evil is beginning to be rectified. For instance, an entire 1999 issue of the *Personality and Social Psychology Review*, the official journal of the Society for Personality and Social Psychology, was devoted to social scientific perspectives on evil and violence.[4]

But why are social scientists so late, and hesitant, in bringing their attention to such an ever-present component of everyday human life? Like many other people, social scientists have had a hard time wrapping their minds around exactly what evil is and is not. Even those relatively few scholars, most housed in religion and philosophy, who write frequently of evil often shy away from a precise conceptual definition. Why? To specifically define the "judgmental" and "moralistic" concept of evil seems to threaten the academic ideal of ethical and value neutrality. To be sure, any definition includes, in part, a value statement reflecting one's own perspective. As Thomas Hobbes, a seventeenth-century English philosopher, wrote, "No man calleth good or evil but that which is so in his own eyes."[5]

To be equally sure, however, this unattainable quest for neutrality has meant that evil has ceased to be a meaningful term. This definitional phobia is a convenient cop-out that keeps us mired on the sidelines of a discussion in which we should be full participants. Though evil may be difficult to define conceptually, we all are aware of its existence and pervasiveness at a concrete level. We know what it looks like, what it feels like, and how it can irrevocably alter our lives. As Susan Sontag has said, "We have a sense of evil," but we no longer have "the religious or philosophical language to talk intelligently about evil."[6]

Most would agree that—in its broadest sense—evil is anything detrimental to the well-being of living things. Following that, we can then distinguish between the two most common categories of evil: natural and human (sometimes called "moral") evil. Natural evil is a function of natural processes of change. It is the evil that originates independently of human actions—events such as earthquakes, tornadoes, floods, fires, pestilence, droughts, and diseases. Natural evil causes harm, but without conscious or unconscious intention. Human evil, in contrast, is evil that we originate. It refers to the destructive things that we do to each other and ourselves.

There is, of course, debate over the exact boundaries of these two subsidiary forms of evil. Because, for instance, human behavior is subject to genetic and physical influences, it becomes hard to strictly distinguish between natural and human evil. Other scholars argue that evil is not so readily located, that it is as much about how we experience suffering as what causes it, as much about a world that cares nothing for humans as it is about humans who care nothing for one another. Some posit a third category of evil representing the combination of the first two—human evil using or taking advantage of natural evil. Still others suggest a divine or metaphysical realm of evil. Each of these is a necessary window to understanding the many facets of evil. It is to the specific question of human evil, though, that this book is addressed.

I define human evil as the deliberate harming of humans by other humans. This is a behavioral definition that focuses on how people act toward one another. The definition includes the creation of conditions that materially or psychologically destroy or diminish people's quality of life—their dignity, happiness, and capacity to fulfill basic material needs. Such conditions include the harming of property (for example, theft or vandalism); psychological harm from threat of physical injury, trauma, or fright; social harm from exploitation, debasement, slander, or libel; or harm that comes from the taking away of an individual's freedom (for example, invasion of privacy, kidnapping, or false imprisonment). At its extreme, the definition also includes killing that is not required for biological survival (that is, murder).

This definition judges as evil any human *actions* leading to the deliberate harming of other humans. What the definition gains in precision, it may lose in exclusions. It does not, for instance, judge evil by conscious intentions. Too often, perpetrators of evil hide their negative intentions from others (and themselves), or justify their negative actions as a necessary route to a greater good, or even defend their harmdoing as the only appropriate response to the victim's evil nature. For them, their conscious intentions are anything but evil. The definition also does not judge evil by motivation. It does not, for example, include cases where people try, but fail, to inflict destruction on other people. These are especially problematic areas because victims and perpetrators are often far apart in their judgments of what the perpetrator's intentions and motives were. Neither does the definition include cases of accidental or unintended harm.

The Nature of Extraordinary Human Evil

Within the broad range of acts defined as human evil, I have chosen to focus this book on *extraordinary* human evil. This focus on human evil writ large is not about the isolated, tabloid cases of serial killers or psychopaths who go berserk in public spaces. Rather, the center of my attention is on the deliberate harm we perpetrate on each other under the sanction of political, social, or religious groups—in other words, the extraordinary human evil perpetrated in times of collective social unrest, war, mass killings, and genocide. I am not referring here to the deliberate harm inflicted in the course of military action against the military forces of an acknowledged enemy. Instead, I am referring to the deliberate harm inflicted against a defenseless and helpless group targeted by a legitimating political, social, or religious authority—human evil *in extremis*.

In this book, my focus is *not* on analyzing the macro-level political, economic, and historical factors that underlie the origins of collective violence in a given society. Understanding the large-scale pressures that animate extraordinary human evil is, obviously, an important issue. Fortunately, much good work has been, and continues to be, done by the historians and political scientists who unpack the myriad macro-level antecedents of mass killing and genocide.

My focus is on the micro-level issue of who actually carries out the violence. History makes clear that political, social, or religious groups wanting to commit mass murder do. Though there may be other obstacles, they are never hindered by a lack of willing executioners. That is the one constant on which they can count. Ultimately, mass killing and genocide happen only because individual human beings kill other human beings in large numbers and over an extended period of time. How are people enlisted to perpetrate such extraordinary evil?

Unlike much of the research on perpetrator behavior, I am not interested in the higher echelons of leadership who structured the ideology, policy, and initiatives behind a particular genocide or mass killing. Nor am I interested in the middle-echelon perpetrators, the faceless bureaucrats who made implementation of those initiatives possible. Rather, I am interested in the rank-and-file killers, the ordinary men and women at the bottom of the hierarchy who personally carried out the millions of executions. These people were so ordinary that, with few exceptions, they were readily absorbed into civil society after the killings and peacefully lived out their unremarkable lives—attesting to the unsettling reality that genocide overwhelms justice.

How many people does it take to commit mass murder? Precise numbers are impossible to come by, but Holocaust scholars estimate that 100,000 to 500,000 killers took part in the Final Solution.[7] More recently, in Rwanda, as many as 75,000 to 150,000 Hutus participated in the slaughter of at least 800,000 Tutsis in just a hundred days. Some Rwandans even maintain that the actual number of perpetrators ran as high as between 1 and 3 million (many of the killings involved groups of people attacking one victim).[8] One point stands clear: to understand the fundamental reality of mass murder we need to shift our focus from impersonal institutions and abstract structures to the actors, the men and women who actually carried out the atrocities.

You could argue that I am guilty of emphasizing the grandiosity and abstractness of evil by focusing the book's attention on the commission of extraordinary human evil. I do recognize that human evil is ubiquitous and that for many of us—especially before September 11—our most direct experiences with evil are the petty cruelties and minor transgressions of everyday life. To be sure, there may be immense value in focusing our attention on everyday evil. It is more common, more is known about it, and it can be studied more easily. Perhaps learning about why people break promises, you could argue, can tell us something about why people come to commit extraordinary evil.

While that may be true, I believe that there is just as much to learn about everyday evil from looking at the extremes of human behavior. Knowing the basics of everyday atmospheric physics, for example, does give us insight into an extraordinary atmospheric event, like a tornado. Studying the physics of tornadoes, though, also gives us a great deal of information about the basics of more everyday atmospheric patterns, like thunderstorms. The extraordinary event—be it a tornado or a human atrocity—is so clear, so exaggerated, and so urgent that it often drives us to a deeper understanding of the ordinary. Over the course of this book, you will see that the causal processes involved in the commission of extraordinary evil will have something in common with the type of everyday evil that you and I commonly commit. In the final analysis, though, the pervasive reality of extraordinary evil offers its own defense for studying it. Unfortunately, extraordinary evil, like a tornado, happens often enough—and is disastrous enough—to merit study for its own sake.

Understanding Evil: A Slippery Slope

I want to recognize two legitimate fears that lie beneath any attempt to understand extraordinary human evil. For many, these fears make any explanation of extraordinary evil intrinsically controversial and, for some, unacceptable. *The first is the fear that to explain the behaviors of perpetrators of extraordinary evil is to justify those behaviors.* In other words, explanation inevitably leads to condoning, pardoning, and forgiving, or—at the very least—a shift in the direction of a more favorable attitude toward the perpetrator. This is why some argue that, rather than studying extraordinary human evil, we should simply recognize it for what it is and condemn it. For instance, Bruno Bettelheim, a survivor of Dachau and Buchenwald, has written: "I restricted myself to trying to understand the psychology of the prisoners and I shied away from trying to understand the psychology of the SS—because of the ever-present danger that understanding fully may come close to forgiving. I believe there are acts so vile that our task is to reject and prevent them, not to try to understand them empathetically."[9]

Similarly, the protagonist of Bernhard Schlink's best-selling novel, *The Reader*, says: "I wanted simultaneously to understand Hanna's crime and to condemn it. But it was too terrible for that. When I tried to understand it, I had the feeling I was failing to condemn it as it must be condemned. When I condemned it as it must be condemned, there was not room for understanding. . . . I wanted to pose myself both tasks—understanding and condemnation. But it was impossible to do both."[10]

Is it really impossible to pose ourselves both tasks of understanding and condemnation? Must one rule out the other? A recent intriguing social psychological experiment by Arthur G. Miller and his colleagues from Miami University in Ohio contends that there *is* ample reason to fear that understanding can promote forgiving. In three experiments designed to explore the exonerating effects of explanations, Miller and his team found "that there are a variety of cognitive and affective processes that, in fact, may produce a relatively condoning attitude toward perpetrators as a result of explaining their actions."[11] Even after a brief exposure to explanations, participants evidenced a significant judgmental shift in the direction of a less harsh or punitive orientation toward a perpetrator. The Miller studies found that social psychological explanations, in particular, ran the risk of reducing the perceived intentionality and responsibility attributed to perpetrators.

Why do our explanations move us closer to justification, forgiveness, or exoneration? In part, because we see explanation only in purely deterministic terms. That is, when we explain a behavior, it is as if the person had no choice but to engage in that particular behavior, and, thus, the behavior is justifiable. In reality, though, only pseudoscience deals in such "certainties." Psychological explanations, when presented responsibly and legitimately, are more probabilistic than deterministic. In other words, they tell us what we are *most likely* to do rather than what we *must* do. Perhaps by knowing the social forces surrounding us, for example, we can indeed develop a reasonable prediction of our capacity to commit extraordinary evil. This is not to maintain, though, that we are *forced* to commit that extraordinary evil. Yes, we are certainly influenced by the constraints of our general culture and a situation's context. But we are just as certainly responsible for our own initiatives in response to those influences. In other words, what perpetrators of extraordinary evil decide to do makes a great difference in what they eventually do. Within the context of our respective freedom, we all are responsible for our deeds—evil or otherwise.

We must continually remind ourselves that a psychological explanation of extraordinary human evil is not exculpatory. We must not, however, unwittingly, buy into a condoning image of perpetrators of extraordinary evil. There are no such things as "perpetratorless" mass killings or genocides. Perpetrators are not just the hapless victims of human nature or their social context. In willfully failing to exercise their moral judgment, they retain full moral and legal accountability for the atrocities they committed. To understand all is not to forgive all. "Explaining is not excusing; understanding is not forgiving," writes Christopher Browning, a professor of history at the University of North Carolina at Chapel Hill. "Not trying to understand the perpetrators in human terms," he continues, "would make impossible not only this study but any history of Holocaust perpetrators that sought to go beyond one-dimensional caricature."[12]

The main goal of this book is psychological understanding, not moral analysis. No one would deny that we have learned a tremendous amount about who we are, and of what the human spirit can endure, by exploring the multidimensional complexity of the victims of extraordinary human evil. It is equally appropriate to believe that there may be just as much to learn by ripping off the masks that disguise perpetrators of extraordinary evil as monsters. In understanding how these ordinary people come to commit extraordinary evil, we get a discomforting glimpse of the depths to which the human spirit can plunge. In short, I do not want to make apologies or offer excuses for perpetrators of extraordinary evil. I do, though, want to understand the processes that produce extraordinary evil. That said, we must then supplement our psychological understanding with the courage to resume the moral condemnation of those terrible acts. As social psychologist Roy Baumeister writes, "It is a mistake to let moral condemnation interfere with trying to understand—but it would be a bigger mistake to let that understanding, once it has been attained, interfere with moral condemnation."[13]

The second fear is that an attempt to explain extraordinary human evil carries with it an inordinate risk of contamination. This fear tempts us to retreat to the safest, and most comfortable, way to deal with the issue—from the heights of moral condemnation rather than the depths of human understanding. At the heart of this fear is the belief that extraordinary human evil is unexplainable. To try and explain the inexplicable only puts you in a position where you will be tainted by the evil itself. I bank my life on the belief that attempting to understand evil does not mean you will become an evil person. At the very least, however, I do recognize that I run the risk of paralysis and falling into a pit of emotional apathy. This is what anthropologist Inga Clendinnen has described as the Gorgon effect—"the sickening of imagination and curiosity and the draining of the will which afflicts so many of us when we try to look squarely at the persons and processes implicated in the Holocaust."[14]

I certainly empathize with this fear. Researching and writing this book exposed me to episodes of inhumanity to which I would rather not have been exposed. It has left me more callused and less easily moved than I should be. For you, reading this book may have a similar effect. Even reduced to black marks on white paper, our inhumane treatment of other humans is enough to darken the brightest day and make uneasy the most comfortable night. You may feel hardened beyond the pull of sentiment. It may be much more difficult than you anticipate to clearly separate *them* from *us*. You will find that when we study the nature of human evil, we inevitably end up examining our own natures.

Our eyes, and hearts, will be scorched by what we see. We must not, though, let that excuse us from the hard task of trying to extract the comprehensible from the unthinkable. We must not let "evil" be a throwaway category for the things we are afraid to understand. We must not let it be the impenetrable term we use when we come to the limit of human comprehension. We must not place human evil beyond human scrutiny. To do so is to give it the benefit of our ignorance. In this sense, our refusal to attempt to understand human evil is a willful failure to know our own hearts and, if anything, only facilitates the continuation of extraordinary evil in human affairs.

Central Argument of the Book

My central argument is that *it is ordinary individuals, like you and me, who commit extraordinary evil.* This argument is difficult to admit, to understand, to absorb. We would rather know Extraordinary Evil as an extra-human capitalization. The embodiment of evil in a hideous creature called IT in Madeleine L'Engle's children's classic *A Wrinkle in Time* is just one example of our preference for knowing evil at a great distance. If we are forced to know IT in human terms, we retreat to our cognitive escape of relating extraordinary acts to correspondingly extraordinary people. We fall back on our belief that the majority of perpetrators of extraordinary human evil throughout history have indeed been extraordinary—sadists, psychopaths, and monsters. But how reasonable is it to believe that there are enough such beasts distributed throughout society to account for the extraordinary human evil that has littered our history?

In reality, a purely evil person is just as much an artificial construct as a person who is purely good. Perpetrators of extraordinary evil are extraordinary only by what they have done, not by who they are. We must not consider them so irrational, so atavistic, as to be beyond human understanding. We must go beyond our tendency to focus on extraordinary evil as a peculiar property or characteristic of despicable individuals and come to focus on the ways in which ordinary individuals become perpetrators of extraordinary evil. Recognizing their ordinariness does not diminish the horror of their actions. It increases it. At the same time, it neither excuses their deeds nor minimizes the threat they pose. On the contrary, it reminds us, in Rabbi Richard L. Rubenstein's words, "how fragile are the bonds of civility and decency that keep any kind of human community from utter collapse."[15]

Part I (chapters 1, 2, 3, and 4) of the book lays out the background for my central argument that it is ordinary individuals, like you and me, who commit extraordinary evil. Chapters 2 and 3 acknowledge that not all scholars agree with this argument. Some maintain that the origins of extraordinary human evil lie not in ordinary individuals but in extraordinary groups, ideologies, psychopathologies, or personalities. Chapter 4 reviews the work of those who argue that extraordinary evil is done by ordinary individuals who have created or activated a second self to commit that evil.

Understanding that ordinary people commit extraordinary evil still begs an explanation. *What factors lead some of us to perpetrate extraordinary evil while others of us stand by indifferently or, occasionally, resist extraordinary evil?* In other words, if we are *all* capable of extraordinary evil, why don't we *all* perpetrate extraordinary evil when given the opportunity? How, *exactly*, do ordinary people come to commit extraordinary evil?

While the chapters in part I are useful in understanding *why* we need a unified theory of perpetrator behavior, readers interested specifically in the question of *how* ordinary people commit extraordinary evil could proceed directly to part II (chapters 5, 6, 7, and 8). These chapters outline an original explanation of extraordinary human evil that considers the wide range of factors involved in the process of ordinary people committing extraordinary evil. Framed in the context of a four-pronged model, this explanation examines the forces relevant to the actor (our ancestral shadow and the identities of the perpetrators), the context of the action (a culture of cruelty), and a definition of the target (social death of the victims) that help shape our responses to authority.

- The first prong of the model (chapter 5) focuses on three tendencies of human nature, or facets of **our ancestral shadow**, that are particularly relevant in shaping our responses to authority: *ethnocentrism* (the tendency to focus on one's own group as the "right" one), *xenophobia* (the tendency to fear outsiders or strangers), and the *desire for social dominance* (often leading to aggression and violence). Studies worldwide show not only that these tendencies are universal in people but also that they start in infancy.

- The second prong (chapter 6) acknowledges that a thorough understanding of extraordinary evil must include a focus on the forces that mold the **identities of the perpetrators** who carry out the atrocities. This prong explores the impact of three such forces: *cultural belief systems* (about external, controlling influences on one's life; authority orientation; ideological commitment), *moral disengagement* of the perpetrator from the victim (facilitated by moral justification, euphemistic labeling of evil actions, and exonerating comparisons), and one's *rational self-interest* (professional and personal).

- The third prong of the model (chapter 7) considers the immediate social context of **a culture of cruelty** in influencing how we think, feel, and behave. Three specific factors are most relevant to the commission of extraordinary evil: the role of *professional socialization* (built on escalating commitments, ritual conduct, and the repression of conscience), the *binding factors of the group* that cement one's adherence to the group and its activities (including diffusion of responsibility, deindividuation, and conformity to peer pressure), and the *merger of role and person* that helps us understand how evildoing organizations change the people within them.

- The fourth and final prong of the model (chapter 8) recognizes that who the victims are, or, at least, who they have been made out to be, is an important piece of understanding how we respond to authority. This prong analyzes three features of the **social death of the victims**: *us-them thinking, dehumanization of the victims* (for example, the use of language in defining the victims as less than human), and *blaming the victims* (a legitimization of the victim as the enemy and, thus, deserving of their victimization).

Part III (chapter 9) concludes the book by addressing the implications of my central argument and explanatory model for how we might live. I realize that my central argument and the corresponding explanatory model are not easy sells. None of us likes to be told that we are capable of committing extraordinary evil. It is a pessimistic point of view that flies directly in the face of our sincere, but misguided, optimism that human evil can be obliterated by reforming society. For some, the explanatory model will dance uncomfortably close to the borders of exoneration. For others, it will smack too much of a "how-to" primer for extraordinary evil. For most, however, the model will be a tool of inflicted self-insight as we are forced to grapple with our own propensity for evildoing in the face of our highly positive, self-serving images of who we wish ourselves to be.

I cannot let the disagreeability of these ideas lead me to turn a deaf ear to what I believe to be the truth about the origins of human evil. In my mind, the pessimism of the argument is more than countered by the realism it engenders. It is only in seeing the limits of who we are that we have a legitimate chance to structure a society in which the gross exercise of human evil is constrained. We cannot begin to command human nature except by obeying the laws under which our human nature operates. If we recognize this fact, then we need not remain helpless in the face of extraordinary evil. I contend that, ultimately, our awareness of our own capacity for evil—and of ways to cultivate the moral sensibilities that curb that capacity—is the best safeguard we can have against future genocide and mass killing.

Between each of the chapters, I have included eyewitness accounts—from perpetrators, victims, and bystanders—of extraordinary human evil perpetrated throughout our history. These accounts—from the Americas to Armenia, from the Ukraine to East Timor, from Cambodia to Guatemala, from Rwanda to the Balkans—offer us the broadest possible picture of our inhumanity to each other and make it exceedingly difficult to isolate extraordinary evil to any particular corner of the world or era of human history.

I do not mean for these accounts to be an impenetrable parade of cruelties that sensationalize or numb. Neither do I, in a book focused on perpetrators, use them as transparent, obligatory gestures of concern for the sufferings of the victims. After all, the underlying motivation of any book on human evil lies, primarily, in our very deep concern for past and future victims. I include the accounts simply as periodic "slaps in the face" to remind us we are dealing with a topic that is not pedestrian. In a way, to understand perpetrators of extraordinary evil is to understand how they think—in a detached, minimalist, insensitive style—about their victims. If this book does its task well, it may seem insensitive to the sufferings of victims. But the eyewitness accounts will remind us that though genocide and mass killing may be motivated by abstractions, they are not abstract. These compelling narratives allow us to make the human connections—

with victims, perpetrators, and bystanders—that lie at the root of all understanding. They tell us that the study of human evil should be objective but must never become dispassionate. It is a flesh-and-bones issue with flesh-and-bones consequences. Too much detachment will only exacerbate our sense of helplessness. In this, it is right not to let our own revulsion slip away.

On a related note, much of the material with which I make my arguments is drawn from the best-documented genocide of this past century—the Holocaust. Of all the cases of mass killing and genocide throughout human history, the Holocaust represents, by far, the largest body of academic scholarship and popular writing that we have. As reflected in part I, it is the singular genocide with which most previous interpretations of extraordinary evil have been concerned. That does not mean, however, that we should restrict our understanding to this one exemplar of extraordinary evil. To do so would be to unnecessarily constrain our investigation. In parts II and III of the book, particularly the chapters detailing my original explanatory model of extraordinary human evil, I have attempted to avoid this constraint by incorporating material from a variety of other cases of mass killing and genocide in the past two hundred years.

So here it begins. I presume that you are reading this because you desire a closer look at the problem of extraordinary human evil. You hope that some blinding insight, flicker of self-knowledge, or clue about how to live in this world will come out of these pages. As we explore the topic together, however, we may find that there are clear limits to our capacity for understanding extraordinary human evil. Our questions may bring us not to definitive answers but only to endless follow-up questions. Our inquiry may be a point of departure, rather than a point of arrival. After all, our understanding of our fellow humans, and ourselves, can never be complete. Those limits will be discovered, though, only at the end of inquiry, not before it begins. We have an obligation to proceed *as if* it were possible to understand and to see our inquiry through to the end.

"Nits Make Lice"

A FTER COLUMBUS "DISCOVERED" the Americas in 1492, he returned the following year to install himself as "viceroy and governor of [the Caribbean islands] and the mainland" of America. From the large island he called "Española" (the modern island of Haiti), Columbus quickly instituted policies of slavery and systematic extermination against the indigenous Taino population. Sources from that time are replete with accounts of Spanish colonists hanging Tainos en masse, roasting them on spits, burning them at the stake, and hacking their children into pieces to be used as dog food. In a mere three years, the Tainos were reduced from as many as 8 million to about 3 million people. Only 100,000 Tainos were left by the time Columbus departed in 1500. By 1520, the number had fallen to just 20,000. Four decades later, only 200 indigenous people were recorded in the Spanish census of Española.[1]

Genocide in the Americas, however, was only just beginning. In 1492, it is estimated that well over 100 million indigenous people inhabited the Western hemisphere. Two centuries later, it is estimated that the indigenous population of the Americas had been diminished by some 90 percent and was continuing to fall steadily. While scholars still debate the exact scale of the population decline, the catastrophic demographic impact of the European exploration and settlement of the New World on the indigenous peoples is undeniable. In the words of Ward Churchill, professor of American Indian Studies at the University of Colorado, Boulder, "The genocide inflicted upon American Indians over the past five centuries is unparalleled in human history, both in terms of its sheer magnitude and in its duration."[2]

Beginning in 1830, the U.S. government undertook a policy of "removing" all indigenous people from the area east of the Mississippi River. In the series of internments and forced marches that followed, entire peoples were decimated. By 1840, with the exception of a handful of tiny Iroquois reservations in upstate New York and the remaining Seminoles in the Florida Everglades, the eastern third of what would become the continental United States had been cleared of its indigenous population. Moreover, it became obvious that the land west of the Mississippi was never seriously intended to be the exclusive domain of the continent's indigenous people.

Generally, in pursuit of their "manifest destiny" to enjoy limitless expansion, the U.S. government did not openly espouse extermination policies against Native Americans. The fact is, though, that the U.S. government was always ready to resort to outright physical eradication of indigenous peoples—genocide—where necessary. Massacres of Indians were well reported in the local press and perpetrators were often paid bounties by the government for the scalps of their victims. No effort was made to intervene or punish the killers. In more than forty military confrontations, or "Indian Wars," it became clear that extermination was the express objective. There were numerous large-scale massacres of Indians—including Horseshoe Bend (1814), Bad Axe River (1833), Bear River (1863), Washita River (1868), Marias River (1870), and the well-chronicled massacre of over 200 Minneconjou and Hunkpapa Sioux at Wounded Knee in 1890—that accounted for untold thousands of Native American dead.

One of the most brutal massacres of Indians occurred at Sand Creek in the Colorado Territory in 1864. The government of the Colorado Territory had created a unit, the Third Colorado Volunteer Cavalry Regiment, expressly for the purpose of killing Cheyennes and any other indigenous people they might encounter over a hundred-day period on the South Platte Trail. Echoing the tenor of the time, William N. Byers, publisher of the *Rocky Mountain News*, wrote: "Eastern humanitarians who believe in the superiority of the Indian race will raise a terrible howl over this policy [of extermination], but it is not time to split hairs nor stand upon delicate compunctions of conscience. Self preservation demands decisive action, and the only way to secure it is [through a] few months of active extermination against the red devils."

Colorado governor John Evans published a proclamation claiming that "the evidence [was] now conclusive" that most Indians on the Plains were "hostile" and calling on whites to "organize [themselves] to pursue, kill and destroy" Cheyennes wherever they might be found. The military commander of this killing unit, Colonel John Milton Chivington (a former Methodist minister now nicknamed "The Fighting Parson"), made clear his intention to kill everyone from the most elderly and infirm to newborn infants—the latter for no reason other than that they would one day grow up to become adult Cheyennes.

At around 8 P.M. on November 28, 1864, Chivington led approximately 700 soldiers out of Fort Lyon and toward an unarmed, noncombatant village of about 500 Southern Cheyenne and Arapaho Indians along Sand Creek in southeastern Colorado Territory. Two-thirds of the village was women and children, purportedly under the protection of the military. So sure were the Indians of their absolute safety that they kept no night watch except of the pony herd that was corralled below the creek. "Kill and scalp all," Chivington instructed his men, "little and big. . . . Nits make lice." Chivington's men struck at dawn on November 29, despite the fact that both American and white flags were flown over the sleeping village. Robert Bent, the mixed-blood son of a local trader and a Cheyenne woman who had guided the troops from Fort Lyon to the village, later described the massacre:

> I saw five squaws under a bank for shelter. When the troops came up to them they ran out and showed their persons, to let the soldiers know they were squaws and begged for mercy, but the soldiers shot them all. I saw one squaw laying on the bank whose leg had been broken by a shell; a soldier came up to her with a drawn saber; she raised her arm to protect herself, when he struck, breaking her arm; she rolled over and raised her other arm, when he struck, breaking it, and then left her without killing her. There seemed to be indiscriminate slaughter of men, women, and children. There were some thirty or forty squaws collected in a hole for protection; they sent out a little girl about six years old with a white flag on a stick; she had not proceeded but a few steps when she was shot and killed. All the squaws in the hole were afterwards killed.

Lieutenant James Connor, a New Mexico volunteer who had ridden along "to gain experience," corroborated Bent's account:

> I did not see a body of man, woman, or child but was scalped, and in many instances their bodies were mutilated in a most horrible manner—men, women, and children's privates cut out, & c; I heard one man say that he had cut out a woman's private parts and had them for exhibition on a stick; I heard another man say he had cut off the fingers of an Indian to get the rings on the hand. . . . I heard of one instance of a child a few months old being thrown in the feedbox of a wagon, and after being carried some distance left on the ground to perish; I also heard of numerous instances in which men had cut out the private parts of fe-

males and stretched them over saddle bows and wore them over hats while riding in the ranks. . . . I heard one man say that he had cut a squaw's heart out, and he had it stuck up on a stick.

John Smith, a frontiersman who served as a scout, also testified:

All manner of depredations were inflicted on the persons. They were scalped, their brains knocked out; the men used their knives, ripped open women, clubbed little children, knocked them in the head with their guns, beat their brains out, mutilated their bodies in every sense of the word . . . worse mutilated than any I ever saw before. . . . Children two or three months old; all lying there, from sucking infants up to warriors.

Amazingly, the majority of villagers at Sand Creek, including many who were severely wounded, somehow escaped the soldiers and survived. After seven hours of attack, at least 150 Cheyennes and Arapahos lay dead. The following day, soldiers and officers roamed the site of destruction scalping and otherwise desecrating the dead—as well as plundering and burning the village in its entirety. As if the true number of deaths (and subsequent mutilation) were not enough, Chivington claimed a body count of "400 to 500" in an after-action report, an estimate he later raised to "500 or 600" during congressional testimony.

The federal government convened three separate investigations of Sand Creek—one each by the House, Senate, and War Department—all of them concluding that Chivington and numerous others were guilty of the atrocities. In the end, however, none of the "guilty" were penalized. Chivington and the others, it was said, were not subject to prosecution in civilian courts because they had been in the military at the time their crimes were committed. Conversely, the military claimed prosecution could not occur because the perpetrators' military commissions had expired prior to the massacre, meaning they were technically civilians at the time it occurred.[3]

The size of the aggregate indigenous North American population in 1500 is estimated at about 15 million. By 1890, it had been reduced by some 98 percent, to less than 250,000. Since then, the ongoing destruction of indigenous people is best characterized as "ethnocide"—that is, the destruction of a culture rather than a people per se. These ethnocidal practices include forced relocation, compulsory transfer of native children into boarding schools designed to assimilate them into non-Indian society, dec-

A child survivor from the Sand Creek massacre of 1864. This Arapaho girl was raised by Miss Ford of Central City, Colo. Photo (taken between 1870 and 1880) by Albert S. McKinney, courtesy of the Denver Public Library Western History Department.

imation of indigenous economies, and forced imposition of new forms of sociopolitical organization in reservation settings that led to the destruction of Indian societies. It was not until 1924 that Native Americans received U.S. citizenship rights, and it was another decade before the government lifted its ban on Native Americans' practice of their traditional religious activities.

Indigenous peoples—sometimes called aboriginals, native peoples, tribal peoples, Fourth World peoples, or "first nations"—generally possess ethnic, economic, religious, and linguistic characteristics that are different from the dominant groups in the societies where they live. Today, 40 percent of the world's countries contain peoples defined as indigenous. In some states—such as Papua New Guinea, Bolivia, and Guatemala—indigenous peoples represent the majority. In most states, however, indigenous peoples are a persecuted minority and stand among the world's most disadvantaged populations. They are usually at the bottom of the socioeconomic ladder in the countries where they live, and they are marginalized politically and socially.

Over the past 500 years, millions of indigenous peoples have had to cope with destruction of their habitats, epidemic disease, hunger, warfare, despair, and gross violations of their human rights. These violations have ranged from forced removals to intentional starvation to torture to extrajudicial executions to large-scale mass killings, and even genocide. The International Work Group for Indigenous Affairs conservatively estimates that the annual deaths of indigenous peoples by violent means total around 30,000.[4]

2

Killers of Conviction

Groups, Ideology, and Extraordinary Evil

A group scarcely distinguishes between the subjective and the objective. It accepts as real the images evoked in its mind, though they most often have only a very distant relation with the observed fact. . . . Whoever can supply them with illusions is clearly their master; whoever attempts to destroy illusions is always their victim.

Gustav Le Bon, *The Crowd*

WHAT ABOUT THE MEN WHO perpetrated the slaughter at Sand Creek? Was it their membership in a collective, the Third Colorado Volunteer Cavalry Regiment, that best accounts for their active and willing participation in the atrocities? Or was it their membership in an even larger collective, the American culture, steeped in an extraordinary ideological hatred against Indians, which made them unusually fit to perpetrate extraordinary evil? This chapter will examine both of these possible explanations: the extraordinary nature of the collective and the influence of an extraordinary ideology.

The Extraordinary Nature of the Collective

One of the ways in which we explain extraordinary human evil is to focus on the means by which groups make that evil possible. Intuitively, many of us recognize that we are vulnerable to losing ourselves in a group. There seems to be something about the nature of the collective—a small band of marauders, an army battalion, a mob, a social or political organization, an office staff, a nation—that brings out our worst tendencies. A long line of scholarly interest in the collective has legitimized that intuition. In 1895, for example, French sociologist and journalist Gustav Le Bon wrote *La psychologie des foules,* which was published in English the following year under the title *The Crowd: A Study of the Popular Mind*. The work became a best-seller, was available in nineteen languages a year after publication, and became enormously influential in the academic origins of crowd psychology.

Le Bon was an anguished French middle-class academic who lived in fear that the mob could seize society at any moment. Le Bon theorized that, in a crowd, the individual's psychology is subordinated to a collective mentality that radically transforms the individual's behavior. "By the mere fact that he forms part of an organized crowd," Le Bon wrote, "a man descends several rungs in the ladder of civilization. Isolated, he may be a cultivated individual: in a crowd, he is a barbarian—that is, a creature acting by instinct."[1]

For Le Bon, the collective is an unreasoning, primitive, fickle, dictatorial, intolerant, and stupid aggregate: "Whoever be the individuals that compose it, however like or unlike be their mode of life, their occupations, their character, or their intelligence, the fact that they have been transformed into a crowd puts them in possession of a sort of collective mind which makes them feel, think, and act in a manner quite different from that in which each individual of them would feel, think, and act were he in a state of isolation."[2] In short, the basic characteristic of crowds—and any group—is the fusion of individuals into a common spirit and feeling that blurs individual differences and lowers intellectual capacities.

Sigmund Freud endorsed Le Bon's controversial view that there is a regression inherent in group behavior and dynamics. As a matter of fact, Freud was so impressed with Le Bon's description of the irrationality of crowds that he devoted a sixth of his classic *Group Psychology and Analysis of the Ego* (1921) to quotations from the Frenchman's work. Freud accepted Le Bon's characterization of the group as credulous, lacking in self-criticism, impulsive, excitable, and suggestive. In a crowd, Freud agreed, individuals lose their own opinions and intellectual faculties, can no longer control their feelings and instincts, and begin to act in a way that surprises both themselves and those who know them.

Freud specifically listed among the characteristic traits of behaviors of persons in groups: (a) the dwindling of conscious individual personality, (b) the focusing of thoughts and feelings into a common direction, (c) the dominance of the emotions and the unconscious over reason and judgment, and (d) the tendency to immediately carry out intentions as they emerge. For Freud, the group is dominated almost exclusively by the unconscious. What we see in a group or crowd, in his view, is a case of temporary regression in which the ego begins to dissolve back into the id from which it came.

Moreover, there also is a degradation of the superego (Freud's name for the individual's conscience and values) as it is externalized, or transferred, to the leader of the group. In other words, each member of the group identifies with the group leader to such an extent that the group begins to share a common superego. Violence in the group becomes possible, therefore, because the individual is no longer checked by his or her own superego but follows the conscience of the leader.

Reinhold Niebuhr, who taught for many years at Union Theological Seminary in New York City, was another vocal proponent of individual regression in groups. In his provocatively titled *Moral Man and Immoral Society*, first published in 1932, Niebuhr argued that there is a "basic difference between the morality of individuals and the morality of collectives, whether races, classes or nations."[3] What is this basic difference? In short, although individuals are capable of goodness and morality, groups are *inherently* selfish and uncaring. There is, Niebuhr argued, a clear distinction between the character of people acting in large social groups as opposed to their character as individual people. "The proportion of reason to impulse becomes increasingly negative," he writes, "when we proceed from the life of individuals to that of social groups, among whom a common mind and purpose is always more or less inchoate and transitory and who depend therefore upon a common impulse to bind them together."[4]

In Niebuhr's view, evil—our pride, pretension, insecurity—is a permanent part of human nature. This view, dubbed "Christian realism," was an update of the centuries-old Augustinian view of human nature after the fall from grace. For Niebuhr, however, this essential baseness of humanity is more massive and obvious in the life of the group than in that of the individual. He saw this as a simple fact about all collectives—they are more arrogant, hypocritical, self-centered, and more ruthless in the pursuit of their ends than the individual. As a result, an inevitable tension exists between individual and group morality. For Niebuhr, this is especially problematic because the claims of a collective far transcend those of the individual. In other words, for its very survival, the individuals involved in a collective are required to do things they would not do (and would not be morally justified in doing) as individuals. As a result, individual capacities for goodness, altruism, and morality are typically subverted to the brutal character of the group.

Moral Man and Immoral Society created a sensation in intellectual circles. Marking the beginning of the end of classical liberalism in American theology, Niebuhr attacked the premise that the steady advance of reason and goodwill in the modern age was capable of eradicating social evils. Where individuals may be reached by reason and a call to justice, Niebuhr held that nations, corporations, labor unions, and other large social groups would be unmoved by such appeals. The collective, he argued, responded to, and could only be dislodged by, one thing—power.

If the evil of the collective is more intractable than the evil of the individual, then noncoercive social institutions are simply not possible. Coercion is necessary to maintain society, and violence is merely the ultimate form of coercion. For Niebuhr, the belief in the possibility of radical societal change by "reorganization of values" or by socializing the young was naively unrealistic.

In the decades following Niebuhr's book, Hitler would move the concept of an immoral society from the realm of the theoretical to the brutal reality of the Holocaust. The general public, hungering for an explanation, latched onto Niebuhr's thinking. No longer was Niebuhr the stark iconoclast who could be vilified as a traitor to progress or, even worse, a fundamentalist. Yes, the social group might curb single individuals with the potential for extraordinary evil. However, the awful reality made clear by Hitler's Nazi Germany was that social groups with the potential for extraordinary evil could run unrestrained and carry out that extraordinary evil.

The notion that the nature of the collective somehow exacerbates or unleashes our worst tendencies was resurrected in M. Scott Peck's 1983 best-seller *People of the Lie: The Hope for Healing Human Evil*. In his discussion of group evil, Peck describes the phenomenon of "group immaturity," or the notion that human groups behave at a level that is more primitive and immature than one might expect. In other words, individuals regress in group settings. Groups, he maintains, are generally less than the sum of their parts.

Framing his point in the context of the 1968 My Lai massacre in South Vietnam, Peck argues that groups allow for the fragmentation of conscience. Not only may individuals in a group forsake their conscience, but also the conscience of the group as a whole can become so fragmented and diluted as to be nonexistent. The fragmentation of conscience described by Peck results, in large part, from the role of specialization in groups. Specialization allows groups to function with far greater efficiency than individuals. It also, however, allows for the compartmentalization of responsibility that Peck has captured in his description of the fragmentation of conscience. In Peck's somber conclusion, "Any group will remain inevitably potentially conscienceless and evil until such time as each and every individual holds himself or herself directly responsible for the behavior of the whole group—the organism—of which he or she is a part."[5]

Peck's choice of framing his discussion in the context of a military massacre is not accidental. The military represents one of our clearest examples of specialization and, as a result, is a real-life laboratory for investigating the fragmentation of conscience. Lt. Col. David Grossman, a professor of military science at Arkansas State University and author of *On Killing: The Psychological Cost of Learning to Kill in War and Society*, contends that it is group absolution that enables sane men and women to do what they do in combat. This notion that "the individual is not a killer, but the group is" echoes Peck's fragmentation of conscience. In addition, Grossman discusses how groups enable killing through developing in their members a sense of anonymity that contributes further to violence. He points out that this group anonymity can even facilitate a kind of atavistic killing hysteria that mimics similar behavior in the animal kingdom. He concludes that "groups can provide a diffusion of responsibility that will *enable individuals in mobs and soldiers in military units to commit acts that they would never dream of doing as individuals* [italics mine]."[6]

Does the Extraordinary Nature of the Collective Best Explain Extraordinary Evil?

Is there a psychological discontinuity between people acting as individuals and people acting as group members? Does membership in a larger collective, and the "mass ego frenzy" of group experience, lead us to do things we would not have done as individuals? Are all collectives inherently capable of such brutality?

The idea that the nature of the collective is immature, even brutal, is a highly pessimistic view. One critic of Niebuhr, Richard Gregg, went beyond the pessimism and maintained that the idea itself was unrealistic: "The statement that human collectives are less moral than the individuals that compose them is a highly doubtful generalization. . . . [It] is not valid. It disregards too much pertinent evidence. It does not square with the results of a wealth of patient and careful biological experiments and observations."[7] Gregg's caution about the broad generalization of the immorality of all human collectives is appropriate. All collectives are not all bad all of the time.

Neither are collectives inherently irrational and frenzied in their actions. Even the most seemingly feverish of groups—ethnic rioters—cannot thoughtlessly be classified as irrational. Donald L. Horowitz, professor of law and political science at Duke University and author of *The Deadly Ethnic Riot*, maintains that there is an important instrumental rationality required to pull off any successful ethnic riot—even though rioters appear to be motivated solely by an emotional torrent. It is a passionate but highly patterned event. Rioters wait until police protection is weak; they choose moments of attack well; they strike against unarmed concentrations of a target group in border neighborhoods; they take great pains to ensure that lives of the attackers are very rarely risked.

On a positive level, we know that groups can develop values, institutions, and practices that promote humanitarian caring and connection. Groups are not inherently selfish and uncaring; they do not always behave at a level that is more primitive and immature than the individuals that comprise the group. Groups can, for instance, help people strengthen their resolve to stop drinking, lose weight, study harder, and expand their spiritual consciousness. Even Le Bon believed that the group's inability to reason meant that they could develop great altruism, something that reason inevitably suppresses but that is a very useful social virtue. At times, groups can even provide the security to *oppose* potentially destructive ideas and practices. Groups brought democracy to Czechoslovakia and Serbia and confronted oppressive governments in China and South Africa.

We also know, however, that groups can certainly develop characteristics that create a potential for extraordinary evil. Laboratory studies indicate that, in groups, we become more aroused, more stressed, and more error-prone on complex tasks. Groups tend to be more antagonistic, competitive, and mutually exploitive than individuals. As Niebuhr pointed out, moral constraints are less powerful in groups than in individuals. As both Peck and Grossman have argued, there is a diffusion of responsibility within groups that can make evildoing a relatively simple matter. In addition, groups have the power to suppress dissent and, thus, encourage the abandonment of the individual self. In so doing, groups provide a moral authority that can give individuals sufficient justification to perpetrate extraordinary evil. Many of these factors help explain how ordinary people come to commit extraordinary evil.

I do quarrel, though, with the idea that it is the *group* rather than the *individuals* in it that best explains extraordinary evil. Being in a group does undoubtedly influence individual behavior. Group dynamics can, to some extent, alter the thoughts, feelings, and behaviors of individuals within a group. While group members may become capable of conduct of which they are incapable individually, I do not believe that being in a group *inevitably* predisposes us to commit acts of extraordinary evil that we "would never dream of doing as individuals." Being in a group *reveals* who individuals are just as much as, if not more than, being in a group alters who they are. In this way, groups can reflect some of the baser characteristics of the individuals within them as well as some of the more noble characteristics. The dynamics of a collective are best understood by the wills and ideologies of the individuals within it. Group processes, like individual processes, are dynamic, not static—changing, not changeless. In short, groups can produce action either heroic or barbaric.

We can gain some insight from group polarization research in social psychology. Decades of experimentation on group decision making show that group discussion typically *strengthens* the average inclination of the individual members in the group. In other words, group discussion tends to strengthen whatever is the initially dominant point of view, whether risky or cautious. It polarizes people's initial tendencies to the extreme. Groups do not *inevitably* make riskier decisions. They *do* inevitably make more extreme decisions. In short, the average of group members' opinions and behaviors becomes more extreme as a result of group interaction.

We can extend these findings beyond the experimental laboratory. In everyday situations, too, group interaction tends to intensify opinions and behaviors. A group, interacting in isolation from moderating influences, becomes progressively more extreme than the sum of its individual members. The result is often extreme acts—good or evil—that the individuals, apart from the group, would never have committed. In groups, not only do risk takers become riskier, but bigots also become despisers, and givers become more philanthropic.

Social psychologists Clark McCauley and Mary Segal analyzed terrorist organizations around the world and found that terrorism arises among people whose shared grievances bring them together. As they interact in isolation from moderating influences, they become progressively more extreme—both as a group and as individuals. The result is violent acts of extraordinary evil that the individuals, apart from the group, likely would never have committed—at least not to the same degree.[8] In this way, a group does become infinitely more dangerous than the same of its individual parts.

It bears repeating, however, that group interaction is a social amplifier that strengthens the preexisting signals of the individuals in the group— whether evil or good. Robert Zajonc, a social psychologist at Stanford, has captured this phenomenon in his concept of *collective potentiation*. Collective potentiation "refers to the augmentation of particular individual actions and lowering of the threshold for these actions in a group, community, organization, or a nation."[9] Under conditions of collective potentiation, more members of a group engage in a specific action, and they do so sooner and more energetically. In other words, the group amplifies individual actions, for good or for evil, through such processes as imitation, definition, celebration, and the sharing of resources.

In summary, when our individual tendencies are negative, groups have the capacity to unleash our worst impulses. However, when our individual tendencies are positive, groups accentuate the best of what we are. Depending on which tendency a group is disinhibiting or magnifying, groups can be very, very bad or very, very good. In other words, it is *not* the nature of the collective that limits our possibility for cooperative, caring, nonviolent relations; it is the nature of the individuals that make up the collective. There *is* a psychological *continuity* between people acting as individuals and people acting as group members.

The Influence of an Extraordinary Ideology

Is there a "national character" that accounts for differences between nations and the people in them? Henry V. Dicks, a British psychiatrist appointed to take over the psychiatric care of Rudolf Hess after his flight to England, certainly thought so. He defined national character as "the broad, frequently recurring regularities of certain prominent behaviour traits and motivations of a given ethnic or cultural group."[10] On the basis of his evaluation of more than one thousand German prisoners of war, Dicks concluded that there was, indeed, a long-standing German national character that lay very close to the political attitudes of the Nazi Party.

To extend Dicks's conclusion, could it be possible that an extraordinary ideology provides the soil for an extraordinary national character that predisposes people in that culture to extraordinary evil? Was Franz Ziereis an inevitable product of an extraordinary German culture shaped from an extraordinary ideological hatred of the Jews? In March 1996, a book was released that raised this very question. Daniel Jonah Goldhagen's *Hitler's Willing Executioners: Ordinary Germans and the Holocaust* stirred a renewed interest in the nature of the collective—specifically the collective of the German people.

In response to the enduring question of how the German people could do the things they did to Jews in the Holocaust, Goldhagen—then an assistant professor of government and social studies at Harvard University—gave a simple and straightforward answer: because they wanted to. Why did they want to? Because they grew up in an extraordinary culture where an unusually virulent form of antisemitism was commonplace. They were heirs to what James M. Glass, professor of government and politics at the University of Maryland, has termed a *Kultur*-group—a group constituted by a set of common or shared beliefs. Most prevalent among these shared beliefs, according to Goldhagen, was a deep-rooted, pathological antisemitism that simply awaited the ascendancy of Hitler and the opportunity of war for its lethal expression.

Following this logic, Goldhagen maintains that ordinary Germans were not forced into performing executions. Rather, they were willing participants in the whole process. These Germans did not view their actions as criminal, nor did they shrink from opportunities to inflict suffering, humiliation, and death—openly, knowingly, and zealously—on their victims. Moreover, many of them were not part of an elite group like the SS. Most were ordinary Germans. Goldhagen posits a minimum figure of one hundred thousand, and says "it would not be surprising if the number turned out to be five hundred thousand or more," who willingly took part in the Final Solution.[11] They were, in his opinion, killers of conviction.

Goldhagen's Central Propositions

Goldhagen offers two central propositions to defend his thesis that an extraordinary culture shaped by an extraordinary ideology can mold ordinary people into extraordinary killers. The first is his concept of the ideology of *eliminationist antisemitism*. Goldhagen argues that from at least the early nineteenth century, over a century before the Nazis came to power, virtually all Germans had come to believe in an "eliminationist" variant of antisemitism. This distinctive and particular German antisemitism held that Jews were different from Germans; that these alleged differences resided in their biology (conceptualized as a race) and were therefore unalterable; that the Jews were evil and powerful, had done great harm to Germany, and would continue to do so. Thus, for Germany to be secure and prosperous, there had to be an elimination of Jewish influence or of Jews themselves from German society.

Moreover, this form of antisemitism was different from all other forms of antisemitism across the world. Goldhagen compares this distinctively lethal German antisemitism with the monomania of Captain Ahab, who was possessed by the irrational passion to avenge himself against Moby-Dick. As with Ahab and the whale, so with Germans and the Jews. The German culture was distinctively possessed of a hallucinatory, lethal view of the Jews. In one critic's terms, Goldhagen depicts the Germans as basically "undifferentiated, unchanging, possessed by a single, monolithic cognitive outlook."[12] The Germans were like nobody else except the Germans. Goldhagen takes great pains to insist that his argument has nothing to do with some immutable German national character. Instead of German national character, he speaks of the character of German nationality. Regardless, his repetitive, even obsessive emphasis on the pervasiveness and depth of this lethal—and singularly German—antisemitism suggests otherwise.

Thus, when Hitler's *Mein Kampf* called for a solution to the Jewish problem, he was preaching to the converted. By the time Hitler came to power in 1933, the eliminationist antisemitism of Germany was already "pregnant with murder." Because virtually all Germans were of "one mind" about the Jews, Hitler had merely to "unshackle" and "unleash" their "preexisting, pent-up" antisemitism to perpetrate the Holocaust. It was not Hitler's willingness to murder the Jews that was crucial. It was the willingness of the German people. As Ron Rosenbaum summarizes, Hitler was more a *facilitator* of an irresistible compulsion rather than a charismatic instigator. The German people were the ventriloquists; Hitler was their dummy.[13]

According to Goldhagen, it was simple enough for the Nazi regime to tweak the eliminationist mind-set toward an exterminationist one. Average Germans, permeated with eliminationist antisemitism, had no moral scruples or reluctance to overcome when faced with the annihilation of the Jews. They were ready, and very willing, to perpetrate evil on Jews. Most would have participated directly in the killing if called on to do so. No process of brutalization was necessary. Hitler's "national project" simply gave the people the opportunity to do what they had wanted to do all along. The preexisting fever of antisemitism erupted into a mass crime of passion.

Summarily rejecting all previous interpretations, Goldhagen's second central proposition designated this *eliminationist antisemitism as the central motive*, or "causal agent," for the Holocaust. According to Goldhagen, this cause outweighs all others, and without it, the Holocaust would have been unthinkable. He writes:

Germans' anti-Semitic beliefs about Jews were the central causal agent of the Holocaust. . . . The conclusion of this book is that antisemitism moved many thousands of "ordinary" Germans—and would have moved millions more, had they been appropriately positioned—to slaughter Jews. Not economic hardship, not the coercive means of a totalitarian state, not social psychological pressure, not invariable psychological propensities, but ideas about Jews that were pervasive in Germany, and had been for decades, induced ordinary Germans to kill unarmed, defenseless Jewish men, women, and children by the thousands, systematically and without pity.[14]

In other words, fueled by this murderous antisemitism, Germans killed Jews because they wanted to kill Jews. They were not faceless cogs of an impersonal bureaucratic abstract system, but individuals acting according to their deep-rooted beliefs. They participated because they thought the Jews ought to die, that the annihilation of the Jews was socially desirable, and that the Jews were a particularly inferior form of subhumans. They simply thought they were doing the right thing. Moreover, the perpetrators engaged in cruelty with zest, enthusiasm, and willingness. Their cruelty, according to Goldhagen, was not a response to orders. They were cruel because of their own free will. They were not subject to forces that made them engage in actions they believed inwardly to be reprehensible. They were eager, even happy, to persecute and murder Jews.

In Goldhagen's view, it was an extraordinary culture driven by an extraordinary ideological hatred against Jews that had shaped an extraordinary people who could carry out such atrocities. No other motive—conformity to peer pressure, obedience to authority, blind acceptance of current political norms, careerism, personal profit, coercion, routinization, brutalization—was necessary. To put it simply, if the perpetrators were antisemites who believed that the extermination of Jews was right, then all the situational factors so commonly asserted to have motivated the killers are irrelevant. Everybody was antisemitic and antisemitism explains everything.

Was Eliminationist Antisemitism Pervasive before the Nazi Takeover?

There is no question that antisemitism, particularly of an "exclusionist" bent, was persistent in Germany prior to the Nazi takeover. There is also no question that, after the Nazi rise to power, the long-standing historical animosity of antisemitism took on a different slant—it became elimin, ation-

ist, even exterminationist. But is Goldhagen correct in asserting that eliminationist antisemitism was a pre-Nazi phenomenon? If he is, it seems that
there would not have been a Jew alive in Germany to persecute in 1933.
Exactly how pervasive was eliminationist antisemitism *before* the Nazi
takeover?

The vast majority of scholars maintain that, regardless of where one
looks, it is hard to find widespread evidence that eliminationist antisemitism was the "culturally shared cognitive model" that Goldhagen
maintains it to be in Germany since the early nineteenth century. In fact,
for a very long time, Germany was thought to be a peculiarly hospitable
and secure place for Jews. German Jews had received legal emancipation in
the second half of the nineteenth century, well ahead of some other European nations. Civil rights for Jews remained on the books until the Nazis
rewrote them. Jews undoubtedly had trouble exercising these rights at
times, but this does not alter the fact that they were granted.

In addition, most scholars agree that Jews were influential out of proportion to their number. In 1933, about 525,000 people, or less than 1 percent of the German population, were registered as Jews. Despite their mea-
ger numbers, Jews were disproportionately active in the cultural, financial,
and political life of Germany. As Marion A. Kaplan, professor of history at
Queens College and the Graduate Center, City University of New York,
writes: "They [Jews] enjoyed general acceptance, even acclaim, in the
worlds of art and culture, participated in center and moderate left politics,
and excelled in the professions of medicine and law. . . . [Jews created] new
forms of German-Jewish culture in literature, music, fine arts, education,
and scholarship."[15] Widespread feverish antisemitism and the achievements
of the Jewish community in Germany stand in impossible contradiction.

A recent study by Arnd Kruger of the University of Göttingen offers
additional support for the assertion that prior to 1933 exclusionist antisemitism did not represent the attitudes of the majority in Germany.[16] In
his analysis of German Jewish sport from 1898 to 1938, Kruger maintains
that exclusionist sentiments were neither weaker nor stronger in Germany
than in other European countries at the turn of the century. As one example, Kruger discusses the German Turner organization. The German Turners (gymnasts) comprised a fiercely nationalistic sport movement that, at the
turn of the century, had six times as many members as all other "sports" combined. In 1889, Austrian clubs—holding membership in the German
Turner organization that comprised the Turners in Germany and Austria—
began a move to exclude Jewish members. This resulted in a split within

the German Turner organization. Though the organization eventually permitted each individual club to include an "Aryan paragraph" in its statutes if it so desired, it did not permit a larger district or region to have such a paragraph in its bylaws.

Eventually, the antisemitic clubs in the German Turners withdrew from the larger organization. The German Turner organization was willing to keep its "handful" of Jewish members, even if it was losing about 15 percent of its membership over the question of an Aryan paragraph. At the turn of the century, when Goldhagen maintains that there existed a rabid eliminationist antisemitism through Germany, exclusionist antisemitism was not even strong enough to sway the German Turners. The pragmatic maintenance of the organization fell second to the moral forces of liberalism, humanity, and sanity. As Kruger points out, this example is especially telling when one considers that athletes and athletic organizations tend to be more conservative in their politics and world outlook than society at large.

Furthermore, Goldhagen does not prove that pre-Nazi German antisemitism was more pervasive than elsewhere in Europe. Doing more comparative work in a larger European context certainly would have modified Goldhagen's extreme views about German antisemitism. The quantity of antisemitic expression in Russia, Romania, and Poland was at least as great as that found in Germany. In Russia, antisemitism was prevalent enough to bring about dozens of violent pogroms, which the Tsarist Minister of the Interior, Count Nikolai Pavlovich Ignatyev, likened to the verdict of a "people's court." Most scholars even contend that *French* antisemitism was far worse, far more virulent, deep-rooted, and bitter than Germany's, in the pre–World War I period.

In addition, Goldhagen's depiction of a pernicious pre-Nazi German antisemitism certainly does not square with most political analyses of the period. Antisemitism was not popular at the German polls before depression struck, nor was it decisive in winning voters over to the Nazi Party. Sociologist William Brustein of the University of Minnesota maintains that as early as 1924–1925, Nazi leaders had concluded that the issue of antisemitism held insufficient appeal for building a national political party attractive to all German classes. In its rise to power, Brustein argues, the Nazi Party increasingly relegated antisemitism to a role as backdrop to other more materialist appeals — particularly economic concerns.[17] In the election of 1930, which won the Nazis their entrée into the political system, political opportunism demanded that the Jewish issue be downplayed. For

Germans, as for most of us, their political affiliation was based on self-interest. And for most Germans, that self-interest was driven by economic, not antisemitic, motivations. Early joiners of the Nazi Party calculated that, of the many competing Weimar political parties, the Nazis offered them the best prospects for a better economic life.

Even given the appeal of the Nazi Party to some Germans, it remains true that the majority of Germans were not moved by the Nazi Party's potential to enrich their lives. In the last free election of the period, in November 1932, the Nazis received only 33 percent of the vote, while the communists and socialists—bitter enemies of each other as well as the Nazis—together garnered 37 percent. Clearly, before 1933, German society was torn with too many social, political, and ideological divisions to ensure a unified brand of eliminationist antisemitism that would find a ready collaborator in the Nazi Party.

As Brustein concludes: "Why has anti-Semitism received so much attention as a theme of the Nazi Party before 1933? The Nazi regime's subsequent systematic policy of liquidating the Jewish people has irrevocably shaped our understanding of Nazism. It is only natural that our view of the Nazis' rise to power is colored by recognition of their profound anti-Semitism. Yet as difficult as it may be for many of us to believe, Nazi anti-Semitism, though a driving force in the foundation of the Nazi Party, hardly explains the NSDAP's spectacular rise to power."[18] Unfortunately, Goldhagen's view of the Nazis' rise to power is overly prejudiced by his exclusive focus on eliminationist antisemitism.

Once in power, of course, the Nazis quickly abandoned their pre-1933 political strategy and pursued their hidden agenda of territorial expansion and racial persecution, including their virulent form of antisemitism. Even as the Nazis gained broad popular support and legitimacy, however, most Germans were drawn to antisemitism because they were drawn to Nazism, not the other way around. In other words, antisemitism was part of the baggage of Nazism.

Indeed, most scholars argue that the majority of ordinary Germans, rather than being eliminationist antisemites, remained simply passive, apathetic, and indifferent to the fate of Jews among them. As historian David Bankier writes, "Ordinary Germans knew how to distinguish between acceptable discrimination . . . and the unacceptable horror of genocide. . . . The more the news of the mass murder filtered through, the less the public wanted to be involved in the Final Solution of the Jewish question."[19] Historian Ian Kershaw likewise concludes, "The 'Jewish question' was of no more than minimal interest to the vast majority of Germans during the war years. . . . Popular opinion, largely indifferent and infused with a latent anti-Jewish feeling . . . provided the climate within which spiraling Nazi aggression towards the Jews could take place unchallenged. But it did not provoke the radicalization in the first place."[20] It is clear that, on the whole, most Germans did not share the fanatical antisemitism—and certainly not the genocidal commitment—of Adolf Hitler and the hardcore Nazis. It is just as clear, however, that their indifference, manifested in a national conspiracy of silence, provided the autonomy for the regime to implement genocidal policies.

It could be argued that this indifference also allowed many ordinary Germans to become part of the destruction process. Perhaps it was not the hateful, rabid, revengeful eliminationist antisemitism that spurred the atrocities. Rather, perhaps it was because the indifference to Jews—motivated, in part, by a "moderate antisemitism"—ran so deep that many ordinary Germans could kill them just as easily as not. So, rather than a deep, preceding ideological hatred, perhaps it was a *lack* of emotional connection that neutralized whatever aversion Germans might otherwise have felt for the Nazis and made such atrocities possible.

Another piece of evidence suggesting that eliminationist antisemitism was not as pervasive as maintained by Goldhagen comes from the secret diaries of Victor Klemperer collected from 1933 to 1945. Klemperer was the son of a Reform rabbi who converted to Protestantism when he was thirty-one years old. After a brief stint as a journalist, he was appointed professor of Romance languages at the Technical University of Dresden in 1920. In 1935, however, the Nuremberg laws on "German Blood and German Honor" defined Klemperer as "un-German." Despite his status as a decorated World War I veteran and his conversion to Protestantism, Klemperer was labeled as a foreigner and a Jew and subject to the anti-Jewish measures sweeping throughout his homeland. In 1935, he was forced by the Nazis to retire from his teaching position at Dresden. He survived twelve years of Nazi rule in Germany only because his wife, Eva Schlemmer, whom he married in 1906, was considered an "Aryan" by the regime.

Goldhagen's depiction of German society as more or less monolithically antisemitic is not confirmed by Klemperer's diary. Rather, his remarkable diary—nearly 1,700 printed pages—reveals a world in which most, but not all, Germans gradually turned their backs on the Jews. To be sure, the Nazi regime's open antisemitism is on display throughout the pages of the two-volume diary. The reaction of ordinary Germans, however, is far different from the violent antisemitism alleged by Goldhagen. "The majority of the people is content," Klemperer records. "A small group accepts Hitler as the lesser evil, no one really wants to be rid of him, all see in him the liberator in foreign affairs, fear Russian conditions . . . believe, insofar as they are not honestly carried away, that it is inopportune . . . to be outraged at such details as the suppression of civil liberties, the persecution of the Jews, the falsification of all scholarly truths, the systematic destruction of all morality. And all are afraid for their livelihood, their life, all are such terrible cowards."[21] Though most found the means to accommodate themselves to the Nazi regime, they were not motivated by a vicious form of antisemitism. Rather, a mix of cowardice, apathy, and slavish obedience to authority motivated them.

Elsewhere Klemperer writes, "I often ask myself where all the wild anti-Semitism is. For my part I encounter much sympathy, people help me out, but fearfully of course."[22] After the introduction of the required yellow star of Jewish identification, Klemperer relates the following incident: "On the park way of the Lothringer Strasse as I came back from the cemetery on Sunday afternoon an old gentleman—white goatee, approximately seventy, retired higher ranking civil servant—came right across the path toward me, stretched out his hand to me, and said with a certain ceremoniality: 'I saw your star and I greet you, I condemn this ostracism of a race, and many others do so likewise.' I: 'That's very kind of you—but you're not allowed to talk with me; it can cost me my life and bring you into prison.'—Yes, but he wanted to, he had to tell me that."[23] Klemperer's perception of a largely indifferent—occasionally even sympathetic—German public contrasts starkly with Goldhagen's image of 80 million willing executioners. Klemperer's firsthand account compellingly demonstrates that not all ordinary Germans were fiercely committed to Nazism and antisemitism.

How does Goldhagen get around this, and other, evidence against his bold claim that eliminationist antisemitism permeated German society? Driven by prosecutorial passion, he pulls a sleight of hand by contending that the cognitive model was so overwhelming that Germans need not *express* antisemitism at all—they were just antisemites. Eliminationist antisemitism was the invisible engine that fueled the German system, from individual souls to state organization. The proof of it, according to Goldhagen, lay in its *absence* from political statements, letters, texts, or creeds. "Notions fundamental to the dominant worldview and operation of a society," he writes, "precisely because they are absolutely taken for granted, often are not expressed in a manner commensurate with their prominence and significance or, when uttered, seen as worthy by others to be noted and recorded."[24]

In short, if you were a German in 1930 and were not *blatantly* antisemitic, it was only because your antisemitism ran so deep that it need not be expressed. Even if expressed, the others around you would not have noted it. You lived in a culture permeated by eliminationist antisemitism, and both its expression and its lack of expression testified to that fact.

Was Eliminationist Antisemitism the Central Motive for the Holocaust?

Even if we accept the spurious concept of a German culture marinated in eliminationist antisemitism, there remain several concerns about raising it as the central motive for the Holocaust. Goldhagen pays no attention, for instance, to the fact that not all the killers in the Holocaust were Germans. The killers included ethnic Germans who lived outside Germany, Romanians, Croats, Ukrainians, Estonians, Latvians, and Lithuanians in significant numbers. How do we ascribe to all these people, who had not been a part of German society, the kind of uniquely German eliminationist antisemitism that Goldhagen maintains to underlie their perpetration of extraordinary evil?

In addition, Goldhagen ignores the fact that German executioners were equally capable of killing millions of non-Jews targeted by the Nazi regime. As historian Christopher Browning points out, the European Jews were only one group of people that became victims of industrially organized killing during World War II. Beginning in 1939, systematic and large-scale mass murder was initiated against mental and physical defectives in Germany (regardless of religion) and Polish intelligentsia; more than 3 million Soviet prisoners of war died from hunger, exposure, disease, and outright execution; Gypsies were included in the genocidal assault; Slavic populations were routinely subjected to selective massacres. All told, the Nazi regime killed approximately 20 million unarmed persons. Yet Jews comprised only a third of the victims, and their mass murder occurred well into the sequence of killing.

Goldhagen does not offer a viable explanation for the victimization of these non-Jewish groups. Did the eliminationist antisemitism spill over to the murder of millions of non-Jewish victims? Is it to be understood as "eliminationist racism" or "eliminationist anti-Bolshevism?" If so, how is it different from "eliminationist antisemitism?" In short, it is not. It is part of a totalistic ideology aimed at a complete reconstruction of Aryan society. In that ideology, hatred of Jews was a part of a hierarchy of hatreds and animosities. To be sure, Jews were selected for the most brutal treatment and were the only group specifically targeted for extermination. This fact cannot, however, be artificially separated from the larger context of which it was a part. Not antisemitism alone, but the much larger scope of Nazi racial ideology played a significant role in the mentality that led to the murder of 15 million victims. As Henry Friedlander, a survivor of Auschwitz and professor of Judaic studies at Brooklyn College of the City University of New York, writes: "One cannot explain any one of these Nazi killing operations without explaining the others. Together they represented Nazi genocide."[25]

More generally, *there are simply too many instances of such mass murders and genocides in history for us to accept a peculiarly German eliminationist antisemitism as the singular, monocausal motivating force.* Instead of probing how humans from a variety of backgrounds have, in a variety of situations, radically violated the norms of "civilized" society, Goldhagen directs all of our attention to trying to understand the radical German violation of the norms — as if German behavior were completely without parallel. He ignores, for instance, the records of the Austrians, Ukrainians, Balts, Croats, French, Hungarians, Romanians, Slovaks, and others that reveal just as much sadism and cruelty as any Germans. If these people perform the same duties and behave in the same way as their German counterparts, then the argument of "specifically German behavioral modes" fails. In addition, other recent historical atrocities — Stalin's terror, the Cultural Revolution in China, the Khmer Rouge in Cambodia — show that mass fealty can be whipped up by a totalitarian leader, operating in an atmosphere of state terror, without any particularly deep, preceding hatred for the victimized groups.

Unfortunately, Goldhagen dismisses as self-serving all German sources that indicate conscience on the part of some German perpetrators or even a gradual hardening of their callousness. He only accepts testimony that is self-condemning. Anything exculpatory or apologetic is dismissed. He also, far less forgivably, disregards the many Jewish sources that testify to the complexity and diversity of the perpetrators' motives. Browning reports two cases of Jewish witnesses (with no self-exculpatory motives) who make it clear that Germans in killing squads differed greatly in their antisemitic outlooks.[26] Survivor testimony is filled with those who recognize this complexity — what Primo Levi has termed the "gray zone" — and speak of watching "decent people become murderers." Yes, there certainly were enthusiastic and sadistic killers. There was not, however, a *uniform and pervasive bestiality* among the perpetrators. Most of them had differentiated reactions, and many of them had a dramatic transformation in character over time. There was no one set of individuals with one set of characteristics that perpetrated the extraordinary evil of the Holocaust. In short, Goldhagen adopts a deterministic methodology that was guaranteed not to reflect diversity of outlook and response and that could confirm no other outcome than his initial hypothesis that all perpetrators acted on prior eliminationist antisemitic beliefs.

Summary

It is tempting to demonize Goldhagen and his work in the same way that, many believe, he demonized the German population. However, he must be granted credit where credit is due. He succeeds admirably in bringing the focus of the investigation of extraordinary evil away from impersonal institutions and abstract structures back to the actors, back to the human beings who committed the crimes and to the populace from which these men and women came. Moreover, he emphasizes personal intent and responsibility in perpetrators.

In addition, he substantiates the important fact that many more Germans were *directly* involved in the killings than has previously been assumed. In so doing, he reminds us that roughly the same proportions of sadists and psychopaths, useful for genocide work, exist across cultures. However, this proportion is not high enough to successfully carry out a mass killing or genocide. You need, as Goldhagen correctly points out, thousands of other "willing executioners." (Unfortunately, he obscures this important point with his obsessive emphasis on the extraordinary nature of the German culture and its extraordinary ideology of eliminationist antisemitism.)

Despite these contributions, Goldhagen's two central propositions remain untenable. First, there is little evidence that the antisemitism of Germans was "eliminationist" aside from the outcome. Germans were not so fundamentally different that it is plausible to attribute to them a single cognitive outlook in stark contrast to the diversity found in the rest of the contemporaneous human community. We will not benefit from an approach that emphasizes uniformity among one particular culture and a sharp difference between "them" and other peoples. We need not invoke a "demonological" hatred of others to explain the commission of extraordinary evil. The existence of widespread negative racial stereotyping in a society—in no way unique to Nazi Germany—can provide fanatical regimes not only the freedom of action to pursue genocide but also an ample supply of executioners.

His second central proposition, that eliminationist antisemitism was the central motive for the Holocaust, fares no better. The fixation on one overarching explanation—rather than many overlapping, reinforcing, perhaps partially competing explanations—is too simplistic. He runs a monocausal thesis into the ground. A singular crime need not be reduced to a singular cause.

Conclusion

What truths can we glean from the argument that the origin of extraordinary evil is in extraordinary groups? First, the extraordinary nature of a collective must be considered in any explanatory model of extraordinary human evil. We must accept the fact that group dynamics can, to some extent, alter the thoughts, feelings, and behaviors of individuals within a group. As Israel Charny writes: "It is a human being who operates through the mechanisms of group behavior to do what he does to fellow human beings, but it is the mechanism of group experience that potentiates, legitimates, operationalizes, and narcotizes the emergence of man's various and often unsavory selves."[27]

We must also accept the fact, however, that being in a group does not inevitably lead us to commit acts of extraordinary evil that we "would never dream of doing as individuals." Being in a group *reveals* who individuals are just as much, if not more, than being in a group alters who they are. In this way, groups can reflect some of the baser characteristics of the individuals within them as well as some of the more noble. The dynamics of a collective are best understood by the wills and ideologies of the individuals within it. To divorce groups from the reality of the nature of the individuals within them is to misplace the blame for the commission of extraordinary evil.

Second, the influence of a culture and its corresponding ideologies must also be considered in any explanatory model of extraordinary human evil. Cultural characteristics are critically relevant in molding the identities of the perpetrators (see chapter 6) and matter in an important way in explaining extraordinary evil. Certainly, for instance, culture and ideology played a partial role in why the Holocaust happened in Germany and nowhere else in Europe.

It is too easy, though, to say that *only* an extraordinary culture, like Germany, and *only* an allegedly extraordinary ideology, like eliminationist antisemitism, could produce a man like Franz Ziereis. We want to assume that mass killing and genocide are simply inherited from cultures and ideologies that preceded a regime's rise to power because then we can believe that extraordinary human evil is curable. Simply change the culture or ideology and you can change the mind-set that leads to something like the Holocaust. Admitting that culture or ideology may be simply the pretext by which we rationalize a more general wish to dominate and destroy is much more discomforting.

Moreover, by ascribing the crimes and their perpetrators to a particular culture or ideology, *their* behavior becomes "unfathomable" and outside of "our" world. Only the Germans could have behaved the way they did; nobody else could have. As a consequence, it cannot be repeated by someone else. Unfortunately, it has been, is being, and will be repeated by many other people. As a result, we must recognize that we are dealing not with "ordinary Germans" but rather with "ordinary people." As Browning writes, "If ordinary Serbs, Croats, Hutus, Turks, Cambodians and Chinese can be the perpetrators of mass murder and genocide, implemented with terrible cruelty, then we do indeed need to look at those universal aspects of human nature that transcend the cognition and culture of ordinary Germans."[28]

Dovey's Story

THE ARMENIANS ARE AN ANCIENT people who, from the first millennium B.C.E., lived in a mountainous plateau in Asia Minor, a country to which they gave their name. They developed their own culture, spoke a unique language, had a distinct alphabet, a native poetry, original folk music, an authentic architectural style, and a series of monarchical dynasties and princely families. Early in the fourth century, the king of Armenia accepted Christianity, making his country the first to formally recognize the new faith. The mountainous country and long, harsh winters reinforced the remoteness, and distinctiveness, of the Armenian civilization.

Over time, however, Armenia proved too small a country to withstand land-hungry outside aggressors. From 1071 on, when Turkish tribal armies prevailed over the Christian forces that were resisting their incursions, the Armenians lived as subjects of various Turkish dynasties. The last and longest lived of these dynasties were the Ottomans. The Ottoman Turks, adherents of Islam, built a vast empire in which Christians and Jews were relegated to second-class status. Despite their inferior status, Armenian communities, as a Christian minority, were tolerated for centuries in the Ottoman Empire and managed to attain an acceptable standard of living.

Armenians welcomed the Young Turk revolution of 1908. Organized in reaction to the autocratic regime of Sultan Abdul-Hamid II, the liberal and egalitarian Young Turks advocated progressive reform that promised to further improve the situation of Armenians. An era of brotherhood and renovation was thought to have begun. Following the Ottoman military disasters of 1908–1912, however, the Young Turk government was taken over by its ultranationalistic, militaristic, and chauvinistic wing led by Enver Pasha, Talaat Bey, and Djemal Pasha. Ottoman tolerance was abandoned for the ideology of pan-Turkism—a version of racial nationalism that emphasized a common culture and language and excluded all minority groups. In April 1915, the Young Turks embarked upon the systematic destruction of the Armenian population.

The procedure for annihilation followed a pattern set by the central government. First writers, poets, jurists, educators, clergy, and community leaders were sent to their deaths. Next, able-bodied men who appeared to be between fourteen and sixty were drafted into special "labor battalions" and set to digging ditches, worked to death, or murdered. Last, women, children, and the aged, on pretext of "relocation," were set on foot toward the Syrian desert. These deportations were mainly intended as death marches. Gendarmes flogged the deportees when they paused to rest; forbade them drink when they passed wells and streams; stole their bread and clothes; tortured, raped, and mutilated them. In these atrocities, the gendarmes often were assisted by prisoners loosed from the jails and by villagers and tribesmen called out to join in the work of killing "by hand."

The Armenian population of the Ottoman Empire was reported at about 2 million in 1915. By 1923, when the Republic of Turkey replaced the Ottoman Empire, virtually the entire Armenian population had disappeared from historic Armenia. In all, it is estimated that up to a million and a half Armenians perished at the hands of Ottoman and Turkish military and paramilitary forces and through atrocities intentionally designed to eliminate the Armenian demographic presence in Turkey.[1]

The following is excerpted from Peter Balakian's award-winning memoir *Black Dog of Fate: An American Son Uncovers His Armenian Past*. This account is a recollection of events from July 1915 in the Armenian province of Diarbekir. It describes the experiences of Dovey, the cousin of the mother of Balakian's Auntie Gladys.

> I could not hear what was being said. Because my father was a spice merchant, he spoke many languages—Turkish, Arabic, Kurdish, French, and English. He was a soft-spoken man who had gone to Euphrates College before he returned to Diarbekir to marry mother and start his business. They talked for several minutes. I heard my father shout: "I was born a Christian and I will die a Christian." Then I heard some footsteps and some clicking of boots on the tiles and the front door closed. It was a big door made of walnut and it had a round silver knocker, and when it closed the knocker slapped the door. I heard the clomping of horses on the cobblestone as they rode away with my father. Then there was silence, and not one of us—my brother Hagop or my sister Takooi or my mother or our servant Dikran—made a move. I went back to bed and lay watching the candlelight flicker against the way, watching the wall turn to purple as the dawn

A family of Armenian deportees walk toward the Syrian desert with no means of shelter from the elements. The woman in the foreground is carrying a child in her arms, shielding it from the sun with a shawl (1915). Photo from the Armenian National Institute (www.armenian-genocide.org), by Armin T. Wegner, courtesy of Sybil Stevens.

hit it, and the next thing I knew I was wakened by a scream. A scream that was my mother's voice. I noticed that my candle had burned down and left a messy puddle of wax on my nightstand. There was a knock at the door and it was Dikran saying, "You must stay in your room."

I put on my riding dress and hurried downstairs. I ran through the courtyard to the foyer and found mother lying unconscious on the green-and-black tiles. Then I saw an object sticking through the door and something that looked like a horseshoe. I walked over to the door and pushed it open. I saw that two horseshoes were nailed to two feet, and my eye followed the feet to the ankles, which were covered in blood, and then to the knees which looked disjointed. I looked up to the genitals, which were just a mound of blood, above which long snake-like lacerations rose up the abdomen to the chest. The hands were nailed horizontally on a board, which was meant to resemble a cross. The hands were clenched like claws around big spikes of iron driven into the board. The shoulders were remarkably clean and white, and the throat had a fringe of beard along the last inch of the body. There was nothing else on the cross. They had left the head near the steps to our house, just at the edge of the street. I could see his nose propped on the step. I could see the beard trimmed neatly along the cheekbones. I could see it was my father. . . .

[About one week later] I walked out of our courtyard through the doorway where my father's crucified body had been left, and into the street. . . . I walked past Saint Giragos, past the Assyrian church and the Mosque, past the archway with the tiled courtyard, and the walls of the city looked even blacker in the heat. Through the doorway of the New Gate I could see how brown the plain was, and in the sun the Tigris looked like floating mud. In the Citadel Gardens nothing was green except the cypress trees. As I passed the Gardens I began to smell the foul odor again. The shops were open, and the rugs and dresses and belts were hanging, and the awnings were stretched out, but there was no one around. The streets were empty. The shops were empty, and the crowd in the southeast corner of the market was growing. I was self-conscious without my charshaff, but no one noticed me as I slipped into the crowd that was making such a commotion in the square.

The crowd lined the square, some people were sitting in chairs, some Arabs selling quinces, people burning incense, the Turkish women in burugs were sitting on hassocks eating simits. The sun was terribly hot, and on the black walls some cranes were perched. In the middle of the crowd there were fifteen or twenty Armenian women, some a little older than me, some my mother's age. They were dressed in their daily clothes. Some in long fine dresses, others, who were peasants, in simple black. They were holding hands and walking in a circle slowly, tentatively, as if they were afraid to move. About six Turkish soldiers stood behind them. They had whips and each had a gun. They were shouting, "Dance. *Giaur.* Slut." The soldiers cracked their whips on the women's backs and faces, and across their breasts. "Dance. *Giaur.* Slut." Many of the women were praying while they moved in this slow circle. *Der Voghormya, Der Voghormya* (Lord have mercy), *Kris-dos bada raqyal bashkhi I miji meroom* (Christ is sacrificed and shared amongst us), and occasionally they would drop the hand next to them and quickly make the sign of the cross. Their hair had come undone and their faces were wrapped up in the blood-stuck tangles of hair, so they looked like corpses of Medusa. Their clothes were now turning red. Some of them were half naked, others tried to hold their clothes together. They began to fall down and when they did they were whipped until they stood and continued their dance. Each crack of the whip and more of their clothing came off.

Around them stood their children and some other Armenian children who had been rounded up from the nearby Armenian school. They were forced into a circle, and several Turkish soldiers stood behind them with whips and shouted "Clap, clap." And the children clapped. And when the soldiers said "Clap, clap, clap," the children were supposed to clap faster, and if they didn't, the whip was used on them. Some of the children were two and three years old, barely able to stand up. They were all crying uncontrollably. Crying in a terrible, pitiful, hopeless way. I stood next to women in burugs and men in red fezzes and business suits, and they too were clapping like little cockroaches.

Then two soldiers pushed through the crowd swinging wooden buckets and began to douse the women with the fluid in the buckets, and, in a second, I could smell that it was kerosene. And the women screamed because the kerosene was burning their lacerations and cuts. Another soldier came forward with a torch and lit each woman by the hair. At first all I could see was smoke, and the smell grew sickening, and then I could see the fire growing off the women's bodies, and their screaming became unbearable. The children were being whipped now furiously, as if the sight of the burning mothers had excited the soldiers, and they admonished the children to clap "faster, faster, faster," telling them that if they stopped they too would be lit on fire. As the women began to collapse in burning heaps, oozing and black, the smell of burnt flesh made me sick. I fainted and your mother's brother Haroutiun found me and took me home.[2]

To date, successive Turkish governments continue to mount increasingly virulent campaigns of denial. Deniers, working from a centrally directed governmental initiative, have ignored extensive documented accounts of foreign diplomatic and mission eyewitnesses; manipulated, altered, and falsified source documents and demographic data; and used flawed argumentation and specious social science to "legitimate" their denials. No other nation in the modern age has engaged in such a massive cover-up campaign about such a heinous crime. Despite their continuing efforts of denial and revisionist interpretation, however, there is now widespread recognition that the Turkish destruction of the Armenians between 1915 and 1923 stands as the first "total genocide" of the twentieth century. On April 24 of each year, Armenians commemorate the genocide at the site of memorials raised by the survivors in their communities around the world.[3]

3

The "Mad Nazi"

Psychopathology, Personality, and Extraordinary Evil

One of the most disturbing facts that came out in the Eichmann trial was that a psychiatrist examined him and pronounced him *perfectly sane*. I do not doubt it at all, and that is precisely why I find it disturbing. If all the Nazis had been psychotics . . . their appalling cruelty would have been in some sense easier to understand.

Thomas Merton, *Reflections*

FOLLOWING THEIR IDEOLOGY OF pan-Turkism, Enver, Talaat, and Djemal set in motion the systematic destruction of the Armenian population. These genocidal plans of the Young Turks were implemented by thousands of commanders, leaders, officers, and rank-and-file soldiers in Ottoman and Turkish military and paramilitary forces. Can the participation of individuals who planned and implemented these atrocities best be explained by equally extraordinary origins? Specifically, can we find the origins of their extraordinary evil in psychopathology (that is, mental illness) or in an extraordinary personality?

Psychopathology

The "Mad Nazi" Thesis

On November 20, 1945, "the greatest trial in history"—the indictment of alleged Nazi war criminals—opened. The Nuremberg Trials, held at the site of annual Nazi Party rallies and one of the few German cities that did not lie in almost total ruins (even after eleven Allied air raids), were the first trials in history for "crimes against the peace of the world." Never before had leaders of a regime been held legally accountable for crimes committed within the framework of their policy. As historian Michael R. Marrus describes the Allies' motivation, "The terrible conflict against Germany, the most destructive war in history, should not end like other wars: It was not a calamity to be overcome, but an unprecedented crime to be punished."[1] It was one of those rare times when humanity itself is put on trial.

The Nuremberg Trials were convened by the International Military Tribunal (IMT), consisting of judges from the Allied powers—Great Britain, France, the Soviet Union, and the United States. The trials were an enormous undertaking that involved 403 open sessions over the course of a year. The tribunal heard 94 witnesses in court (33 for the prosecution and 61 for the defense) and received written responses to interrogatories of an additional 143. In addition, the IMT received tens of thousands of affidavits and scrutinized thousands of pages of documents, briefs, and motions.

Some major Nazi figures, such as Hitler, Himmler, and Joseph Goebbels, had escaped trial by committing suicide. Others, such as Reinhard Heydrich, were assassinated during the war. At Nuremberg, twenty-two high-ranking Nazi leaders stood in the dock. (Two additional leaders were accused, but one, Robert Ley, committed suicide, and the other, Gustav Krupp, was considered too physically infirm to stand trial.) These members of the Nazi elite were responsible not merely for following orders but also for issuing them. Each of the defendants was tried on one or more of the following charges: (1) crimes against the peace, (2) war crimes, (3) crimes against humanity, and (4) conspiracy to commit any of these crimes.

The announcement of the verdicts was completed on October 1, 1946. Appropriately, this date fell on Yom Kippur, the climax of the High Holy Days in Judaism. This sacred Day of Atonement is the day to face up to one's sins and their consequences. On this day, the tribunal would announce the consequences of the sins committed against humanity by the twenty-two Nazi defendants. The IMT acquitted three of the defendants. Twelve others were condemned to death by hanging. Martin Bormann, Nazi Party secretary and chief aide to Hitler, was tried in absentia and missing from the group of the condemned, and Hermann Göring, Reichsmarschall and the highest-ranking Nazi official after Hitler, escaped the gallows when he killed himself by swallowing cyanide on the eve of his execution day. The remaining seven defendants received prison terms that ranged from ten years to life.

Rudolf Hess, Hitler's private secretary and the third-ranking Nazi official, was one of the defendants sentenced to life in prison. For the final five years of the war, Hess had occupied a succession of British jails and military hospitals. He was judged somewhere between eccentric and mad. At Nuremberg, Hess took advantage of the latter suspicion and feigned insanity—or, at the very least, incompetence to stand trial—during much of the proceedings. With a mad stare in his eyes, he pretended that he was unaware of what was going on and had lost his memory. Throughout most of the trial, Hess read novels in the courtroom. At the reading of his verdict, he refused to put on his earphones and rocked back and forth. The court was not so equally swayed. In reading their verdict, they maintained there was nothing to show that Hess did not realize the nature of the charges against him or was incapable of defending himself. Hess spent the rest of his life in Spandau prison, allegedly dying by his own hand in 1987 at the age of ninety-three.

Hess's calculated portrayal of the "mad Nazi" had fooled several of the Allied mental health professionals. Even after Hess's dramatic courtroom admission that his reasons for simulating loss of memory were of a tactical nature, at least a couple of professionals still clung to their diagnosis of an insane "hysterical amnesiac" who was mentally unfit to stand trial. As historian Joseph E. Persico has concluded, however, "one cannot read the literally hundreds of letters that this man wrote, from the time of his internment in England in 1941, throughout the trial, and during the Spandau years, without concluding that here was a clear mind at work. If there was anything mad about Rudolf Hess it was his decision to act mad for nearly half a century."[2]

Indeed, Hess was clever as a fox—especially in his attempt to take advantage of the general perception that only pathological people could have implemented and participated in these atrocities. Another defendant—Karl Donitz, Hitler's actual successor and commander of the German U-boat fleet—also had unsuccessfully played the "mad Nazi" card. "Two companions and I," Donitz confessed to a prison psychiatrist, "decided it might aid our efforts to escape if we were adjudged insane. We walked about, our heads hunched down, going 'Bzzzz, Bzzzz,' and insisting we were U-boats. The British doctors were too smart for us. We didn't get anywhere. Solitary confinement cured our 'mental state' in no time."[3]

These defendants were building on a tradition of Allied propaganda that portrayed the Nazi leaders as a group of uniquely diabolical, sinister, viciously sadistic, and demonically deranged lunatics. In 1943, noted American psychologist Henry Murray suggested how deep ran the well of psychopathology in Germany: "We must realize that we are dealing with a nation suffering from paranoid trends: delusions of grandeur; delusions of persecution; profound hatred of strong opponents and contempt of weak opponents; arrogance, suspiciousness and envy—all of which has been built up as a reaction to an *age-old inferiority complex and a desire to be appreciated* [italics in original]."[4]

Similarly, long-winded psychoanalytic conjectures hypothesized that the Nazis had personalities that were, if not outright pathological, at least deeply disturbed. In a 1950 article, for example, British psychiatrist Henry V. Dicks suggested that

> Nazis were likely to be men of markedly pregenital or immature personality structure in which libido organisation followed sado-masochistic pattern, based on a repression of the tender tie with the mother and resulting typically in a homo-sexual paranoid (extra-punitive) relation to a harsh and ambivalently loved and hated father figure, with its attendant sadism towards symbols of the displaced bad portion of this figure; in increased secondary ('defensive') narcissism, in libido splitting *vis-à-vis* female love objects; and in tendencies towards hypochondrical (internal prosecutor) and schizoid or hypomanic (guilt denial) features.[5]

The October 25, 1945, suicide of Robert Ley, leader of the German Labor Front and one of the Nuremberg accused, added fuel to the fire of the "mad Nazi" thesis. A postmortem autopsy of Ley's brain revealed a "long-standing degenerative process of the frontal lobes." The announcement that one Nazi's brain did show neuropathology confirmed the widespread notion that the Nazi atrocities could be relegated to abnormal, diagnosable conditions—even something as quantifiable as "brain damage." A later announcement that Ley's brain was not as abnormal as most people had made it out to be drew very little attention.

The only lesson the world wanted to learn was simple: keep insane people out of high office and the atrocities of Nazi Germany will never happen again. In fact, for most of the mental health professionals assigned to Nuremberg, the question was not *if* they would find psychopathology among the defendants, but simply *how much* psychological disturbance they would find. The notion that any of the defendants would test as seemingly normal and ordinary people was simply not considered. It was beyond the realm of rational possibility. Why? Primarily because it was, and is, more comforting to believe that no "normal" or "healthy" person would be able to engage in such atrocities against humanity. It makes it easier for us to distance ourselves from the Nazi atrocities by regarding all perpetrators as inherently evil, psychopathic killers.

But how valid would the "mad Nazi" thesis prove to be? Millions waited in anticipation as a contingent of Allied mental health professionals, led by Douglas M. Kelley and Gustave Gilbert, descended on Nuremberg to plunge the depths of what most assumed to be the darkest psychopathology imaginable. The U.S. Army assigned Kelley, a psychiatrist, and Gilbert, a German-speaking psychologist, to the Nuremberg jail. They were involved (likely at their own initiative) in the administration of psychological tests, primarily intelligence and Rorschach inkblot tests, to the accused war criminals.

Gilbert assumed the responsibility of administering IQ tests to the twenty-one internees at Nuremberg. He utilized the best test in the world at the time of the trials—the Wechsler-Bellevue Intelligence Test, Adult Form I. Since a formal German translation was not yet available, Gilbert had to rely on a homemade translation. In addition, he was forced to eliminate three of the eleven subtests on the standardized test that, in his opinion, were culturally biased. Fortunately, Gilbert could at least still norm the Nuremberg defendants against a 1944 U.S. sample of 1,081 individuals.

Gilbert computed that the average IQ for the twenty-one Nazi defendants, with a high of 143 and a low of 106, was 128—falling in the superior to very superior range of intellectual abilities. (For purposes of comparison, the average IQ is 100; that of college graduates is 118; that of doctoral students is 125.) Perhaps, as some suggest, the scores were slightly inflated because of the lack of standardization for this particular test. Regardless, not only were the Nuremberg defendants intelligent enough to know the difference from right and wrong, but they tested as *unusually* intelligent—eleven of them obtained IQ scores that were in the superior range, and a few could have even been described as "geniuses." If they were "mad Nazis," they were certainly very smart "mad Nazis." These findings obviously did not fit public opinion very well. It would have been better for the "mad Nazi" thesis if the defendants were in some way mentally deficient and the crimes committed by them could be related to their impoverished cognitive state. As a result, the findings were not widely reported.

The second test of the "mad Nazi" thesis would fall to the Rorschachs. The Rorschach technique, developed in the 1920s by Swiss psychiatrist Hermann Rorschach, was the instrument of choice in clinical psychology during the 1940s and 1950s. It is an assessment technique utilizing ten cards containing bilaterally symmetrical inkblots—five black and white, five with blobs of red, blue, or yellow. The subject is handed the cards one at a time and asked, "What might this be?" The inkblots are not intended to look like anything, so there is no right or wrong answer (though there are *more* common/typical and *less* common/typical responses). The Rorschach takes approximately one hour to administer and includes a period of free association followed by an inquiry phase during which the examiner reviews the responses with the examinee for clarification. In addition, the examiner notes time of responses, position or positions in which cards are held, spontaneous remarks, emotional expressions, and other incidental behaviors of the examinee during the test session. Responses are later categorized and scored and a final description of the personality as a whole is offered.

The Rorschach technique belongs to the larger category of "projective" techniques that rely on relatively vague and unstructured stimuli to open the psychological door for projection to occur. In responding to the ambiguous stimulus of an inkblot, for instance, the examinee must convert—or disambiguate—the blot into something that it is not. In so doing, they are assumed to project aspects of their personality into their responses. (This is a good place to note that we should always be cautious about assessing personality with *one* testing instrument. Responsible personality assessment generally involves the application of several complementary testing instruments as well as everyday observations of a person's behavior and interpersonal relations. Unfortunately, such a broad bank of assessment and observation was not easily available for the perpetrators of the Holocaust and, for that matter, would be difficult to assemble for perpetrators of any mass killing or genocide.)

During his five-month stay at Nuremberg, Kelley—well trained in the technique—administered the Rorschach instrument to seven defendants. During his year-long stay at Nuremberg (overlapping for two months with Kelley), Gilbert—decidedly less familiar with the technique—administered Rorschachs to sixteen defendants (including four of those whom Kelley already had tested). All testing was virtually completed before the beginning of the trial so that the validity of the tests would not be compromised by the stress of the courtroom proceedings. The psychological testing protocols themselves were never used in the trials—the prosecution team at Nuremberg was resistant to anything that would introduce insanity as a defense—and therefore were not mentioned in the official proceedings.

Personal animosities kept Kelley and Gilbert from collaborating on both the administration and the interpretation of the Rorschachs. It was only after they left Nuremberg that, separately, they began to disseminate their conclusions. Kelley first concluded that the Rorschachs revealed little evidence of psychopathology among the defendants. In a brief 1946 article in the *Rorschach Research Exchange*, Kelley wrote that the Nuremberg defendants "were essentially sane and although in some instances somewhat deviated from normal, nevertheless knew precisely what they were doing during their years of ruthless domination. From our findings we must conclude not only that such personalities are not unique or insane but also that they could be duplicated in any country of the world today."[6] He went on to suggest: "We must also realize that such personalities exist in this country and that there are undoubtedly some individuals who would willingly climb over the corpses of one half of the people of the United States if, by doing so, they could thereby be given control of the other half."[7]

That same year, in an interview with the *New Yorker*, Kelley continued his dismissal of the "mad Nazi" thesis: "With the exception of Dr. Ley, there wasn't an insane Joe in the crowd. That's what makes this trial important—there are twenty-one ruthless people with counterparts all over the world, none of them sufficiently deviate to be locked up by society under normal conditions."[8] In the following year, 1947, Kelley published a book, *22 Cells in Nuremberg: A Psychiatrist Examines the Nazi War Criminals*, that provided a more general overview of his time in Nuremberg.

Gilbert also was quick to rush into print with his Nuremberg experiences. In 1947 he published a book, *Nuremberg Diary*, describing his work as the prison psychologist, and in 1948 he published an article, "Hermann Goering, Amiable Psychopath," in the *Journal of Abnormal and Social Psychology*. He released a second book, *The Psychology of Dictatorship: Based on an Examination of the Leaders of Nazi Germany*, in 1950. In each of these early publications, as well as several presentations at professional conferences, he gave only brief and fragmentary commentaries on the Rorschach tests. Most of his analyses came from his own more casual, personal impressions of the Nazi elite formed during his year-long stay at Nuremberg. For instance, his nineteen-page article on Göring includes only one paragraph on the Rorschachs. It is replete, though, with psychodynamic speculations on Göring's fantasy life and aggressive egotism as derived from Gilbert's numerous informal conversations with him. For example, Gilbert offers the following explanation for Göring's motives in joining the Nazi Party: "After the defeat and flight of the Kaiser, Goering's essentially infantile emotional dependence was left without an authoritarian figure to cling to. In Hitler, he recognized such a potential figure."[9]

Finally, in 1963, in response to the Eichmann trial, Gilbert published a short article in *Yad Vashem Studies* that would come closest to a broad psychological explanation of the Nuremberg defendants. Gilbert maintained that the Nazis had cultivated a deviate personality type that lacked empathy and conscience. In his tellingly titled article "The Mentality of SS Murderous Robots," Gilbert described this new inhuman personality type as "the unfeeling, mechanical executioner of orders for destruction no matter how horrible, who goes on and on with this ghastly work as though he were a mere machine made of electrical wiring and iron instead of a heart and a mind, with no qualms of conscience or sympathy to restrain him once someone has pressed the button to put him into action with a command."[10] Clearly invoking a medical model of psychopathology, Gilbert suggested that this deviate personality type is principally the reflection of "diseased elements of the German culture inflamed to epidemic proportions under the Nazi regime."[11]

How do we explain the dramatic interpretative differences between Kelley and Gilbert? Fortunately, the scientific enterprise is a collaborative effort open to all members of the academic community. So how would other experts interpret these same records? Gilbert's records were made available to a group of ten Rorschach experts in 1947. The plan was for each expert to react to the protocols and to submit their reactions to the group. Their comments would then be included in a report at the first International Congress of the World Federation of Mental Health in London the following year. Amazingly, however, not one of the experts undertook the task of examining the Rorschach records that they had received.[12]

Why the unexpected and uniform lack of response? Most cited a lack of time and other personal involvements. Could it be, however, that after examining the records each expert realized that the Rorschachs did not reveal the homogenous group of psychologically disturbed individuals for which the public clamored? Molly Harrower, vice chair of the committee that initiated the project, certainly believed so. "Over the years," she wrote nearly thirty years later, "I have come to believe that our reason for not commenting on the test results was that they did not show what we expected to see, and what the pressure of public opinion demanded that we see—that these men were demented creatures, as different from normal people as a scorpion is different from a puppy."[13] Elsewhere, she reiterated her admission: "As experts in 1946 we operated on the assumption that a sensitive clinical tool (which the Rorschach unquestionably is) . . . must also be able to demonstrate moral purpose, or lack of it, in persons of various assets and liabilities. . . . Implicit also at that time was the belief that this test would reveal an idiosyncratic psychopathology, a uniform personality structure of a peculiarly repellent kind. We espoused a concept of evil which dealt in black and white, sheep and goats. . . . This concept of evil was such that it was ingrained in the personality and therefore must be a tangible, scorable, element in psychological tests."[14]

In other words, the risk—or, perhaps, the reality—of finding no psychopathology in the Nuremberg Rorschachs was paralyzing. If no deep psychological disturbances were found, then the very nature of the Rorschach technique, not to mention the profession's assumptions about human evil, would be called into question. It is likely that none of the experts wished to go on record as stating that, according to psychological test data, many of the Nazis may actually have been normal or even well-adjusted. People wanted psychological distance from the perpetrators; they did not want to believe that the potential to act like a Nazi could exist in them or their neighbor. To deflate the myth of the "mad Nazi," to say that they were not a homogeneously sinister and psychologically deranged group, promised to have a discrediting impact on one's professional career as well as the broader profession of psychological testing.

The opportunity lost in terms of the London conference would mean that the Nuremberg Rorschachs would not be published until three decades after the end of the war. During this time, even as interpretative techniques for the Rorschach continued to mature in sophistication, this treasure trove of Rorschach data lay unanalyzed and unpublished. Why? Part of the answer lies in a silly professional feud, motivated by greed and academic ambition, between Kelley and Gilbert. Another part lies in the reality that increasing numbers of behavioral scientists turned their attention to broader issues of authoritarianism, dogmatism, obedience to authority, the "banality" of evil, and more behavioristic procedures of assessment.

In 1975, however, Florence R. Miale and Michael Selzer reopened the Nuremberg Rorschachs and published verbatim the sixteen Gilbert records in their book *The Nuremberg Mind: The Psychology of the Nazi Leaders*. Miale, a psychologist and experienced Rorschach expert, and Selzer, a political scientist and author of several books on Jewish affairs, were driven to reexamine the records for evidence of severe psychopathology. They concluded that fifteen of the sixteen Nuremberg defendants were, in varying degrees, "psychopathic." As a highly distinctive group, their most prevalent emotional characteristic was depression (not terribly surprising, given the stress of awaiting trail and the possibility of eventual execution). The second most prevalent characteristic was a proclivity for violence. In short, they were vicious, opportunistic psychopaths who felt no real sense of guilt for their atrocities. The defendants not only shared a "common ideology with their most devoted followers, but a similar personality structure as well."[15] The authors boldly concluded: "The answer can be stated briefly and decisively. The Nazis were not psychologically normal or healthy individuals."[16]

Other researchers quickly stepped in to challenge this reemergence of the "mad Nazi" thesis. The following year, Harrower published an article in the *Journal of Personality Assessment* showing that Rorschach experts could not differentiate Nazi records from those of normal individuals. Furthermore, she asserted that the Nuremberg Rorschachs showed far greater variation than they did uniformity. In other words, the individual differences in the Rorschachs significantly outweighed any similarities. As a result, Harrower maintained that there was no single, uniform, abnormal personality that could serve to explain the atrocities committed by the Nazis. To look for such a personality was, in her opinion, a misguided approach.

In Harrower's analysis, the Nazi crimes were in no way related to the presence of a mental disorder or insanity. Removed from the post-Nuremberg need for psychological distance, she was able to write: "The Nazis who went on trial at Nuremberg were as diverse a group as one might find in our government today, or for that matter, in the leadership of the PTA."[17] She cautioned that "well-integrated, productive and secure personalities are no protection against being sucked into a vortex of myth and deception, which may ultimately erupt into the commitment of horror on a grand scale."[18] Harrower concluded by soberly reminding readers that "it [state-sponsored mass murder] *can* happen here."[19]

Why such continuing discrepancy of interpretation around the Nuremberg Rorschachs? Harrower, along with many others, suggested that too often the interpretations reflected the interpreters' values, prejudices, and prior expectations about Nazi mentality more than the personalities of the defendants. In other words, projective test results may tell us more about the *examiners* than the *examinees*. If you hold, for instance, a preexisting belief that only psychopaths could act in the manner in which the Nazi war criminals acted, then you will inevitably conclude that the defendants were psychopaths. You do not need the Rorschach tests to reach such a conclusion—unless, of course, you can interpret the tests in a way that supports your preexisting conclusion.

While the role of personal bias is undoubtedly important, the discrepancies also sprang from four significant methodological issues. First, the original records were not collected under standardized conditions. Gilbert, especially, was quite candid in reporting that his testing procedures differed significantly from standard professional clinical practice. Unfortunately, subsequent interpreters had to play the hand they were dealt and take this into account in determining the degree of confidence they, and others, could have in their conclusions. Second, many of the interpretative studies had not consistently employed blind evaluation techniques; that is, the evaluation of the records without knowledge of the subject's identity or group membership. The lack of a blind evaluation of the records makes it especially easy to fit the data to previously held biases, consciously or unconsciously. Third, standardized procedures of scoring and interpretation were not used consistently from study to study. This lack of consistency made comparative critiques, and replications, especially problematic. Finally, many studies lacked explicit norms for comparison and analysis. Though the establishment of an appropriate comparison group for Nazi war criminals is certainly no easy matter, it must be done to give the conclusions of a particular study any meaning.

In the mid-1980s, Harrower joined psychologists Eric A. Zillmer, Barry A. Ritzler, and Robert P. Archer in addressing these weaknesses in yet another reanalysis of the Nuremberg Rorschachs. Their work stands as the definitive study of the psychological functioning of Nazi war criminals. Their comprehensive study took advantage of the most recent advances in Rorschach administration, scoring, and interpretation. These advances, known as Exner's Comprehensive System (CS), make the Rorschach technique more standardized, objective, and empirical. Using the CS, many scholars maintain there is ample evidence to demonstrate the Rorschach's diagnostic and heuristic value. (It should also be noted, however, that the CS is currently engulfed in a scientific controversy. The points in contention include such fundamental issues as accuracy and cultural generalizability of the CS norms, scoring reliability, validity, clinical utility, and accessibility of supporting research. A recent review commissioned by the American Psychological Society concluded: "Despite its continued widespread use by clinicians, the Rorschach Inkblot Test remains a problematic instrument from a psychometric standpoint. Although many psychologists initially believed that the CS remedied the Rorschach's primary shortcomings, the scientific status of this system appears to be less than convincing.")[20]

Obviously, Zillmer and his colleagues could not go back and readminister the Rorschachs to the Nuremberg defendants. Thus, an "official" diagnosis cannot be given because no interaction is possible; historical subjects cannot respond to clarifying questions. We must be satisfied to glean whatever information we can from what previous researchers have left behind. In this spirit, Zillmer and colleagues could take advantage of the strides promised by the CS in standardizing and validating the scoring and interpretation of the responses. In addition, they could then compare their reevaluations of the Nuremberg Rorschachs with large banks of normative data for both pathological and normal populations.

Based on their extensive research, Zillmer and colleagues concluded that the leaders of Nazi Germany were anything but "mad Nazis." They were, for the most part, extremely able, intelligent, high-functioning people. They were average German citizens—products of a rigid, paternalistic, male-dominated society. There was no evidence of thought disorder or psychiatric conditions in most of these men. In short, a contemporary reanalysis of the Nazi Rorschachs, based on the latest scientific progress, shows that the "mad Nazi" thesis holds little water for the Nazi elite tried at Nuremberg. In the authors' concluding words, "High-ranking Nazi war criminals . . . participated in atrocities without having diagnosable impairments that would account for their actions. In this sense, the origins of Nazi Germany should be sought for primarily in the context of social, cultural, political and personality, rather than clinical psychological factors."[21]

But did the Nuremberg defendants accurately reflect the entire culture of cruelty that they created? In other words, how far can we generalize the conclusions drawn from the Nazi elite? Can they be generalized to the psychological functioning of the broader population of Nazis? Returning to the main focus of our investigation, if the "mad Nazi" thesis did not hold true for the Nazi elite at Nuremberg, does that necessarily mean that it also would not hold true for the rank-and-file killers?

To answer these questions, Zillmer and colleagues examined another large bank of nearly 200 Rorschach records of rank-and-file Nazis. These records came from tests administered at the war crimes trials in Copenhagen in 1946. The Rorschach records were those of Danish citizens convicted of collaborating with the Nazi occupation and German military personnel who were sentenced for war crimes committed in Denmark. Their conclusions suggest that these rank-and-file Nazis showed some unusual thought patterns (for example, rigid and pessimistic thinking), but not enough to indicate grossly disturbed thinking. Neither did the perpetrators' responses demonstrate any particular inclination toward violence. In short, consistent with the Nuremberg Rorschachs, there was a lack of evidence for obvious and severe psychopathology in the Copenhagen Rorschachs. The "mad Nazi" thesis applied no better to the rank and file than it did to the Nazi elite.

We should remember, however, that the most egregious cases of extraordinary evil in the Holocaust were not performed on Danish soil. So, we should be cautious about generalizing these findings to the rank-and-file perpetrators in the East who actually carried out the mass executions, dropped the gas pellets, and manned the crematory ovens. However, a 1971 book by the German journalist Heinz Hohne suggests that the results from the Copenhagen Rorschachs may be more applicable to the killers in the East than we might like to believe.

In analyzing the membership of the Einsatzgruppen killing units, Hohne concludes that there is no evidence to show that either the commanders or rank-and-file personnel were specially selected brutes or sadists. "The Jew-liquidators," he writes, "in fact were a curious collection—highly qualified academics, ministerial officials, lawyers and even a Protestant priest and an opera singer. Even among the rank and file, enthusiasm for Heydrich's duty in the East was so small that he had to comb all the Gestapo, Kripo, and SD offices to obtain the necessary personnel. He was even compelled to scratch men out from the *Ordnungspolizei* and Waffen SS; a Berlin Police Battalion was disbanded and distributed by platoons to the individual *Einsatzgruppen*."[22]

The "necessary personnel" sought for this duty were not sadists and psychopaths. As a matter of fact, a systematic effort was made to weed out all those who might derive pleasure from what had to be done. There was a fear that they would not be as efficient, effective, and dependable as killers for this special operation. "Ordinary" and "sane" people, whose loyalty was to a worthy cause and who could be bent to the commission of extraordinary evil in support of that cause, were thought to be much better candidates.[23] As Hohne concludes: "The system and the rhythm of mass extermination were directed not by sadists . . . [but by] worthy family men brought up in the belief that anti-semitism was a form of pest control, harnessed into an impersonal mechanical system working with the precision of militarised industry and relieving the individual of any sense of personal responsibility."[24]

Raul Hilberg likewise argues:

> The German perpetrator was not a special kind of German. . . . We know that the
> very nature of administrative planning, of the jurisdictional structure, and of the

budgetary system precluded the special selection and special training of personnel. Any member of the Order Police could be a guard at a ghetto or on a train. Every lawyer in the Reich Security Main Office was presumed to be suitable for leadership in the mobile killing units; every finance expert to the Economic-Administrative Main Office was considered a natural choice for service in a death camp. In other words, all necessary operations were accomplished with whatever personnel were at hand. However one may wish to draw the line of active participation, the machinery of destruction was a remarkable cross-section of the German population. Every profession, every skill, and every social status was represented in it.[25]

These results are also consistent with the work of Christopher Browning, who investigated one of the many units that was called to Eastern Europe to shoot thousands of defenseless Jews at point-blank range and then allowed to return to their normal civilian lives and families in Germany. Reserve Police Battalion 101 was a unit of German Order Police—rear-echelon reserve policemen—from the port city of Hamburg, one of the least Nazified cities in Germany. Called to Poland in June 1942, the men of this battalion participated in the direct shooting deaths of at least 38,000 Jews and the deportation to Treblinka's gas chambers of 45,000 more, a total body count of 83,000 over a sixteen-month period for a unit of less than 500 men.

What type of men could engage in such wholesale slaughter? In the case of Reserve Police Battalion 101, they were middle-aged family men, German civilians, of working- and lower-middle-class background. They had been deemed too old for combat service and were drafted instead into the Order Police (Ordnungspolizei or Orpo). Their ranks included dockworkers, truck drivers, artisans, salesmen, waiters, teachers, and clerks. They were raw recruits with remarkably little or no ideological indoctrination or training. Most had no experience with German occupation methods in Eastern Europe or—with the exception of the very oldest, who were World War I veterans—any kind of military service. In short, the men of Reserve Police Battalion 101 were the unlikeliest of mass murderers. They did not represent special selection or even random selection. For all practical purposes, they represented negative selection for the task at hand. In Browning's words, "The battalion was the 'dregs' of the manpower pool available at that stage of the war."[26] They were simply ordinary people who went about completing the murderous tasks assigned them with considerable indifference.

The diversity of the demographic profile of Holocaust perpetrators also is reflected in the perpetrators of the Rwandan genocide. At one end of the social spectrum were the hundreds of thousands of Hutu peasants and unemployed city youth whose major motivation for killing was to steal their victims' property—land, furniture, radios, or what little cash they carried. At the other end of the social spectrum were numbers of intellectuals and professionals—doctors, teachers, journalists, and even priests—who participated in the massacres. As *New York Times* correspondent Raymond Bonner wrote, "It was not just a few young toughs and uneducated peasants who killed. The guilty cut across the social and economic strata."[27]

Further evidence of perpetrators' lack of overt psychopathology is found in reports of their early reactions to the human suffering caused by their extraordinary evil. A wide range of perpetrator accounts reveal that initial involvement in killing often led to nightmares, anxiety attacks, debilitating guilt, depression, gastrointestinal problems, temporary impotence, hallucinations, substance abuse, numerous bodily complaints, and many other signs of stress reactions. As just one of a score of examples, Browning reports that "repression during waking hours could not stop the nightmares. During the first night back from Jozefow, one policeman awoke firing his gun into the ceiling of the barracks."[28] Such reactions are hardly consistent with our general notions of pathologically disturbed individuals. Rather, this perpetration-induced traumatic stress is consistent with how we expect ordinary, psychologically "normal" people to react to traumatic events outside the realm of ordinary experience.[29]

Moreover, not only does the claim of widespread psychopathology among perpetrators contradict the available evidence, but it also contradicts all diagnostic and statistical logic. The *Diagnostic and Statistical Manual of Mental Disorders* (*DSM-IV-TR*) of the American Psychiatric Association is the professional guidebook for diagnosing psychopathology and specifying its prevalence in general and clinical populations. Of its sixteen major diagnostic classes (for example, Substance-Related Disorders, Mood Disorders, and Anxiety Disorders), the most relevant for considering perpetrator psychopathology would be Personality Disorders. A Personality Disorder is defined as "an enduring pattern of inner experience and behavior that deviates markedly from the expectations of the individual's culture, is pervasive and inflexible, has an onset in adolescence or early adulthood, is stable over time, and leads to distress or impairment."[30]

Of the ten Personality Disorder categories, the most applicable psychopathology for perpetrators of extraordinary evil is *Antisocial Personality*

Disorder (APD). A pervasive pattern of disregard for, and violation of, the wishes, rights, or feelings of others characterizes this disorder. Persons with APD may blame the victims for being foolish, helpless, or deserving their fate; they may minimize the harmful consequences of their actions; or they may simply indicate complete indifference. Individuals with this disorder show little remorse for the consequences of their acts. The terms "sociopath" (emphasis on social and environmental forces) and "psychopath" (emphasis on personality structure of the individual) are often used interchangeably with APD. The *DSM-IV-TR*, however, has moved away from the clinical use of those commonly known, and even more commonly misused, terms in favor of the more appropriate and descriptive classification of Antisocial Personality Disorder.

APD is much more common in males than in females. The *DSM-IV-TR* indicates that the incidence of APD among the general population of American males is approximately 3 percent. (As is typical of other personality disorders, higher prevalence rates are associated with clinical populations such as those found in substance abuse treatment settings and prison or forensic settings.) If we begin with the assumption that military personnel are a fairly representative smaller sample of the larger general population, we can hypothesize that approximately 3 percent of the perpetrators might be classified as APDs.

By their very nature, however, APDs are not easily used in military and paramilitary organizations. Such people rebel against authority, are consistently and extremely irresponsible and, according to the *DSM-IV-TR*, "may receive dishonorable discharges from the armed services." Thus, there is no reason to expect that the distribution of APD among perpetrators of genocide is any greater than that of the general population; there are actually very good reasons to expect that the distribution is *less* than that of the general population. In other words, we could expect that less than three out of one hundred perpetrators of extraordinary evil would be diagnosable APDs.

Even were we to broaden our search for psychopathology beyond APD, it is doubtful that rates of abnormality among perpetrators run any higher than what we find among the general population. For instance, Ella Lingens, a physician imprisoned in Auschwitz, testified: "I know of almost no SS man who could not claim to have saved someone's life. There were few sadists. Not more than 5 or 10 percent were pathological criminals in the clinical sense. The others were all perfectly normal men who knew the difference between right and wrong."[31] Another physician imprisoned at Auschwitz, the noted psychiatrist Viktor Frankl, also recalled some guards who were capable of acting with genuine kindness toward inmates. Most perpetrators, even the ones who acted brutally, were not sadists outside the context of the camps and, after the war, did not engage in disproportionately high rates of criminal activity.

Obviously, some former prisoners offer substantially different accounts, and much higher rates, of sadism among perpetrators. In general, however, the late historian George M. Kren and psychologist Leon Rappoport conclude that the general trend of testimony by survivors indicates "that in most of the camps, there was usually only one, or at most a few, SS men known for their intense outbursts of sadistic cruelty. The others were not always decent persons, but their behavior was at least considered comprehensible by the prisoners. . . . Our judgement is that the overwhelming majority of SS men, leaders as well as rank and file, would have easily passed all the psychiatric tests ordinarily given to American army recruits or Kansas City policemen."[32]

Extraordinary human evil can never be simply distilled to one particular psychiatric diagnosis. To do so is to project evil exclusively onto some small segment of the population instead of acknowledging its imminent presence in each of us. As historian Dick de Mildt argues, "By converting the criminal actors of the story into demon-like lunatics, we distance ourselves from them in a radical fashion, assuming them to belong to a different species which only remotely resembles us in physiognomy."[33] Clearly there were some perpetrators involved in the Third Reich who were deranged psychopaths or otherwise psychologically disturbed. Were there enough, though, for us to responsibly consider psychopathology a predominant cause of participation in extraordinary evil? The Nuremberg and Copenhagen Rorschachs, coupled with other historical and eyewitness testimony, make it clear that most perpetrators could not be considered psychopathological. There is no sufficient data to conclude that the vast majority of Nazi perpetrators, whether high-ranking officials or members of the rank and file, were significantly abnormal in any psychological or mental way. In short, where they existed, perpetrators characterized by extraordinary psychopathology were far too few to account for the litany of atrocities that occurred in the name of the Third Reich. As much as we may wish it to be true, the Nazis cannot so easily be explained away as disturbed, highly abnormal individuals.

An Extraordinary Personality

The Search for the "Nazi Personality"

Early attempts at understanding the perpetrators of the Holocaust were a search for homogeneity. In other words, they were a search to defend our general belief that *all* Nazis were very similar to each other and very different from each of us. As we have seen, however, the perpetrators of the Holocaust were not uniformly similar in ideology or, certainly, in psychopathology. But didn't it stand to reason, many suggested, that the Nazis *would* be characterized by a homogenous, nonpathological personality structure? Moreover, wouldn't this personality structure—though not abnormal in a clinical sense—be extraordinarily different from the personality structure of the rest of us? In other words, wouldn't they have more in common with each other than with any other group of people? In short, wasn't there a single Nazi personality—aggressive, militaristic, disciplined, undemocratic, and antisemitic in nature—that made the perpetrators more susceptible to committing extraordinary evil?

Between the autumn of 1942 and the spring of 1944, British psychiatrist Henry V. Dicks examined 138 German prisoners of war. The method of examination was a prolonged, personal, nondirected interview with each prisoner. No formal psychological testing procedures or scripted questions were used. As a matter of fact, the interviewer merely represented himself as an officer privately interested in the prisoners as men—not as a psychiatrist or mental health professional. The lack of professionalism, both in data gathering and ethical practice, is appalling. Thus, it comes as little surprise that Dicks found exactly what he expected, and wanted, to find—a homogeneous personality structure that existed in greater concentration in more "Nazi" personalities than in other Germans.

What was this homogeneous personality structure? Labeled the "High F Syndrome" (F for "fanatical"), it was very similar to the "average" member of the Wehrmacht described by Dicks in a 1944 War Office Research Memorandum titled *Psychological Foundations of the Wehrmacht*. Dicks, adopting a decidedly psychoanalytic approach, wrote:

> The "average" member of the Wehrmacht can be described as tense, earnest, industrious, meticulous, over-respectful to authority and anxious to impress. He is a martinet in his dealings with his social inferiors and his subordinates. He is very touchy about status. He requires uniformity and order, and is uneasy in unforeseen situations. . . . He idealises his women in their role as mothers and as objects

towards whom libidinal aim-inhibition is demanded; but he also deprecates them socially and sexually on the plane of reality. . . . Conformity and "loyalty," as of a servant to his master, are rated among the highest virtues. . . . A weak authority is despised. . . . Allegiance to paternal authority is furthered by the projection of the German's own repressed aggressive feelings to the authority itself.[34]

Unfortunately, Dicks did not use a control or comparison group. As a result, one is left to wonder if his description of the "High *F* Syndrome" does not, in fact, characterize the military personnel of most nations. Fortunately, such slippery and ill-founded descriptions of the "Nazi Personality" would not go unchallenged. They would be confronted by the same extensive data bank that was used to confront the "mad Nazi" thesis—the Rorschach records of Nazi war criminals. In addition to gauging psychopathology, the Rorschach test also allows for a comprehensive description of an individual's personality—an estimate of cognitive and emotional resources, perceptual accuracy, information processing, stress tolerance, problem-solving style, modulation of affect, goal orientation, self-esteem, interpersonal relations, and so on. In short, the Rorschach gives us a window onto an individual's most striking or dominant personality characteristics, those that are relatively consistent over time and across different situations, those that differentiate him from others.

Returning to our discussion of the Nuremberg Rorschachs, recall that Gilbert advanced the notion of a "new inhuman personality type" that he designated "the murderous robots of the SS." He clearly located one origin of this personality type in psychopathology—specifically, the schizoid personality.[35] However, he also clearly designated two nonpathological social influences on this personality type: an extreme authoritarianism and a belief in the hostile racial ideology of Nazism. He believed that the SS selected for, and reinforced, this specific personality type.

Similarly, Kelley—although adamant in his denial of psychopathology in the Nazi war criminals—was still at least willing to admit to a cluster of homogeneous personality traits among the defendants. In *22 Cells in Nuremberg*, Kelley wrote: "No, the Nazi leaders were not spectacular types, not personalities that appear only once in a century. They simply had three quite unremarkable characteristics in common—and the opportunity to seize power. These three characteristics were: overweening ambition, low ethical standards, a strongly developed nationalism which justified anything done in the name of Germandom."[36]

Zillmer and his colleagues' reanalysis of the Nuremberg Rorschachs confirmed the presence of two personality characteristics that, while not abnormalities in a psychiatric sense, were present in many of the defendants. The first major personality characteristic they noted was the *overall problem-solving style* of the defendants. Among the sixteen Gilbert records, they reported that an unusually high number of the Nazis (nine) tested as ambitent. Ambitents have failed to develop a consistent preference or style in their coping behaviors when confronted with difficult tasks. In other words, these are individuals who essentially have no mind of their own. They rely heavily on others as well as on an external structure for guidance in problem solving. Generally, this leads to less efficiency and more vacillation in decision-making operations.

Zillmer and colleagues describe the ambitent tendencies of the Nazi elite as a "chameleonlike" personality that allowed the defendants to adopt the beliefs and objectives of whatever leadership was in power at the moment, rather than basing their judgments on an "internal compass." Very few showed well-established, but reasonably adaptable, problem-solving skills. Again, this is not a measure of psychopathology but simply a particular problem-solving style that is a relatively stable psychological feature of the individual—that is, a personality trait.

Zillmer and his coauthors also present a second, less stable personality characteristic that broadly defined many of the Nuremberg defendants: *overconfidence*. This was manifested in an increased self-esteem that may have included a sense of entitlement and an overvaluing of self. Related to this, the Nuremberg group as a whole was more likely than a comparison control group to blame the Rorschach test itself, the testing situation, or the examiner for any uncertainty or uneasiness they felt about the quality of their responses.

With the exception of these two characteristics, however, the authors conclude that "research on the records of the Nazi elite failed to identify a homogenous Nazi personality. In fact, the differences among the members of this group by far outweighed any similarities. . . . The Nazi elite demonstrated a complex range of personalities and cannot be simply defined in strict terms."[37]

The Nuremberg defendants were the architects of the Holocaust. But what about the rank-and-file individuals who actually carried out mass murder? Did they all exhibit a common personality style in which the essential feature was a pervasive pattern of dependent and submissive behavior? Again, the Copenhagen Rorschach records of Danish citizens convicted of collaborating with the Nazi occupation and German military personnel offer insight.

Providing a much larger data bank than the Nuremberg Rorschachs, the Copenhagen records reveal a cluster of personality traits that characterized many, but not all, of the Danish perpetrators. Among these are the findings that many rank-and-file Nazis were not deep thinkers and may have had difficulty in making their own decisions; were deficient in stress tolerance and vulnerable to even typical levels of subjective stress; showed coping deficits; showed signs of social skill deficits that may have been manifested in an inability to form close, supportive attachments outside the structure of the Nazi organization; appear to have had low self-esteem with a tendency to view themselves as victims of circumstances; had an inconsistent and ineffectual problem-solving style (that is, "ambitent"); were more likely to experience anxiety or feelings of depression (that is, emotional stress) rather than suffering from worry or other negative thoughts and preoccupations (that is, cognitive stress); tended to process information simplistically and unimaginatively, making them particularly susceptible to prejudice and bigotry; and had indications of rigid and pessimistic thinking.

Perhaps the most telling personality characteristic, however, was the tendency for the Copenhagen subjects to view themselves and others as simple, incomplete part-objects. Zillmer and his coauthors argue that a "strong case can be made that the Nazis were not capable of perceiving themselves and other human beings as complex, integrated personalities. Such overly simplistic attitudes lend themselves to arbitrary, prejudicial beliefs about the integrity of human beings and may make it possible for individuals such as the Danish collaborators to treat others as if they were not human."[38]

While certainly not desirable, we are reminded that these personality characteristics are not—in and of themselves—pathological. Neither are they prevalent enough throughout the sample to define a homogenous rank-and-file "Nazi personality" profile. Few, if any, of the Rorschach protocols contain all—or even most of—the constructs identified as "common" in the sample. Indeed, the variations from person to person are much more striking than the similarities.

At best, we can see these as a number of personality traits that may have served as predisposing factors for having participated in Third Reich atrocities. Collectively, they may represent a general susceptibility to the influences of the Nazi movement. As the authors conclude: "The above personality traits may nevertheless serve as predisposing characteristics. In this sense the presence of them may make individuals more vulnerable to the influences of a Nazi movement, or for that matter, any political movement. . . . We must therefore conclude that under certain social conditions, just about anyone could have joined the Nazi movement, but that there were individuals who were more likely to join."[39]

Even here, though, we must keep in mind the scores of people *with* this same cluster of traits who did not participate in the atrocities as well as the scores of perpetrators *without* these specific traits who did participate in the atrocities. In summary, when looking at the perpetrators, we do not find homogeneity of personality traits. Rather, we are confronted by a disturbing heterogeneity that undermines the notion of a uniform "Nazi personality."

The Authoritarian Personality

Historically, social psychologists—including myself—have been drawn to the phenomenon of prejudice. Many important questions have emerged from this study: Do there exist individuals who regularly and consistently display prejudice? In other words, is there a singular, homogeneous personality type that is characteristically predisposed to prejudicial thoughts, feelings, and behaviors? Is there a uniform personality that consistently and regularly accepts those who are similar to them and rejects those who are different from them? In short, are there people who are predisposed toward being prejudiced simply because of the kind of people they are? Moreover, does this personality make them more susceptible to fascist ideology, criminalization or, perhaps, the commission of extraordinary evil? Several noted psychoanalysts and psychologists addressed these questions—Erich Fromm, Erik Erikson, Wilhelm Reich, Abraham Maslow, and Ross Stagner, among others. In the 1940s, however, it would fall to a group of researchers at the University of California at Berkeley—two of whom had fled Nazi Germany—to build on these works and offer the first quantitative conceptualization of a fascism-prone personality.

The Berkeley researchers—Theodor Adorno, Else Frenkel-Brunswik, Daniel Levinson, and Nevitt Sanford—were initially drawn to uncovering the psychological roots of an antisemitism so poisonous that it led to the Holocaust. Eventually, however, their investigation broadened to outline a personality that would be predisposed to a wide variety of hatred—in other words, not a personality that was descriptively prejudiced but a personality that predisposed one to prejudice. They eventually discovered that individuals who harbor prejudicial attitudes toward one group (that is, Jews) tend to be the same individuals who harbor prejudicial attitudes toward other groups (blacks, Hispanics, Mormons, socialists, etc.). In 1950, their findings, and the explanation for those findings, were published in a book titled *The Authoritarian Personality* (*TAP*). Over five years in the making, and nearly 1,000 pages in length, *TAP* became an instant landmark in the field of social psychology.[40]

How did they come to these findings? Adorno and his colleagues first identified a group of individuals who possessed antisemitic attitudes and then assessed the extent to which these people also possessed a general aversion to all people who diverge from white, middle-class American norms and values. By comparing responses from a newly developed antisemitic questionnaire to those from a well-established scale measuring ethnic prejudice, Adorno and his colleagues discovered a consistent pattern of prejudicial attitudes. Apparently, according to the criterion of consistency across targets, a prejudiced personality does indeed exist. Prejudice appeared to be less an attitude specific to one group than a general way of thinking about those who are different.

Having identified the existence of a prejudiced personality, these researchers turned their attention to the origins of this personality. In the late 1940s, psychoanalysis was at the peak of its popularity in academia. Fittingly, the authors of *TAP* were themselves psychoanalytically oriented; three of them were personality psychologists, and the fourth, Adorno, was a philosopher specializing in the ethics of music. Utilizing the theoretical ideas of Freudian personality dynamics, they postulated that the origins of this personality were in the innate, and socially unacceptable, drives of sex and aggression. When the restraints against the expression of these drives are unusually harsh, the individual becomes anxious, insecure, and unusually attuned to external authority sources for behavioral guidance. This reverence for authority goes far beyond the normal, balanced, and realistic respect for valid authority that most of us have; it reflects an exaggerated, emotional need to submit.

Prejudiced individuals, according to the four researchers, were the children of domineering fathers and punitive mothers who engaged in unusually harsh child-rearing practices. These practices involved a combination of threats, coercion, and the deliberate use of parental love and its withdrawal to promote obedience. In other words, authoritarian parents are not able to show their children affection without reservation; it is contingent on the child's good behavior. The result is children who are decidedly insecure and, paradoxically, extremely dependent on their parents. Moreover, such children fear their parents and experience unconscious hostility toward them.

Adorno and his colleagues claimed that these unconscious childhood conflicts led insecure and dependent children to grow up to be adults who were excessively submissive and obedient to those in positions of power and authority. Similarly, the fear and hostility of their childhood years become a well of repressed resentment within them. This hostility is displaced and finds it way into aggression toward members of minority groups and other people perceived to be less powerful than themselves—even while the individual maintains an outward respect, and desire, for authority. These are people inclined to obey authority and to act aggressively toward people not in authority. To those above, they bow; those below, they kick. In short, bigotry addressed and, to some extent, resolved their deepest needs.

As adults, these individuals displayed the behavioral elements of a syndrome that was first called the *fascist character*, then the *anti-democratic*, and, finally, the *authoritarian personality*. Adorno and his colleagues identified nine a priori clusters of personality dimensions—many surprisingly similar to Dicks's "High *F* Syndrome"—that made up the authoritarian personality:

1. *Conventionalism*: Rigid adherence to conventional middle-class values.
2. *Authoritarian Submission*: Submissive, uncritical attitude toward idealized moral authorities of the in-group.
3. *Authoritarian Aggression*: Tendency to be on the lookout for, and to condemn, reject, and punish, people who violate conventional values.
4. *Anti-Intraception*: Opposition to the subjective, the imaginative, the tender-minded.
5. *Superstition and Stereotypy*: The belief in mystical determinants of the individual's fate; the disposition to think in rigid categories.
6. *Power and "Toughness"*: Preoccupation with the dominance-submission, strong-weak, leader-follower dimension; identification with power figures; overemphasis on the conventionalized attributes of the ego; exaggerated assertion of strength and toughness.

7. *Destructiveness and Cynicism*: Generalized hostility, vilification of the human.
8. *Projectivity*: The disposition to believe that wild and dangerous things go on in the world; the projection outward of unconscious emotional impulses.
9. *Sex*: Exaggerated concern with sexual "goings-on."

These clusters were conceptualized as a single syndrome, a more or less enduring structure in the person that renders her receptive to "antidemocratic" propaganda.

To assess the authoritarian personality, Adorno and his coauthors constructed a thirty-eight-item scale (later trimmed to thirty items) that they named the *Implicit Antidemocratic Trends* or *Potentiality for Fascism Scale* because they believed that the authoritarian personality makes individuals susceptible to antidemocratic or fascist propaganda. Over time, it simply became known as the *F* scale.

What else do we know about a person when we know his or her score on the *F* scale? Research utilizing the *F* scale suggests people who are high on authoritarianism do not simply dislike Jews or dislike blacks, but, rather, show a consistently high degree of prejudice against *all* minority groups (including, recent studies indicate, AIDS patients). Any selection of a *particular* hate target is guided by convenience and social convention. In addition, research suggests that high-scoring individuals display considerable cognitive rigidity and intolerance for ambiguity, as well as the firm belief that other people tend to think and feel as they do. High authoritarians tend to reject minorities and foreigners, accept the attitudes of those in power, and identify with authoritarian characters in television situation comedies (for example, Archie Bunker).

Although authoritarianism will not always coincide with authoritarian behavior, high authoritarians also are more obedient to authority and more likely to raise their own children in an authoritarian manner. On the political front, supporters of extreme right-wing parties, candidates, and programs have sharply higher *F* scale scores than those who support prodemocratic and liberal points of view. Finally, it also has been shown that high authoritarians were more likely to support the Vietnam War; oppose socialized medicine; favor faculty loyalty oaths during the McCarthy era; and advocate severe sentences for various criminal acts, especially for criminals of perceived lower social status.

When *TAP* was published, reactions to the book were quick, strong, and numerous. The project was praised as a model of imaginative and integrative work. It generated a blizzard of empirical studies that lasted through the 1960s. By the early 1970s, however, interest had waned. Why? Much of the answer lies in the fact that its reception was influenced by the prevailing ideological climate and by the state of social science at the time.

On the ideological level, initial critics of *TAP* had charged that the research concentrated exclusively on the political "right-wing" authoritarians (the fascists), while neglecting the political authoritarians on the Left (the communists). Given the nine defining traits of the authoritarian personality, some argued, are not communists necessarily nonauthoritarian? After all, communist ideology stresses equality above all and stands opposed to hierarchy and the superiority of a master race.

At the height of the Cold War, at a time when anticommunism had come to the fore as the engine of U.S. foreign policy and efforts to rearm the defeated Germans were under way, Adorno and his colleagues were at least implicitly accused of facing the wrong enemy. Fascism had been defeated; the new enemy was communism (though, as in the case of the Soviet Union, some left-wing communists became the political right wing almost as quickly as they achieved power). Communism, the critics shouted, had been completely disregarded when it was the greater threat. In short, the *F* scale had captured only one kind of extremist (the fascist), and the "wrong" one at that.

On the social scientific level, mirroring the general positivist-empiricist emphasis in psychology at the time, critics attacked various technical problems of the *F* scale. The most serious of these problems was what psychologists call a "response set." A response set is a tendency for individuals to develop a pattern in responding to a questionnaire or survey. For example, some respondents may consistently agree or disagree with survey statements regardless of their content. Others may consistently respond in an unusual or deviant fashion. Still others may respond in ways that present themselves in an unusually good light. Regardless of their specifics, response sets are a major threat to the validity of any questionnaire or survey.

The problem of response set is particularly relevant to the *F* scale because all of the items were worded in the same direction. In other words, all items were worded so that agreement indicated a high (or prejudiced, fascist, authoritarianism) score. As a result, it was easy for researchers to demonstrate that the scale did not measure ideological content but only a tendency to agree—with anything. In short, the scale encouraged a response set of positive answers. Instead of identifying genuine authoritarians, perhaps the *F* scale simply singled out some very agreeable persons without strong opinions. Such critiques were strengthened by the facts that many of the follow-up empirical studies yielded only trivial, if statistically significant, results, and reversed items were commonly shown to be less effective measures of authoritarianism than items stated in the authoritarian direction.[41]

Both of these ideological and social scientific attacks were critical in derailing continuing research on the authoritarian personality. After the concept languished for years, however, the 1980s—and the reappearance of fascism in various countries—brought authoritarianism once again into the spotlight of research. In hindsight, the methodological objections raised against the *F* scale seemed less damaging than originally thought. In the Netherlands, for instance, Jos D. Meloen conducted an extensive meta-analysis of studies done over forty years using the *F* scale and found considerable evidence for the validity of the scale as a measure of antidemocratic and fascist tendencies.[42]

Despite this revival of interest, however, the original hypotheses about the psychodynamics of the authoritarian personality have yet to be validated. Psychologist Bob Altemeyer of the University of Manitoba is one of many critics to point out that the tracing of authoritarian personalities to unconscious dynamics established from early childhood experiences has not been very successful. He maintains that the basic psychoanalytic orientation of *TAP* is obsolete. Rather than tapping into unconscious personality dynamics, Altemeyer focuses on social learning theory models that emphasize parental modeling and the transmission of social norms through school, the media, peer groups, and the overall zeitgeist (that is, the intellectual spirit and philosophical outlook characteristic of the country and the era).[43]

Altemeyer's social learning argument is supported by research on postwar authoritarianism in German adolescents. Following World War II, West Germany went through several decades of antiauthoritarian reform aimed at changing attitudes about the exercise of authority. Gerda Lederer found a decline in authoritarianism among German youth from 1945 to 1978 that could be due to changes in child-rearing practices in (the former) West Germany. This attitudinal change was not only significant relative to the Germans' former views but actually reflected attitudes that were very similar to those of their American contemporaries; in some cases, scores even showed German adolescents to be *less* authoritarian than Americans. Lederer's findings suggest that the authoritarian personality is far less fixed and durable than the authors of *TAP* had anticipated. This research strongly points to the direct and sustaining influence of the social system in which the individual lives as a major predictor of authoritarian attitudes.[44]

This does not mean, however, that research on the relationship between personality type and prejudice has been summarily discarded. One example of ongoing research in this area is Altemeyer's work on Right-Wing Authoritarianism (RWA). He has found inconsistent support for the nine-cluster psychological syndrome described in *TAP*. His thirty-item RWA scale (with balanced item wording and higher reported reliability and validity than the *F* scale), however, does suggest the presence of three enduring and distinctive traits from the original syndrome — conventionalism, authoritarian submission, and authoritarian aggression. Altemeyer's resulting conceptualization of Right-Wing Authoritarianism — developed on the premise that some persons need very little situational pressure to submit to authority, while others often require significantly more — is both simpler and better documented than the nine-cluster syndrome of the traditional authoritarian personality described in *TAP*.

Today, the traditional authoritarian described in the pages of *TAP*, as one critic said, "now seems a bit quaint." Indeed, contemporary social psychology texts either ignore *TAP* altogether or devote only a few paragraphs to it. As social psychologist Neil Kressel of the William Paterson College of New Jersey concludes, "More than four decades later, one remains uncertain about which aspects of the authoritarian personality, if any, actually predispose a person to authoritarian behavior. Punitive tendencies, dogmatic habits of thought, submissiveness, a tendency to project one's inner conflicts outward, conventionalism, and cynicism may *jointly*, or *individually*, bear on participation in mass atrocities under different circumstances."[45]

While there may be no homogenous authoritarian personality, we can at least say that people differ in the degree to which they hold beliefs that are authoritarian. These differences in degree reflect a particular orientation to authority. Moreover, we can say that these differences in orientation to authority affect the way they relate to ideas as well as people — especially people with differing authority or status. Some people clearly do prefer hierarchical relationships with a clear delineation of spheres of power. Some of us enjoy obeying authority and enjoy exercising power over those below us. Thus, we are wise to at least consider orientation to authority as *one* of several factors — including low intelligence, low education, lack of political sophistication, and external threats of specific kinds (for example, economic threat) — predisposing people to accept fascist ideology.

How Applicable Is TAP *to Perpetrators of Extraordinary Evil?*

Even if the construct of the authoritarian personality were valid, how applicable would it be to explaining the activities of perpetrators in mass killing and genocide? Unfortunately, researchers have devoted very little attention to understanding the role played by authoritarianism in extraordinary human evil.

The original studies of the *TAP* relied on a sample of white California residents in the 1940s, but the authors used the results to imply that the character of the German people, in part, explained the Germans' acceptance of such a strong and demented leader as Adolf Hitler. The image of the authoritarian German was emblematic of the German culture and often the subject of German literature (for example, Heinrich Mann's *Little Superman*, 1918). The strict parenting practices of Germans were believed to make German children particularly susceptible to real and imaginary threats. Moreover, these same parenting practices were thought to lead children to seek out strong authority figures in search of protection and relief. In short, it was generally assumed that the traditional emphasis on obedience that had prevailed in German society had paved the way for fascism and the Holocaust.

To address this assumption at the level of the Nazi elite, psychologist Mark N. Resnick compared the protocols of the sixteen Nuremberg Rorschachs to the nine dimensions of the authoritarian personality. He hypothesized that the Nazi elite would score high on the authoritarianism scale because a pro-authoritarian set of beliefs exemplifies the dogmatic mind-sets that will readily comply with the commands of an authority without question or protest. Contrary to his hypothesis, however, the Nazi elite converged on only three of the nine dimensions of authoritarianism—anti-intraception, superstition and stereotypy, and projectivity. Resnick concluded that the authoritarian personality more accurately defines the *leader* of a fascist or totalitarian regime than it does the rank and file.[46]

But what about the rank and file? Two decades after the war, John M. Steiner—a sociologist and a former inmate of five concentration camps—administered a questionnaire containing, among other questions, twenty-one items selected and translated from the American original of the *F* scale to two groups—former members of the SS and the Wehrmacht (the regular German armed forces in the Nazi period). Over two hundred analyzable questionnaires were received from each group. The average authoritarianism score of former SS men was significantly higher than that of the former

Wehrmacht members. In both samples, findings indicated a syndrome of the following characteristics: loyalty and honor held in higher esteem than justice; Hitler's book *Mein Kampf* read before 1933; personal military or semimilitary past regarded with satisfaction; tendency to prefer a dictatorial or monarchic form of government.

Later, Steiner posited a distinct authoritarian personality type, "authoritarian sleepers," to describe this group of men who had volunteered for the SS. "We propose," Steiner wrote in a 1980 article, "to advance the concept of the 'sleeper' who lies dormant until circumstances or specific events will activate him or her and produce behavioral traits not apparent before. . . . The shifts occurring in the display of personality characteristics when social conditions change radically is absolutely striking."[47] In other words, Steiner argued that these early volunteers had certain personality characteristics of violence-prone individuals that remained latent until activated under certain conditions. Nazism roused these "authoritarian sleepers" and, in particular, drew them to the SS and the opportunity to fulfill their violent interests and inclinations for which they had no other outlets. In short, they were "self-selected" for participation in extraordinary evil as a result of their authoritarian personality.

Psychologist Ervin Staub of the University of Massachusetts, Amherst, accepts the notion that some people become perpetrators as a result of their personality. He directly challenges, however, the uniqueness of Steiner's "authoritarian sleeper." "Most persons," Staub writes, "are sleepers to some degree, inasmuch as they have a violent potential that can be triggered by specific conditions. Only a limited number of SS members were likely to have sleeper characteristics to a high degree. Others had to evolve more. . . . Thus, self-selection does not mean that most who joined the SS were ready to become mass murderers as soon as their environment allowed it."[48] In other words, most people—under particular circumstances—have a capacity for extraordinary evil. To relegate that capacity to only the exceptional "authoritarian sleepers" among us is hopeful but wrong.

The work of historian George C. Browder of the State University of New York, College at Fredonia, also stands in direct contrast to Steiner's insistence on a definite self-selection process in the degree of authoritarianism of early volunteers flocking to the SS. While focusing on the same general topic, the data banks utilized by Steiner and Browder differed significantly. Steiner's data were drawn from several decades of informal postwar interviews with a self-selected group of former SS and Wehrmacht members. Browder's data, in contrast, came from the personnel files of 526 men who joined the SS Security Service between 1932 and the end of 1934. Rather than self-report data colored by postwar reflections of the few SS men who survived the war (a sampling problem, to say the least), Browder had the advantage of archival, prewar, quantifiable data of those members drawn to the SS Security Service in its earliest years. Though not a random sample, it certainly is more representative than Steiner's sample. Browder's analysis is especially telling because these early affiliates were more likely to be volunteer-activists, while the later joiners were more likely to be conformist-opportunists. Steiner's sample included no data on Nazi Party membership and date of joining it or its subsidiaries (though it did, curiously, ask for musical preferences). In addition, Browder's sample was much more exhaustive than Steiner's, including 99 percent of the officers (for all practical purposes, a total population) and about 62 percent of the total membership by the end of 1934.

As we have seen, certain features of our sociocultural environments are more conducive to the production of an authoritarian personality than others. These features go beyond the authoritarian family to include broader environmental deprivations. Browder examined several of these features—low level of education, age, rural background, membership in disadvantaged minority, dogmatic religion, lower socioeconomic origin, authoritarian family background, military service, and authoritarian occupation—as a test for arguments that authoritarian personalities prevailed among the SS Security Service members.

Browder concluded that few of these features offer significant predictive reliability. In other words, there was no single sociocultural environment that gave rise to a particular personality—authoritarian or otherwise—that characterized the majority of SS Security Service personnel. If anything, the data suggest that this sample of personnel should actually have been *less* likely than the general population to exhibit traits associated with the authoritarian personality. In Browder's words: "With respect to all early formative experiences . . . the membership sample should have been subjected significantly less than the general population to deprivations that enhance 'authoritarianism.' "[49] In short, Browder found little support for the construct of the authoritarian personality.

Also consistent with the findings of the Nazi Rorschachs, Browder finds more variability than he does consistency. More evidence for heterogeneity than he does homogeneity. For every possible trend in one direction, there is a countertrend in the other direction. Furthermore, Browder maintains that this heterogeneity reflects the fact that the recruitment and training of SS Security Service personnel did not make any special appeal to certain personality types. This, at least partially, contradicts Zillmer and his coauthors' contention that there was a particular personality type that was more susceptible to participation in the Nazi movement. As Browder concludes: "The causes of their [SS Security Service personnel] behavior apparently lie not in defective personalities, but in the processes they experienced that legitimized participation in mass inhumanity."[50]

In his analysis of Reserve Police Battalion 101, Browning likewise found scant evidence to support the authoritarian personality thesis. He concludes: "Indeed, if Nazi Germany offered unusually numerous career paths that sanctioned and rewarded violent behavior, random conscription from the remaining population—already drained of its most violence-prone individuals—would arguably produce even less than an average number of 'authoritarian personalities.' Self-selection on the basis of personality traits, in short, offers little to explain the behavior of the men of Reserve Police Battalion 101."[51] In sum, authoritarian *behavior* is often found in people otherwise devoid of preexisting authoritarian *personality traits*.

Summary

To bluntly suggest that all Nazis had a common, homogenous extraordinary personality that predisposed them to the commission of extraordinary evil is an obvious oversimplification. Just because they shared, to some degree, a common pattern of behavior does not mean that they also shared a common underlying personality. As we have seen in the above discussion, we cannot justifiably speak of a psychological coherence or homogeneity among perpetrators as a group. In short, the Nazis were not a homogenous group of individuals who had more in common with each other than with any other group of people. They were, quite simply, a representative cross section of the normal distribution of humans.

Even where there is homogeneity of personality characteristics, we are still faced with another, equally important, question. Are these commonalties in psychological functioning *unique* to the perpetrators as a group, or do we also find these characteristics in nonperpetrator groups (for example, high-level business executives and bureaucrats, nonkilling military personnel, lawyers, teachers, psychiatrists, etc.)? In other words, do these characteristics discriminate, or differentiate, perpetrators of extraordinary evil from groups of nonperpetrators? Clearly, the answer is no. The few personality structures that describe the psychological organization of a majority of the perpetrators (for example, problem-solving style) are also common to millions of other individuals who may have done nothing more criminal in their lives than commit a parking meter violation.

Conclusion

A myopic focus on the proposed psychopathology of perpetrators, or on their alleged extraordinary personalities, tells us more about our own personal dreams of how we wish the world to work than it does about the reality of perpetrator behavior. In that role, such explanations satisfy an important emotional demand of distancing *us* from *them*. The truth seems to be, though, that the most outstanding common characteristic of perpetrators of extraordinary evil is their normality, not their abnormality. Browning's conclusion to his study of Reserve Police Battalion 101 is as disturbing as it is insightful: "If the men of Reserve Police Battalion 101 could become killers under such circumstances, what group of men cannot?"[52]

Indeed, if the violent, aggressive, and antisocial behaviors displayed by perpetrators of extraordinary evil are not exclusively attributable to gross psychopathology or a homogeneous personality syndrome that predisposes one to accept fascist ideology, then to what other influences or factors can such behaviors be attributed? As Zygmunt Bauman writes, "Cruelty correlates with certain patterns of social interaction much more closely than it does with personality features or other individual idiosyncrasies of the perpetrators. Cruelty is social in its origin much more than it is characterological."[53] In other words, Bauman affirms that the cause of most extraordinary evil does not lie in a pathological or faulty personality. Rather, it lies in the truth that "well-adjusted" people can get caught up in a tangle of social forces that may lead them to act in concert with their leaders to massacre opponents. As we will see in chapter 4, scholars have provided sufficient evidence to accept the view that under specific circumstances ordinary, "normal" people can commit acts of extraordinary evil. While the evil of genocide is not ordinary, the perpetrators most certainly are.

The Massacre at Babi Yar

THE GERMAN INVASION OF THE Soviet Union, code-named Operation Barbarossa, began on June 22, 1941. More than 3 million German soldiers, reinforced by half a million auxiliaries from Germany's allies, attacked the Soviet Union across a broad front, from the Baltic Sea in the north to the Black Sea in the south. Special action squads followed the German forces as they advanced east. These squads, the Einsatzgruppen, were composed of four battalion-sized operational groups. The total strength of the four Einsatzgruppen execution units was about three thousand men.

With the Einsatzgruppen, a new stage in the Nazi process of destruction began. The Einsatzgruppen were mobile killing units charged with the murder of anyone whom the Nazis deemed racially or politically unacceptable. These included Soviet political commissars and other state functionaries, partisans, prisoners of war, Roma (Gypsies), and Communist Party leaders. Specifically targeted for annihilation were all Jews in the occupied Soviet territories. Under cover of war and confident of victory, the Germans turned from the forced emigration and imprisonment of Jews to mass murder.

The first sweep of killing began on June 22, 1941, and was completed toward the end of 1941. During this sweep, the mobile killing units reported approximately 100,000 victims a month. The second sweep of killing began in the Baltic area in the fall of 1941 and spread through the rest of the occupied territory during the following year. All told, about 1.3 million Jews and hundreds of thousands of other innocent people were killed, one by one, by the three thousand men in the four Einsatzgruppen, their support troops, local police, and collaborators.[1]

Einsatzgruppe C began operations from the western Generalgouvernement of Poland and fanned out across the Ukraine toward Kharkov and Rostov-on-Don. It carried out mass-murder operations in Lvov, Tarnopol, Zolochev,

Kremenets, Kharkov, and elsewhere. Its bloodiest work, though, was done in Kiev, the Ukraine's capital city. German forces entered Kiev in September 1941. During the first days of the occupation, several buildings used by the German army were blown up, apparently by the Soviet Secret Police. The Germans, however, blamed the Jews for the explosions and, ostensibly in retaliation, decided to kill the 60,000 Jews of Kiev. Detachments of Einsatzgruppe C, together with Ukrainian auxiliary units, were assigned to carry out the massacre.

In late September, the Germans posted notices requiring all Jews in Kiev to report for resettlement. On September 29, 1941, masses of Jews reported and were directed to proceed northwest along Melnik Street toward the Jewish cemetery. From there, they were marched in groups of thirty to forty people to a ravine called Babi Yar, about six miles from the center of the city. There, the Jews were directed to hand over all their valuables and to disrobe. They were then forced through a gauntlet of baton-wielding soldiers. Those who survived the gauntlet were taken to the ravine and shot.

The bloodiest shooting massacre of the Holocaust continued for two days between the Jewish New Year and the Day of Atonement. A concise report to the chief of the Security Police and Security Service in Berlin included the following cryptic notation: "Sonderkommando 4a in collaboration with Einsatzgruppe HQ and two Kommandos of police regiment South, executed 33,771 Jews in Kiev on September 29 and 30, 1941."[2]

The following eyewitness account comes from the 1959 testimony of a German, Fritz Hofer, who was a truck driver in Sonderkommando 4a:

> One day I was instructed to drive my truck outside the town. I was accompanied by a Ukrainian. It must have been about 10 o'clock. On the way there we overtook Jews carrying luggage marching on foot in the same direction that we were travelling. There were whole families. The further we got out of town the denser the columns became. Piles of clothing lay in a large open field. These piles of clothing were my destination. The Ukrainian showed me how to get in there.
>
> After we had stopped in the area near the piles of clothes the truck was immediately loaded up with clothing. This was carried out by Ukrainians. I watched what happened when the Jews—men, women and children—arrived. The Ukrainians led them past a number of different places where one after the other they had to remove their luggage, then their coats, shoes and overgarments and also underwear. They also had to leave their valuables in a designated place. There was a special pile for each article of clothing. It all happened very quickly and anyone who hesitated was kicked or pushed by the Ukrainians to keep them moving. I don't think it was even a minute from the time each Jew took off his coat

before he was standing there completely naked. No distinction was made between men, women and children. One would have thought that the Jews that came later would have had a chance to turn back when they saw the others in front of them having to undress. It still surprises me today that this did not happen.

Once undressed, the Jews were led into a ravine which was about 150 meters long, 30 meters wide and a good 15 meters deep. Two or three narrow entrances led to this ravine through which the Jews were channelled. When they reached the bottom of the ravine they were seized by members of the Schutzpolizei and made to lie down on top of Jews who had already been shot. This all happened very quickly. The corpses were literally in layers. A police marksman came along and shot each Jew in the neck with a sub-machine gun at the spot where he was lying. When the Jews reached the ravine they were so shocked by the horrifying scene that they completely lost their will. It may even have been that the Jews themselves lay down in rows to wait to be shot.

There were only two marksmen carrying out the executions. One of them was working at one end of the ravine, the other at the other end. I saw these marksmen stand on the layers of corpses and shoot one after the other.

The moment one Jew had been killed, the marksman would walk across the bodies of the executed Jews to the new Jew, who had meanwhile lain down, and shoot him. It went on in this way uninterruptedly, with no distinction being made between men, women and children. The children were kept with their mothers and shot with them.

I only saw this scene briefly. When I got to the bottom of the ravine I was so shocked by the terrible sight that I could not bear to look for long. In the hollow I saw that there were already three rows of bodies lined up over a distance of about sixty meters. How many layers of bodies there were on top of each other I could not see. I was so astonished and dazed by the sight of the twitching blood-smeared bodies that I could not properly register the details. In addition to the two marksmen there was a "packer" at either entrance to the ravine. These "packers" were Schutzpolizisten, whose job it was to lay the victim on top of the other corpses so that all the marksman had to do as he passed was fire a shot.

When the victims came along the paths to the ravine and at the last moment saw the terrible scene they cried out in terror. But at the very next moment they were already being knocked over by the "packers" and made to lie down with the others. The next group of people could not see this terrible scene because it took place around a corner.

Most people put up a fight when they had to undress and there was a lot of screaming and shouting. The Ukrainians did not take any notice. They just drove them down as quickly as possible into the ravine through the entrances. From the undressing area you could not make out the ravine, which was about 150 meters away from the first pile of clothes. A biting wind was blowing; it was very cold. The shots from the ravine could not be heard at the undressing area. This is why

I think the Jews did not realize in time what lay ahead of them. I still wonder today why the Jews did not try and do something about it. Masses kept on coming from the city to this place, which they apparently entered unsuspectingly, still under the impression that they were being resettled.

Kurt Werner was a member of Sonderkommando 4a and an active participant in the executions:

> That day the entire Kommando with the exception of one guard set out at about six o'clock in the morning for these shootings. I myself went there by lorry. It was all hands to the deck. We drove for about twenty minutes in a northerly direction. We stopped on a cobbled road in the open country. The road stopped there. There were countless Jews gathered there and a place had been set up where the Jews had to hand in their clothes and their luggage. A kilometer further on I saw a large natural ravine. The terrain there was sandy. The ravine was about 10 meters deep, some 400 meters long, about 80 meters wide across the top and about 10 meters wide at the bottom.
>
> As soon as I arrived at the execution area I was sent down to the bottom of the ravine with some of the other men. It was not long before the first Jews were brought to us over the side of the ravine. The Jews had to lie face down on the earth by the ravine walls. There were three groups of marksmen down at the bottom of the ravine, each made up of about twelve men. Groups of Jews were sent down to each of these execution squads simultaneously. Each successive group of Jews had to lie down on top of the bodies of those that had already been shot. The marksmen stood behind the Jews and killed them with a shot in the neck. I still recall today the complete terror of the Jews when they first caught sight of the bodies as they reached the top edge of the ravine. Many Jews cried out in terror. It's almost impossible to imagine what nerves of steel it took to carry out that dirty work down there. It was horrible. . . .
>
> I had to spend the whole morning down in the ravine. For some of the time I had to shoot continuously. Then I was given the job of loading sub-machine-gun magazines with ammunition. While I was doing that, other comrades were assigned to shooting duty. Towards midday we were called away from the ravine and in the afternoon I, with some of the others at the top, had to lead the Jews to the ravine. The Jews were led by us up to the edge of the ravine and from there they walked down the slope on their own. The shooting that day must have lasted until . . . 17.00 or 18.00 hours. Afterwards we were taken back to our quarters. That evening we were given alcohol (schnapps) again.[3]

In the months that followed the massacre, thousands more Jews—as well as Roma and Soviet prisoners of war—were shot at Babi Yar. Until the liberation of Kiev by the Red Army on November 5, 1943, almost 150,000

A woman holds photos of her brother and aunt, who were killed by the Nazis in the September 1941 massacre of more than 33,000 Jews at Babi Yar. In the background, people lay flowers at the ten-foot-high menorah monument in Kiev (September 28, 1997). Photo by AP Photo, Efrem Lukatsky.

people were murdered in Babi Yar. Among the victims were at least 80,000 Jews from Kiev and its surroundings, Ukrainian citizens of both sexes, prisoners of war, sailors from the Dnieper fleet, and Roma.

Following the war, the first trial of Einsatzgruppen members was conducted in Nuremberg by the American Military Tribunal from September 15, 1947, through April 10, 1948. In contrast to the major war criminals, whose trials were more widely publicized, the defendants in the Einsatzgruppen trials had been *directly* involved in the supervision and implementation of mass murder, war crimes, and genocide. Of the twenty-four accused, twenty-one were sentenced. Among those, two commanders, ten leaders, and two officers were sentenced to death. One commander and one leader were sentenced to life imprisonment. Two other leaders and one officer were sentenced to twenty years imprisonment, and two officers to ten years. Most relevant to the Babi Yar massacre, one of the men sentenced to death was Paul Blobel, leader of Sonderkommando 4a of Einsatzgruppe C at Kiev. The commander of Einsatzgruppe C, Otto Rasch, did not stand trial due to his health. He died in prison during the trial.

In 1966, a memorial to the victims of Babi Yar was erected by the Soviets. In remembering the victims, it mentioned "citizens of Kiev and prisoners of war," but not Jews. In 1991, Jewish groups erected their own memorial, a ten-foot-high menorah less than a mile away from the Soviet monument.

4

The Dead End of Demonization

> By describing the Nazi criminal, his acts and his mode of thinking in
> a language replete with metaphors of the most bizarre nature, they
> turn him into a one-dimensional incarnation of absolute evil. In this
> way the Nazi killer acquires the amalgamated characteristics of the bo-
> geyman, the demon and the lunatic. With the appearance of this
> pitch-black culprit, however, the possibility of identification and, thus,
> worldly judgement, vaporises into thin air.
>
> Dick de Mildt, *In the Name of the People*

W E HAVE SEEN THAT THE ORIGINS of extraordinary evil cannot be isolated in the extraordinary nature of the collective, the influence of an extraordinary ideology, psychopathology, or a common, homogenous, extraordinary personality. We are then left with the most discomforting of all realities—ordinary, "normal" people committing acts of extraordinary evil. The notion of the "ordinariness" of those who commit extraordinary evil was first given life in the early 1960s when a noted political philosopher posited an obedient, indifferent, and mundane personality to explain the atrocities of the Holocaust. The philosopher's name was Hannah Arendt, and her concept of the "banality of evil" would fundamentally challenge our understanding of who commits extraordinary human evil.[1]

Hannah Arendt was one of about 37,000 German Jews who emigrated from Germany in 1933. She first went to France, where, with Youth Aliyah, she worked for the immigration of Jewish refugee children into Palestine. Interned during the war at Gurs, in Vichy France, she escaped, made her way to the United States in 1941, and secured U.S. citizenship in 1951. Arendt's field of study was philosophy, and she counted among her mentors Rudolf Bultmann, Martin Heidegger, and Karl Jaspers. Over time, she became a prominent political philosopher and theoretician who focused much of her very productive academic life on the question of behavior in totalitarian regimes.

In 1961, Arendt—then numbered among the most important intellectuals in the United States—was commissioned by the *New Yorker* magazine to cover the sensational trial of Adolf Eichmann in Jerusalem. Eichmann was a major bureaucrat in the Final Solution. After serving as an SS corporal at Dachau concentration camp, he found a less monotonous position in the powerful SS security service. While there, Eichmann gradually became the acknowledged "Jewish specialist" of the Third Reich. With the takeover of Austria in 1938, he was sent to Vienna to promote Jewish emigration. Eichmann developed a method of "forced emigration" that was financed by confiscation of Jewish property—simultaneously putting fear into the Jewish population *and* destroying their economic well-being. He was later named head of the Department for Jewish Affairs in the Gestapo (Department IV B 4), a position he would hold from 1941 to 1945. In that role, Eichmann was responsible for the implementation of Nazi policy toward the Jews in Germany and all occupied territories—including the deportation of millions of Jews to concentration and extermination camps. By all accounts, he carried out his assigned duties with unyielding persistence, considerable ingenuity, and undying loyalty to the vision of the Final Solution.

Following the defeat of Nazi Germany, Eichmann was arrested and confined to an American internment camp. Because his name and role were not yet well known, however, Eichmann managed to escape and flee to Argentina. Eventually abducted by Israeli intelligence agents in Argentina in May 1960, he was brought to Israel to stand trial. He was charged with fifteen counts of crimes against the Jewish people and against humanity, and of war crimes. Eichmann's trial opened on April 11, 1961, and ended on August 14 of the same year. He was found guilty and sentenced to death (Israel allows the death penalty only for crimes of genocide). An appeal of his death sentence was rejected in May 1962. Eichmann was hanged in the Ramla prison on the night of May 31, 1962. His body was cremated and his ashes spread over the sea, outside the territorial waters of Israel.

While covering the legal and technical aspects of the Eichmann trial, Arendt also explored the wider themes inherent in the trial—the nature of justice, the behavior of Jewish leadership during the Nazi regime, and the nature of evil itself. In 1963, the five articles serialized in the *New Yorker* were published, in revised and expanded form, as a book, *Eichmann in Jerusalem: A Report on the Banality of Evil.* The next year, a follow-up version appeared that carried a postscript and reply to the heated controversy that followed Arendt's original work.

What were the critics so exercised about? A substantial number of critics questioned her explanation of the *why* of the Holocaust. Arendt located the *why* in the nature of the bureaucratic mind—a world of operations without consequences, information without knowledge: in other words, mindless perpetrators doing what they are ordered to do and expected to do without being personally involved, committed, or aware of the terrifying destruction they are executing.

Arendt argued that what was frightening about Eichmann was not how unusual or how monstrous he was but, rather, how extremely *ordinary* he was. In his personal manner, he had little in common with the dramatic antisemitism or florid lust for killing of some other Nazi leaders. He was not evil personified. Neither was he a deranged Jew-killer. Half a dozen psychiatrists had certified him as "normal"—"more normal, at any rate, than I am after having examined him," one of them was reported to have said.[2] Eichmann was, in Arendt's view, a drab drone committed to industriousness and efficiency, a featureless functionary particularly steadfast in obeying and carrying out assigned duties and orders. "Except for an extraordinary diligence in looking out for his personal advancement," Arendt wrote, "he had no motives at all."[3] It was the discovery that there was nothing to discover that turned the Eichmann trial into such a shocking experience.

The "banality" of Eichmann's evil, his breathtaking human mediocrity, was what most struck Arendt—and infuriated her critics. Exactly what did Arendt mean by the "banality of evil"? The phrase did not appear in the *New Yorker* articles. Notwithstanding its prominence in the subtitle, and hints of the concept from the first chapter on, the phrase itself only appeared once in the book, at its very end: "It was as though in those last minutes he was summing up the lesson that this long course in human wickedness had taught us—the lesson of the fearsome, word-and-thought-defying *banality of evil* [italics in original]."[4] Arendt must have thought that the meaning of her phrase was obvious, since she did not define or explain it. Most, however, were—and still are—puzzled by the exact meaning of the "banality of evil."

We can begin to unpack Arendt's conception of the banality of evil by saying that it seems clear she did *not* mean several things. She did not mean that Eichmann's evil was trite, hackneyed, or stale. She also did not mean that his evil was not immoral or grossly wrong. Nor did she use the word, as some critics charged, as a form of clever apologetics to make Eichmann into an everyday functionary—interchangeable with other unimportant people and their passive followers. Nor did she use it to mean that evil itself was banal or to make the Holocaust just one more example of everyday evil in human history. Finally, she obviously did not use it to hide or reveal any particular thesis or doctrine or as a precise theoretical explanation.

So what did Arendt mean by the "banality of evil"? By "banal," she meant a strictly factual contrast with "diabolical," "demonic," or "evil instincts." She meant to counter the prevailing tradition of thought—literary, theological, and philosophical—about the phenomenon of evil and place it more squarely in "the ordinary." Psychoanalyst Elisabeth Young-Bruehl affirms that, for Arendt, the term "banal" did not mean "commonly occurring" but, rather, meant "commonplace" or "ordinary."[5] Peter Novick, professor of history at the University of Chicago, wove together Arendt's remarks from other publications and lectures to argue that by "the banality of evil" Arendt meant

> the phenomenon of evil deeds, committed on a gigantic scale, which could not be traced to any particularity of wickedness, pathology, or ideological conviction in the doer, whose only personal distinction was a perhaps extraordinary shallowness. . . . However monstrous the deeds were, the doer was neither monstrous nor demonic. . . . [Evil] can spread over the whole world like a fungus and lay waste precisely because it is not rooted anywhere. . . . It was the most banal motives, not especially wicked ones (like sadism or the wish to humiliate or the will to power) which made Eichmann such a frightful evil-doer.[6]

Perhaps the greatest clarification, however, comes from the recognition that Arendt's conception of "banality" was less a description of the nature of evil and more a description of the nature of the man who committed the evil. In other words, she applied the term "banal" not to the crimes themselves but, rather, to the origins—the causes and motivations—behind the man who perpetrated them. For Arendt, the "ordinary" banality of Eichmann's evil was twofold. First, Eichmann's evil was normal, prosaic, or matter-of-fact within the disfigured reality of the Nazi worldview. Second, Eichmann's evil was rationalized as good because it was obedient or because it served a larger purpose. Rather than a sadistic monster, Eichmann was a person strongly committed to personal fulfillment through a bureaucratic career—not a raving ideologue animated by demonic antisemitism or a deranged madman, but simply an ambitious bureaucrat who did his duty and followed orders.

Contrary to expectations, Eichmann also was *not* a man without a conscience. As a matter of fact, it was his "good" conscience (though certainly not one that valued all of human life) that compelled him to follow what he felt to be his "duty" toward his superiors. In other words, his conscience worked "the other way around." He had organized the killing not because he particularly hated Jews or because he had somehow been forced to do so. Rather, he did his job simply, and thoughtlessly, because he was a person "duty bound" to a social hierarchy committed to such extraordinary evil. The banality of his personality kept him from having compunction or even second thoughts about his "job." Arendt wrote, "He would have had a bad conscience only if he had not done what he had been ordered to do—to ship millions of men, women and children to their death with great zeal and meticulous care."[7] This is why Eichmann continually made it clear that he felt he did no wrong. He would not have felt the slightest remorse if the Nazis had won and he had been able to carry out the Final Solution.

Arendt reasoned that anyone could have filled Eichmann's role and that his evil was "banal" precisely because insertion into a social hierarchy committed to such evil made it normal and legitimate. This is why, in her view, Eichmann was not a madman. His deeds were monstrous, but Eichmann himself was thoroughly ordinary. In Arendt's words: "The trouble with Eichmann was precisely that so many were like him, and that the many were neither perverted nor sadistic, that they were, and still are, terribly and terrifyingly normal."[8]

Arendt's conception of evil was almost entirely new. As Stephen Miller has pointed out, before the Enlightenment, most literary, theological and philosophical thinking about the nature of evil rested on the assumption that evildoing is the product of strong passions—pride, ambition, envy, or hatred.[9] During the Enlightenment and well into the nineteenth century, Western thinkers began to suggest that evil grew less out of our dark passions and more from unjust social conditions. This belief sounded a more hopeful note: it held out the possibility of eradicating evil through social and political transformations. The events of the Holocaust, though, shattered this more hopeful conception and cried out for a new conception of evil. For many, it appeared that Arendt had found one.

To be sure, there is debate over how applicable Arendt's concept of the "banality of evil" is to Eichmann specifically. The eminent Holocaust historian Raul Hilberg, for one, believes that Arendt did not recognize the magnitude of what Eichmann had done in the Final Solution in organizing the mass deportations of Jews from all corners of occupied Europe to the Polish extermination camps. "She did not," Hilberg wrote, "discern the pathways that Eichmann had found in the thicket of the German administrative machine for his unprecedented actions. She did not grasp the dimensions of his deed. There was no 'banality' in this 'evil.'"[10] Similarly, Norman Podhoretz wrote that "no person of conscience could have participated knowingly in mass murder: to believe otherwise is to learn nothing about the nature of conscience. . . . No banality of a man could have done so hugely evil a job so well; to believe otherwise is to learn nothing about the nature of evil."[11]

On a more general level, Arendt's "banality of evil" concept also may be subject to qualifications in describing the larger category of perpetrators of extraordinary evil. Though it may be more broadly applicable than the homogenous vicious, sadistic, and antisocial "Nazi personality" or the submissively conventional "authoritarian personality," it should be remembered that Arendt's hypothesis of the obedient, indifferent, and mundane banal Nazi certainly does not apply to all Nazis. Such a sweeping judgment can lose the important distinctions, exceptions, qualifications, and nuances that are inherent in the complexity of understanding perpetrators of extraordinary evil.

As it turns out, however, the awkward truth of the banality of Eichmann's evil is much more accurate and broadly applicable than we would hope. It had been apparent in the courtrooms at Nuremberg, and it had surfaced again and again in the subsequent German postwar trials against other perpetrators of Nazi genocidal policies. Recent research by historian Dick de Mildt, for example, meticulously reviewed the cases of 129 German citizens put on trial in the late 1940s and early 1950s before West German courts on suspicion of involvement in the mass murder policies of Nazi Germany. The trial sentences analyzed by de Mildt concerned two related aspects of the Nazi genocidal program — the *"Euthanasia" Aktion*, or mercy killing program, primarily directed against the inhabitants of Germany's mental institutions and *Aktion Reinhard*, the extermination of Jews in Nazi-occupied Poland and one of the largest murder campaigns of the Final Solution.

De Mildt concluded that, by and large, the background profiles of the men and women who were involved in either one — or both — of these mass murder campaigns evidenced the same banality of evil that Arendt used to characterize Eichmann. They were not idealists or killers of conviction. Rather, they were killers by circumstance and opportunity. "Instead of matching the image of the paranoiac ideological warriors so often invoked when describing the fieldworkers of Nazi genocide," de Mildt writes, "their background profile far more closely matches that of rather ordinary citizens with a well-developed calculating instinct for their private interests. . . . The key word which springs to mind when reviewing the criminal biographies of the 'Euthanasia' and *Aktion Reinhard* hangmen is not 'idealism' but 'opportunism.'"[12]

More recently, the "ordinariness" of the perpetrators of the Holocaust has been yet again confirmed by an exhibition on the history of the Wehrmacht. The Wehrmacht—referring to the regular German armed forces, comprising the land army, navy, and air force—was the institution where all German men did their military service. About 20 million men were in service during World War II, of which roughly 13 million fought or served "in the East" at one point or another. The exhibition, created by the Institute for Social Research in Hamburg, Germany, and titled *The German Army and Genocide: Crimes against War Prisoners, Jews, and Other Civilians, 1941 to 1944*, opened to a storm of public interest in Hamburg in March 1995. As of July 1999, the exhibition had drawn approximately 860,000 visitors in many of Germany's and Austria's leading cities.

The exhibition also had become a center of national controversy, even resulting in a debate in the German Bundestag, the national parliament, in Bonn on March 13, 1997. The controversy centered on the legend of the "unsullied Wehrmacht." Prior to the exhibition, the German Wehrmacht was generally presented to the German public, and to the world, as a skilled, professional, military organization that had little in common with the twisted ideological worldview and criminality of the Nazi regime. They were the relatively "heroic" organization least contaminated by the barbaric Nazis and most representative of the ordinary German. For decades, it had been a national taboo in Germany to seriously question the role of the Wehrmacht in the Nazi regime.

The Hamburg exhibition was the first public display of documents and photographs culled from German archives, and especially the heretofore inaccessible archives of the former Soviet Union and other East European countries formerly under communist domination, concerning the criminal conduct of the Wehrmacht in the East during World War II. It made clear that the Wehrmacht had come under the influence of the Nazi regime from early on and was a major tool in the implementation of Nazi policies until the end of the war. On display were scores of documents and haunting amateur photographs that testified to the Wehrmacht's direct and systematic involvement in the criminal atrocities perpetrated during the war in the East. The extraordinary evil perpetrated in the East could no longer be confined to specialists from the elite death squads of the SS or to physicians who executed ruthless experiments on prisoners. The exhibition made clear what much of the German public had long suspected but refused to acknowledge: troops of the Wehrmacht were directly involved in the genocide of the Jews and widespread crimes against enemy soldiers and the civilian population, acting both on orders by their superiors and also, in some instances, on their own initiative.

On display in the exhibition are descriptions of events, the documentation of orders, and letters from soldiers. Most captivating, though, are the nearly 800 photographs illustrating what the texts document: German soldiers photographing, seemingly without the least compunction or guilt, other German soldiers committing extraordinary atrocities—massacres, hangings, and torture. Given the numbers of active soldiers on the Eastern front, Germans' discussion about the crimes of the Wehrmacht automatically became a discussion about the possible links between these crimes and one's own father, grandfather, uncle, or brother. Indeed, a few visitors discovered their relatives in some of these photographs. Some older visitors even saw themselves—literally.

In a figurative sense, you could say that *all* of the visitors to the exhibition saw themselves in the photographs. Each was the victim of an inflicted self-insight. As Michael Geyer writes in his foreword to the companion text to the exhibition:

> For it is one of the most disturbing features of these photographs that they neither show cartoon stereotypes of vicious and sadistic brutes nor haughty officers and SS supermen. These soldiers are people quite unlike anything movies, television, and quite a few books would like to make us believe. They look in uniform much like what they would become in postwar life—your average Fritz, Franz or Otto. They look perfectly normal, but committed extraordinary atrocities. We would not recognize them for what they did—were it not for the photographs that depict what they did, but did not see for themselves, until years later.[13]

In summary, perhaps Arendt's coinage of the phrase "banality of evil" was unfortunate. Its lack of clarity certainly leaves it open to many interpretations. For all of her critics, though, her *conception* of the banality and ordinariness of perpetrators of extraordinary evil has withstood the test of time. Its durability is especially notable because it directly contradicts our tenacious desire to believe in the extraordinariness of people who perpetrate such extraordinary evil. We would rather maintain that extraordinary individuals, very much *unlike* you and me, commit extraordinary evil. We can then distance *us* from *them* and rest in the reassurance that extraordinary evil cannot be duplicated in "ordinary" groups or cultures or in individuals with seemingly "normal" human capacities. As the novelist Leslie Epstein wrote in 1987, "The outrage . . . that greeted Arendt's thesis when applied to Adolf Eichmann indicates the depth of our need to think of that bureaucrat as different from ourselves, to respond to him, indeed, as a typical character in Holocaust fiction—a beast, a pervert, a monster."[14]

The banality of Eichmann's evil leaves us with the real possibility that the potential for committing extraordinary evil exists in each of us. Arendt, correctly in my view, reminds us that perpetrators of extraordinary evil are not that fundamentally different from you and me. She suggests that the commission of extraordinary evil transcends groups, ideology, psychopathology, and personality. Arendt leaves us with the crucially insightful recognition that ordinary people in extraordinary circumstances can perform extraordinarily evil deeds.

This insight, though, still begs an explanation. *How do ordinary people come to commit extraordinary evil?* This question remains a matter of contentious debate within the academic community. In the rest of this chapter, we examine the well-known work of two theorists who argue that extraordinary evil is done by ordinary individuals who activate or create a second self to commit that evil.

Obedience to Authority: Milgram's Agentic State

While the Eichmann trial was still in progress, Stanley Milgram, a young social psychologist at Yale University, was beginning a three-year program of study (1960–1963) that would lend considerable support to Arendt's concept of the banality of evil. Milgram's experimental studies on obedience to authority remain one of the most widely cited, and controversial, programs of studies in psychology. They seem without parallel as a catalyst of scholarly and public debate. Indeed, they have become part of our society's shared intellectual legacy. The studies have been the focus of a 1976 televised drama with William Shatner (*The Tenth Level*), a CBS *60 Minutes* feature, a dramatic play by Dannie Abse (*The Dogs of Pavlov*), articles in *Harper's* and *Esquire*, an interview in *Psychology Today*, and a forum on political authority with John Dean. Milgram's 1974 book, *Obedience to Authority*, has been translated into German, French, Japanese, Dutch, Danish, Italian, Spanish, Swedish, Portuguese, Indonesian, and Serbo-Croatian.[15]

Milgram's experiments on obedience to authority posed a simple but intriguing question: *How far would ordinary Americans go in inflicting serious harm on a perfectly innocent stranger if they were told to do so by an authority figure?* To test this question in the initial experiment, Milgram recruited forty males from New Haven, Connecticut, and the surrounding communities to participate in what was described to them as a study of memory and learning. Volunteers were promised four dollars for an hour of their time, plus fifty cents carfare. They were a broad spectrum of ordinary men drawn from working, managerial, and professional classes and ranging from twenty to fifty years of age. One had not finished elementary school, and some held doctorates and other professional degrees. On arrival at the Interaction Laboratory at Yale University, each of two volunteers was told that the study was concerned with the effects of punishment on learning. The study required one volunteer to play the role of a "teacher" and the other to play the role of a "learner." Out of fairness, roles were randomly assigned by the volunteers selecting slips of paper, one with the word "teacher" and the other with the word "learner," from a hat.

Immediately after the drawing, the teacher and learner were taken to an adjacent room, and the learner was strapped into an "electric chair" apparatus with thick leather restraints. An electrode was attached to the learner's wrist, and electrode paste was applied "to avoid blisters and burns." Subjects were told that the electrode was attached to a shock generator in the adjoining room. In response to a question from the learner, the experimenter declared that "although the shocks can be extremely painful, they cause no permanent tissue damage."

The teacher was then taken to the adjoining room where he was shown an ominous-looking electrical generator bearing a precision engraved label from the fictional "Dyson Instrument Company, Waltham, Mass." The generator had thirty different switches running in fifteen-volt increments from 15 to 450 volts. The higher levels of shock were labeled in big letters as "Intense Shock," "Extreme Intensity Shock," "Danger: Severe Shock," and, ominously, "XXX." When a switch was depressed, an electric buzzing was heard, lights flashed, and various relay clicks were sounded. To strengthen their belief in the authenticity of the generator, each teacher received a sample shock of 45 volts, a level strong enough to be distinctly unpleasant.

Both teacher and learner were then introduced to the learning task—

a "paired-associate" test in which the teacher was instructed to read a series of word pairs to the learner and then to read the first word of a pair and four possible associations. The learner was to indicate which of the four associations originally had been paired with the first word. The experiment asked the teachers to inflict on the learner increasingly painful shocks in response to wrong answers. The learner was to receive the shocks, graduating one 15-volt increment in intensity with each wrong answer, when he failed to memorize word pairs. The teacher was instructed to announce the voltage level before administering each shock. If the teacher reached the thirtieth shock level (450 volts), he was instructed to continue the procedure using this maximum voltage.

When the experiment began, the learner's answers to the paired-associate test flashed silently on a signal box on top of the shock generator. The learner did fairly well at first, then began to make frequent mistakes. The teacher found himself administering higher and higher shock levels. At 300 volts, the learner vigorously pounded on the laboratory walls in protest. From this point on, the learner's answers no longer appeared on the signal box. The learner's pounding was repeated after 315 volts. Afterward, he was not heard from again, nor did his answers reappear on the signal box. Teachers were instructed to regard these nonresponses as incorrect and to continue the procedure. Throughout the experiment, in response to the teachers' increasing anxiety and occasional refusal to continue, the experimenter (the role of "Authority") responded with four scripted, increasingly strident verbal prods: "Please continue" or "Please go on"; "The experiment requires that you continue"; "It is absolutely essential that you continue"; and, finally, "You have no other choice, you *must* go on." If the teacher refused to obey the experimenter after the fourth prod, the experiment was terminated.

In reality, the real focus of the experiment was the teacher. The drawing was rigged so that the roles of teacher and learner were prearranged. One of the "volunteer" subjects was actually an accomplice of the experimenter, and the other was the "real," naive subject. Both slips of paper in the hat read "teacher," so that the real subject would always assume that role and Milgram's accomplice, a forty-seven-year-old accountant of Irish-American descent who was seen by most observers as "mild-mannered and likeable," would be assured the role of the learner. In addition, the shock generator was not wired to give any shocks to the learner. The learner, trained for the role, simply acted as if he was receiving the shocks. The learner's responses to both the test (a prearranged pattern of approximately three wrong answers to one correct answer) and the "shocks" were carefully scripted and rehearsed.

Before disclosing the results, Milgram presented the details of this experiment to a group of 110 psychiatrists, college students, and middle-class adults. He asked each to "reflect on the experiment, then privately record how he himself would perform in it." *Each* of the 110 respondents saw himself disobeying the experimenter at some point in the command series—that is, exhibiting defiance. Only four of the respondents reported a willingness to go as high as 300 volts. These respondents were then asked how *other* people would perform in the same experimental situation. They predicted that virtually all subjects would refuse to obey the experimenter; only a pathological fringe, not exceeding 1 or 2 percent, was expected to administer the highest shock on the board.

How close were these predictions to the results of Milgram's initial experiment? Not very. In the initial experiment, despite the learner's distress and cessation of responding, *twenty-six out of forty participants (65 percent) obeyed the experimenter's orders that they shock, in steadily increasing magnitude, the learner to the point of maximum, perhaps even life-threatening, punishment—450 volts*. To be sure, the teachers complained, hesitated, and refused to take responsibility. There were fits of nervous laughter and giggling. The teachers sweated furiously, trembled, stuttered, bit their lips, groaned, and paced the floor as if they are going to walk out of the door. Milgram reported the conflicted reactions of one typical subject: "I observed a mature and initially poised businessman enter the laboratory smiling and confident. Within 20 minutes he was reduced to a twitching, stuttering wreck, who was rapidly approaching a point of nervous collapse. He constantly pulled on his earlobe, and twisted his hands. At one point, he pushed his fist into his forehead and muttered: 'Oh God, let's stop it.' And yet he continued to respond to every word of the experimenter, and obeyed to the end."[16] Despite their hesitancies, most subjects persisted in their obedience to authority. All they had to do to end the experiment was just say no—and mean it. Far fewer than half, though, did. Even those heroic subjects who defied the experimenter's demands never left their seat to help their victim without first being given permission to do so by the experimenter.

With this startling degree of obedience as the baseline, Milgram then carried out more than twenty subsequent studies to clarify the influence of situational factors on obedience to authority. He found, for instance, that obedience decreased somewhat as the physical closeness of the teacher and learner increased. In a condition where the teacher could actually hear the learner screaming and demanding to be set free, for example, "only" 25 out of 40 participants remained fully obedient. In another variation, requiring the subject to have physical contact with the victim in order to give him punishment, full obedience was exhibited by only 12 of 40 subjects. Milgram even tried, in yet another condition, to encourage disobedience by having the learner claim a preexisting heart condition. Even here, however, obedience remained at a substantially high level—26 of 40 went all the way to 450 volts. Utilizing a Bridgeport office building, Milgram also found that obedience did not require that the study be conducted at a prestigious university—19 of 40 subjects were fully obedient. All told, it was difficult for Milgram to devise an experimental variation in which at least some subjects would not exhibit full obedience to the experimenter. Clearly, obedience runs deep and insidious in our behavioral patterns.

In short, Milgram's basic findings held, without regard to age, gender, or level of education of the subjects, in a range of obedience conditions that tested more than a thousand individuals at several universities. His main findings have been replicated at least forty times. Moreover, subsequent research has demonstrated that these rates of obedience have shown no systematic change over the years since Milgram's original studies. International studies have confirmed a cross-cultural potential for obedience to destructive authority. One study of German citizens in Munich, for example, found an 85 percent rate of full obedience under the exact experimental setting used in Milgram's initial study.[17]

The data that carried the greatest impact—on other psychologists and on the general public—came from Milgram's initial experiment. Of a sample of average Americans, nearly two-thirds were willing to administer what they believed to be life-threatening shocks to an innocent victim, well after he lapsed into a perhaps unconscious silence, at the command of a single experimenter with no apparent means of enforcing his orders. It was the extreme willingness of adults to go to almost any lengths on the command of an authority that drew the world's interest to Milgram's studies.

So powerful were Milgram's conclusions that they were adopted as defense strategies in several notable court cases. Lt. William Calley unsuccessfully used the "obedience to authority" defense during the trials concerning the 1968 My Lai massacre—and a large portion of the American public judged his defense appropriate. In 1989, South African courts accepted "obedience to authority" as one of several extenuating factors in two separate trials where thirteen defendants were accused of committing murder as part of a mob; nine were saved from the death penalty.[18]

What Can the Milgram Studies Teach Us about Perpetrators of Extraordinary Evil?

Despite its impact and incredibly broad range of (mis)applications, there is, obviously, no comparison between the scale of events in Milgram's laboratory and the enormity of the Holocaust or other cases of genocide. Milgram himself was well aware of this: "Is the obedience observed in the laboratory in any way comparable to that seen in Nazi Germany? (Is a match flame comparable to the Chicago fire of 1898?)"[19] But is there anything about the underlying psychological processes that is common to the subjects' behavior in Milgram's laboratory and the extraordinary evil perpetrated in cases of genocide and mass killing? What are the real, and apparent, limitations in using Milgram's research to understand perpetrators of extraordinary evil?

There are at least four ways in which the general conditions of the Milgram experiments do not correspond well to those of mass killings and genocides:

1. The destructive consequences of Milgram's subjects' actions were by no means certain. They were assured, by an authority figure representing a generally benevolent institution, that no permanent physical damage would result from their actions. Perpetrators of genocide can rely on no such assurances. They know they are not only inflicting pain but also destroying human life.

2. Milgram's subjects had no previous exposure to their victims and, one could argue, were strongly opposed to harming the victim. When offered the slightest excuse to avoid obedience (for example, when the experimenter was out of the room), they did so. Perpetrators of genocide, conversely, often have an intense devaluation of the victims—built up over years and years—prior to action against them. It is not uncommon for perpetrators to display destructive obedience when no authority figure is physically present.

3. Milgram's subjects exhibited great anguish and conflict in delivering dangerous shocks to their victims. This sharply contrasts with the sadism sometimes exhibited by perpetrators of mass killing and genocide. (There was some indication, though, that Milgram's subjects became angry with the learner as the experiment progressed. They became angry with him for, as they saw it, making the mistakes that caused them to be sub-

jected to such stress. It is entirely possible to see how this anger, roused in the limits of one laboratory hour, could progress to sadistic behavior over the course of an extended period of time and contact.)

4. The entire Milgram study lasted about an hour; most perpe-trators commit their crimes time and time again over a period of months or years. Milgram's subjects had little time to con-template the implications of their behavior. Over an extended period of time, it would be harder—though not impossi-ble—for a perpetrator to avoid such contemplation.

In short, it would be inaccurate to characterize the subjects' motiva-tions and behavior in Milgram's Yale laboratory as exactly equivalent, either morally or psychologically, to that of those who commit atrocities in mass killing and genocide. However, it is just as inaccurate to say that Milgram's research is without relevance to our study of extraordinary evil. He correctly focuses our attention on the social and situational pressures that can lead ordinary people to commit extraordinary evil.

It is incredibly insightful to realize that Milgram's subjects—with no obligatory military, cultural, or ideological commitments and without prior training or conditioning—were willing to inflict excruciating pain on someone just like themselves, against whom they had no animus at all. In Milgram's words: "After witnessing hundreds of ordinary people submit to the authority in our experiments, I must conclude that Arendt's concep-tion of the banality of evil comes closer to the truth than one might dare imagine. . . . That is, perhaps, the most fundamental lesson of our study: ordinary people, simply doing their jobs, and without any particular hos-tility on their part, can become agents in a terrible destructive process."[20] He concludes, "While there are enormous differences of circumstance and scope, a common psychological process is centrally involved in both [his laboratory experiments and Nazi Germany] events."[21]

The Agentic State

What is this common psychological process that is centrally involved in both Milgram's laboratory and events in Nazi Germany? This takes us to the level of explanation. *How and why did the subjects so readily delegate their moral decision making, and behavior, to an authority? Why didn't they walk out of the laboratory once they recognized what was developing in terms of their inner moral conflict? What were the mechanisms that mediated the link between his scripted paradigm and the subjects' responses? Why is submission to authority such a powerful and potent condition in humankind?* Milgram answered these questions by invoking several social and situational causal forces. Among this itemized list were the socialization of obedience, self-generated binding factors (or "cementing mechanisms") that exerted a pressure for the subject to remain in the unpleasant situation, and the process of gradual escalation and entrapment that was inherent in the sequential nature of the task.

More relevant to our discussion, and often neglected by contemporary commentators, Milgram also explained destructive obedience to authority as deriving from a fundamental human disposition to be obedient under appropriate circumstances. Milgram recognized that humans must often function within organizations. He argued that an evolutionary bias favors the survival of people who can adapt favorably to hierarchical situations and organized social activity. As a result, according to Milgram, we have developed an evolutionary potential for obedience. It is not a simple instinct for obedience, he asserts, but a *potential* for obedience that interacts with the influence of society and situations. In short, the standard workings of evolutionary selection pressures have left us with an inherent propensity, a deeply ingrained behavior tendency, to obey those positioned hierarchically above us.

But what is the mechanism of this proclivity for obedience? Milgram postulated, as the "keystone" of his 1974 analysis, the existence of a discontinuous, altered cognitive state that he called the *agentic state*. The agentic state, activated by one's integration into a hierarchy, occurs when one "sees himself as an agent for carrying out another person's wishes."[22] In the agentic state, one is in a state of openness to regulation by an authority; it is the opposite of the state of autonomy. It is a change in one's self-perception, a cognitive reorientation induced when a person occupies a subordinate position in a hierarchical system.

In the agentic state, inner conflict is reduced through the abrogation of personal responsibility. Unable to defy the authority of the experimenter in Milgram's study, subjects attributed all responsibility to him. In Milgram's words: "The most far-reaching consequence of the agentic shift is that a man feels responsible *to* the authority directing him but feels no responsibility *for* the content of the actions that the authority prescribes [italics in original]."[23] In the agentic state, Milgram argued, we are not governed by the operations of our own conscience; instead, our conscience has been momentarily switched off or given over to the "substitute" conscience of the authority. Consistent with Arendt's depiction of Eichmann, we become more preoccupied with duty than with matters of our personal conscience.

Milgram argues: "Moved into the agentic state, the person becomes something different from his former self, with new properties not easily traced to his usual personality."[24] Explaining the shift from normal autonomous functioning to the agentic state, Milgram suggests transformations, beyond our technical skill to specify, at the chemoneurological level. For Milgram, shifts in patterns of neural functioning are the "triggers" that allow us to toggle between normal and agentic functioning. It is a dichotomous and all-or-nothing proposition—we are either in one state or another at any given time. Milgram's notion of an "on-off" switch reflects the acutely abrupt nature of the agentic shift—a necessary conceptualization given that Milgram's subjects began and completed their task of administering what they regarded as life-threatening shocks to an innocent victim within the window of one laboratory hour.

Although logically compelling, the empirical evidence supporting the agentic shift is, in fact, weak or contradictory. Some critics asserted that transcripts of subjects' conflicted comments and behaviors during the experiment—hesitation, tentative refusals, and extreme anxiety—raised doubts about an entire shift into an agentic state, or, at the very least, concerns about the transient in-and-out nature of the agentic shift even in the context of one abbreviated laboratory hour. Even Milgram's own empirical support, based on postexperimental judgments of the subjects, found that both obedient and defiant subjects attributed virtually identical levels of responsibility to the experimenter. This runs counter to the "agentic shift" hypothesis, which would predict far more responsibility to be assigned to the experimenter by obedient subjects (looking to rationalize their obedience) than by defiant subjects.

More crippling to the agentic shift hypothesis was a 1976 study by German psychologists David Mark Mantell and Robert Panzarella. Their major finding, also based on postexperimental debriefings, was that there was *no* relationship between the degree of obedience exhibited by subjects and the subjects' assignment of responsibility. There were both obedient and defiant subjects who accepted 100 percent of the responsibility, and there were those who accepted none at all. In their words: "A monolithic view of the obedient person as a purely passive agent who invariably relinquishes personal responsibility is a false view. There are people who obey and continue to hold themselves responsible as well as people who obey and relinquish responsibility. Similarly, among people who initially obey but then defy, there are those who accept full responsibility and those who accept none at all for the actions they performed prior to their defiance."[25]

The lack of empirical support makes it clear that the agentic shift is *not* essential to all acts of obedience. At times, people will obey authority without relinquishing a sense of personal responsibility for their action to a superior. In other words, there is not always a strong correlation between the amount of responsibility attributed to the authority and the amount of obedience exhibited. For example, some may feel an obligation to comply arising from a norm of reciprocity ("I did that for you, so you should feel obligated to do this for me"). Others may respond to a norm of equity ("I have worked hard and suffered, so I have a right to ask you to do something to make up for it"). Neither of these norms need stem from relative positions in a social hierarchy. In short, shifting from an autonomous to an agentic state is *not* a necessary precondition for obedience to destructive authority.

Despite the lack of empirical evidence for "something different" from a former self in explaining Milgram's results, both scholars and laypeople have continued to hold on to the notion that there is a mystical shift from one self to another that enables a person to commit extraordinary evil. There seems to be something emotionally compelling about the idea that extraordinary evil is committed by a "double" of some sorts—ourselves become not ourselves.

Separating Home from Hell: Lifton's Doubling

Robert Jay Lifton, professor of psychology and psychiatry at John Jay College and the Graduate Center of the City University of New York, maintains that the Nazi state could be viewed as a "biocracy." "Just as in a theocracy, the state itself is no more than a vehicle for the divine purpose," he writes, "so in the Nazi biocracy was the state no more than a means to achieve *'a mission of the German people on earth'*: that of *'assembling and preserving the most valuable stocks of basic racial elements in this* [Aryan] *people . . .* [and] *raising them to a dominant position'* [italics in original]."[26]

Central to the enactment of this biological mission were doctors. Given the important role the state assigned to them, it comes as little surprise that 65 percent of German doctors became Nazi Party members. This was the highest ratio of party members of all professions—twice the proportion of teachers who became Nazis, even though teachers had the important role of indoctrinating Germany's youth in Nazism. Some of the

Nazi doctors chose to follow their biological mission to its inevitable conclusion—state-sponsored killing operations.

In October 1939, Hitler authorized a systematic Nazi medical program to eliminate *lebensunwertes Leben* (life unworthy of life). His rare written directive authorized selected physicians "to administer to incurably sick persons a mercy death." The directive, predated September 1, 1939, to coincide with the beginning of the war and mask the program as a wartime economy measure, was written informally on his personal writing paper. What Hitler envisioned with this directive had nothing whatsoever to do with the common understanding of "euthanasia"—painlessly ending the life of a terminally ill person either at his or her own request or with the consent of their relatives. Rather, "euthanasia" was a euphemism for state-sanctioned murder.

At first, the intention was to apply this directive only to Germans with mental afflictions. Eventually, however, the program broadened to encompass the "euthanasia" of severely handicapped children in hospital wards as well as a wide variety of other institutionalized patients—senile persons, epileptics, sufferers from Huntington's chorea, encephalitics, the criminally insane, and individuals who had been institutionalized for at least five years: in short, anyone that suffered some disability that stigmatized them in the eyes of their persecutors as "life unworthy of life."

Under the codename "T4," after the address of the project's offices in a confiscated Jewish villa in Berlin, this "euthanasia" program was history's first technological killing operation. Those selected to die were transported to one of six "euthanasia" centers in Germany and Austria: Hartheim, Sonnenstein, Grafeneck, Bernburg, Hadamar, or Brandenburg. Medical personnel at these centers first used starvation, pills, and lethal injection (morphine and, occasionally, the direct injection of phenol into the heart) to kill many of the selected patients. Later, gassing with carbon monoxide—in specially constructed chambers with false showerheads—became the more efficient method of choice. The bodies were removed and burned in an attached crematorium, but not before all gold teeth had been extracted and some of their brains had been removed for purposes of "scientific research." Families then received a death certificate fraudulently listing the cause of death as natural—pneumonia, typhus, meningitis, bronchitis, carbuncles, seizures, and so on—along with an accompanying letter justifying the cremation as necessary for public health reasons.

Under pressure from Germany's Roman Catholic and Lutheran leaders, T4 was "officially" halted on August 24, 1941. Before that time, however, the program resulted in the murder of 70,000 to 80,000 people, including 4,000 to 5,000 Jews. Unfortunately, Hitler's stop order did *not* end the destruction of those considered "life unworthy of life." The stop order applied only to the killing centers; mass murder of the handicapped continued by other means. In fact, more victims of euthanasia perished *after* the stop order was issued than before. All told, T4 and the subsequent "wild" euthanasia programs of Nazi Germany murdered between 200,000 and 250,000 people. In administration, technology, and vision, this spree of medicalized killing prefigured the Final Solution and became a model for all that followed. At the institutional heart of this extraordinary evil were the Nazi doctors.[27]

Doubling

How could this "unique" category of ordinary people, men and women pledged to the ideals of the Hippocratic Oath and the preservation of human life, come to kill and do so in the name of healing? That was the question addressed by Lifton's compelling book *The Nazi Doctors: Medical Killing and the Psychology of Genocide.* Drawing on extensive, face-to-face interviews with twenty-nine medical professionals involved at high levels in Nazi medicine, twelve former Nazi nonmedical professionals of some prominence (lawyers, judges, economists, teachers, architects, administrators, and Party officials), and eighty former Auschwitz prisoners who had worked on medical blocks (more than half of them doctors), Lifton advances the explanatory concept of "doubling" to answer the question of how ordinary people come to commit extraordinary evil.

What is doubling? The roots of the concept are apparent in the work of early psychologists, such as William James, and many psychoanalysts, such as Otto Rank (particularly in his classic study *The Double*). It was psychoanalysis that gave us the related concept of a *personal shadow*—the negative emotions and behaviors that lie concealed just beneath our surface, masked by our more proper selves. Beginning in childhood, many forces play a role in forming our shadow selves—parents, siblings, teachers, clergy, and friends. Through this socialization, we learn to bury in our shadow those qualities that do not fit our self-image. Occasionally, some psychoanalysts suggest, we will even deposit in the dark treasury of our shadow some undeveloped talents and gifts. In short, our shadow self contains unexpressed potentials of all kinds that the conscious personality chooses to neglect, forget, and hide. Most psychoanalysts even maintain that the shadow self is *necessary* to the human psyche; the loss of one's shadow or "double" means death.

Doubling's strongest roots, however, lie in the psychiatric concept of dissociation. From a clinical perspective, dissociation occurs when a group of mental processes are separated (or split) from the remainder of the person's activity. These mental processes coexist or alternate without becoming connected or influencing one another. In contemporary psychiatry and clinical psychology, the concept of dissociation remains central in a broad category of unconscious defense mechanisms such as "repression," "isolation," and "splitting." These defense mechanisms often are adaptive, even life-saving, short-term strategies for dealing with severe trauma. Excessive reliance on these defense mechanisms, however, may result in a dissociative disorder. Such clinical dissociative disorders are characterized by a severe disruption in the usually integrated functions of consciousness, memory, identity, or perception. This disruption leads to an amnesia, or nonawareness, of a segment—or segments—of one's activity.

The *DSM-IV-TR* identifies four categories of dissociative disorders: (1) Dissociative Amnesia, (2) Dissociative Fugue (wandering states), (3) Dissociative Identity Disorder (formerly Multiple Personality Disorder), and (4) Depersonalization Disorder. (There is an additional catchall category, Dissociative Disorder Not Otherwise Specified.) Such dissociation of personality is a particularly disturbing phenomenon because it calls into question a basic assumption about human nature—namely, that for every body there is but one person; that each of us, despite the passage of time, remains the same person, with a single biography and store of memories.

Lifton posits dissociation as the most frequent psychological adaptation utilized by the Nazi doctors. He avoids the overgeneralization of a pathological condition to scores of perpetrators, however, by differentiating the distinctive dissociation involved in evildoing from clinical dissociative disorders. Lifton presents the dissociation in evildoing as involving a dialectic, or awareness, between the split selves. In other words, the dissociation employed by the Nazi doctors was a split leading to a second self that "had to be both autonomous and connected to the prior self that gave rise to it."[28] This form of dissociation is vastly different from a clinical dissociative disorder in which multiple selves are *disconnected from*, and *nonaware of*, the other selves. Pathological forms of clinical dissociation and Lifton's dissociation also differ in that the former are lifelong patterns and the latter a more focused and temporary form of adaptation that "occurs as part of a larger institutional structure which encourages or even demands it."[29]

Lifton is clear regarding the ordinary origins of this extraordinary evil: "Participation in mass murder need not require emotions as extreme or demonic as would seem appropriate for such a malignant project. Or to put the matter another way, ordinary people can commit demonic acts."[30]

In his later discussion, Lifton introduces the principal unconscious defense mechanism used in the Nazi doctors' unique brand of dissociation. This mechanism, a variant of splitting termed "doubling," is defined as "the division of the self into two functioning wholes, so that a part-self acts as an entire self."[31] Lifton maintains that doubling involves five characteristics:

1. There is a dialectic between two selves in terms of autonomy and connection. There is a primary, prior self that is both autonomous and connected to the evildoing, second self.

2. Doubling follows a holistic principle. This holistic principle differentiates doubling from "splitting." Rather than a "split-off" element of the self that ceases to respond to the environment, Lifton focuses on a holistic view of the self in which doubling is simply part of the universal potential for opposing tendencies in the self. In other words, the potential for doubling is part of being human.

3. Doubling has a life-death dimension. An evildoing self is created on behalf of what one perceives as one's own healing or survival. Doubling protects the perpetrator from his or her own death anxiety.

4. A major function of doubling is the avoidance of guilt. The evildoing, second self is the one performing the "dirty work." It is not the *elimination* of conscience that allows the perpetrator to commit extraordinary evil; it is the *transfer* of conscience to the second self that frees the primary self from responsibility.

5. Doubling involves both an unconscious dimension—taking place largely outside of awareness—and a significant change in moral consciousness.

In sum, doubling maintains that the doctors created a second dissociated self to do evil, related to, but more or less autonomous from, the prior self. This fractured identity was formed as the perpetrator internalized many of the patterns and assumptions of the Auschwitz environment. This compartmentalized Auschwitz self took shape over months or years as an adaptation to an extreme environment in which healing and killing were reversed. And yet an Auschwitz doctor's primary or prior self was operative when he visited his wife, children, and parents when on leave for a few days every month.

These dual selves, one an atrocious perpetrator active in mass killing and the other an ordinary human being, coexisted simultaneously through the psychological mechanism of doubling. As Lifton relates from a conversation with Dr. B., "Each SS doctor could call forth two radically different psychological constellations within the self: one based on 'values generally accepted' and the education and background of a 'normal person'; the other based on 'this [Nazi-Auschwitz] ideology with values quite different from those generally accepted.'"[32] The two selves are encapsulated, walled off from each other to avoid internal conflict. The second self is a complete functioning self that has its own psychological framework (divided from the prior self), within which ordinary intellectual and moral standards are annulled. The two selves may eventually merge again when the situation producing the doubling is temporary and rectifiable; when the situation is lasting and beyond remedy, however, so are the dissociative inner divisions of the self.

Lifton's use of the verb form, as opposed to the more usual noun form found in literature (that is, "*the* double"), makes it clear that doubling is *not* a metaphor but rather an active psychological explanation of evildoing. In addition, it is equally clear that his concept of doubling is *not* limited to one personality type or the extreme case of the Nazi doctors. Lifton contends that doubling occurred in people of varied psychological characteristics and extensively in nonmedical Auschwitz personnel as well. Elsewhere, however, Lifton does suggest that doctors and other professional groups (for example, psychologists, physicists, biologists, clergy, generals, statesmen, writers, artists, nuclear weapons designers and strategists) have a special capacity for doubling, as do some cultures, such as the German and the Japanese.

Critique

There are four critical questions to raise concerning Lifton's conception of doubling as a psychological explanation for how ordinary people commit extraordinary evil. First, should doubling be understood as a legitimate psychological explanation of *how* ordinary people commit extraordinary evil or simply as a coping mechanism by which perpetrators evade the guilt of their evildoing? In other words, rather than an explanatory mechanism, might we better think of doubling as a defense mechanism by which perpetrators psychologically distance themselves from the evil they commit and, later, use that distance to avoid moral self-accusations?

Lifton's theory, through the creation of a second self, posits a way of permitting one to engage oneself systematically in evil actions while avoiding a sense of one's own evil. Indeed, Lifton lists guilt avoidance as a "major function" of doubling and one of its five basic characteristics. Nowhere is the use of doubling in guilt avoidance more evident than in the various statements of Nazi doctors interviewed by Lifton. Ernst B., for instance, states that as a Nazi doctor in Auschwitz "you were caught and had to go along"—a statement that Lifton interprets to mean that one had to create a second Auschwitz self.[33] Lifton again: "The feeling was something like: 'Anything I do on planet Auschwitz doesn't count on planet Earth.' And what one does not believe, whatever the evidence of one's own actions, one does not feel. That is why Dr. Tadeusz S. could say, of Nazi doctors, with bitter irony: 'They have no moral problems.'"[34]

Doubling, rather than a *cause* of evildoing, can easily be seen as a *consequence*. In other words, it is an adaptation that does not explain *how* ordinary people commit extraordinary evil, only how they cope with their participation in evildoing once it has commenced. It is important to distinguish between psychological defense operations and the complex construction of an entirely new self. While doubling may have merit as a guilt avoidance strategy, it offers little as an explanatory mechanism for how ordinary people commit extraordinary evil.

Second, even if understood as an adaptive mechanism, how essential is doubling in allowing perpetrators to divorce their evildoing self from their ordinary self? As Lifton points out, the two separate selves, one for ordinary living and the other for evildoing, have a dialectic in terms of connection. How do the separate, yet connected, selves reconcile their own very disparate activities? How does one self maintain its standing as a kind and loving husband, father, and son in the screaming face of a dissonant second self that perpetrates extraordinary evil? In a way, one could argue that Lifton's postulation of a second self is actually *less* preferable as an adaptive device than would be a true dissociative state in which the two selves are disconnected.

How necessary is doubling as a short-term adaptive mechanism? For Lifton, doubling is the *only* means by which one can perpetrate the evil required by an extreme environment. It is clear, however, that for perpetrators of extraordinary evil, doubling is only one of many short-term adaptive mechanisms. For instance, Lifton often speaks of the high rates of alcohol abuse among the Nazi doctors. Similarly, Browning recounts that the men of Reserve Police Battalion 101 ate little but drank heavily after the Jozefow massacre. Why the heavy drinking if perpetrators have a second, compartmentalized self that is responsible for their evildoing? It reveals more than, as Lifton maintains, a pattern of male bonding. Rather, it is another example—one of many (for instance, structural diffusion of responsibility)—of an adaptive short-term mechanism to the dissonance raised by the perpetration of extraordinary evil. As such, it illustrates that doubling is not sufficient to stand as the only, or even the central, psychological mechanism of *even* short-term adaptation.

As a long-term adaptation, doubling fares even worse. Social psychological evidence has strongly demonstrated the marked inability of human subjects to withstand even minimal and innocuous levels of inner dissonance for sustained periods. Experimental participants who are *forced* to argue a position inconsistent with their own, for example, often subsequently evidence substantial attitudinal change in the direction of the position they were forced to argue. If, by simply advocating a position in which we do not believe, we find the inner dissonance so intolerable that we will modify our previously held beliefs to be more consistent with that position, then the extreme inner dissonance required by Lifton's theory cannot be validated as a sustained form of adaptation to evildoing. The human psyche simply cannot tolerate long-term dissociative inner divisions in the manner in which Lifton suggests. People tend toward integration, not compartmentalization. Even Lifton, in a coauthored work with Erik Markusen, speaks of the "always fragile human aspiration for wholeness."[35]

Again, so strong is our desire for integration and wholeness that a dissociative process like doubling could only work as one means of short-term adaptation. Over the long run, the changes that occur in the primary self of perpetrators of extraordinary evil are much deeper and long-lasting. As Ervin Staub points out, perpetrators "develop unitary selves by changes in their motives, world views, and beliefs and by achieving highly differentiated orientations to different groups of people."[36]

Third, what are the long-term implications of doubling as an adaptive mechanism? Lifton states that doubling can be both "prolonged and temporary, not necessarily permanent" and that "one can cease being an evil person when one's life returns to ordinary pursuits, even without confronting the evil one had been part of."[37] Consistent with these notions, Browning states that one of the disturbing features of the perpetrators in his study was how easily they reaccommodated and readapted to the nonlethal situation following the war and returned to lead seemingly normal lives. De Mildt also affirms the relative ease of perpetrators' reconversion to their role as law-abiding citizens once killing was no longer a state-sponsored affair.

It is reasonable, however, to question whether the primary self can remain unaltered after participation in extraordinary evil. Can the human psyche effectively reorganize itself so as to essentially erase the legacy of an evildoing "Auschwitz self"? Certainly, some psychological reorganization can and does take place after participation in evildoing. But can it be so pervasive as to erase the tremendous guilt of participation and leave the individuals committing the evil unchanged?

Interestingly, Lifton himself did not see many signs of extensive psychological reorganization on the part of the Nazi doctors. He admits that "the residual Nazi or Auschwitz self has remained with them and significantly affected their attitudes and their lives."[38] The existence of a residual self decades after their evildoing betrays the fundamental and long-lasting alterations that the perpetrators had experienced. The consequence of this relative permanence, in Darley's words, is to make "the individual so socialized permanently susceptible to being caught up in harmdoing institutions in the future."[39] In the grip of similar social forces, all would commit evil again—perhaps even more readily. John M. Steiner, in his postwar study of former SS men, agrees: "What has been observed . . . is a continuation of what can be described as authoritarianism and the pursuit of occupations in which aggression is socially acceptable, even desirable."[40] The men in his sample, for instance, still advocated "dictatorship" instead of "monarchy" or "democracy"—even after twenty postwar years of democracy. Though the majority of these men successfully integrated into postwar German society, it is clear that their evildoing left an imprint on their attitudes, beliefs, and vocations. In short, perpetrators are themselves changed—in fundamental and relatively permanent ways—by their participation in extraordinary evil.

Fourth, and finally, doubling rests on the uneasy legs of ideological commitment. For Lifton, the Nazi doctors were ideologically committed to their biological mission and it was this deep devotion to the Nazi cause that prepared them for their participation in evildoing. Lifton even speaks of an "ideological call to doubling." In other words, the Nazi doctors became killers because they followed a "biomedical vision," approaching their task as a "therapeutic imperative." It was this ideological commitment that gave the killing the status of right, justice, and truth. It was this same commitment that sustained the Nazi doctors in their continued participation in the healing-killing paradox. Though, as Lifton maintains, the Nazi doctors were not generally full ideologues, they certainly saw themselves as "ideological fighters" in the struggle for the purity of the Aryan race.

As was pointed out in chapter 2, however, ideological commitment has its clear limits in explaining the perpetration of extraordinary evil by ordinary people. Ideologies are rarely coherent, nor are ideologues consistent. Moreover, Henry Friedlander maintains that Nazi doctors collaborated in killing operations for many personal reasons unrelated to their ideological commitment. "Of course," he points out, "it is undoubtedly true that the participating physicians believed in the racial and eugenic goals of the Nazi regime . . . [but] a physician could refuse to participate in killings even if he subscribed to the ideology of racial science."[41] De Mildt's analysis, discussed earlier in this chapter, agrees that these were not killers by conviction but killers by circumstance and opportunity. In short, for the Nazi doctors, ideological commitment was no more a predictor of involvement in mass killing than was family background, economic position, or academic achievement.

Given the critique discussed above, how might we accommodate Lifton's concept of doubling in a larger, explanatory model? One way would be to understand doubling as one of the initial tools of adaptation to evildoing. It is possible that such a short-term adaptation could have more than intuitive or metaphorical appeal—it could very well be a part of the human repertoire of responses to our own atrocities, a temporary frame of emotional security.

Over time, however, fundamental internal alterations in the psychological framework of the perpetrators will increasingly diminish the need to compartmentalize. Harming victims can become "normal" behavior. The human psyche, driven by integration toward a unitary self, ultimately must change to diminish the dissonance. Even Lifton acknowledges that "to chart their involvement in a continuous routine of killing, over a year or two or more, one needs an explanatory principle that draws upon the entire, functioning self."[42] The concept of doubling offers no such explanatory principle.

Conclusion

As we have seen in the previous chapters, there is a pervasive bias toward attributing the commission of extraordinary evil to equally extraordinary origins as the primary causes of such behavior. As this chapter has shown, however, the combined work of Hannah Arendt and historians such as Dick de Mildt and those involved in the exhibition *The German Army and Genocide* gives the lie to that bias. Buttressing their historical arguments is the psychological evidence from the work of Stanley Milgram and Robert Jay Lifton. Both Milgram and Lifton, in very disparate ways, have described the reality of the propensity for ordinary people to commit extraordinary evil. Their work illustrates what I call "divided self" understandings of extraordinary human evil.

Our fascination with the notion of a divided self, or two selves occupying the same person, is reflected in impressive mythological and literary roots. Throughout history, the divided self has appeared via the human imagination as a monster, a dragon, a white whale, an extraterrestrial, or a man or woman so evil that we cannot see ourselves in him or her. The idea of a divided self or "double" still flourishes in superstitions, fairy tales, and folklore throughout the world. These allusions, fascinating in and of themselves, are important because of how they influence cultural and professional acceptance of a divided self as an acceptable explanation for human (mis)behavior. Indeed, fiction sometimes can teach us more about life, or what we think we know about life, than life itself.

In addition, a new breed of "postmodern psychologists" is redirecting the social scientific discussion to the concept of multiple selves. They maintain that we have no single, centralized, unified, coherent self. Rather, we have a community of selves, each with its own desires and motives, which have been created to relate to different aspects of our multifaceted lives. It's not just that we each have different sides to our personality; it's that we have no central personality in relation to which all our varied behaviors might be seen as just "sides." Such a postmodern conception of human identity challenges the comfortable assumption of a single self that is basic to Western culture. It argues that there are only multiple and fragmented selves that form and reform momentarily in response to a complex relational field. In other words, our personality is a system of selves-in-relation. Psychological health involves a relatively fluid access to this multiplicity of selves, and a general sense of comfortable containment of them.

But should the unitary self be a dead notion? The vast majority of social scientists think not. They maintain a firm belief in the existence of a coherent, authentic, integrated self that is essential to normal, psychological functioning. This self may have a fluid, evolving character that is in a continual process of becoming. Along the way, this self may play different roles in different settings—but it is one unitary self nonetheless. In addition to the specific critiques of the agentic state and doubling, there are at least three more general reasons that mainstream social scientists remain committed to the notion of a unitary self.

First, the complexity inherent in divided self theories is unnecessary. Driven by the law of parsimony, most social scientists can find no justifiable reason to assume the existence of separate selves or states of being. As Berel Lang puts it: "It is more plausible to infer a single moral agent—one that granted greater conviction to evil than to good—than two independent moral domains that were constantly being traversed."[43] In other words, there is no credible reason to believe that we *temporarily* become wholly different people, with different ways of thinking, feeling, and behaving, when we commit extraordinary evil. It is more plausible to believe that we have one unitary self that is forever altered by participation in extraordinary evil.

Second, there is a moral problem: divided self theories diminish individual responsibility for perpetrating extraordinary evil. Milgram's subjects, in an agentic state, could easily defer their destructive behavior to a higher authority. Although they did horrible things in Auschwitz, doubling allowed the Nazi doctors to continue to see themselves as decent and even moral people in private. Though both Milgram and Lifton emphasize that perpetrators make *choices* to enter the agentic state or invoke a second self, it is easy to see how divided self theories lead to a subjective experience of the evildoing act as not really *real* and not really *mine*. One could authentically experience oneself as innocent of acts committed by divided selves.

Finally, many social scientists suggest that the presuppositions regarding human nature that underlie divided self theories are increasingly out of step with contemporary social scientific understandings of human nature. This is an important recognition of the fact that the question of the nature of humankind lies at the heart of our discussions about evildoing. While affirming that evil is an ever-present potentiality in each of us, divided self theories maintain that evil can only be committed from something outside our ordinary selves—namely, a fragmented, altered, dissociated, discontinuous second self. The assumption is that our "ordinary" or "true" self is good and we can only commit evil deeds by acting independently of or contrary to this self. In essence, we never become completely evil because the "ordinary" or "true" good and moral self is patiently waiting to once again predominate. While Lifton may claim evil is neither inherent in the self nor foreign to it, his assumption of the primary self as a good self is clear throughout his work. Such a depiction of humankind's essential goodness is not universally shared among social scientists and, as we will see in chapter 5, is increasingly incongruent with much of what we are learning about the nature of human nature from the contemporary field of evolutionary psychology.

In conclusion, emphasizing that ordinary people commit extraordinary evil does not preclude the possibility that certain types of individuals may be more likely than others to engage in destructive obedience. Nor does it deny that there are evil people. Rather, it simply affirms the uncomfortable reality, based on the historical and social psychological evidence, of our capacity for inhumanity toward each other. This reality is not well explained by reference to the extraordinary nature of the collective; the influence of an extraordinary ideology; psychopathology; a common, homogeneous extraordinary personality; or the elaborate creation of a divided self. The limits of these perspectives call for a new explanation of how ordinary people commit extraordinary evil. That explanation is the focus of part II of this book.

The Invasion of Dili

T HE ISLAND OF TIMOR LIES LESS THAN four hundred miles north of Australia, at the southeastern extremity of the Indonesian Nusa-tenggara island group. In this archipelago, it is located at the opposite end to the island of Bali, one of Asia's best-known tourist attractions. In about the middle of the seventeenth century, Timor was divided into two almost equal parts by the Dutch (West Timor) and Portuguese (East Timor) colonial administrations. Throughout its history, East Timor remained poor, underdeveloped, remote, and unconnected to the global network of commercial and tourist communications. It had little strategic or economic importance and no political independence.

All of this promised to change in April 1974, when a cartel of Left-leaning generals overthrew the Portuguese dictator Marcelo Caetano in Lisbon. The new regime made it known that it would free the remaining scraps of Portugal's once extensive colonial empire — Angola, Mozambique, Guinea-Bissau, and East Timor. In anticipation of independence, two major political parties quickly emerged in East Timor — the Timorese Democratic Union (UDT) and the Revolutionary Front for East Timor Independence (FRETILIN). In January 1975, the two parties formed a coalition for independence and prepared for statehood.

Unfortunately, Indonesia — East Timor's powerful neighbor — had other plans. Directed by military leaders who were determined to control East Timor, Indonesian agents sabotaged the region's peaceful progress toward independence by dividing the UDT and FRETILIN. They accomplished their divide-and-conquer plan by combining a propaganda offensive against FRETILIN with a sustained courting of UDT leaders. By May 1975, talks between the UDT and FRETILIN had broken down, and the UDT withdrew from the coalition.

Spurred by Indonesian-planted rumors that FRETILIN planned to launch a coup, the UDT launched a preemptive coup of its own in Dili in

August 1975. Within three weeks, however, the party and its followers had been overwhelmed by FRETILIN. UDT forces and their families were driven over the border into West Timor. On November 28, 1975, FRETILIN unilaterally declared East Timor an independent republic. The Indonesian military, its plan for control of East Timor having backfired, lost no time in responding. Claiming that intervention was necessary to restore peace and security in East Timor, Indonesia invaded the capital city of Dili on December 7, 1975.

In the very first days of the invasion, rampaging Indonesian troops engaged in an orgy of indiscriminate killing, rape, and torture. Large-scale public executions of from 20 to more than 100 persons were carried out. In some villages, whole communities were slaughtered, except for young children. Mass "disappearances," often of the educated and those with leadership ability, were common.

The following is a summary of the testimony of Etelvina Correia, a survivor of the Dili invasion:

> The attack on Dili began at about 4 A.M. on 7 December. Etelvina Correia was in the Church, which is located in the waterfront area. Some time later paratroops began to land (some of them dropped into the water). At 7 A.M she saw paratroops shoot a woman in the parish garage and later 3 women in front of the Church, although their hands were raised. The Indonesian soldiers then ordered all of the people in the vicinity of the Church to go inside. Next day, Etelvina and the others were ordered by troops to go to the wharf area. There 20 women — Chinese and Timorese — were taken out in front. Some of them had children who were weeping. The soldiers tore the children from the women who were then shot one by one, with the crowd being ordered to count after each execution. At 2 P.M. on the same day 59 men, including Chinese and Timorese, were taken to the wharf and executed in the same way. Again the witnesses were ordered at gunpoint to count. They were told that these killings were in reprisal for the killing of a paratrooper near the Toko Lay shop in Dili.[1]

Outraged by these atrocities, the small but determined Timorese army bitterly contested the advance of the invading forces. Retreating to terrain ideal for guerrilla warfare, they were able to deny the Indonesian military effective control outside the main towns and administrative centers. The result, however, was a harsh, oppressive, and prolonged occupation beginning with the July 1976 annexation of East Timor to Indonesian territory as its twenty-seventh state.

In 1991, Dili would again be the scene of a large-scale massacre. On November 12 of that year, several hundred Timorese gathered at the Santa Cruz cemetery to peacefully demonstrate against Indonesia's forced integration of East Timor. For two or three minutes, Indonesian troops fired into the crowd, expending perhaps 1,000 rounds of ammunition. Two hundred seventy-one unarmed East Timorese civilians, mostly young people, were killed. Three hundred eighty-two others were wounded. Two hundred fifty more just "disappeared."

Zito Soares was one of the demonstrators that survived the Santa Cruz massacre. A young East Timorese student, he was twenty years old at the time:

> After all this happened many, many people of all ages joined Sebastiao's [Sebastiao Gomes was murdered by the Indonesian military] funeral, when he was taken to Santa Cruz cemetery. It was then that the arrangements were made, among the youths, for a demonstration that would happen 14 days after Sebastiao's death—the 11th of November. But that was postponed to November 12th, after the celebration Mass for Sebastiao's Soul. The reason was the presence of Holland's Foreign Minister, who would be in East Timor from October 10th on. He was to come as a representative of a Human Rights Committee. . . .
>
> Then [November 12] we arrived and went inside the cemetery. We then started praying, saying the Rosary—in Portuguese. . . . That was when the first military truck arrived, carrying Indonesian policemen. But they couldn't get to the street because of the crowd. Two more trucks arrived afterwards [from battalion 303], most of the men wore uniforms, some didn't wear shirts, and all of them were armed. These two groups were military. They all went inside the other cemetery, the Army cemetery, which is right in front of Santa Cruz. There they aligned by the wall overlooking the street, preparing to shoot at the demonstrators. The wall of this cemetery is very close to the street, we people stood very close by, [the soldiers were] at a distance of barely 5 or 6 steps away from some of us. So, there they were prepared to shoot.
>
> Some of our fellows who had a megaphone told the crowd that the military wouldn't shoot at us because we were only peacefully demonstrating, with a clear intention: "Let's stay quiet, let's keep on praying, and then we will carry on with the demonstration until the afternoon."
>
> It was then that the Indonesians started their gunfire. They shot from the wall of the other cemetery at the demonstrators who were near the gate of Santa Cruz. There was a great commotion among the crowd of demonstrators. I heard much shouting, many people crying for their mothers and fathers.
>
> I was outside the cemetery, 20 meters away or so, in the main street; at that moment I just took one or two steps forward and then threw myself at the

ground. All that came into my mind was "I am going to die now; or if I don't, I will be arrested." Then I turned my face back and saw the first soldiers. They had ran [*sic*] out of bullets and were using their bayonets now. They first bayoneted a friend of mine. Fortunato, who later lost his arm due to the wounds. From that moment on, I could only think about either running away or dying there with the others. "If I run away I'll be shot and die at once, whereas if I stay here I'll suffer much more." So I sprang to my feet and ran towards the smaller side door of the cemetery. That was when I got my arm wounded. But I was able to run across the cemetery, and escape to Bishop Belo's house. . . .

After the treatment [medical treatment at the Urgent Care Unit], the soldiers would arrest the people immediately and took them at once to the military hospital. . . . The army hospital is some 500 meters away from the cemetery. After the massacre, from November 13th on, the Indonesians began to enclose the hospital, putting security battalions around the area. . . . As soon as the 13th November, large stones had been used to kill those who were still alive inside the hospital.[2]

Since the Indonesian military invaded in 1975, Amnesty International places the loss of life at more than 200,000 (the Indonesian government puts the number at 100,000). In awarding the 1996 Nobel Peace Prize to national liberation activists Bishop Carlos Filipe Ximenes Belo and Jose Ramos-Horta of East Timor, the Nobel Committee wrote that "a third of the residents of East Timor have lost their lives because of hunger, infectious epidemics, war and terror."[3]

Since the initial invasion, the case of East Timor was on the UN's agenda. From 1977 on, Indonesia and the international community were repeatedly advised of the humanitarian consequences of this process of annexation and subjugation. Internationally, East Timor was never recognized as part of Indonesia. Generally, however, the West—including the United States—continued to support Indonesia as a valuable ally in the war against communist expansion in Southeast Asia and as a lucrative trading partner, providing its government and military with funding, training, and weapons.

For two and a half decades, the East Timorese continued to suffer under the Indonesian occupation. This was different from the Armenian genocide and the Holocaust because there was no evidence that the Indonesian government sought, as a matter of deliberate policy, to destroy the Timorese people as a race or ethnic group. However, Indonesia's occupation strategies, and the behavior of the military, seemed bound to achieve that end. In addition to the widespread killing, for example, mass sterilization of Timorese women occurred without consent during surgical operations to decrease the

An East Timorese child holds a sign that reads "Deepest sympathy to our friends who died in the Santa Cruz tragedy" during a memorial service at Santa Cruz cemetery in Dili on the tenth anniversary of the massacre (November 12, 2001). Photo by Reuters NewMedia Inc./CORBIS.

Timorese population. Accompanied by a state-sponsored program of mass migration of Indonesians to East Timor, the East Timorese were rendered a minority in their own country. Moreover, the Indonesian newcomers were very much the ruling class, dominating the military, civil government, and economy. This deliberate "Indonesianization" of East Timor, together with ongoing attempts to eliminate support for a separate Timorese state, threatened to submerge Timorese culture and ultimately destroy it — in short, a cultural genocide.

On August 30, 1999, spurred by escalating expressions of worldwide concern and protest, the United Nations sponsored a ballot in which the East Timorese were asked to either accept or reject integration with Indonesia. The East Timorese voted overwhelmingly for independence from Indonesia. A wave of violence by militias, the Indonesian National Army, and the police followed. Amnesty International documented accounts of systematic and widespread human rights violations — including extrajudicial executions, rape, and forcible expulsions. More than 300,000 people fled, or were forcibly expelled from, East Timor. In response to the backlash of violence, the UN Security Council authorized the establishment of a multinational force that was deployed on September 20.

Following the ratification of the ballot results by the Indonesian Parliament on October 19, authority for East Timor was transferred to the UN Transitional Administration in East Timor. Today, the East Timorese people and the UN administrators are working to build a nation from scratch. East Timor faces a dearth of skilled labor in virtually every civil institution and every part of its infrastructure. Rural areas, still subject to blackouts and shortages of water, complain that reconstruction funds have mainly been directed toward Dili. Though many refugees have returned to East Timor, thousands more—particularly those who voted against independence—remain displaced because of fear of reprisals. The persecution of East Timor's Muslim minority, many who relocated under Indonesia's policy of diluting the native population, is emerging as a key test of religious and political tolerance. An 80 percent unemployment rate, coupled with the UN's inability—some say, unwillingness—to recruit East Timorese in the reconstruction efforts, leave many on the island feeling a lack of ownership in the fate of their hard-won fledgling nation.

Hope does, however, appear on the horizon. On March 22, 2002, an eighty-eight-member democratically elected assembly overwhelmingly accepted the final draft of a charter for East Timor's first constitution. As of this writing, campaigning for elections to decide the nation's first president is under way. East Timor is slated to become the world's newest nation on May 20, 2002.[4]

II

BEYOND DEMONIZATION: HOW ORDINARY PEOPLE COMMIT EXTRAORDINARY EVIL

A Model of Extraordinary
Human Evil

A S WE LOOK AT PERPETRATORS OF extraordinary evil, we need no longer ask *who* these people are. We know who they are. They are you and I. There is now a more urgent question to ask: *How* are ordinary people, like you and me, transformed into perpetrators of extraordinary evil?

The precise "how" of the transformation process by which ordinary people come to commit extraordinary evil remains veiled from us, as it may have remained veiled from the men and women who experienced it. Regardless, we are now in a position to advance some hypotheses. We do know, for instance, that the process is far too complex to be reduced to one factor alone, such as the nature of the collective; the influence of an extraordinary ideology; psychopathology; a common, homogeneous extraordinary personality; or the elaborate creation of a divided self. We also suspect, however, that some of these factors may contain a grain a truth that—when combined with other dispositional, situational, and social factors—will help advance our understanding of perpetrators of mass killing and genocide.

In other words, it is not that all of the existing theories are completely *wrong*; rather, each of them is *incomplete*. It is in looking at their incompleteness that we most clearly see the need for a new understanding—in all its depths and particulars—of how ordinary individuals come to commit extraordinary human evil. There is a call to find order where there appears to be none. We need a unified theory in which all of us, "normal human beings," must confront our universal potential for extraordinary evil. Such a new theory, an attempt to synthesize and systematize the diversity of explanations into one coherent whole, is the focus of part II of this book.

Chapters 5, 6, 7, and 8 outline an original explanation of extraordinary human evil that considers the wide range of factors involved in the process that transforms ordinary people into perpetrators of extraordinary evil. The

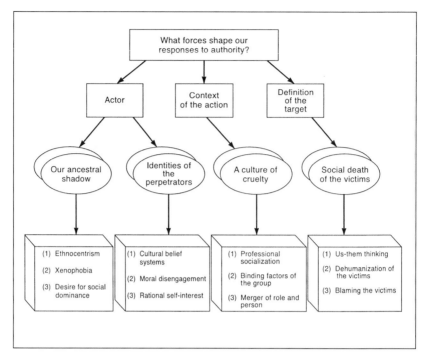

Figure 1. A Model of Extraordinary Human Evil

model should, for the general reader, shed light on how ordinary people commit extraordinary evil and, also, why most people do not. For the specialist, the model should provide a theoretical and conceptual framework that stimulates additional research to clarify its various components.

The model (see figure 1) specifically explicates the forces that shape our responses to authority. It does so by looking at who the perpetrators are (actor), the situational framework they are in (context of the action), and how they see the "other" (definition of the target). In addressing the actor, I examine the universal forces that make us the same (our ancestral shadow) and those particular forces that make us different (identities of the perpetrators) in our thoughts, feelings, and behaviors. I frame the context of the action as a culture of cruelty and examine the immediate situational influences that facilitate the commission of extraordinary evil by ordinary people. Finally, I conceptualize the definition of the target as the social death of the victims and examine the psychological processes by which victims are excluded from the moral universe of perpetrators.

The model—drawing on existing literature, eyewitness accounts of extraordinary evil by killers and victims from a wide range of genocides and mass killings in the twentieth century, and classic and contemporary research in social psychology—is not an invocation of a single broad-brush psychological state or *event* to explain extraordinary human evil. Rather, it is a detailed analysis of a *process* through which the perpetrators themselves—either in committing atrocities or in order to commit atrocities—are changed. An ordinary person becomes something different; a new self takes shape, and the extraordinarily evil acts become part of that self. In short, the model lays out the factors that help shape our responses to authority and unleash our destructive capacities.

Finally, I conclude with a point which I asserted in chapter 1 and to which I will return again in chapter 9: a psychological explanation of extraordinary evil is not exculpatory. In trying to understand the processes that produce extraordinary evil, we are not making apologies or offering excuses for perpetrators. On the road to extraordinary evil, there are many choice points for each perpetrator. What perpetrators of extraordinary evil decide to do makes a great difference in what they eventually do. As a result of willfully failing to exercise their moral judgment, perpetrators retain full moral and legal responsibility for the atrocities they committed; no explanatory model can ever take that away.

5

What Is the Nature of
Human Nature?

Our Ancestral Shadow

The real problem is in the hearts and minds of men. It is not a problem
of physics but of ethics. It is easier to denature plutonium than to denature the evil spirit of man.

Albert Einstein

IN SOME UNIQUE WAYS, EACH OF US is like *no other* human being. In
other ways, each of us is like *some other* human beings. And, in yet some
other ways, each of us is like *all other* human beings. The question of the
nature of human nature is captured in this final statement. In what ways are
we like *every other* person that has gone before us and will come after us?
This question is particularly relevant to our discussion of extraordinary
human evil. The issue is not whether we can do good or evil, because each
of us is certainly capable of either in any given situation. Rather, the issue
is what, by our nature, we are most *prone* to do.

Is there an endowment with which each of us begins our life that is important in understanding how ordinary people commit extraordinary evil?
Is there a basic inborn proclivity or tendency of human nature that limits,
or enables, the possibility of cooperative, caring, nonviolent relations between social groups? Could there be a universal human condition that is antecedent to all extraordinary evil and from which all extraordinary evil is
derived? These are vital questions because how we answer them significantly shapes our realities and determines how we perceive others' actions—particularly the actions of those who perpetrate extraordinary evil.

Many philosophers, social thinkers, and psychologists assume that
human nature is intrinsically neutral and has no predisposing inclinations.
In this view, we become that to which we are exposed. We are a blank slate,

virtually free of content until written on by the hand of experience. Our malleable capacities for goodness and evil are simply reflections of our socialization and experience. Psychoanalyst Eric Fromm succinctly summarizes this view: "Man is neither good nor evil. If one believes in the goodness of man as the only potentiality, one will be forced into rosy falsifications of the facts, or end up in bitter disillusionment. If one believes in the other extreme, one will end up as a cynic and be blind to the many possibilities for good in others and in oneself. A realistic view sees both possibilities as real potentialities, and studies the conditions for the development of either of them."[1]

Others more optimistically maintain that our basic predisposition is toward goodness. In many religious worldviews, it is common to find concepts of a depth of godliness and an intrinsic goodness in every soul from the beginning of its creation. This godly potential, which must be diligently protected from the specter of equally potent evil forces, lies at the heart of our human nature. In secular circles, it is even more common to find assumptions that humans are naturally good. Humanistic psychologists and self-help theorists, for example, assume a well of goodness in human nature that must simply be tapped by a person wishing to attain self-fulfillment or self-actualization. Individuals choose to do evil, of course, but if we would simply choose to live by the goodness of our inherent nature, then the world could liberate itself from extraordinary evil. Hope springs eternal; things have to get better because people are ultimately good.

Still others argue for a more pessimistic conception of humans as essentially evil, dangerous, or impulse-ridden—a recognition of our basic natural proclivity to turn ugly. Theologians of many faiths, and philosophers of many stripes, have maintained as much for centuries. Saint Augustine, the famed Christian theologian of the fourth and fifth centuries, held that human evil was a direct consequence of the misuse of God-given human freedom in the Garden of Eden. Adam and Eve's disobedience was so severe that it corrupted their nature and, with it, the nature of all their descendants. As a result of this historical corruption of our original goodness, we are born with a nature that, in order to fulfill itself, will inevitably commit evil. Twelve centuries later, Thomas Hobbes argued that we are basically unconcerned about others' welfare and will therefore do anything to satisfy our own interests—*homo homini lupus* (man is a wolf to his fellow man). Society and the state, to prevent us from harming others in fulfilling our own interests, must control us externally. Most social theorists since that time have reiterated Hobbes's claim that the state of nature, prior to the social contract, is the war of each against all, and, as a result, coercion is necessary to maintain society.

Finally, many thinkers affirm the existence of *both* good and evil inclinations in humankind and focus on the eternal struggle between these two universal aspects of human nature. In John Steinbeck's words: "We have only one story. All novels, all poetry, are built on the never-ending contest in ourselves of good and evil."[2] This view depicts a natural competition between an intrinsic potential for good and an intrinsic potential for evil, a competition that is determined to a large extent by the influences of the environment or by free choice. Jewish tradition, for example, speaks of two inclinations, called the *yetzer ha-ra* and the *yetzer ha-tov*, literally, the "bad inclination" and the "good inclination," respectively. In this view, we are given free will to choose to follow either of these rival character endowments. We are left alone with these two inclinations, one for evil and one for good, and the choice between the two is ours alone.

How do modern social scientists respond to the question of the nature of human nature? Do they believe there is a dominant propensity for good, or evil, in each of us? Most are hesitant to directly engage the topic. There is something too "personal" and "subjective" about it that makes it seem out of bounds. It is mistakenly assumed to be a question of metaphysics that cannot be addressed using the methodology of the social sciences. In reality, though, all social scientists have, and regularly employ, conceptions of human nature. As Franklin Littell, emeritus professor of religion at Temple University, writes: "The hidden agenda is disagreement about the nature and destiny of Man, and of such mysteries as Sin and Evil."[3] It is precisely these underlying assumptions that must be faced as we begin to construct an explanatory model of how ordinary people commit extraordinary evil.

The Nature of Human Nature in Modern Social Science

René Descartes, the noted French philosopher and mathematician of the seventeenth century, argued that humans alone are capable of rational thought and reflective reasoning. Descartes, and most thinkers after him, conceived of human nature around the belief that we, as humans, act out of our own volition, that we think about and will our behaviors. Conversely, so-called lower animals are mere machinelike automata whose every response is controlled and directed by instinct. In other words, humans are something more than animals. We are animals *plus*. There is a gap that contains some kind of special human essence that has been added to the baseline of our animal nature. This Cartesian gap between humans and animals was fundamentally challenged by the rise of evolutionary thought in the mid–nineteenth century.

Charles Darwin was not the first to advance the idea of evolution—that is, changes over time in organic structure. His important contribution was to offer a compelling and lucid explanation, a causal mechanism, of how evolution works—his theory of natural selection. Darwin's theory of natural selection had three essential ingredients: variation, inheritance, and selection. First, the *variation* evidenced by animals within a species (for example, wing length, bone mass, fighting ability) provides the raw materials for evolution. Second, only those variations that are the product of *inheritance* play a role in the evolutionary process. Third, *selection* pressures work to ensure that the strongest live and the weakest die. By "strongest," Darwin meant the best adapted to the environment. "Best adapted" refers to appropriateness of design toward particular ends—that is, the sum of features that increase the likelihood of survival and reproduction. In short, natural selection is the process whereby organisms that are better adapted outbreed those that are less well adapted.

Nowhere within Darwin's *On the Origin of Species by Means of Natural Selection* (1859) is natural selection applied to understanding the nature of human nature. The concluding paragraph of the volume promised only that the theory of natural selection would be important in securing a foundation for the new field of psychology and would shed light on human origins. Twelve years later, however, with his publication of *The Descent of Man*, Darwin explicitly depicted human beings, along with all other animals, as shaped by natural selection. His theory of natural selection unified all living creatures, from single-celled amoebas to multicellular mammals, into one great tree of descent.

Biographers of Darwin note that actually he had included humans in evolution long before either of these two books was published. In his personal notebooks of the late 1830s, Darwin was already seeing connections between human beings and animals. "If we choose," he wrote in one of these notebooks, "to let conjecture run wild, then animals, our fellow brethren in pain, disease, suffering, and famine—our slaves in the most laborious work, our companions in our amusements—they may partake of our origin in one common ancestor—we may be all melted together."[4]

It is clear that Darwin had a strong determination to demonstrate the continuity between animals and human beings. The most straightforward feature of this continuity was morphological—showing how the physical shape of human beings was derived from animal ancestors. Darwin also sought, however, to extend this physical continuity between animals and humans into the realms of behavior and mental and moral habits. Darwin maintained that in all these ways—physical, behavioral, mental, and moral—humans could observe their primitive selves in animals. With the Cartesian gap between "lower animals" and humans obliterated, it opened a new avenue for understanding the nature of human nature.

Darwinian evolution insisted on the assumption that much of human behavior was dependent on the same thing that drove much of animal behavior—instinct. In other words, if humans were simply now one species of animal, and if animal behavior was motivated in large part by instinct, then much of human behavior could now be understood in instinctual terms as well. What did Darwin mean by "instinct"? He devoted an entire chapter to the concept in *The Origin of Species* but refused to offer a specific definition of instinct. In addition, he confined his discussion of instinct to lower animals. Only in attempting to clarify his use of the term "instinct" did he consider the case of humans: "If Mozart, instead of playing the pianoforte at three years old with wonderfully little practice, had played a tune with no practice at all, he might truly be said to have done so instinctively."[5] Darwin's understanding of instinct is clear—instincts are actions that are inborn and carried out without necessary prior practice or experience. While instincts may vary somewhat among members of a species, the same way that ears or noses do, instinctual acts will be generally very similar in different individuals of the same species.

It can be argued that, for all the areas of thought stirred by the controversy of Darwinian theory, no realm was more challenged than our conception of the nature of human nature. Indeed, the notion that humans are driven by an instinctual legacy from our animal ancestry may well be the most radical component of the most revolutionary theory in modern history. At the turn of the twentieth century, the emerging field of psychology—steeped in the confidence of Darwin's theory of evolution—welcomed the advent of instinct theory in explaining the complexities of human behavior.

William James, the father of American psychology, gave a central place to instinct theory in his seminal book *Principles of Psychology*, written in 1890. James defined instinct simply "as the faculty of acting in such a way as to produce certain ends, without foresight of the end, or without previous education in the performance."[6] Instinct, James contended, drawing directly from Darwin, was common to both animals and human beings. Where others saw humans ruled by "reason" and few instincts, James argued that human behavior is more intelligent than that of other animals because we have *more* instincts than they do, not fewer. James's peers judged his emphasis on instinct in accounting for human behavior as a fundamental insight of the emerging science of psychology. His work set the stage for a proliferation of instinct theories and catalogs throughout the social sciences.

Of all the instinct theories at the turn of the twentieth century, it was the theory of Sigmund Freud, the founder of psychoanalysis, which most fundamentally revolutionized our understanding of human nature. By "instinct," Freud did not mean what biologists mean—specific forms of behavior coded into the genes. Rather, Freud used the term "instinct" to denote "impulse," "moving force," or "drive." For Freud, instincts were the pent-up forces within the mental apparatus, and all the "energy" in our minds comes from them alone. Although Freud admitted that we could distinguish an indeterminate number of instincts, he believed that they all were derived from a few fundamental instincts.

In the beginning, Freud assumed that the most basic instinct animating human life was sexual. In his original theorizing, sexual instincts made up the sum total of psychic energy. In *Civilization and Its Discontents*, he admitted, "It seemed for a time inevitable that libido should become synonymous with instinctual energy in general."[7] Later, Freud would add other "self-preservation" instincts, such as hunger, to his concept of libido to form one basic "life" instinct (Eros). For twenty years, he resisted acknowledging any other competing instinct that would be equated with destruction or aggression.

Freud's later research, however, convinced him that there is indeed a second, opposing instinct at play in humankind—an instinct to destroy. The horrendous bloodshed of World War I and his clinical work on "repetition compulsions" (tendencies to repeat self-defeating or painful acts) were particularly influential in shaping his thinking on this destructive instinct. "I drew the conclusion," he wrote, "that, beside the instinct preserving the organic substance and binding it into ever larger units, there must exist another in antithesis to this, which would seek to dissolve these units and reinstate their antecedent inorganic state. That is to say, a death instinct as well as Eros."[8] Freud's concept of the "death" instinct (Thanatos) as an innate universal urge across humankind encompassed all impulses toward hostility, sadism, aggression, and, even, he tentatively suggested, a mysterious drive toward one's own death. Thanatos fulfilled a primordial drive toward reconciliation with, or completion of, the inevitable process of death that awaited each living creature.

Freud, countering the prevailing sentiments of the nineteenth century, posited an animal essence at the core of the unconscious, an inborn inclination for aggression. According to Freud, humans are not content only to defend themselves when attacked, but are so constituted "that a powerful measure of desire for aggression has to be reckoned as part of their instinctual endowment."[9] In Freud's view, "the tendency to aggression is an innate, independent, instinctual disposition in man," and this innate tendency leads "to aggression, destruction, and, in addition, cruelty."[10] Elsewhere, Freud describes the inclination toward aggression as "an original, self-subsisting instinctual disposition in man."[11]

The mind, for Freud, was a place of conflict between animal impulses and social reality. The veneer of civilization is thin, however, and our innate, brutal urges push hard to break through. Freud, working from the same foundational assumption as Hobbes, made the case for an internal control of this destructive instinct through the acquisition of a conscience molded by socialization. Externally, Freud argued, it is the purpose of civilization to keep this aggressive impulse in check.

While few have accepted Freud's specific concept of a death instinct, many have embraced the notion that human nature has a tendency toward aggression. Recognizing that aggression can be closely linked with self-preservation and self-affirmation reminds us that it need not be derived from a "death instinct." Regardless, Freud's influential, and controversial, work on the instinctual bases of human nature guaranteed that the nature of human nature had a foothold as a useful concept in the emerging social sciences.

That foothold, though, would be swept out by the behaviorist revolution of the early 1920s. Behaviorism, which dominated social science for the next fifty years, spoke of a formless human nature given form by reward and punishment. It threw out the assumption that much of human behavior was dependent on instinct. Darwin's assertion of continuity between animals and human beings was considered irrelevant by leading behaviorists such as John B. Watson. The behaviorist revolution replaced the notion of *a* human nature with a focus on environment, and culture, as the underlying cause of human behavior.

In what is perhaps the most famous single passage in the history of American psychology, Watson wrote in his 1924 book *Behaviorism*: "Give me a dozen healthy infants, well-formed, and my own specified world to bring them up in and I'll guarantee to take any one at random and train him to become any type of specialist I might select—doctor, lawyer, artist, merchant-chief, and, yes, even beggar-man and thief, regardless of his talents, penchants, tendencies, abilities, vocations, and race of his ancestors."[12] Another section of his book was tellingly titled "Concept of Instinct No Longer Needed in Psychology." Watson had little or no evidence for his assertions of extreme environmentalism. This book, though, was a fierce counter to the arguments of those who asserted an instinctive basis for human behavior and illustrated a dramatic and rapid shift in how a new generation of psychologists, and social scientists, were coming to think of human nature—or the absence of *a* human nature.

In psychology, the concept of "instincts" was driven underground, to be replaced by more "scientific" explanations for human behavior like "motivation," "drive," or "reinforcement." The general trend in social sciences away from instinct and toward cultural determinism was aided by the tremendous influence of Margaret Mead's 1928 book, *Coming of Age in Samoa* (though Mead would later be proved spectacularly wrong in many of her claims about Samoan life). By the mid- and late 1930s, instinct theory and evolutionary thinking had all but disappeared from most psychological and social scientific journals. Through the 1950s and 1960s, the popularity of B. F. Skinner's theories of environmental conditioning kept the idea of human nature outside the boundaries of social science. There was no inherent human nature driving human behavior; rather, our essential nature was to be driven by rewards and punishments. This paradigm shift in American social science was reinforced by broader changes in social and political thought that downplayed an instinctive or biological basis for human behavior.

In sum, these trends led to the general development of what came to be called the Standard Social Science Model (SSSM).[13] The SSSM, pervading all of the social sciences from the opening of the 1930s through the end of the 1960s, rested on the twin beliefs that (1) all humans have similar potential and (2) the only thing that separates us is culture, not biology. In other words, the nature of humans is that they have no nature; culture is the fundamental determinant of human behavior. Human nature is essentially an empty container waiting to be filled by socialization. Why study paper (human nature) when what is interesting is the writing on it and the author (socialization)? Such a belief system—inundating our methodologies, theories, and interpretations—left generations of social scientists blind to the role of human nature in shaping our thoughts, feelings, and behaviors.

At the beginning of the 1970s, however, the discussion of the nature of human nature returned to the social sciences. The work of ethologists—such as Nikolaus Tinbergen's *Study of Instinct* (1951), Konrad Lorenz's *On Aggression* (1966), and Desmond Morris's *The Naked Ape* (1967), about instincts in animals (and human beings)—led many social scientists to rethink the SSSM. We began to revisit Darwin and his insistence on the continuity between human and animal nature. Subsequently, three decades of research in cognitive psychology, artificial intelligence, psycholinguistics, evolutionary biology, paleoanthropology, and neuroscience have legitimated the study of evolution-produced instincts in humans and "other animals." We have been reminded that no longer can we grossly underestimate the impact of *what* we are on *who* we are; no longer can we relentlessly insist that everything about us is attributable to something that happened either in school, in our relations with our parents, or in some other aspect of our environment or culture.

To be sure, there remains a gulf between humans and animals that is far from closed. The edges of this gulf, though, continue to move closer to one another. As they do, the concept of a human nature has returned to the front of the academic conversation in the social sciences. As Carl Degler, Margaret Byrne Professor of American History Emeritus at Stanford University, writes: "The movement began three decades ago to follow out the implications of Darwinian evolutionary thought and to restore biology to the definition of man seems likely to persist and, perhaps, to advance further in the direction Darwin had pointed, a direction which still delineates a conception of human nature more radical than many can accommodate."[14]

Leading this charge into the twenty-first century is the field of *evolutionary psychology*—a hybrid of the natural (evolutionary biology) and social (cognitive psychology) sciences. One critic explicitly identified this field as "the territory on which the coming century's debate about human nature will be held."[15] Another wrote: "Evolutionary psychologists have become the new cosmologists. They help us make sense of ourselves and our role in the universe. Even magazines for teenage girls now rely on them to explain why guys behave the way they do."[16] What is evolutionary psychology, and what does it have to say about the nature of human nature?

Evolutionary Psychology

Evolutionary psychology (EP) is a multidisciplinary approach within the Darwinian paradigm that seeks to apply theories of evolutionary biology in order to understand human psychology. EP is not a specialized subfield of psychology, such as personality psychology or social psychology. Rather, EP is best seen as a different way of thinking about the *entire* field of psychology, a way of thinking in which knowledge and principles from evolutionary biology are put to use in research on the structure of the human mind. The specific goal of EP is to discover and understand the design of the human mind in terms of Darwinian evolution. In EP, the mind is *not* the brain; rather, the mind refers to what the brain does—that is, information processing or computation. EP is really engineering in reverse. In forward engineering, we design a machine to do something. In reverse engineering, we figure out what a machine—in this case, the human mind—was designed to do.

The research of EP, in describing the psychological mechanisms that give rise to our natural instincts or tendencies, cuts straight to the heart of the nature of human nature. In EP—as conceptualized by psychologist Leda Cosmides and anthropologist John Tooby, two pioneers of evolutionary psychology at the University of California at Santa Barbara—human behavior is driven by a set of *universal reasoning circuits* that were *designed by natural selection* to solve *adaptive problems* faced by our *hunter-gatherer ancestors*.[17] We can unpack this statement by discussing its four central components.

1. Universal Reasoning Circuits

Universal reasoning circuits are best thought of as a set of information-processing machines, or minicomputers, in the brain. Just as a computer has circuits, our brain has circuits as well. The essence of a computer, however, lies not in the materials from which it is made but in the programs it executes. Correspondingly, just as a computer's circuits determine how it processes information, so do our neural circuits determine how our brain processes information. The brain—our wet computer—is composed of a large collection (hundreds, perhaps even thousands) of these circuits, with different circuits specialized for solving different problems. Our brain's neural circuits are designed to generate behavior that is appropriate to our environmental circumstances. In so doing, these universal reasoning circuits organize the way we interpret our experiences, place certain recurrent concepts and motivations into our mental life, and give us universal frames of meaning that allow us to interpret the actions and intentions of others.

Universal reasoning circuits are one specific example of a general category known as "adaptations." Adaptations are inherited mechanisms that are here because they have, in the past, increased the likelihood of survival and reproduction among our ancestors. There must be genes for an adaptation because such genes are required for the passage of the adaptation from parents to offspring. Adaptations tend to be typical of most or all members of a species but need not be present at birth. Many adaptations—for instance, walking and breast development—develop long after birth.

Generally, it makes little sense to speak of adaptations as behaviors. Rather, the proper focus should be on adaptations and the behaviors they generate—that is, behavior as the *product* of adaptations. In other words, natural selection cannot design behavior directly. It designs adaptations that produce adaptive behavior. In the case of universal reasoning circuits, behavior is the product of evolved psychological adaptations.

While bearing all the hallmarks of what we commonly call "instincts," these universal reasoning circuits should not be seen as rigid, genetically inflexible behavior patterns that are inevitably expressed and impenetrable to environmental, social, and cultural influences. To say that something is an adaptation is not to say that it is unchangeable. Adaptations bear functional relationships to aspects of the environment of any particular organism. Adaptations will change in time because the environment is changing all the time. Most adaptations, for a number of reasons, are not perfect; some are actually quite imperfect. In the words of psychologist David Buss and his colleagues: "Adaptations are not optimally designed mechanisms. They are better described as jerry-rigged, meliorative solutions to adaptive problems constructed out of the available materials at hand, constrained in their quality and design by a variety of historical and current forces."[18]

2. Designed by Natural Selection

Where did these universal reasoning circuits, or "instincts," come from? EP maintains that these circuits were *designed by natural selection*. The word "design" is not implying that the process is purposeful or forward-looking. Natural selection is not intentional and cannot look into the future to foresee distant needs. Rather, "design" is shorthand to refer to the adaptive product of the evolutionary process—an inanimate process, devoid of consciousness.

By virtue of natural selection, species undergo changes in their adaptations over time. Most adaptations designed by natural selection are physiological—for example, changes in beak structure, neck size, and so on. These changes evolve because they help the individuals who possess them to survive and reproduce. EP proposes that—just like physiological structures—cognitive structures have been designed by natural selection to serve survival and reproduction. EP is firm in its belief that there is no fundamental or qualitative difference between these psychological adaptations and any other type of physiological adaptations. Thus, EP sees natural selection as the principal guiding force in the creation of complex, functional, problem-solving mechanisms such as universal reasoning circuits.

3. Adaptive Problems

Natural selection designed universal reasoning circuits to solve *adaptive problems*. What is an adaptive problem? Adaptive problems have two defining characteristics. First, they are the problems that crop up again and again during the evolutionary history of a species. Second, they are problems whose solution impacts the survival and reproduction of individual organisms within a species.

At its most concrete, adaptive problems have to do with how an organism makes its living—what it eats, who it mates with, who it socializes with, who it aggresses against, how it communicates, and so on. Simply put, they are problems that an organism needs to solve in order to survive and reproduce. The only kinds of problems that natural selection can design circuits for solving are adaptive problems. This leads to, in the words of Cosmides and Tooby, a conclusion that the brain "is a naturally constructed computational system whose function is to solve adaptive information-processing problems."[19]

4. Hunter-Gatherer Ancestors

Finally, these adaptive problems, for which natural selection designed our universal reasoning circuits, are, unfortunately, problems most relevant to our *hunter-gatherer ancestors*. It is important to realize that well over 99 percent of our species' evolutionary history has involved living as foragers in small nomadic bands. In their lifelong camping trip, our Pleistocene ancestors faced some daunting adaptive problems. Among others, these included problems like detecting and avoiding predators and other dangerous animals, gathering and eating the right foods, forming friendships, developing alliances to defend oneself against aggression, helping children and other kin, communicating with other people, and selecting mates—all, ultimately, having an impact on the survival and reproduction of our species over time.

Our ancestral history must be coupled with the reality that natural selection is a slow and imperfect process occurring over many generations. In physical evolution, it takes a long time to change a leg into a wing or a flipper. Likewise, there will often be a lag in time—very substantial in the case of human evolution—between a new adaptive problem and the evolution of a mechanism designed to solve it. As a result, there just haven't been enough generations for natural selection to design universal reasoning circuits that are well adapted to all aspects of our modern environment. Fewer than 10,000 generations separate everyone alive today from the small group of ancestors who are our common ancestors—the blink of an eye, in evolutionary terms. In other words, most of our human nature evolved during the hunter-gatherer period of our ancestral history—known as the Environment of Evolutionary Adaptedness (EEA). Too little time has elapsed since then for substantial evolution of human nature to take place. In Cosmides and Tooby's words, "Our modern skulls house a stone age mind."[20] They continue: "In many cases, our brains are better at solving the kinds of problems our ancestors faced on the African savannahs than they are at solving the more familiar tasks we face in a college classroom or a modern city."[21]

In some aspects, our modern environment does not radically diverge from the human EEA. So, some of the circuits developed by natural selection to deal with the problems of our EEA still serve us well today. In many other aspects, however, our modern environment does diverge quite radically from the human EEA. As a result, we are not perfectly adapted to our modern environments, nor will we ever be—certain imperfections of design are the inevitable results of the inherent limitations of natural selection. For example, automobiles kill far more people today than do spiders or snakes. But people are far more averse to spiders and snakes than they are to automobiles. Why? Because in our EEA spiders and snakes were a serious threat to our survival and reproduction, whereas automobiles did not exist. Thus, it was possible—not to mention advantageous for our survival and reproduction—for us to evolve an innate aversion to spiders and snakes, but not to automobiles. While natural selection continues its glacial process of building circuits that are more suited to a modern environment, our ability to solve other kinds of more modern problems is best seen as a side effect or by-product of circuits that were designed to solve the adaptive problems of our hunter-gatherer ancestors.

I want to restate this point because it is vital to the first component of our explanatory model of extraordinary human evil. Human behavior in the *present* is generated by universal reasoning circuits that exist because they solved adaptive problems in the *past*. As a result, these past-oriented circuits will not always necessarily generate adaptive behavior in the present. In some cases, what the circuits were designed to accomplish in the hunter-gatherer context even can lead to maladaptive behavior in response to contemporary environmental contexts. In other words, any organism can possess adaptations that no longer serve any survival or reproductive function— some of these adaptations even can impede survival and reproduction. For example, we have lungs now because oxygen existed in our atmosphere in the past, not because oxygen exists in the immediate present. Should oxygen somehow disappear from the atmosphere, we would still have lungs— they just wouldn't work and we would quickly become extinct.

EP makes clear that our universal reasoning circuits inject certain motivations into our mental life that directly influence our behavior. There is a universal, evolved psychological architecture that we all share by virtue of being humans—*a* human nature. This human nature includes hundreds, perhaps even thousands, of universal reasoning circuits that are domain-specific and functionally specialized to facilitate our survival and reproduction. In other words, instead of having a single, central general-purpose reasoning machine, we have a massive collection of special-purpose modules, each one designed to solve a specific adaptive problem. Famously, Cosmides and Tooby compare the massive modularity of our mind to a Swiss Army knife with lots of gadgets, each one designed for a specific task.

How Can EP Help Us Understand Extraordinary Human Evil?

To begin, we must remember that competition lies at the heart of the natural selection that designs the universal reasoning circuits used to solve adaptive problems faced by our hunter-gatherer ancestors. We must also recognize that not only do individuals compete with other individuals in the same group, but groups also compete with other groups.

In our Pleistocene environment, it is likely that we were gathered into small groups numbering no more than a couple of hundred people. Most of those we lived among were relatives. What happened to them, happened to us. What we did to others, we did to ourselves. Our increasing mobility, however, meant that we occasionally found ourselves among strangers—other groups with whom we were not familiar and against whom we competed, probably fiercely, for scarce resources. The results of this competition were significant because the winners not only obtained material benefits, but—in some cases—also got rid of their competitors. In this context, hurting individuals in other groups solved adaptive problems faced by our group and, ultimately, was selectively advantageous. Organisms survived and reproduced, to some extent, at one another's expense. In short, competition—often escalating into intergroup conflict—was a major fact of life for many of our ancestors. In a sense, all of us today owe our existence to having "winners" as ancestors, and each of us today is designed, at least in some circumstances, to compete.

This is, essentially, the concept of *group selection*—adaptation in which aggregates of individuals constitute the unit of selection. Most evolutionary biologists, however, reject the concept of group selection. They point out that *individual* variation, *individual* fitness, and *individual* selection are at the heart of Darwin's theory. There are thousands of instances in Darwin's writings where it is perfectly clear that his theory was firmly built on the individual. Consistent with this overarching emphasis, contemporary evolutionary biologists maintain that—though possible in theory—it is hard to imagine the special circumstances in which group selection would spread some trait that individual selection on its own would not favor.

Darwin himself only made one exception to his exclusive focus on the individual as the unit of selection. That exception was to explain the way some insects (such as ants, bees, and termites) live "selflessly" in large colonies, most of them sterile servants to a single fertile queen. Darwin suggested that this striking behavioral adaptation was for the good of the colony: even though they themselves could not bear offspring, the workers' "selfless" dedication ensured the survival of the larger community or group to which they belonged. Though Darwin would later suggest that natural selection sometimes acts on groups just as it acts at other times on individuals, his practice was to appeal to the concept of group selection only rarely. Generally speaking, most contemporary evolutionists follow Darwin's practice and believe that natural selection is primarily sensitive to differences in individuals and seldom sensitive to differences among groups.

Recently, however, an increasing number of evolutionists are advancing the argument that group selection does have the power to produce group-level adaptations. In other words, the idea that some adaptations exist for the good of the group. After all, it is likely that the small social group has been one of the few constants in our evolutionary history. We have evolved in the context of group living. It would be irresponsible to simply assume that living in these groups has not somehow produced group-level adaptations in human behavioral evolution. Adaptation to group living promoted individual survival, particularly in settings where collective action facilitated defense or the acquisition of food. If the universal reasoning circuits of the mind are engineered by natural selection, then our social motives should be strategies that are tailored to the group environments in which we have evolved and live.

As one example, philosopher Elliott Sober of the University of Wisconsin and evolutionary biologist David Sloan Wilson of Binghamton University advance a modified group selection model to explain the origins of evolutionary and psychological altruism. They argue against the belief that behaviors that seem to benefit others at the expense of self are only "apparently" altruistic, with "genuine" altruism in nature remaining elusive. In its place, Sober and Wilson maintain that the process of group selection, favoring traits that maximize the relative fitness of groups, can be sufficiently strong for true altruism to evolve in a species. They conclude, "At the behavioral level, it is likely that much of what people have evolved to do is *for the benefit of the group* [italics in original]."[22]

Even more recently, psychologist Henry Plotkin of University College London has laid out a strong theoretical argument for the existence of group selection as a relatively common phenomenon in species like ours. Plotkin maintains that it is perfectly possible "for traits that favour the group to have higher fitness value for the ultimate survival of individuals in the group than do traits that favour the individual at the expense of the group."[23] In his view, the group *can* be considered, in the same way we consider an individual, as a unitary vehicle on which natural selection acts. "Human evolution," he concludes, "will have favoured behavioural traits that enhance the fitness of individuals, but some of these will do so because they operate at the group level."[24]

The role of group selection in shaping characteristics of human nature remains a matter of debate—often contentious—within the scholarly community. Most would at least agree, though, that natural selection is certainly not as efficient at crafting adaptations at the level of the group as it is at the level of the individual. So it seems safest to proceed on the understanding that the evolution of group life depends, ordinarily and primarily, on the psychological adaptations promoted in individuals.

What are some of the psychological adaptations that enhance the fitness of individuals within a group? These likely include love, friendship, cooperativeness, nurturance, communication, a sense of fairness, and, even, self-sacrifice—the things that hold society together. Indeed, Cosmides and Tooby argue that adaptations for the expression and regulation of cooperation and altruism are expected design features of social organisms. Natural selection does not forbid such prosocial adaptations; it does, however, make them difficult engineering problems. We should remember that even these "good" behavioral traits did not evolve for the good of the *species*, but rather for the good of a particular *group* within a species and—most important—a particular *individual* within that group. Moreover, as Sober and Wilson remind us, concern for others is only *one* of the ultimate motives that people *sometimes* have.

Our adaptations also include some darker ultimate motives that people sometimes have—intergroup competition for dominance, boundary definition, and fear of social exclusion. These behavioral traits foster a hostility to other groups that often tears society apart. In the words of Sober and Wilson: "Group selection does provide a setting in which helping behavior directed at members of one's own group can evolve; however, it equally provides a context in which hurting individuals in other groups can be selectively advantageous. Group selection favors within-group niceness *and* between-group nastiness."[25] Similarly, Steven Pinker writes: "For what it's worth, the theory of a module-packed mind allows both for innate motives that lead to evil acts and for innate motives that can avert them."[26]

For us, the critical question is not whether every human in every culture engages in extraordinary evil, because they certainly do not. Rather, the more illuminating question is whether every human in every culture comes *endowed* with psychological mechanisms that leave us capable of committing extraordinary evil when activated by appropriate cues. People in all cultures feel that they are members of a group (a band, tribe, clan, or nation) and feel animosity toward other groups. Clearly then, intergroup relations include some significant adaptive problems. What kinds of selection pressures sustain such aggressive intergroup behavior in the face of its tremendous cost to some individuals? To restate in the words of our con-

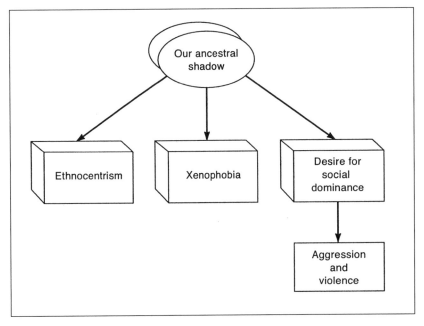

Figure 2. What Is the Nature of Human Nature?

ceptualization of EP, *what set of universal reasoning circuits were designed by nat-ural selection to solve the adaptive problems of intergroup relations faced by our hunter-gather ancestors?*

Of the many we could explore, I believe there are three innate, evolu-tion-produced tendencies of human nature that are most relevant to un-derstanding our capacity for extraordinary evil—ethnocentrism, xenopho-bia, and the desire for social dominance (see figure 2). Studies worldwide show not only that these tendencies are universal in people, but also that they start in infancy. These are the powerful, innate, "animal" influences on human behavior that represent evolved social capacities lying at the core of human nature. They are the underlying, distant capacities that, in concert with other immediate and proximal influences, help us understand our ca-pacity for our extraordinary evil toward one another.

Ethnocentrism and Xenophobia

Human minds are compelled to define the limits of the tribe. Knowing who is kin, knowing who is in our social group, has a deep importance to species like ours. We construct this knowledge by categorizing others as "us" or "them." As we will see in chapter 8, we tend to be biased toward "us" and label "them"—those with whom "we" share the fewest genes and least culture—as enemies. We have an evolved capacity to see our group as superior to all others and even to be reluctant to recognize members of other groups as deserving of equal respect. A group of the !Kung San of the Kalahari call themselves by a name that literally means "the real people." In their language, the words for "bad" and "foreign" are one and the same. Similarly, the cannibal inhabitants of the delta area of Irian in Indonesian New Guinea call themselves the Asmat, which means "the people—the human beings." All outsiders are known very simply as Manowe—"the edible ones."

Biologist Lyall Watson calls our tendency to divide the world into "us" and "them" one of the few true human universals. Anthropologist Donald Brown likewise includes in his characteristics of Universal People (features all people have in common) the following: "Important conflicts are structured around in-group–out-group antagonisms that characterize the UP. These antagonisms both divide the UP as an ethnic group as well as set them off from other ethnic groups. An ethical dualism distinguishes the ingroup from the out-group, so that, for example, cooperation is more expectable in the former than with the latter."[27]

What are the universal human tendencies that underlie our innate capacity for "us-them" thinking? I believe there are two complementary psychological adaptations that are most relevant. First, *ethnocentrism* refers to the tendency to focus on one's own group as the "right" one. Anthropologist W. G. Sumner first coined this term in 1906 and defined it as "a differentiation that arises between ourselves, the we-group, or in-group, and everybody else, or the others-group, out-groups. The insiders in a we-group are in a relation of peace, order, law, government, and industry to each other. . . . Ethnocentrism is the technical name for this view of things in which one's own group is the center of everything, and all others are scaled and rated with reference to it. . . . Each group nourishes its own pride and vanity, boasts itself superior, exalts its own divinities, and looks with contempt on outsiders."[28]

Ethnocentrism is a universal characteristic of human social life and, as often as not, it is fairly harmless. From an evolutionary perspective, there is an advantageous reinforcement of communal identity and "we-ness" when groups consider their ideas, their cultures, their religions, or their aesthetic standards to be either superior to others, or at least in certain ways to be preferential or noteworthy in comparison to other groups. As R. A. Hinde writes: "It is not unreasonable to entertain the possibility that natural selection acted on individuals to enhance this identification with groups and to augment the (real or perceived) superiority of the group with which they identified."[29]

Ethnocentric loyalties show themselves early in life. The importance of both the caretaker-infant bonds and stranger anxiety reactions of the first year of life demonstrate a universality of the us-them differentiation process. By age six or seven, children exhibit a strong preference for their own nationality—even before the concept of "nation" has been fully understood. Experimental social psychologists have even demonstrated that classifying individuals into *arbitrary* groups in the laboratory (for example, giving one group red labels and the other group green labels) can elicit ethnocentric reactions. Other recent social psychological experimental evidence suggests that the concepts "us" and "them" carry positive emotional significance that is activated automatically and unconsciously.[30] Once identified with a group—even in the complete *absence* of any links, kinship or otherwise, among individuals in that group—individuals find it easy to exaggerate differences between their group and others.

Included with ethnocentrism is a second universal adaptation— *xenophobia*, the complementary tendency to fear outsiders or strangers. It can even be said that in forming bonds we deepen fissures. In other words, defining what the in-group *is* also requires defining what it is *not*. As psychologists Henri Tajfel and J. P. Forgas put it, "We are what we are because *they* are not what we are."[31]

Matt Ridley contends that xenophobia is a by-product of the evolution of cooperative society. For Ridley, a coalitionist or "tribal" instinct, evolved in the context of sexual selection pressures, is at the core of human nature. But the dark side of this sociability is a fear of, and even an intolerance for, outsiders or strangers. In Ridley's view, sociality promotes ethnocentric conflict by providing a critical building block for in-group amity and out-group hostility. In other words, the evolution of sociability, altruism, and the instincts for coalitions goes hand in hand with hostility to outsiders. We cooperate to compete. There is no "us" without a corresponding "them" to oppose.[32]

The widespread rise of domestic violence seems, at first glance, to go against our evolutionary instruction to favor "us" and oppose "them." On closer analysis, however, psychologists Martin Daly and Margo Wilson of McMaster University in Canada found that once the urge to kill exists, genetic factors come into play in the choice of a victim. In cases of domestic homicide, family members who are not blood kin—such as spouses—are eleven times more likely to be killed than are family members who are blood kin. Even in cases where the victim *is* blood kin, there are very often factors involved that make biological, if not moral, sense.[33]

On a broader societal level, governments, propaganda, and militaries can easily evoke our evolved capacities for ethnocentrism and xenophobia. At the extreme, these capacities may even translate into a genocidal imperative as they are used to forge in-group solidarity and undermine the normal inhibitions against killing out-group strangers. As anthropologist Michael Ghiglieri writes: "Xenophobia and ethnocentrism are not just essential ingredients to war. Because they instinctively tell men precisely whom to bond with versus whom to fight against, they are the most dangerously manipulable facets of war psychology that promote genocide. Indeed, genocide itself has become a potent force in human evolution."[34]

In short, we have an innate, evolution-produced tendency to seek proximity to familiar faces because what is unfamiliar is probably dangerous and should be avoided. More than two hundred social psychological experiments have confirmed the intimate connection between familiarity and fondness. This universal human tendency is the foundation for the behavioral expressions of ethnocentrism (focusing on our group as the "right" one) and xenophobia (fearing outsiders or strangers).

Desire for Social Dominance

The primary hostile force of nature encountered by humans is other humans. One of the robust findings of EP is that, aside from the sexual drive, one of the most powerful motivating forces in animals is the *desire for social dominance*. This desire, leading to differences in rank and status, can be defined as the set of sustained aggressive-submissive relations among a group of animals. These relations form a hierarchical structure, commonly called a dominance hierarchy. Dominance hierarchies arise in group-living organisms to minimize the aggression that occurs between individuals competing for limited resources. Dominance hierarchies based on relatively stable relationships have been observed in numerous avian and mammalian species as well as some reptilian species.

As psychologists Steven Gaulin and Donald McBurney argue, social dominance hierarchies have an adaptive, perhaps even cooperative, function of efficiency: "Individuals inevitably compete with other members of their species for scarce resources. If two individuals had to fight every time they both wanted the same food item, the same mate, or the same nesting site, they would waste valuable time and energy, as well as run the risk of injury or even death. To avoid needless fighting a great many social animals establish pecking orders."[35] As organisms become more complex, they are able to remember interactions with different individuals and do not have to engage in fighting after their initial encounter. While humans do not have rigid pecking orders, all of our societies recognize some kind of social dominance hierarchy—particularly among men.

Is there a universal reasoning circuit for social dominance? Some evidence from research with preschool children suggests so. In one study, children as young as four years of age were able to rank members of their preschool class for toughness. The children's rankings agreed with one another as well as with an adult observer's measure of dominance on the basis of their play interactions. A wide range of cross-cultural research with adults shows a high degree of agreement about physical features of the face that convey dominance status. Other studies report that these facial features—particularly traits associated with physical maturity (proportionately thin lips and eyes, receding hairline) and physical strength (wide face, square jaw)—are reliable predictors of professional and reproductive success. Height is another major influence on social dominance hierarchies—particularly in human males. In an array of situations, increased male height confers an economic, political, and social advantage. In the United States, for instance, taller men are hired more, are promoted more, earn more (in annual salary, $600 per inch over the mean height of five feet, eight inches), and—amazingly enough—are elected president more (the taller candidate won twenty of the twenty-five elections between 1904 and 2000) than shorter men.[36]

So we seem to have innate tendencies to assume that physical traits constitute a reliable cue to social dominance. More relevant to our inquiry, what are the *behavioral* consequences of a psychological adaptation of a desire for social dominance? How does our prideful pursuit of rank and status impact our relationships with others? Occasionally, our desire for social dominance has prosocial consequences as we realize that helping others creates friendships and coalitions that are useful in our struggle for power. At other times, however, our evolved desire for social dominance means that we have a predisposition to respond to certain kinds of situations aggressively (sometimes even violently) to get our way. Violence works as a means of getting some contested resource by increasing the cost of that resource to another individual. Moreover, once an organism gets past initial inhibitions against aggressive and violent behavior, such behavior rapidly escalates and increases over time and seems, in part, to become self-reinforcing. In short, aggression and violence often result from our desire for social dominance.

The first suggestion that aggression and violence might have an instinctual basis came from the work of Konrad Lorenz, an influential figure in the field of ethology (the scientific study of animal behavior). Lorenz concentrated his research on aggression between members of the *same* species. He found that, despite the ubiquity of aggression among vertebrate animals, it is extremely rare for an adult animal to be killed or seriously injured in the wild by members of its own species (except in cases of territorial overcrowding). To be sure, many animal species kill, but usually that killing is directed toward other species, toward prey. Most aggressive behavior between animals of the same species, conversely, takes the form of threats or pursuits, rather than actual physical combat.

Why? Lorenz argued that evolution has produced a "ritualization" of fighting so that aggression can grant fitness advantages without actually causing substantial physical injury or death. Necessary to this process are mechanisms by which aggression can be inhibited. Typically, these mechanisms include an appeasement gesture or ritual submission—a signal that one competitor gives up—by which one animal can inhibit the aggression of another. Because of these mechanisms of inhibition, fighting adults of almost all species normally stop at winning. They do not go on to kill.

Lorenz extrapolated his research to humans. Like other animals, he maintained, humans have an innate drive to aggressive behavior toward our own species as well as some evolved mechanisms of inhibition—particularly culturally imposed inhibitions institutionalized by religion, education, laws, and everyday codes of human social behavior. Unfortunately, however, the biological equilibrium between killing other people and inhibition is upset in humans. Relative to other animals, humans are physically quite weak and it is difficult for one human to kill another in unarmed combat. We are not designed for it. Our claws and teeth just are not up to the job of killing. As a result, Lorenz argued, there was no evolutionary need for very strong inhibition mechanisms to moderate aggression among our hunter-gatherer ancestors.

In modern times, however, this lack of inhibitory mechanisms has been dangerously coupled with technological development that puts lethal weapons in our hands—arrows, swords, rifles and guns, dynamite, and chemical and nuclear weapons. For Lorenz, the dissonance between our low inhibitions against moderating aggression and our increasing technological capability for mass destruction is why human beings are the only animals to indulge in mass slaughter of their own species. In other words, we have a capacity for destruction without precedent and, unfortunately, also without the strong inhibitory mechanisms that accompany most animals' natural weaponry.

Lorenz's work has been subject to much criticism and debate. In *On Aggression*, for instance, he takes most of his examples from fish and birds, rather fewer from mammals, and hardly any from our closest genetic relatives, the modern great apes (orangutans, gorillas, chimpanzees, and bonobos). On that point alone, there is considerable doubt about the validity of Lorenz's extrapolations from other animals to humans. But, fortunately, we now do have some detailed studies from the modern great apes that shed light on our instinctual basis for aggression and violence and call into question the popular myth that humans are unique in the animal kingdom in our capacity for aggression against members of our own species.[37]

On the early afternoon of January 7, 1974, in Gombe National Park, Tanzania, something was to happen that would make us rethink the nature of animal nature and, by extension, the nature of human nature. Godi was an ordinary chimpanzee male, a young twenty-one-year-old adult in the Kahama community. As Godi ate alone that day, a group of eight chimpanzees from a neighboring community—well beyond their normal border zone—attacked him. Although he fled, his pursuers chased after him, grabbed him, and held him captive. They inflicted appalling wounds on his face, body, and limbs. Godi was heavily bruised and bled from dozens of gashes, cuts, and punctures. After ten minutes, the attackers left and eventually returned to their own range. Godi was never seen again. Given the grievous nature of his wounds, he surely died within a few days.

As anthropologist Richard Wrangham and science writer Dale Peterson explain, the attack on Godi was a first—certainly not the first such attack in chimpanzee history, but the first *humanly observed* instance of lethal raiding among chimpanzees (observed by Hillali Matama, the senior field assistant from Jane Goodall's research center in Gombe).[38] Subsequently, other research sites in the world where chimpanzees live with neighboring groups have yielded similar results: a propensity for within-species aggression and lethal violence that rivals the bleak picture of our own inhumanity to each other. These observations verify that chimpanzees are a second species—in addition to humans—that deliberately seek out and kill members of their own species. The remarkable violence of humanity is not uniquely ours. The species most closely related to us genetically—chimpanzees, with whom we share 98.4 percent of our DNA—also have a dark side to their nature.

The Kahama killings and other chimpanzee observations made credible the idea that our aggressive and violent tendencies go back into our prehuman past. In Wrangham and Peterson's words, "The idea that humans might have been favored by natural selection to hate and to kill their enemies has become entirely, if tragically, reasonable."[39] Elsewhere: "Modern chimpanzees are not merely fellow time-travelers and evolutionary relatives, but surprisingly excellent models of our direct ancestors. . . . Chimpanzee-like violence preceded and paved the way for human war, making modern humans the dazed survivors of a continuous, 5-million-year habit of lethal aggression."[40] In short, our ape ancestors have passed to us a legacy of aggression and violence, shaped by the power of natural selection.

Summary

We have been fighting and killing other humans for thousands upon thousands of years. Why? Animals—including humans—have been selected over evolutionary time to do whatever it takes to better their own chance for survival and reproduction. At times, those actions may be contrary to the well-being of the species as a whole. However, if psychological adaptations like ethnocentrism, xenophobia, and a desire for social dominance enhanced our ancestor's survival and reproductive success in a world of limited resources, then they were favored—regardless of their impact on other members of the species. In short, natural selection has left deep traces of design in our minds and at least some of those designs leave us evolutionarily primed with the capacity to perpetrate extraordinary evil against each other.

Critique

We should remember that EP is still in its infancy. The best it offers now is a promissory note. In this early stage of development, EP suggests many hypotheses that have yet to be subjected to empirical verification. As with any emerging theoretical perspective, there is often controversy about the meaning and scientific utility of EP's new explanatory concepts. The most vociferous critics maintain that the claims of evolutionary psychology rest on shaky empirical evidence, flawed premises, and unexamined political and social presuppositions.

At present, EP is best seen as neither pseudoscience nor hard science, but as "protoscience," or science in the making. As such, EP should continue to be held to a rigorous theoretical and empirical standard—particularly given its potentially volatile ramifications for understanding the nature of human nature. It also is true that, as an emerging field, EP is often caricatured and maligned as something that it is not. The ongoing debate between EP's proponents and detractors is a good, old-fashioned scientific brawl.[41] Let's look at four of the most common, and controversial, questions raised in that discussion.

Is EP Guilty of "Pan-Adaptationism" and "Ultra-Darwinism"?

EP has been criticized for ignoring alternative explanations of human behavior, especially in its singular focus on adaptations in explaining human behavior. Some critics especially take EP to task for believing that *everything* is an adaptation—that is, "pan-adaptationism." They maintain that too much credit has been given to adaptation and that many, if not most, of the complex designs of the human mind may not necessarily have arisen as adaptations. In other words, the critics argue, EP must not assume that there is a specific mechanism for every complex capacity. Some capacities are just side effects or by-products of mechanisms that *are* adaptations. Noted paleontologist Stephen Jay Gould has even proposed names for such side effects and by-products—spandrels and exaptations—and maintains that they may be more important tools in understanding human behavior than the concept of adaptation.[42]

Is EP guilty of pan-adaptationism? In truth, evolutionary psychologists are reluctant to call something an adaptation unless there is firm, and universal, evidence to show that it is. Most evolutionary psychologists follow the conservative guideline suggested by biologist George Williams: adaptation is a distinctive concept that should be used only where it is really necessary.[43] They accept that much of human behavior today is a side effect or by-product—or even a malfunction—of adaptations designed for other purposes.

Critics also bristle at the notion that evolutionary explanations must necessarily rely on natural selection as the only force capable of producing complex behavioral patterns. In this sense, critics maintain, EP's overreliance on explanation in terms of adaptation is "ultra-Darwinian," in suggesting that natural selection is the only force responsible for the range of behaviors that we observe today in humans. Even Darwin himself expressed frustration at those who claimed that only natural selection caused all evolutionary changes. Ultimately, the critics argue, EP's overreliance on natural selection—its "Darwinian fundamentalism"—leaves it incapable of accounting for the wide range of human behavior.

Is EP ultra-Darwinian? Not really. EP is pluralistic in maintaining that natural selection is not, of course, the only cause of evolutionary change. Other events—such as mutation, accidental change, and environmental catastrophes—also alter the course of our evolutionary history. Natural selection, however, is the only evolutionary force that acts as a "designer" in engineering mechanisms to solve adaptive problems. In other words, it is the only known causal process capable of producing complex functional organic mechanisms.

Despite the massive modularity of our mind, EP holds strongly the understanding that not *all* of contemporary human behavior can be explained in evolutionary terms. EP is a powerful tool to explain thoughts, feelings, and behaviors that have significant consequences for our fitness. Other psychological adaptations that have little to do with fitness, however, may be beyond the reach of EP. In other words, psychological adaptations that have no effect on fitness are likely invisible, or immune, to selection pressures. (It also bears remembering, however, that even if an adaptation is not strongly linked to fitness now, one cannot assume that it *never* had any impact on fitness.)

Is EP Guilty of Greedy Reductionism?

Science is an attempt to reduce complex phenomena to their most basic, fundamental underlying principles. In this sense, despite its bad press, "reductionism" is just good science. At times, however, reductionism can reach absurd proportions and come at the expense of accuracy. In these cases, to paraphrase philosopher Daniel Dennett, "greedy reductionism" is bad science.[44] Is EP guilty of greedy reductionism—particularly in positing a genetic basis of our most complex social behaviors? Neuroscientist Steven Rose certainly believes so: "Far from creating a genuine integration, it [evolutionary psychology] offers yet another reductionist account in which presumed biological explanations imperialize and attempt to replace all others."[45]

Evolutionary psychologists certainly *are* reductionists, in the good sense that they attempt to reduce complex phenomena to their most basic, fundamental underlying principles. It is not necessarily true, however, that they are greedy reductionists. Evolutionary psychologists do not *over*simplify the complex phenomena with which they are dealing—certainly not to the degree of focusing only on nature at the exclusion of nurture.

We should remember that adaptations are not immutable genetic programs; they are predispositions to learn. As such, our universal reasoning circuits should be seen as information-processing devices that are the joint, interactive product of genes and environment. EP understands nature and nurture to be inseparable. Biology is as much a product of culture as culture is a product of biology. Trying to pull apart their separate effects is illogical and obscures the causes that linked them.

The EP perspective is voluntaristic. EP can only suggest why certain needs and desires have the appeal they sometimes have and their probable evolutionary origins. It does not entail acceptance of heredity as fate. It does not say that we only respond to iron instinct. We are not constrained by our innate psychological mechanisms. As a matter of fact, the *more* psychological adaptations we have, the more capabilities we have. In other words, we are not slaves to an unyielding genetic leash; rather, our genes endow us with a capacity to learn and to adapt to life in a variety of environments. EP emphasizes the uniqueness of humans as flexible animals with a vast range of potential behaviors.

There is no gene for genocide. Ethnocentrism, xenophobia, and our desire for social dominance are tendencies, not triggers that lead to mechanical causation or reflex action. They help us understand that we have been endowed by evolution with a host of needs and desires, such that it is often difficult for one person to pursue his or her needs and desires without coming into conflict with other people. On this, evolutionary psychologists actually agree with an assertion from one of their most vocal critics, Stephen Jay Gould, who wrote: "The statement that humans are animals does not imply that our specific patterns of behavior and social arrangements are in any way directly determined by our genes. *Potentiality* and *determination* are different concepts."[46] In other words, we should not mistake enablement for causation.

Is EP Guilty of Justifying Social Inequality?

Does EP defend existing social arrangements as biologically inevitable? There are certainly those who do use evolutionary studies to lend authority to sexist, racist, and capitalist ideologies. In a 1989 meeting of the American Association for the Advancement of Science, for example, J. Philippe Rushton argued that some human populations are more "advanced" than others on a wide variety of personal and population attributes (for example, intelligence, sexual restraint, social organization) because of their evolutionary history. Rushton specifically maintains that "Orientals" are slightly superior to "Whites," and both groups are considerably superior to "Blacks." Today, Rushton continues his controversial work through his Charles Darwin Research Institute, "a charity set up to guarantee academic freedom for research on race differences."[47]

Rushton's use of evolution to explain genetic differences between groups of individuals certainly has an air of an earlier Social Darwinism that many today find downright offensive. We should remember, however, that most of today's evolutionary psychologists are concerned with the *universals* of human nature, not the differences. EP mainly focuses on adaptations that are *common* to all people. EP is not, in general, concerned with individual or group genetic differences—though many popularizers of EP have traded on the supposedly universal behavioral differences between males and females.

To reiterate, EP is concerned with similarities, or universals, across human nature. Evolutionary psychologists are interested in the basic mechanisms of the mind that all humans share. Moreover, the more important a mechanism is, the less individual variation we expect to find in it. EP maintains that genetic differences among individuals are quite minor compared to our genetic commonalities. In other words, all of us possess essentially identical adaptations, psychological or otherwise. To be sure, individual differences among people could very well come from random variations in the assembly process or from different life histories. In general, though, the psychological mechanisms posited by EP are installed in every neurologically normal human being. Anthropologist Edward Hagen of the University of California, Santa Barbara, draws the following analogy: "Although there are no doubt minor differences in heart morphology that have a genetic basis, all hearts are built and function in exactly the same way. Similarly, psychological adaptations, should they exist, must also be built and function in the same way across individuals, although there will, no doubt, be minor differences attributable to underlying genetic differences."[48]

Finally, we also should remember that a denial of human nature, just as much as an emphasis on it, can be used to justify social inequality. As James Wilson writes: "If science tells them [despots] that biology is nothing and environment everything, then they will put aside their eugenic surgery and selective breeding programs and take up instead the weapons of propaganda, mass advertising, and educational indoctrination."[49]

Is EP Guilty of Justifying Our Antisocial Behaviors?

The difference between using innate, psychological mechanisms to *explain* behavior and using those same mechanisms to *excuse* behavior is tremendous and has been an ancient theme of moral reasoning. EP explains behavior; it does not justify it. In other words, EP describes what human nature is like—it does not prescribe what humans should do. Imagining that it does is known as the *naturalistic fallacy*. The naturalistic fallacy confuses "is" with "ought." In other words, it confuses the situation that exists in the world with our moral judgment about that situation.

We should remember that nothing says that adaptations produced by natural selection are morally correct. Simply because a set of traits is "natural" does not make it good. What happens in nature is not always right. What people are driven to do is not necessarily what they ought to do. If we understand those drives, however, we are in a better position to encourage the desirable behaviors and discourage the undesirable ones.

EP does not blame antisocial behavior on our genes. Psychological adaptations are one of many causes of human behavior—each of which raises the question of free will and responsibility. As Steven Pinker argues: "Science is guaranteed to appear to eat away at the will, *regardless* of what it finds, because the scientific mode of explanation cannot accommodate the mysterious notion of uncaused causation that underlies the will."[50] This reality is what Dennett has called the "Specter of Creeping Exculpation."[51]

How do we reconcile EP with responsibility and free will? Science and morality are separate spheres of reasoning. The former searches for the physical processes (genetic, environmental, social) that cause behavior, the latter for an assignment of moral value to behavior based on the behavior's inherent nature or its consequences. Perhaps the idealization, or even the delusion, of free will is an adaptation designed to hide some of our baser motives from our conscious awareness. Regardless, as Pinker concludes, only by recognizing science and morality as separate spheres of reasoning can we have them both.

Conclusion

As we have seen, the conventional wisdom in the social sciences has historically been that human nature is a blank slate, simply an imprint of an individual's background and experience. The emerging field of EP, however, has led social scientists to rethink the nature of human nature. EP says that human nature is not blank at all; it consists of a large number of evolved psychological mechanisms. EP reminds us that we are part of the natural world and, like other animals, we have our own particular psychological tendencies that animate many of our behaviors. We are obligated to examine the impact of *what* we are on *who* we are in understanding how ordinary people commit extraordinary evil. To not seek such evidence is like failing to search a suspect for a concealed weapon.

At first glance, some of the evolved psychological mechanisms posited by EP appear to affirm our capacity for cooperative, caring, nonviolent relations — for example, love of kin, preferential altruism directed toward kin, reciprocal altruism, enduring reciprocal alliances or friendships, compassion, and so on. In many ways, we owe our success as a species to these prosocial instincts. Ridley has even argued that it is our instinctive cooperativeness that is the very hallmark of humanity and what sets us apart from other animals.

But EP also warns us that self-congratulation about our human nature is premature. In Ridley's words: "We have as many darker as lighter instincts. The tendency of human societies to fragment into competing groups has left us with minds all too ready to adopt prejudices and pursue genocidal feuds."[52] In other words, beneath our social surface is a seamy underside of human nature that is much less flattering. The reality is that we tend to reserve major doses of "goodness" either for close kin or for non-kin who show signs of someday returning the favor. Underlying even our acts of "charity" for other organisms are a strain of selfish and aggressive traits that are part of our inherently self-centered human nature; sometimes altruism and cooperation turn out to be the most effective ways to compete. In short, however deeply buried, the capacities for extraordinary evil are within all of us. We have a hereditary dark side that is universal across humankind. Acts of extraordinary evil are not beyond, beneath, or outside ordinary humanness.

Should we really be surprised by the unflattering depiction of human nature that EP provides? In some ways, probably not. We already know that we have such nefarious capacities because history provides so many examples of their actualization. Perhaps as a result of our history of brutal inhumanity to each other, this view of human nature certainly has the weight of intellectual tradition on its side. Theologians beat evolutionary psychologists to the discovery of the "animal in humans" by several centuries. Indeed, the idea that human nature contained innate drives similar to those in animals is a central element of the traditional Christian view of human nature, often captured in the doctrine of original sin. As historians Kari Konkola and Glenn Sunshine conclude, "The hottest field in modern science [evolutionary psychology] is just in the process of discovering the part of human nature which Christianity used to call 'original sin!' "[53] Others agree that, regarding the nature of human nature, religion and evolutionary psychology converge to a surprising extent—though members of either field fiercely refuse to acknowledge such a convergence.

EP, in spite of its youth, is lending substantial credibility to the perception of a fundamental unity among human beings. While the roots of extraordinary evil cannot be distilled solely to natural selection, we can no longer dismiss as an unsupportable theological or philosophical assumption the idea that human nature has a dark side. No longer can we evade the possibility that there is an essentialist trait underlying our inhumanity to each other that makes each of us, ultimately, capable of committing extraordinary evil. We must at least partially ground our evil deeds in our evil human natures and recognize the possibility that we *do* evil because we *can*. In other words, while an impulse to do evil may not be *the* defining characteristic of human nature, such an impulse certainly qualifies—at the very least—as a human capacity.

The nature of our human nature is only one component in understanding how ordinary people commit extraordinary evil. Natural selection may have designed certain adaptations that give us the capacity for extraordinary evil, but the fact remains that no other species shows the degree of premeditated mass killings of its own species that humans have shown over the centuries. Indeed, on this level, it really is quite unfair to these other species to compare them with humankind. On the scale of extraordinary evil, *Homo sapiens* stands alone. As Edmond Mrugamba, a Tutsi in Rwanda, asks: "An animal will kill, but never to completely annihilate a race, a whole collectivity. What does that make us in this world?"[54]

Indeed, what does that make us? We all have dark sides to us, and, given the right confluence of contributing factors, we are all capable of some terrible deeds. Human nature contains some built-in mechanisms that can be adapted and recruited into the service of extraordinary evil. EP offers, at best, a distal explanation for what enables our participation in extraordinary evil. While it describes the foundational capacities common to all of us, it doesn't explain why only some of us actually perpetrate extraordinary evil. To understand that, we need to investigate the more immediate and proximal factors involved in leading ordinary people to commit extraordinary evil. Specifically, what are the dispositional, situational, and social factors that activate our underlying capacity for extraordinary evil? In chapter 6, continuing with our emphasis on the *actor*, we will shift our focus from the universal forces that make us the same to the particular forces that make us different.

The Tonle Sap Massacre

THE KHMER EMPIRE THRIVED FROM the ninth century to the fifteenth century. At its height, it stretched across Southeast Asia from present-day Thailand to Vietnam. Its trading networks reached as far as China. The empire's crown jewel was its capital, Angkor. In the twelfth century, it is estimated that Angkor may have been home to a population of 1 million. By comparison, Paris—one of the great cities in Europe at the time—had a population of perhaps 30,000. Angkor included a seventy-five-square-mile complex of more than one hundred elaborate Hindu temples. These temples were part of a vast network of dams and canals that captured water flowing from nearby hills, enabling the Khmer to enjoy an extra rice harvest each growing season. It was such vision and planning that helped sustain the empire for more than 500 years.

Pol Pot (born Saloth Sar in 1928) wanted to return twentieth-century Cambodians to the symbolic grandeur of their glorious past through an extremist agrarian revolution. The centerpiece of his revolution was a campaign aimed at ridding the country of those deemed not *borisot* (pure). These included the educated, those "tainted" by anything foreign (including knowledge of a foreign language), and a wide range of "heredity enemies," especially the Vietnamese and other ethnic minorities (persons of Chinese, Thai, or Lao ancestry, as well as the Muslim Cham). To accomplish his genocidal vision, on April 17, 1975, Pol Pot's Khmer Rouge Communist Party overthrew the U.S.-backed regime of Gen. Lon Nol. Pol Pot, "Brother Number One," installed himself as prime minister of Cambodia, proclaiming the new state of Democratic Kampuchea. In that position, Pol Pot conceived and directed the genocide in Cambodia from 1975 to 1979.

Immediately after their seizure of power, the Khmer Rouge executed a ruthless evacuation of the 2 million inhabitants of the capital, Phnom Penh. Thousands died of exhaustion and starvation. In the next weeks, the remainder of the nation's cities were evacuated in a "forced rustification," hospitals were emptied, schools were closed, factories were deserted, money and wages were abolished, monasteries were emptied, and libraries were scattered. Purges began among the Khmer Rouge leadership and ethnic minorities and then extended to the general population.

The Khmer Rouge cut Cambodia off from the world. Foreign and minority languages were banned, and neighboring countries were attacked to regain ancient "lost territory." Free speech and free travel, even between villages, were eliminated. Cambodia's Theravada Buddhist religion—to which roughly 90 percent of the nation's population claimed adherence—was banned as reactionary. Following the lead of Maoist China, farming was completely collectivized, with peasants forced into unpaid collective labor. In the four years of the Khmer Rouge reign, no Cambodian was free. There were no political, civil, or human rights. There were no practicing lawyers, doctors, teachers, engineers, or scientists because it was presumed that any peasant could pick up the "simple" truths of these professions through experience.

In this prison camp state of 8 million inmates, Ben Kiernan, founder of the Cambodian Genocide Program at Yale University, conservatively estimates that 1.7 million people (nearly one-quarter of the total population) were worked, starved, or beaten to death in "the Killing Fields." Fewer than 2,000 of Cambodia's 70,000 Buddhist monks survived the reign of the Khmer Rouge; the rest either were massacred or succumbed to hard labor, disease, or torture. Other scholars suggest that Pol Pot was responsible for the murders of between 3 and 4 million of his fellow Cambodians due to disease, starvation, overwork, torture, and execution.[1]

Ronnie Yimsut was thirteen years old when the Khmer Rouge swept into Phnom Penh in 1975. He and his extended family were removed from their homes in Siem Reap, near the famed ruins of Angkor, and forced to work in collective camps. During the last week of 1977, Ronnie's family was relocated, for the twenty-fifth time, to the Tonle Sap. The Tonle Sap, the Great Lake, dominates the center of Cambodia. It was to the Khmer what the Nile was to the ancient Egyptians. Yimsut, along with seventy-eight others, were told they were being moved to the Tonle Sap to catch fish for the government. The following is excerpted from his testimony:

> They took us south through a familiar muddy road toward the lake, which was about six or seven miles away. The last time I walked on this very same road was just last the year before, when I was on another Mobile Brigade project. The longer we were on that road, the more relaxed we were. Perhaps they were telling

Up to 20,000 people were tortured and killed by the Khmer Rouge at Tuol Sleng prison from 1976 to 1979. Mugshots of Tuol Sleng prisoners, taken by a Khmer Rouge photographer (1978). Photo courtesy Ben Kiernan, Tuol Sleng Museum, 1980.

us the truth? We seemed to be heading in the right direction. There were only five of them. They couldn't possibly kill all 79 of us—could they?

. . . They wanted us to move on quickly before the setting of the sun. They asked all the able men, both young and old, to come and gather in front of the group. The men were then told to bring their tools, especially any knives and axes they had with them. They said that the men needed to go ahead of the group to build a camp for the rest of us. The men were soon lined up in a single file with their tools in hand. I watched my brother Sarey as he walked reluctantly to join the line after saying goodbye to his pregnant wife, Oum. I told him that I would take good care of my sister-in-law. The group disappeared shortly in the darkening sky. That was the last time I ever saw Sarey and the rest of the men again. . . .

It was about 7 or 8 o'clock in the evening when we were ordered to move on again. By this time the children who still had enough energy to cry were crying and screaming as loud as they could. It was mainly from hunger and exhaustion, but also from the attack by the swamping mosquitoes. Amidst the crying of the children I could hear the sobbing and weeping of the people who lost their loved ones. I still had my doubts about the whole situation, although the odds were stacked against us. If we didn't die of starvation, exhaustion, or mosquito bites, there was a good chance that we might be killed by the hands of the soldiers.

The thought of me actually coming face to face with death now terrified me for the first time. I had thought of escaping right then, but could not do it after a long consideration. I didn't have the heart to leave my family, especially my pregnant sister-in-law who was already a week overdue. Besides, where would I go from here? I would eventually be recaptured and killed later on. If I were to die, I preferred to die among my loved ones. There were plenty of opportunities for me to escape, but I just couldn't do it. So I reluctantly trekked with the rest of the group, with my sister-in-law Oum over my right shoulder and a small bag of belongings on my left. Somehow it seemed ironic; we were knowingly walking toward our deaths just like cattle being herded towards a slaughterhouse. We all knew where we were heading; even the children seemed to know it as well. I still had a little doubt despite everything I had seen and heard thus far. Perhaps it was a faint hope—a hope that these Khmer Rouge soldiers were not the cold-hearted killers we thought they were. Perhaps . . .

We were no more than 300 yards off the main road when they asked us to sit down on the edge of a small shallow canal that ran east to west. Both of our legs stretched forward; we had to shut up or they would beat us up. In a matter of minutes a large group of at least 50 people suddenly emerged from a hidden place in the nearby forest. It was really dark by that time, but I could tell from their silhouettes that they were soldiers with AK-47 rifles, carbines and large clubs in their hands. One of them began to shout loudly at us as the rest surrounded the group with their rifles, aiming directly at us. People began to plead for their lives. The soldiers screamed for all of us to shut up. They said that they only wished to ask a few questions—that was all they wanted. They also said that this was an interrogation and that they suspected there were enemies among us. They claimed there were Vietnamese agents in our group, which I knew was a bogus claim since we all had known each other for many years. It was all a tactic, a dirty trick to keep us calm, weak and under their control. But the tactic had been very effective because all the strong men who could have risen against them were the first ones to go. Those people left in my group were women and children, the sick and the weak. They had us right where they wanted. It was all a premeditated plan.

A soldier walked towards me, yanking away a cotton towel and shredding it into small strips. I was the first one to be tied up tightly by the soldiers with one of the strips. I was stunned and quite terrified. I began to resist a little. After a few blows to the head with rifle butts, I could only let them do as they pleased with me. My head began to bleed from a wound. I was still semi-conscious—I could feel the pain and blood flowing down on my face. They were using me as [an] example of what one would get if they got any kind of resistance. They quickly tied the rest of the group without any problems. By this time it was totally chaotic as people continued to plea for their lives. I was getting dizzier as blood continued to drip across my face and into my right eye. It was the first time that I had tears in my eyes—not from the blood . . . [or] the pain, but from the reality that was now setting in. I was numb with fear.

I was beyond horrified when I heard the clobbering begin. Somehow, I knew that this was it. Oum's elderly father was next to me and his upper torso contracted several times before he fell on me. At that moment, I noticed a small boy whom I knew well get up and start to call for his mother. Suddenly there was a warm splash on my face and body. I knew it was definitely not mud—it was the little boy's blood, perhaps his brain tissue scattering from the impact. The others only let out short but terrifying sputtered sounds. I could hear their breathing stop cold in its tracks. Everything seemed to happen in slow motion; it was so unreal. It happened in a matter of seconds but I can still vividly remember every trifling detail. I closed my eyes, but the terrifying sounds continued to penetrate my ear canals, piercing my eardrums. The first blow came when I was lying face down to the ground with a corpse partially covering my lower body. It hit me just below my right shoulder blade—I remember that one very well. The next one hit me just above my neck on the right side of my head. I believe it was the one that knocked me out that night. The rest of the clubbing, which included at least 15 blows, landed everywhere on my skinny little body. Fortunately, I did not feel them until much later. I do not remember anything after that, except that I slept very well that night, unconscious from the beating. . . .

The faint light of a new dawn broke through the sky, revealing my shriveled, blood-soaked body in the mud. It must have been about 4 or 5 o'clock in the morning, January 1, 1978. "Not a Happy New Year today," I thought. It was still dark and cold. My motor skills came back little by little until I was able to move with great difficulty. I pushed myself to sit up by supporting myself on the pile of dead bodies. I began to work to untie myself from the cloth rope. I broke the rope after a few painful tries. My eyesight was also back, but I wished then that I was blind after seeing the scattered bodies laying at every direction. Some of them were beyond recognition. Some were completely stripped naked. Bloodstains which had already turned to a dark color gave the area a new dimension. It definitely was not a sight for sore eyes.

I wanted to look around for my relatives, but was unable to turn around. My neck was stiff with pain. My head hurt—oh how it hurt so badly. I could only feel around me with my two hands. Everywhere I touched was cold flesh. My hands were both trembling and I could not control them from shaking. I cried my heart out when I recognized a few dead bodies next to me, one of which was Oum and her unborn child. I suddenly remembered the bare foot I saw when I woke up—it was hers. Her elderly father and her two sisters were all piled on top of each other and side by side as though they were embracing just before they lost their lives. I could not go on. My cries turned to a sobs; it was the only sound around besides the mosquitoes which continued to torment my almost bloodless body. I began to fade and feel as though my life was slipping away. I passed out again on top of the dead bodies. I was totally out cold.[2]

Of the dozens killed at Tonle Sap Lake on that December day, only Yimsut survived. He eventually found his way to a refugee camp near the Thai-Cambodian border. Sponsored by a cousin and her husband, Yimsut came to America in October 1978. Today he is a landscape architect for the National Forest Service. He lives in Bend, Oregon, with his wife and two children.

In 1978, Vietnam invaded Cambodia to stop the Khmer Rouge from attacking its borders. The following year, Phnom Penh fell to the Vietnamese, who installed a puppet regime—the People's Republic of Kampuchea—consisting largely of Cambodian communists who had deserted Pol Pot in 1977–1978. Pol Pot was forced to flee to the hill country bordering Thailand. There, the Khmer Rouge set up guerrilla bases and continued to be recognized as Cambodia's legal representative to the UN for fourteen years. During this period, the Khmer Rouge received millions of dollars from foreign powers anxious to oppose Vietnam—including the United States. By 1997, the Khmer Rouge had splintered, and Pol Pot's last loyalists had fled. Pol Pot was captured by other Khmer Rouge, given a perfunctory show trial, and placed under house arrest. In April 1998, Pol Pot was reputed to have died from undisclosed medical difficulties, and his body was reportedly burned in the presence of Thai officials. Many of his senior colleagues remain alive.

In 1997, Cambodia officially requested assistance from the United Nations to convene a genocide tribunal. Unfortunately, the negotiations ran into numerous difficulties, including whether foreign or Cambodian judges and prosecutors would participate. Finally, on April 29, 2000, Sen. John Kerry (D-Mass.) announced that the United Nations and the Cambodian government had reached a tentative agreement to try Khmer Rouge leaders on genocide charges. On February 8, 2002, however, the United Nations—fearing that the complicated formula for a court with Cambodian and foreign judges and prosecutors may not provide impartial justice—reneged on this agreement. As of this writing, it appears that the international community—including the United States—has given up on its efforts to bring the leaders of the Khmer Rouge to justice. Consequently, healing and genuine national reconciliation in Cambodia now seem to be faded, even unattainable dreams.

6

Who Are the Killers?

Identities of the Perpetrators

> If only there were evil people somewhere, insidiously committing evil
> deeds, and it were necessary only to separate them from the rest of us
> and destroy them. But the line dividing good and evil cuts through the
> heart of every human being. And who is willing to destroy a piece of
> his own heart?
>
> Alexander Solzhenitsyn, *The Gulag Archipelago*

SOCIAL PSYCHOLOGISTS HAVE LONG been torn between internal and external explanations of the forces that shape our responses to authority. In our parlance, we have referred to internal influences as *dispositional*, external influences as *situational*. Generally, we have a preference for seeking causal explanations in forces outside the individual—particularly features of the immediate situation. As a result, social psychologists, by and large, do not think of evil actions as the product of evil dispositions or personalities. In truth, though, any complete explanatory model of human behavior—including one of extraordinarily evil human behavior—must include both dispositional and situational components. We simply cannot ignore the interactional reality of the internal *and* external forces that shape our thoughts, feelings, and behaviors.

Ultimately, a contest between dispositional and situational explanations is not productive. Overreliance on either type of influence runs the risk of unnecessarily constraining our understanding of how ordinary people commit extraordinary evil. Instead, what we should be concerned with is the *relative* importance of dispositional *and* situational factors in explaining extraordinary human evil. Not only do situations affect the person, but people also influence situations, primarily by our choice or creation of situations most conducive to the expression of our personalities. In other

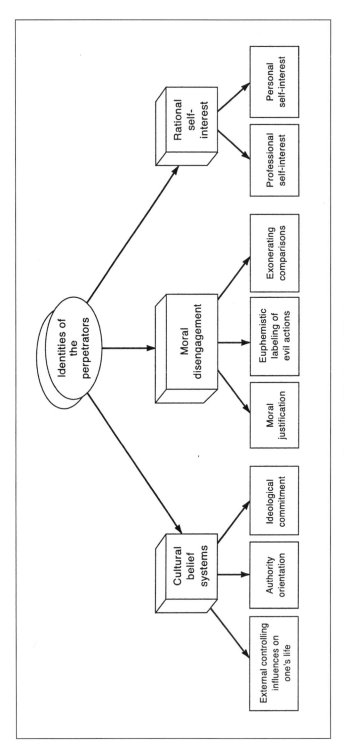

Figure 3.   Who Are the Killers?

words, we are partly the products of our situations, but we are producers of our situations as well. This perspective stresses the importance of viewing any human behavior—including the perpetration of extraordinary evil—as a product of both personal dispositions and situational factors.

In chapter 7, we will examine the power of the situation in influencing how ordinary people commit extraordinary evil. In this chapter, we will begin our interactional approach by recognizing that the dispositions and personalities of perpetrators *do* matter; there *are* personality issues involved in the commission of extraordinary evil that must be clarified. There is certainly something about *who* the perpetrators are that must be taken into account in understanding how ordinary people commit extraordinary evil. Individuals do differ in how they assess authority situations and their responsibilities within them. What are the dispositional influences in responding to authority that are most relevant to understanding perpetrators of extraordinary evil?

In chapter 5, we started at the most logical place—examining the nature of human nature. As Christopher Browning wrote in a 1996 editorial: "Any attempt to understand perpetrators of the Holocaust—not just Germans, but all those recruited into its machinery of destruction—requires an investigation of human nature. We will add little to our ability to understand either the Holocaust or the events of killing and genocide reported on the front pages of our daily newspapers if we ignore that task."[1] Having taken on that task, we found that genocidal evil is readily available in our human potential.

But, as I noted at the end of chapter 5, understanding the universal dispositional nature of human nature only tells us that we all are *capable* of extraordinary evil. Our instinctual "pushes" are too diffuse to tell us everything we need to know about the direction, form, and targets of our violent behavior. Moreover, the universal dispositional nature of human nature does not explain why only *some* of us actually perpetrate extraordinary evil and, in fact, why the great majority of us never do. To explain why some do perpetrate extraordinary evil but most do not requires sharpening our focus to the more *particular* dispositional influences that mold the identities of ordinary people. This chapter will focus on three such dispositional influences—cultural belief systems, moral disengagement, and rational self-interest (see figure 3).

Cultural Belief Systems

All cultures, communities, and family systems leave their fingerprints on the members within them. One such set of prints is the cultural belief systems we hold—our thoughts, values, and principles, which constitute a primary feature of our disposition or personality. By the phrase "cultural belief systems," I am referring to the stable and enduring information a person has about other people, objects, and issues. The beliefs themselves may be factual, or they may be only one person's opinion. Furthermore, the beliefs may be linked with positive, negative, or no evaluative feelings for the target of the beliefs. Finally, the beliefs typically are organized in some form of associative network or system.

There are three specific cultural belief systems that are most relevant to understanding how ordinary people commit extraordinary evil: cultural belief systems about (1) external, controlling influences on one's life; (2) one's orientation to authority; and (3) ideological commitment.

1. External, Controlling Influences on One's Life

Thomas Blass reviewed several dispositional variables that are theoretically relevant in shaping our responses to authority—interpersonal trust, level of moral judgment, social intelligence, and individual differences in hostility. While results of studies related to these variables are, at best, suggestive, Blass does lay out a compelling case for the influence of one particular group of dispositional variables in shaping our responses to authority: one's cultural belief systems about *external, controlling influences on one's life.*

Blass analyzed four relevant studies bearing on the hypothesis that beliefs about external, controlling influences on our life shape our responses to authority. Three of the studies focused on "locus of control," in which the source of external controlling influence was chance, luck, or fate. The fourth study, utilizing religious dispositional variables, focused on enduring belief systems related to divine influence and authority. "What three out of four of these studies suggest," Blass concludes, "is that beliefs about ceding versus retaining personal control seem to be salient and predisposing factors in obedience to authority. The evidence, in this regard, is clearest with religious variables, that is, variables centered around the belief that one's life is under divine control."[2]

In other words, there is a central importance to underlying, cultural belief systems—particularly those focused on external, controlling influences—in shaping our responses to authority. Hitler, for example, often revealed an enduring belief system about external, controlling influences on his life—and Germany's destiny. Once at the dinner table, when he thought about the destruction of the Jews, he remarked with stark simplicity: "One must not have mercy with people who are determined by fate to perish."[3] Similarly, the traditional belief system in Rwanda has pronounced tendencies toward fatalism. Most Rwandans are brought up to accept fate rather than to challenge it, believing that neither natural events nor individual destiny can be humanly controlled.

In the particular study reviewed by Blass that focused on religious dispositional variables, those that scored high on many of the religious variables were more accepting of the commands of an authority than were those who scored lower or were indiscriminately antireligious. In other words, enduring religious belief systems emphasizing divine influence and authority may be particularly relevant in shaping our responses to *worldly* influence and authority. This finding is congruent with a wealth of social psychological research suggesting that religious belief systems influence individuals' proneness to prejudice. While the teachings of most religious belief systems are replete with affirmations of the dignity of human life and the responsibilities of human beings to respect and preserve that dignity, a basic and quite consistent finding is that church members tend to be more prejudiced than nonmembers, irrespective of the target of prejudice (though frequent church attenders are less prejudiced than occasional attenders). The most pervasive levels of prejudice are found in very strict and fundamentalist Protestant churches and sects.

The finding that enduring religious belief systems make us more amenable to the commands of authority also is affirmed by the historical realities surrounding many cases of mass killing and genocide. Just as religious belief systems are an element in the impulse to heal, they also can be an element in the impulse to kill. There is a dark side to religious belief systems, which are often fused with ethnic and national identities. In this sense, religion is epiphenomenal—attached to and living off other phenomena. As such, religious belief systems do not always liberate humanity from extraordinary evil. Rather, they are often part of the problem—if not as a primary cause, certainly as something that worsens rather than mitigates conflict.

Just as religious belief systems can be an epiphenomenal element, however, they also can be *the* phenomenon, the main inspirer or motivator of extraordinary evil. Most religious belief systems are, by their very nature, ethnocentric and, in the extreme, may even foster a devaluing effect on the human life that falls outside the veil of the faithful. They distinguish all too clearly between "us" and "them," between the committed and the nonbelievers, between those whom the gods love and those whom they hate. They can be perverted to justify and reward the most horrendous of human deeds.

We must bear in mind, however, the reality that religious belief systems do not kill people. People who are religious may kill other people in the name of religion. It is in that context that enduring religious belief systems must be understood as one of the significant dispositional influences that shape our responses to authority.

In summary, those who have cultural belief systems that see control as external tend to react passively to authoritative orders rather than proceed on the assumption that they can redefine situations through their own actions.

2. One's Orientation to Authority

As we saw in chapter 3, the concept of a global authoritarian personality has been very controversial. Generally, research findings have disconfirmed several aspects of the original theory. However, it does at least seem tenable, as social psychologist Ervin Staub suggests, to consider *one's orientation to authority* as one predisposition of ordinary people who become perpetrators. Staub defines authority orientation as "a person's tendency to order the world and relate to people according to their position and power in hierarchies."[4] In other words, people high in authority orientation prefer hierarchical relationships with a clear delineation of spheres of power. They enjoy obeying authority and exercising power over those below them. They prefer order and predictability. In short, individual differences in authority orientation affect the way we relate to people with differing authority or status—even the way we relate to ideologies and other components of our social world.

Each of us comes into contact with a multiplicity of authority hierarchies; it is unavoidable, part of living together with other human beings. As a result, a certain degree of authority orientation is required in all social systems. Indeed, in most cultures, an authority orientation favoring obedience is a major cultural value. Without it, group life is impossible. In a culture that inculcates an excessively strong authority orientation, however, it is less likely that individuals will oppose leaders who scapegoat, or advocate violence against, a particular target group. Indeed, in most cases of mass killing and genocide, the culture has been characterized by a strong authority orientation.

An individual's orientation to authority is influenced by a global pattern of socialization practices inherent in child rearing, schools, and other social institutions. As one example, David Norman Smith, a sociologist at the University of Kansas, points out that exceptionally intense violence occurs with significantly greater frequency in cultures where children are routinely physically or emotionally abused or denied affection. In analyzing the origins of the Rwandan genocide, Smith asserts that centralized family systems in which the patriarch can capriciously favor, or disfavor, his wives and sons in any way he likes are often fraught with exceptionally sharp tensions that could promote authoritarian child rearing—in short, family systems bereft of emotional involvement. Families in such cultures, of which Rwanda is one illustration, typically value children primarily as helpers, while placing extreme stress on obedience toward authority.[5]

Similarly, in his analysis of the origins of genocide, Staub maintains that the strong authority orientation of German culture was reinforced by family dynamics. As he points out, numerous sources have maintained that obedience to parents, especially to the father, was the highest value in German family systems. According to Blass, generations of German children grew up on cautionary tales whose moral was that disobedience could lead to rather drastic, violent consequences. In such a setting, it is difficult for a strong, independent, individual identity to develop. Children raised in this way, Staub contends, are likely to prefer hierarchical systems—that is, they are likely to develop a strong authority orientation.

Perhaps an even more relevant socialization practice for one's orientation to authority is the particular cultural tradition of obedience and identification with the state. Both obedience to authority and giving oneself over to a leader had positive value in German culture, since at least the late nineteenth century. Historically, influential German thinkers viewed the state as an organic entity, superior to any individual. In this view, the state was not a servant of the people but an entity to which citizens owed unquestioning obedience. During his interrogation, Adolf Eichmann even suggested that his unflagging obedience was part of the nature of the German: "All my life I have been accustomed to obedience, from early childhood . . . used to being led, in business and in everything else. . . . That's how it has always been. Little by little, we were taught all these things. We grew into them, all we knew was obedience to orders."[6] In Eichmann's case, as could be argued with many other perpetrators, a cultural tradition was unfortunately complemented by a simplistic cognitive miserliness that made him particularly susceptible to obedience to authority.

Nazi ideology certainly capitalized on this legacy of strong authority orientation. For example, the first of twelve commandments listed in a primer used to indoctrinate Nazi youth was: "The leader is always right." It can even be argued that the authority orientation to the state in German culture was so highly valued that it contributed to the rise of the Nazi movement and its leaders through an "authoritarian counterurge"—a reversion to an authoritarian form of government that resulted from a too drastic attempt to impose democratic rule on Germany after World War I.

Staub also traces the role of authority orientation in several other cases of mass killing and genocide. During the Turkish genocide of the Armenians, for example, the Ottoman Empire was a monolithic, theocratic society. The society was feudal and hierarchical and had a strong authority orientation (stemming from, in part, a religious basis). Similarly, the role of the king in Cambodian society provided a cultural blueprint for a strong authority orientation. This blueprint was taken to its extreme in the totalitarian system created by Pol Pot and his Khmer Rouge regime.

Rwanda also had a strong state authoritarian tradition going back to the roots of their culture. The early Tutsi kings were definitely not constitutional monarchs, and killing was even an accepted sign of their political health. Obedience to the political authority of the state was woven into the fabric of Rwandan society. Journalist Philip Gourevitch reports an interview with a Rwandan lawyer who said: "Conformity is very deep, very developed here. In Rwandan history, everyone obeys authority. People revere power, and there isn't enough education. You take a poor, ignorant population, and give them arms, and say, 'It's yours. Kill.' They'll obey."[7]

While Staub, and others, focus on authority orientation at a cultural level, we also should note that the concept has its impact on cultures because of its impact on individuals. Just as authority orientation helps us understand why a particular culture may foster genocidal tendencies, it also helps us understand the individual differences in perpetrating such extraordinary evil. Differences in one's orientation to authority may provide the impetus certain people need to translate their feelings of hate into action.

3. Ideological Commitment

Finally, *ideological commitment* also shapes perpetrators' responses to authority. Here I am referring to cultural belief systems about an ideal social organization and way of life. As Staub points out, it is helpful "to distinguish between the *existing culture*, which consists of beliefs, meanings, values, valuation, symbols, myths, and perspectives that are shared largely without awareness, and *ideology*, which I [Staub] define as a primarily consciously held set of beliefs and values."[8] As a cultural belief system, ideology can give meaning and direction to life—both positive and negative. Indeed, mass killing and genocide are often ideologically inspired crimes. There certainly is no reason to simply assume that those who carried out the crimes were ideologically unmotivated and only thoughtlessly following orders.

As we saw in chapter 2, however, the perpetration of extraordinary evil cannot be reduced only to the influence of an extraordinary ideology. Unwavering ideological commitment simply is not *the* answer to the question of why hundreds of thousands of people come to perpetrate extraordinary evil. For most, their behavior was not solely the expression of some inner inspiration based on a belief in an insane ideological commitment. To restate, we do not find in perpetrators of extraordinary evil the uniformly high level of ideological commitment that Goldhagen hypothesized in his study of Holocaust perpetrators. Instead, we find more heterogeneity than we do homogeneity. Quite simply, some specific individuals are more deeply and consciously committed to a particular ideology than are others—regardless of how pervasive the ideology is in the general culture.

As Christopher Browning points out in his analysis of Reserve Police Battalion 101 (see chapter 3), ideological indoctrination certainly influenced the policemen in a general way—particularly with a sense of their own superiority and racial kinship contrasted against Jewish inferiority and otherness. However, most of the indoctrination circulars and pamphlets were clearly inappropriate or irrelevant to men of their age and standing. Most notably, the indoctrination material was absent of anything designed to explicitly prepare the reservists for the task of killing Jews. This contrasts notably with the two-month indoctrination period given the Einsatzgruppen before they entered Soviet territory, during which considerable effort was made to explicitly prepare those men for the mass murder they were going to perpetrate. This comparison makes clear the fact that ideological indoctrination and commitment varied substantially among perpetrators in the Holocaust.

Regardless of the variability in commitment, we should acknowledge that ideologies do play at least a partial role in understanding perpetrators of extraordinary evil. In examining cultural preconditions for war, for example, Staub focuses on an ideology of antagonism—built on differences in values, beliefs, and ways of life; devaluation; and a past history of antagonism—as a powerful impetus for extraordinary evil. "When an ideology of antagonism exists," he writes, "anything good that happens to the other inflames hostility. The ideology makes the world seem a better place without the other."[9]

Psychologist Robert Sternberg of Yale University goes qualitatively beyond mere antagonism and maintains that the most powerful force underlying mass killings and genocide is an ideology of *"hate* [italics mine] that is carefully nurtured and shaped in order to accomplish ends that are mindfully, planfully, and systematically conceived."[10] Indeed, extraordinarily evil ideologies often are based on hate and communicated through laws and courts, social learning, and propaganda distributed by the mass media.

In his soon-to-be-published conceptual model, Sternberg suggests three components of hate. The first, *negation of intimacy*, involves the seeking of distance from a target individual. This component of hate is affective; it is experienced as a negative emotion. The second component, *passion*, expresses itself motivationally as intense anger or fear in response to a threat. The final component, *decision/commitment*, is characterized by cognitions of devaluation and diminution toward the targeted group. This is the cognitive component that is often nurtured by institutions.

For Sternberg, the most dangerous hate, what he calls "burning hate," occurs when all three components of hate are present and feeding off each other. In those cases, the haters may feel a need to annihilate their enemy. The communication of ideology through hate propaganda is central to the development of "burning hate." Such propaganda functions to negate the intimacy toward the targeted entity, generate passion, and generate commitment to false beliefs through the implantation of false presuppositions.

In Rwanda, for instance, the quasi-official radio network of the Hutu ruling party, the Radio Télévision Libre des Mille Collines (RTLMC), was the only source of insight into the larger world of public affairs for most Hutus. What the radio said is what the Hutus heard. And what the radio said was coarse, violent, and full of anti-Tutsi demonology. Tutsi were often reviled as "vipers, drinkers of untrue blood" that were plotting the wholesale slaughter of Hutu innocents. In this unrelenting message of hate propaganda, no Tutsi were to be trusted. All Tutsi were, actually or potentially, traitors and mass murderers. The RTLMC generated in many Hutu a passionate, ideological commitment that their lives were menaced from inside and outside Rwanda by Tutsi infiltrators (as well as Hutu supporters of democracy). Such an ideological commitment became the match that started the fire of burning hate that would eventually consume Rwanda.

The role of ideological commitment in shaping perpetrator behavior is perhaps most clearly delineated in the Holocaust. Nazi ideology, first laid out in Hitler's *Mein Kampf* in the fall of 1925, centered on the notion that race is the foundation of all culture. Racial purity was the highest ideal of this ideology, and it carried dual obligations to promote racial purity wherever possible and destroy whatever—and whomever—threatened racial purity. According to this ideology, the fate of people who did not preserve their racial purity could be seen in the examples of Sparta and Rome. The committed ideologist, unless he was willing to abandon the comfort of his ideology and admit he was wrong, had to destroy all threats to that ideology. Perpetrators of extraordinary evil easily drew on this overarching ideology to justify and support their atrocities.

Finally, we should note a recent line of research directed at understanding some of the individual differences in ideological commitment. A team of psychologists at Stanford University, headed by Felicia Pratto and Jim Sidanius, theorize that individuals differ in the degree to which they want their own group to be superior to other groups and to dominate those groups. These individual differences in *social dominance orientation* (SDO) have important implications for one's acceptance or rejection of various social and political ideologies that support group-based hierarchies. People high in SDO, for example, show more antiblack racism, more belief in the existence of equal opportunities, more patriotism, more political-economic conservatism, less support for social programs and women's rights, less tolerance for diversity, and less altruism.[11] In short, people high in SDO generally are attracted to social and political ideologies that foster group inequalities and pave the way for a moral disengagement of the perpetrator from the victim.

Moral Disengagement

Albert Bandura, a social psychologist at Stanford University, maintains that people generally refrain from behaving in ways that violate their moral standards because such conduct will bring self-condemnation. He also notes, however, that moral standards are not invariant internal regulators of conduct. Our moral standards do not operate unless they are activated. As Bandura's extensive program of research on moral agency reveals, there are many social and psychological mechanisms by which moral standards can be selectively engaged or, most relevant to our discussion, disengaged.[12] *Moral disengagement* is not simply a matter of moral indifference or invisibility. Rather, it is an active, but gradual, process of detachment by which some individuals or groups are placed outside the boundary in which moral values, rules, and considerations of fairness apply.

Most great crimes in human history come in moralistic dress. How do perpetrators of extraordinary evil regulate their thinking so as to disengage, or not feel, their moral scruples about harming others? How do they overcome the lingering effects of thousands of years of social morality and ethics? What do their evil actions mean to them? How do they make extraordinary evil look good in their eyes?

The cultural belief systems, in part, lay the foundation for a moral disengagement from the perpetration of extraordinary evil. How does this moral disengagement come about? Following Bandura, there are three disengagement practices necessary for perpetrators to make their reprehensible conduct acceptable and to distance them from the moral implications of their actions: (1) moral justification, (2) euphemistic labeling of evil actions, and (3) exonerating comparisons.

1. Moral Justification

People do not ordinarily engage in extraordinary evil until they have justified to themselves the morality of their actions. How do perpetrators redefine extraordinary evil to avoid recognizing it as immoral? In part, their conduct is legitimized by the conviction that killing, or being willing to kill, members of another group of people is necessary for the safety and security of one's own group. As Gourevitch recounts in his chronicle of the Rwandan genocide, "Perpetrators of a slaughter like the one just inside the door where I stood need not enjoy killing, and they may even find it unpleasant. What is required above all is that they want their victims dead. They have to want it so badly that they consider it a necessity."[13]

So, the perpetration of extraordinary evil is made personally and socially acceptable by portraying it as serving socially worthy or moral purposes. Perpetrators may believe this rationalization to such an extent that their evil is not only morally justifiable but becomes an outright moral imperative. Perpetrators can then justify their evil as essential to their own self-defense—to protect the cherished values of their community, fight ruthless oppressors, preserve peace and stability, save humanity from subjugation, or honor their national commitments. In some cases, perpetrators' sense of vulnerability in the world is actually based in the reality of their past victimization. In most cases, though, perpetrators' sense of vulnerability is a self-justifying mental gymnastic—not accurately reflecting reality—that comes easily from the part of our psyche that wants to view ourselves as victims or potential victims.

Social psychologist Robert Zajonc of Stanford University believes that moral imperatives are actually better understood as *motives* than they are rationalizations. For Zajonc, moral imperatives are the key force for mobilizing a collectivity for extraordinary actions. Moral imperatives can be generated by political forces, economic circumstances, nationalist ideologies, religious fervor, ecological pressures, health conditions, welfare policies, and countless other circumstances. They specify what is good, what is right, what is evil, and what is dangerous. In some cases, moral imperatives may even emerge as laws of the state, with institutional support granting them exceptional legitimacy. Once in place, moral imperatives can provoke a collectivity to engage in acts of uncommon virtue or unspeakable atrocity. They are, in Zajonc's words, "above all summons for action—action that is seen as right, necessary, and fulfilling a high purpose."[14]

For Zajonc, the moral imperative can develop on different bases—eliminationist, religious, ideological, supremacist, segregationist, economic, or nationalist. Zajonc cites the American doctrine of Manifest Destiny as a clear example of a religious moral imperative. Indiana senator Albert J. Beveridge, speaking at the turn of the nineteenth century, proclaimed, "God has marked the American people as His chosen nation to finally lead in the regeneration of the world. This is the divine mission of America, and it holds for us all the profit, all the glory, all the happiness possible to man." In his conclusion, Zajonc maintains that he has "not encountered a single instance of massacre that was not preceded by extensive development of moral imperatives."[15]

We should note that the moral imperative only goes so far. Some perpetrators who commit extraordinary evil may do so in the name of a moral imperative, but others certainly use it as an excuse to grab land, personal property, money, homes, and professional advancement. We also should note that there is not, as some would argue, an actual diminishment of moral standards in the perpetrators. Rather, the moral justification necessary for perpetrating extraordinary evil is accomplished, in Bandura's words, "by cognitively redefining the morality of killing so that it can be done free from self-censure."[16] By this redefinition, extraordinary evil gets clothed in the moral wrappings of good, and, thus, perpetrators preserve their view of themselves as moral agents even while they are inflicting extraordinary evil on others.

Raul Hilberg also addresses the use of moral justification by perpetrators in his analyses of the Holocaust.[17] He points out that the Germans employed two types of rationalization to justify their perpetration of extraordinary evil. The first, focused on the Jew, was an attempt to explain why the Jews had to be destroyed. It was a process of defining Jews as the "other" (see chapter 8) that relied on widespread propaganda—simple, single-minded, and uncompromising messages penetrating all domains of life—to inflame the passions nurtured by centuries of paranoid antisemitism.

The second type of rationalization focused on the perpetrator and justified individual participation in the destruction process—from a bureaucratic signature on a piece of paper to the brutal squeeze of a trigger. Often, this rationalization came from without. For instance, one high-command message relayed from Hitler to troops on the front lines in the Soviet Union said: "The troops must have the right and duty to use, in this fight, any means, even against women and children, provided they are conducive to success. Scruples, of any sort whatsoever, are a crime against the German people and against the front-line soldier. . . . No German participating in action against bands or their associates is to be held responsible for acts of violence either from a disciplinary or a judicial point of view."[18]

More often, however, the rationalization came from within. Hilberg subdivides perpetrator rationalization into five categories of self-deception: (1) the doctrine of superior orders, (2) impersonal duty, (3) shifting moral standards, (4) powerlessness and diffusion of responsibility ("no man alone can build a bridge"), and (5) the combative reality of nature. Obviously, such rationalizations gave perpetrators the necessary and sufficient moral justification for their commission of extraordinary evil.

2. Euphemistic Labeling of Evil Actions

Activities can take on very different appearances depending on what they are called. Perpetrators facilitate moral disengagement by using euphemistic language to make their extraordinary evil respectable and, in part, to reduce their personal responsibility for it. By camouflaging their extraordinary evil in innocuous or sanitizing jargon, the evil loses much of its moral repugnancy. In this way, language can obscure, mystify, or otherwise redefine acts of extraordinary evil.

Bandura gives several examples: "Soldiers 'waste' people rather than kill them. Bombing missions are described as 'servicing the target,' in the likeness of a public utility. The attacks become 'clean, surgical strikes,' arousing imagery of curative activities. The civilians whom the bombs kill are linguistically converted to 'collateral damage.'"[19] Similarly, during the revolutionary period after 1918 in the USSR, kulaks were not murdered, they were "liquidated." Mass murder in Bosnia was "ethnic cleansing," and in Rwanda it was "bush clearing." Studies of torturers have revealed an equally highly specialized vocabulary referring to methods of torture, for example, as "the tea party," "the dance," "the birthday party," "the telephone," "the submarine," and "the airplane." The camouflage vocabulary used by the Nazis to cover their extraordinary evil was especially striking— "final solution," "special treatment," "evacuation," "spontaneous actions," "resettlement," and "special installations," among many others. Raul Hilberg has said that he examined "tens of thousands" of Nazi documents without once encountering the word "killing," until, after many years, he finally did discover the word—in reference to an edict concerning dogs.

Bandura also maintains that the agentless, passive style often used in depicting events of brutality serves as another linguistic tool for creating the appearance that extraordinary evil is the work of nameless forces rather than of people. It is as though perpetrators are not really the agents of their own extraordinarily evil acts. As a matter of fact, it is not uncommon in perpetrator testimony for perpetrators to speak of their atrocities in the third person (he, she, they, them) rather than the first (I, me, we, us).

Perpetrators do not, of course, literally believe the euphemistic labels given to their extraordinary evil. Even the most self-deluded of perpetrators are aware of what the euphemisms cover. At the same time, however, the euphemisms give perpetrators a discourse in which extraordinary evil need no longer be experienced, or even perceived, as extraordinary evil. As they live within their euphemistic labels, and use them with each other, perpetrators become bound to a psychologically safe realm of dissociation, disavowal, and emotional distance.

3. Exonerating Comparisons

Finally, how behavior is viewed is colored by what it is compared against. Psychologists refer to this as the *contrast effect*. Research in learning has found that shifts in the amount of reward we receive can dramatically influence performance. For example, when laboratory animals are shifted from a small reward to a larger reward, there is an increase in their performance to a level greater than that of subjects consistently receiving the larger reward. Conversely, when subjects are shifted from a large reward to a smaller reward, their performance decreases to a level lower than that of subjects consistently receiving only the smaller reward. The general principle underlying the contrast effect is that the perceived merit—or lack thereof—of our behaviors is relative to other experiences. In contrast to our other experiences, our behaviors can be exaggeratedly good or evil, or understatedly good or evil.

By exploiting the contrast effect, extraordinary evil can be redefined as acceptable, even benevolent, in the face of comparison with actual or perceived threats by one's enemies. Such comparisons are exonerating for perpetrators of extraordinary evil and help us understand the significant degree to which perpetrators go on dehumanizing and demonizing their victims (see chapter 8). In so doing, their extraordinary evil becomes benign or even worthy. Terrorists, for instance, justify their behavior as acts of selfless martyrdom by comparing them with widespread cruelties inflicted on the people with whom they identify. Similarly, in contrast to the possibility of communist enslavement, American military intervention in Vietnam—and its resulting massive destruction—was a worthy endeavor.

As Bandura points out, exonerating comparisons rely heavily on moral justification by utilitarian standards. Such justification is facilitated by two sets of judgments. "First," Bandura writes, "nonviolent options are judged to be ineffective to achieve desired changes, thus removing them from consideration. Second, utilitarian analyses using advantageous comparisons with actual or anticipated threats by one's adversaries affirm that one's injurious actions will prevent more human suffering than they cause."[20] As others have pointed out, however, there is much subjectivity and bias in estimating the gravity of potential threats and, as a result, related judgments are often suspect at best. Regardless of their accuracy, however, exonerating comparisons still serve their function of neutralizing self-censure and preserving self-esteem in perpetrators of extraordinary evil—functions clearly in the perpetrators' rational self-interest.

Rational Self-Interest

We are purposeful, goal-oriented actors. Though our goals vary from context to context, generally we prefer more wealth, power, prestige, and esteem to less wealth, power, prestige, and esteem. If we believe one particular course of action will produce more positive outcomes, we will choose that course. In this way, our choice may be considered rational in that we have chosen to behave in a way that we believe will produce desired outcomes. Note that the rationality of our choice is determined solely by our subjective calculation that the expected benefits will exceed the expected costs. In other words, the rationality of our choice is not defined by others or by its actual, objective outcome. To say that we act out of *rational self-interest*—particularly in cases that can promote our material or psychological well-being—is not to say that those behaviors always end up promoting our self-interest.

It is important for us to examine the ways in which perpetrators believed they were acting out of rational self-interest when they committed atrocities. We must recognize that some atrocities are performed because of the positive outcomes—be it material expropriation or career advancement or power—they promise for the perpetrators' self-interest. Extraordinary evil certainly may be brought into being when people do not examine the ramifications of choices made on the basis of rational self-interest. Specifically, there are two levels of rational self-interest that must be considered: (1) professional and (2) personal. These levels of rational self-interest can help explain both the initial willingness of perpetrators to participate in extraordinary evil as well as the enormous vested interest that promotes their sustained involvement.

1. Professional Self-Interest

As we have seen, the relational context in which mass killing and genocide occur varies. For example, many of the atrocities committed in Cambodia, Bosnia, Rwanda, and Sierra Leone were inflicted on neighbors by neighbors, and even by one's own close relatives. Generally speaking, however, most perpetrators of mass killing and genocide commit their extraordinary evil within the context of a military or paramilitary organization. In that context, there is a logic of incentives enmeshed with professional self-interest—ambitions, advancement, careerism—that certainly plays a role in understanding evil behavior.

Several prominent historians have recognized the role of professional self-interest as a motivating force for participation in extraordinary evil. For instance, Henry Friedlander, in his analyses of physicians involved in the T4 program (see chapter 4), concluded: "Career considerations were undoubtedly the most important reason why the T4 managers agreed to direct the killings. A job at the KdF [Chancellery of the Fuhrer] placed them close to the center of power. These young men had reached positions commonly considered important and influential. In addition, these jobs involved an assignment that was secret, sensitive, and significant. They operated at the center of events."[21]

Similarly, Gerhard Weinberg, professor emeritus of history at the University of North Carolina, Chapel Hill, cited professional self-interest as motivating the creativity and persistence of the killers in the Holocaust. He writes:

> By 1944, it was obvious to all of them that this was their road to advancement and to medals. It is not a coincidence that promotions and decorations invariably occupy such a central place in military and pseudomilitary hierarchies; these are the visible signs of success. Furthermore, every individual involved in the program to kill all the Jews the Germans could reach knew very well, most especially by the summer of 1944, that this was not only the route to higher rank and higher decorations but the best chance of exemption from conscription if he was still in a civilian position and from far more dangerous duty at the front if he was in uniform.[22]

Finally, a testimony from an SS-Scharführer (sergeant) and Kriminal-Assistant in the General-Gouvernement speaks directly to the role of careerism in his perpetration of extraordinary evil: "I thought that I ought not to say anything to Leideritz because I did not want to be seen in a bad light, and I thought that if I asked him to release me from having to take part in the executions it would be over for me as far as he was concerned and my chances of promotion would be spoilt or I would not be promoted at all. That is what I thought at the time and that is why I did not say anything to Leideritz."[23]

As John Keegan concluded in *A History of Warfare*, professional soldiers, from the Romans to the present, are attracted to and sustained in military life by pride in belonging to a valued group, concern over winning admiration and fellowship of colleagues, accumulation of honor, and largely symbolic recognitions of success.[24] In short, there are myriad professional incentives that make it in the best rational self-interest of many perpetrators to participate in extraordinary evil. Moreover, there often is a mutually reinforcing, and deadly, compatibility of one's professional self-interests with a larger political or social interest in annihilation of a specific target group.

2. Personal Self-Interest

Professional self-interest is not easily separated from personal self-interest. Regardless, in his detailed analysis of the Gestapo and the SS Security Service, George Browder goes a step beyond professional self-interest and contends that affiliation with military and paramilitary organizations fulfilled, or shaped, one's personal self-interest—particularly one's significant ego needs (that is, need for status, power, brutality, etc.). Building on the work of John Steiner, Browder suggests that specific organizational affiliations are linked with specific identity potentials. These "ego-organizational links" help us understand why certain persons join certain organizations: because the organizations promise to fulfill their ego needs—in short, to enhance their self-esteem.[25]

Roy Baumeister is a social psychologist at Case Western Reserve University who has investigated the relationship between self-esteem and aggression. Baumeister discredits the prevailing wisdom that low self-esteem causes aggression. He points out that none of the patterns associated with low self-esteem—such as uncertainty and confusion, shyness, modesty, orientation toward avoiding risk and potential loss, emotional instability, and lack of confidence—seem likely to increase aggression. As a matter of fact, many of these patterns seem more likely to discourage aggression.

Baumeister's research brings him to a counterintuitive conclusion. "Violent acts," he writes, "follow from high self-esteem, not from low self-esteem. This is true across a broad spectrum of violence, from playground bullying to national tyranny, from domestic abuse to genocide, from warfare to murder and rape. Perpetrators of violence are typically people who think very highly of themselves."[26] In other words, perpetrators of violence do not lack for self-esteem; if anything, they have too much self-esteem (though this may be compensatory rather than genuine). He also cautions, however, that implicating high self-esteem as an inevitable, unrelenting cause of aggression is too simple. High self-esteem is characteristic both of highly aggressive individuals and of exceptionally nonaggressive ones, and as a result of this heterogeneity, high self-esteem offers no more predictive value for aggression than does low self-esteem.

In the place of self-esteem, Baumeister suggests that the link between self-regard and aggression is best captured by his theory of *threatened egotism*. Egotism simply means thinking well of yourself, regardless of whether those thoughts are justified or not. How do we defend a highly favorable view of self against someone who seeks to undermine or discredit that view? One option is to lower how we think of ourselves. The more common option, Baumeister maintains, is to defend our ego by responding aggressively against the specific threat. While it may be true that aggressive, violent people hold highly favorable opinions of themselves, it also seems true that they behave aggressively only when these favorable opinions are disputed or questioned by other people—in short, when their ego is threatened.

Baumeister goes on to argue that narcissism—grandiose views of personal superiority, an inflated sense of entitlement, low empathy toward others, fantasies of personal greatness, and so on—is the specific form of self-regard most closely associated with violence. Narcissists have high ego needs. They are heavily invested in their high opinion of themselves and are equally, if not more, invested in wanting others to share and confirm this opinion. In defense of their self-view, Baumeister contends, narcissists will behave aggressively against the specific people who undermine their flattering self-portrait.

Baumeister even maintains that threatened egotism is operative at a group level. "When large groups of people differ in self-esteem," he writes, "the group with the higher self-esteem is generally the more violent one."[27] He argues that threatened collective egotism may lie at the heart of extreme nationalism (that is, a belief in the superiority of one's nation over others). Baumeister also notes that nationalism is positively correlated with individual aggressive tendencies. He concludes, "Feelings of collective superiority are linked to violent, militaristic inclinations, ranging from personal conflicts to nuclear war."[28]

Staub's analysis of four genocides repeatedly refers to the perpetrators' sense of being superior and being better, a sense that is often aggravated by threatening conditions. In each of the four cases, the genocides were perpetrated by nationalities and regimes that believed strongly in their own innate superiority but that had suffered some threat to their sense of superiority. For instance, Staub points out that Germans had an extremely positive view of themselves. The ideas of Germanness and German *Kultur* (literary, musical, artistic achievements) carried with them a romanticized sense of pride, satisfaction, and superiority. The Nazis were able to build on this sense of superiority, especially the mystical idea of a *Volk*, or special people, to rally the German populace in the face of the "threat" posed by enemies.

In sum, self-esteem is not an independent and direct cause of violence. Rather, the major cause of violence is high self-esteem combined with an ego threat. "When favorable views about oneself," Baumeister writes, "are questioned, contradicted, impugned, mocked, challenged, or otherwise put in jeopardy, people may aggress. In particular, they will aggress against the source of the threat."[29] Returning to Browder's concept of ego-organizational links, perpetrators could fulfill their narcissistic needs by joining an organization that promoted those needs. Committing extraordinary evil against a perceived ego threat achieves a symbolic dominance over that threat and affirms one's esteem to the extent of being superior to the victim. Genocides are replete with the rhetoric of threat. Extraordinary evil often is upheld as a response to impure, evil, decadent threats against the superiority of a "master race." In addition, extraordinary evil often is a means of satisfying the wish to blame one's ego-threatening misfortunes on a scapegoat who could then be punished.

We intuitively understand how our internal ego needs govern our external behaviors and roles in a given organization. It makes sense that people join an organization because it is consistent with the needs they are looking to fulfill. Some dedicated and enthusiastic perpetrators actually value evildoing. These persons, living manifestations of our darkest nightmares, freely select participation in situations or organizations that give vent to their evildoing dispositions. As we have seen, however, most perpetrators are less fully committed and require a less "demonized" analysis of their evildoing. Many perpetrators initially engage in evildoing for reasons completely unrelated to their attitudes or beliefs. As we will see in chapter 7, ego-organizational linkages also help us understand how evildoing organizations *shape* the ego needs of perpetrators who may be less committed.

In summary, an identity fulfilled or shaped by affiliation with an organization may, in Browder's words, "retard or reinforce the mechanisms for authorization, bolstering, routinization, and dehumanization."[30] He maintains that ego-organizational linkages provide the best hope of explaining how mature, strong personalities could have involved themselves in extraordinary evil. If membership in a military or paramilitary organization furthered their ego needs, then their ego-organizational links could become extremely powerful. These linkages could become powerful enough, in fact, to account for the unwillingness to risk any loss of their identity by withdrawing from the organization. The power of the ego-organizational links did not only lie in the power perpetrators had over their victims. It also was found in the perpetrators' perceived access to power above them and the hope of actively shaping their society through that access to power. In short, individual differences in linkages between one's ego and the organization to which one belongs are relevant to understanding how susceptible one is when called to obey.

Evelin Gerda Lindner even suggests that perpetrators' ego investment was so intense that—after the fact—they are best understood as humiliated victims of seduction and abandonment by despotic dictators.[31] Lindner's seduction theory certainly understates the moral responsibility required of perpetrators even as it overstates the persuasive appeal of dictators. It does, however, remind us that ego investment in a military or paramilitary organization is an important part of understanding how ordinary people come to commit extraordinary evil.

Conclusion

We began this chapter by emphasizing the importance of an interactional approach in which we look at both the person and the situation. While it is not always easy to cleanly distinguish between the two, this chapter focused on three dispositional influences relevant to understanding how ordinary people commit extraordinary evil: (1) *cultural belief systems* about external, controlling influences on one's life, authority orientation, and ideological commitment; (2) *moral disengagement* (moral justification, euphemistic labeling of evil action, and exonerating comparisons); and (3) *rational self-interest* (professional and personal).

We must recognize that these dispositional influences are by no means confined to extraordinary circumstances. From early on in our lives, these influences operate in everyday situations in which we routinely do things that bring us gains at the sake of costs to others. For instance, Craig Haney, a psychologist at the University of California, Santa Cruz, has even applied the mechanisms of moral disengagement to understand how normal, law-abiding citizens can condemn their fellow citizens to death in a capital punishment case.[32]

We must also recognize, again, that these dispositional influences do not occur in a vacuum. Their influence must be considered *relative* to the power of situational influences. In chapter 7, we will turn to the situational influences that interact with these dispositional influences to give us a fuller understanding of extraordinary evil.

Death of a Guatemalan Village

THE INDIGENOUS PEOPLES OF Guatemala, a country no larger than Ohio, are descendants of the Mayan civilizations that sought to re-establish their identities and land claims after the collapse of the Mayan empire and before the arrival of the Spaniards. Their Mayan ancestors had the glory of great social and political organizations, military strength, and extraordinary technical achievements. They were a culture of uncommon accomplishments, especially in agriculture, textiles, and medical practices. Today, however, the lives of the approximately 10 million Mayan inhabitants in Guatemala—representing more than half of Guatemala's total population—are a far cry from those of their ancestors. The political, social, and economic persecution of indigenous peoples in Guatemala is unparalleled in the contemporary world.

Over 60 percent of the Guatemalan population lives in dispersed rural communities of less than 2,000 people. Health and educational services are scarce to nonexistent in most of those communities. All told, 45 percent of the population lack minimal health services and the mortality rate for children under age five was 67 per 1,000 live births in 1995—one of the highest such rates in the industrialized world. Only about 48 percent of the adult Guatemalan population can read, and in the rural areas, illiteracy rises to 72 percent. Approximately 65 percent of the arable land in the country is held by 2 percent of the population. The inequity in land ownership at least partially corresponds with the fact that 36 percent of the urban population and 71 percent of the rural population live in extreme poverty.

Such deprivations have fueled periodic rebellions and, most recently, an armed insurgency that ran from 1960 through the end of 1996. In that thirty-six-year period of internal conflict, more than 440 rural villages were razed, more than 40,000 people "disappeared," and between 150,000 and 200,000 Guatemalans were killed. These actions resulted in more than 200,000 orphans, 80,000 widows, and the internal displacement of nearly

1 million people and the fleeing of several hundred thousand others to other countries. Various international human rights organizations estimate that between 100,000 and 140,000 of the dead, most residing in small countryside villages, were the victims of extrajudicial killings, large-scale massacres, and, ultimately, genocide perpetrated by Guatemalan government death squads in the 1980s and early 1990s.[1]

Efrain Rios Montt, a former army general who assumed power of the Guatemalan government in a March 1982 coup d'état, led many of the military counterinsurgency efforts aimed at leftist guerrillas. Under his direction, government soldiers and paramilitary patrols engaged in scorched-earth campaigns in which hundreds of Mayan villages were destroyed, thousands of people killed, and hundreds more driven from their homes and into exile. The Guatemalan army considered Mayans subversives, and considered subversives guerrillas; it drew no distinction between civilians and combatants. Justifying his atrocities, Montt was famously quoted as saying: "We do not have a policy of scorched earth. We have a policy of scorched Communists."[2]

Victor Montejo was a primary school teacher in a remote Guatemalan village. On September 9, 1982, the civil patrol of his village (civilians appointed by a military commander to "defend themselves against subversion") mistook an army detachment dressed in olive fatigues for leftist guerrillas and mobilized for defense. Partially in reprisal, but primarily to fulfill their "objective," the army detachment carried out a series of extrajudicial killings of alleged leftist sympathizers, including Montejo's brother, and unleashed a wave of violence and terror that decimated the village. The following is excerpted from Montejo's account of the night of his capture.

> It was two A.M. when I checked my watch again. Most of the soldiers were asleep, and the few standing guard in the patio and corridor laughed and cursed in shrill voices that failed to perturb the placid sleep of their fellows, who lay inert on their bunkbeds with their Galil rifles by their sides. . . .
>
> [They] lifted me by the arms, then dragged me outside, past the pillar I had been tied to and across the patio to the rim of a foul cesspool filled with mud, water and garbage. As they held me at the rim I heard a muffled cry rise from the depths and a head broke the surface, struggling to free itself from that horrible captivity. . . . "T-t-take me out or shoot me, but don't leave me in here," he wailed pitifully. One of the soldiers leaned over the rim the man was clinging to and hit him in the face with his rifle butt, sinking him once again into the dark murky waters of the pit. "Shut up, turd . . ."
>
> All at once a piercing scream tore through my thoughts and caused my heart

to pound violently; it was like a howl from the world beyond. The soldiers had become so inured to these hair-raising screams, not one of them stirred in his bunk. They all kept on snoring, impervious to what was happening in the adjoining torture chamber. . . . I shuddered to think of the fate of that luckless man after they finished with him. First they cut out one eye, then the other. Then the nose, lips, the tongue, ears and testicles, and at last they slice off his head. It is a slow, excruciating death, conceived to make a human being die in the greatest possible pain. . . .

The screams of that night have become forever engraved in my memory. I thought disconsolately on all the horrendous crimes that have been committed since the army set up base in our town.

The incinerated corpses of the victims are thrown into a pit the military dug on the edge of a nearby ravine. "Forbidden Zone—No Trespassing," read the signs they put up, to prevent people from stumbling on the clandestine cemetery that has grown day by day in our community. . . .

For those who have to die, it is far better to be shot attempting to escape than to be killed slowly, staring up at your executioners' faces as they cut you open.

Fernando, a poor neighbor of ours and father of six children, was cruelly tortured and then decapitated. They removed his teeth one by one and forced him to swallow them, like hard pellets. They cut off his tongue, pierced his eyes. Yet he died bravely, like a man. . . .

Why was it, I repeatedly asked myself, that the soldiers harbor so much hatred in their hearts and behave so drastically toward their own people, while obeying the criminal orders of their superiors? Most of these men who kill and maim come from the same remote villages and belong to the same wretchedly poor families as do the condemned ones with whose blood they have stained their hands.

A friend who is an ex-soldier had told me one afternoon, not long before: "They brainwash and indoctrinate us in such a way that we could torture our own parents, if we were ordered to. I spend three years in the barracks, and what did I learn? Fucking zero. The only thing you are taught is to kill and kill, again and again."[3]

Victor Montejo survived that dark night of terror and eventually was reunited with his wife and children. After later learning that his name was on a death list, Montejo fled with his family to America. Today, Montejo is an assistant professor of Native American studies at the University of California, Davis. He remains active in issues of human rights and the resettlement of Guatemalan Mayan peoples.

On December 29, 1996, a peace accord was signed between the leftist rebels and the government. The agreement included economic and agrarian re-

Indigenous men and women of Mayan descent from the Guatemalan province of Quiche march to downtown Guatemala City on February 25, 1999, where Guatemala's "Truth Commission" was due to present its 3,600-page report, titled *Guatemala: Memory of Silence*, to UN officials. The report concluded that 83 percent of the more than 200,000 people who died during the country's thirty-six-year civil war were Mayans and that over one hundred massacres took place in the Quiche province alone. Photo by AFP/CORBIS.

forms, the protection of human rights, and the establishment of a commission to investigate war crimes. A National Reconciliation Law was ratified and took effect in December 1996 that protected rebels from arrest. At the same time, the Guatemalan government issued a blanket amnesty for those involved in many atrocities—with the supposed exclusion of torture, genocide, and forced disappearance.

In February 1999, Guatemala's Commission for Historical Clarification, also know as the "Truth Commission," concluded that more than 200,000 Guatemalan civilians were killed over a period of some thirty-six years. More than 90 percent of the 42,000 human rights violations examined by the Truth Commission were attributed to the U.S.-backed Guatemalan government or its paramilitary supporters. Moreover, the Truth Commission's 3,600-page report asserted that some of the state's counterinsurgency operations could be correctly deemed genocidal in intent.

In 1999, Rigoberta Menchu, a Mayan Quiche Indian and winner of the 1992 Nobel Peace Prize, filed genocide charges with Spain's National Court against Rios Montt and his predecessor, ex-president Romeo Lucas Garcia, and six other military figures. The court rejected the case, ruling that Menchu had made no effort to prosecute the accused first in Guatemala. In June 2001, judges in Guatemala City finally ordered an investigation of Montt and Garcia in response to criminal complaints filed by human rights groups. This marked the first time Guatemalan courts have agreed to investigate former dictators for atrocities committed during the thirty-six years of civil war.

As of this writing, most international observers believe there are still signs that the Guatemalan military wields significant and abusive power in the country. The impunity that continues to cover human rights and other crimes, an increase in human rights violations and death threats apparently related to judicial proceedings against human rights violators, and recent rumblings of military power struggles within the new administration of President Alfonso Portillo have renewed questions about the military's commitment to civilian rule. Terrorist actions and extrajudicial killings, some by paramilitary forces with historical ties to the government, are still being reported in various areas of Guatemala.[4]

7

What Is the Immediate
Social Context?

A Culture of Cruelty

There must be a moment at the beginning,
where we all could have said no.
But somehow we missed it.

Tom Stoppard, *Rosencrantz and*
Guildenstern Are Dead

A S I POINTED OUT IN CHAPTER 6, mainstream social psychology
has long believed that what really matters is not who you are, but
where you are. Decades of research have hammered home the power of the
situation in influencing our thoughts, feelings, and behaviors. Generally,
social psychologists believe that personality variables have little predictive
utility because they depend on forecasts of future actions based on past reactions in *similar* situations—but rarely based on the *exact* situation currently being encountered. Thus, predictions based mainly on personality
variables often misinterpret or underestimate the dominating and pervasive
impact of the immediate social context.

In trying to understand the causes of complex human behavior, most
social psychologists start with a situational analysis and yield to the dispositional only when the situational fails to offer a satisfactory explanation.
We operate with the beliefs that dispositional variables only explain a small
portion of the variance in social behavior and that the greatest insights will
come from an analysis of the immediate social context. This directly counters the predominant view—inherent in much of psychology, psychiatry,
religion, and the law—that behavior is primarily under the influence of
dispositional factors.

A situationist perspective is *not* an unconscious, unstated, hush-hush
presupposition of social psychology. It is fundamental to what we do and

how we do it, and generations of social psychologists have not been shy at all in advocating a situationist perspective. Consider the words of Stanford social psychologist Philip Zimbardo: "Individual behavior is largely under the control of social forces and environmental contingencies rather than personality traits, character, will power or other empirically unvalidated constructs."[1] Likewise, Stanley Milgram:

> Many people, not knowing much about the experiment [obedience to authority], claim that subjects who go to the end of the board are sadistic. Nothing could be more foolish than an overall characterization of these persons. It is like saying that a person thrown into a swift-flowing stream is necessarily a fast swimmer, or that he has great stamina because he moves so rapidly relative to the bank. The context of action must always be considered. The individual, upon entering the laboratory, becomes integrated into a situation that carries its own momentum.[2]

So how does a situationist perspective inform our understanding of extraordinary evil? The immediate social context of extraordinary evil is a culture of cruelty (by "culture," I am not referring to the macro level of societies but rather to the micro level of groups within societies). Sociologist Fred Katz describes a culture of cruelty as

> systematically organized to reward individuals for their acts of cruelty: for being creative at inventing cruelties and for establishing a personal reputation for their particular version of cruelty. Here cruelty can be a macabre art form: one's creativity at inventing new forms of cruelty is socially recognized and rewarded. Here, too, cruelty can be a distinctive "economy," where one's credit rating depends on one's level of cruelty—the more cruel, the higher one's standing. By contrast, acts of kindness can lead to publicly declared bankruptcy, and in some situations the punishment for this bankruptcy is a death sentence.[3]

Perpetrators create, and are created by, a culture of cruelty that helps them initiate, sustain, and cope with their extraordinary evil. Such a culture makes each perpetrator believe that all men are capable of doing what he does. It is an inverted moral universe, shaped by a process of brutalization, in which right has become wrong; healing has become killing; and life has become death. This chapter will focus on three momentum-inducing features of a culture of cruelty that are most relevant to understanding how ordinary people commit extraordinary evil—professional socialization, binding factors of the group, and the merger of role and person (see figure 4).

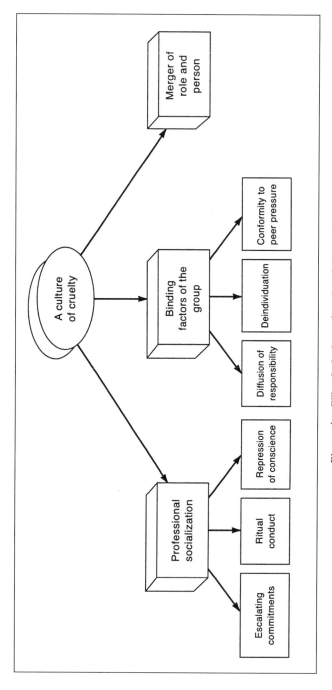

Figure 4. What Is the Immediate Social Context?

Professional Socialization

Most people take military and paramilitary organizations, at least on the face of it, to be legitimate. This legitimacy is conferred and reinforced by a process of *professional socialization* into the organization. Newcomers are typically in the position of not knowing their way around. It is natural for newcomers to seek information from others to learn which behaviors are acceptable or not acceptable in the organization. In this sense, even extraordinarily evil behavior can be socialized—particularly during a period in which recruits are brought to full commitment—as the professionally acceptable norm to newcomers. Specifically, three mechanisms, often institutionalized in military or paramilitary organizations, serve to socialize perpetrators into a culture of cruelty—(1) escalating commitments, (2) ritual conduct, and (3) repression of conscience.

1. Escalating Commitments

The road to extraordinary evil often takes the form of a sequence of seemingly small, innocuous incremental steps—a series of *escalating commitments*. In contemporary social psychology, the process of engaging in escalating commitments has been conceptualized as the foot-in-the-door phenomenon. The foot-in-the-door phenomenon refers to the tendency for people who have first agreed to a small request to comply later with a larger request. Considerable research has demonstrated that people are more likely to donate time, money, blood, and the use of their home and other resources once they have been induced to go along with a small initial request.[4]

In these studies, the initial compliance is always voluntary, never coerced by threat or bribe, yet creates a mounting momentum of compliance. As a consequence, later behaviors may be shaped by gradually escalating commitments. One of the most striking aspects about the foot-in-the-door phenomenon is its generality. Agreement with an initial request breeds compliance with a larger request, even when the second request concerns a different topic than the first, the requests come from different people, and the time between the requests is varied.

The empirical and theoretical literature on escalating commitments makes it clear that an initial, relatively inconsequential, evil act can make later evildoing easier. Once one has taken the initial step, one is in a new psychological and social context in which the pressures to continue are quite powerful. Ervin Staub describes the importance of escalating commitments in joining a system or movement: "Small, seemingly insignificant acts can involve a person with a destructive system: for example, accepting benefits provided by the system or even using a required greeting, such as 'Heil Hitler.'"[5] Robert Jay Lifton even allows for "the slow emergence of a functional 'Nazi self' via a series of destructive actions, at first agreed to grudgingly, followed by a sequence of assigned tasks each more incriminating, if not more murderous, than the previous ones."[6] Princeton social psychologist John Darley summarizes the role of escalating commitments in evildoing as follows: "The essence of the process involves causing individuals, under pressure, to take small steps along a continuum that ends with evildoing. Each step is so small as to be essentially continuous with previous ones; after each step, the individual is positioned to take the next one. The individual's morality follows rather than leads."[7]

From 1967 through 1974, the process of escalating commitments was used by the military regime then in power in Greece to train torturers. In a systematic process of escalating commitments, recruits underwent physically brutal initiation rites. At the same time as they were cursed, punched, kicked, and flogged, they were told how fortunate they were to be invited into such an elite organization. They were subjected to torture themselves (as if it were a normal act), then assigned to guard prisoners, then to participate in arresting squads, then ordered to hit prisoners, then to observe torture, and, finally, to practice torture in group beatings and a variety of other brutal methods. Once the training was complete, a carrot-and-stick strategy of special benefits coupled with threats and punishment for disobedience kept the perpetrators committed to their tasks.

It is important to note that the researchers—Janice Gibson and Mika Haritos-Fatouros—found no evidence of sadistic, abusive, or authoritarian behavior in the Greek soldiers' histories prior to their training. There was nothing in their family or personal histories to differentiate them from the rest of the nation's male population of their age at that time. In their training as torturers, the process of escalating commitments was used to fundamentally alter who they were.[8]

Perpetrator testimony in a wide range of mass killing and genocide is replete with examples of escalating commitments. These commitments took perpetrators to acts of atrocities that they hardly anticipated when they joined the ranks of the military or paramilitary organizations to which they belonged. For many who had voluntarily began these commitments, it became exceedingly difficult—though by no means impossible—to extricate themselves from the escalating series of more severe commitments that culminated in the perpetration of extraordinary evil.

2. Ritual Conduct

A significant aspect of professional socialization into a culture of cruelty is what anthropologists have identified as *ritual conduct*. Ritual conduct refers to behaviors that are apparently excessive or unproductive but which nonetheless are persistent. In other words, ritual conduct is persistent indulgence in apparently noninstrumental exercises—exercises that consume radically limited energies and resources not only of the victims but also of the perpetrators themselves. As Inga Clendinnen points out, ritual conduct is based on an established script that is "the heart-made creation of whatever group it is we are trying to understand."[9] Such behaviors, however theatrical they may seem to outsiders, carry significant meaning and rewards for those who perform them in a culture of cruelty. In short, they are rituals—often repeatable, choreographed experiences—enacted for the psychological benefit of the perpetrators rather than as instrumental exercises in discipline. In Nazi concentration and death camps, for instance, ritual conduct included the roll calls, camp parades, meaningless physical exercises, and the stripping and beating of victims already marked for death.

How did ritual conduct benefit Nazi perpetrators? Clendinnen suggests that "the rounds of disciplinary procedures so ardently enforced by the Auschwitz SS not only met cultural criteria of discipline and punishment, but were also consciously theatrical, and that these pieces of SS theatre, constructed and enacted daily, reanimated the SS sense of high purpose and invincibility, authenticated the realism of their absurd ideology, and sustained both morale and self-image in what was, indubitably but inadmissibly, psychologically a hardship post."[10] In so doing, ritual conduct enabled the perpetrators to carry out their acts of extraordinary evil. For instance, when journalist Gitta Sereny asked Franz Stangl, commandant of Treblinka, why the killing of Jews was organized so as to achieve the maximum humiliation of the victims, he replied, "To condition those who actually had to carry out the policies. To make it possible for them to do what they did."[11]

At times, ritual conduct takes on the face of macho competition among comrades. Historian David Stannard, for instance, recounts the story told by a cavalry major who was reporting to Congress on the Indian wars in

Colorado in 1864. One morning, soldiers attacked an Indian village mostly comprising old folks, women, and children. The officer recalled seeing a particular child, "about three years old, just big enough to walk through the sand," running along after some of the Indians who were fleeing the attack. The major watched one cavalryman get down off his horse, aim his rifle, and shoot. He missed the child, who was now toddling along the sand about seventy-five yards away. Another cavalryman rode up and said, "Let me try the son of a bitch; I can hit him." He dismounted and fired from a kneeling position. He too missed the child. A third man came up and boasted that he could be more accurate. He took careful aim and fired, "and the little fellow dropped."[12]

In short, ritual conduct, whether officially structured or informally spontaneous, reinforces a culture of cruelty that helps perpetrators initiate, sustain, and cope with their extraordinary evil.

3. Repression of Conscience

Finally, professional socialization into a culture of cruelty, fostered by escalating commitments and reinforced by ritual conduct, carries with it a *repression of conscience* where "outside" values are excluded and locally generated values dominate. Raul Hilberg argues that the repression used by Holocaust perpetrators, for instance, proceeded through five stages. The first stage was to shut off the supply of information from all those who did not have to know it. Whoever did not participate in the culture of cruelty was not supposed to know. The second stage was to make sure that whoever knew would participate. This ensured that no one was free to talk and accuse because he was not himself involved. The third stage in the process of repression was the prohibition of criticism—particularly criticism aimed directly at the destruction process itself. In its fourth stage, repression removed the destruction process as a subject of social conversation. In Hilberg's words, "There are some things that can be done only so long as they are not discussed, for once they are discussed they can no longer be done."[13] Finally, the fifth stage of the repression process was to omit mention of "killings" or "killing installations" even in the secret correspondence in which such operations had to be reported. This was accomplished through the use of euphemisms and a camouflage vocabulary (see chapter 6).

Though continuous, the process of repression is never absolute. Extraordinary evil can never be hidden completely—either from the world or from oneself. Regardless, the *attempt* at repression that is encouraged by professional socialization into a culture of cruelty does serve a self-protective function. This is illustrated in the testimony of Theodore Nyilinkwaya, a survivor of the Rwandan genocide: "Everyone was called to hunt the enemy. But let's say someone is reluctant. Say that guy comes with a stick. They tell him, 'No, get a *masu* [a club studded with nails].' So, OK, he does, and he runs along with the rest, but he doesn't kill. They say, 'Hey, he might denounce us later. He must kill. Everyone must help to kill at least one person.' So this person who is not a killer is made to do it. And the next day it's become a game for him. You don't need to keep pushing him."[14]

As this testimony reveals, the repression of conscience had a progressively desensitizing effect on the perpetrators. It is clear that perpetrators can become accustomed to their shocking atrocities and cease to react strongly to them. As our psychological system grows used to events that initially produced a strong reaction, extraordinary evil becomes habitual and routinized. The fiftieth time we kill is certainly easier than the first time. Christopher Browning writes of this in his analysis of Reserve Police Battalion 101: "Once the killing began, however, the men became increasingly brutalized. As in combat, the horrors of the initial encounter eventually became routine, and the killing became progressively easier. In this sense, brutalization was not the cause but the effect of these men's behavior."[15] This meshes with the views of a number of scholars who maintain that many perpetrators often experienced severe initial distress in carrying out their atrocities, only to become increasingly desensitized to those atrocities over time. It is worth recalling the extreme distress that Milgram's subjects evidenced in the obedience to authority experiments (see chapter 4) and theorizing that these reactions would likewise have eventually faded into an ordinary routine over the course of sustained involvement.

All available evidence certainly points to the fact that, though the atrocities were initially shocking, extraordinarily evil actions quickly become routinized and habitual for all but the most sensitive of perpetrators. One of the Nazi doctors interviewed by Lifton, for instance, said: *"In the beginning it was almost impossible. Afterward it became almost routine. That's the only way to put it* [italics in original]." Similarly, Johann Paul Kremer was an SS physician who was assigned to Auschwitz for about three months and kept a detailed diary covering his service there. His first two diary entries speak of "the most horrible of horrors," a mass execution by gassing, in which he was forced to participate. "By comparison," he wrote, "Dante's *Inferno* seems almost a comedy." Astoundingly, throughout the remainder of his diary, Kremer never again comments on his sense of horror or revulsion about his continuing involvement in such atrocities—even while he goes on at length about the most mundane details of camp life. Kremer's desensitization to evil was nearly immediate and certainly pervasive.[16]

For those to whom desensitization did not come as quickly and as easily, alcohol played a ready substitute. Scores of records of Nazi perpetrators reveal that they often committed their extraordinary evil drunk or got drunk immediately after it. Some of the physicians interviewed by Lifton cited heavy alcohol use as an occupational hazard of their work—as if it were unthinkable that one might remain sober in committing extraordinary evil. In his autobiography, Rudolf Hess reported what he had heard from Eichmann's descriptions: "Many members of the Einsatzkommandos, unable to endure wading through blood any longer, had committed suicide. Some had even gone mad. Most of the members of these Kommandos had to rely on alcohol when carrying out their horrible work."[17] Alcohol facilitates desensitization by deflecting thinking away from the self so that one does not have to dwell on issues of personal identity and individual responsibility.

Most problematic is the fact that desensitization to violence gradually extinguishes inhibitions among many perpetrators, blunting their sensitivity to the suffering of their victims. In this way, desensitization offers an explanation for the cruelty, sadism, and zest that pepper many accounts of perpetrator behavior. Brutality comes to be considered an accomplishment, a mark of distinction, in a process of brutalization that has left its participants habituated and desensitized to the extraordinary evil they commit. Once habituated to extraordinary evil, the prevailing mind-set becomes how to do it better, not whether to do it at all. Desensitization makes it possible for perpetrators to act, on their own initiative, with greater brutality than their orders call for.

It is through desensitization that ordinary people commit extraordinary evil in excess. In Auschwitz, for instance, the supervisor of the large crematoria would place four persons in a row, one behind another, at the edge of a burning pit and then shoot all four with a single bullet. Whoever tried to escape this form of death was thrown alive into the fire. This same man also hung a prisoner by his arms and shot repeatedly at the man's arms until they ripped apart. After that, he repeated the same procedure, hanging the man by his legs. In the Warsaw ghetto, the company captain openly encouraged shooting at the ghetto wall. A mark was made on the bar door for each Jew shot, and "victory celebrations" were reportedly held on days whenever a high score was reached.

American cavalrymen in nineteenth-century genocidal campaigns against Native Americans showed similarly brutal effects of desensitization. One report from the massacre at Sand Creek included the following:

> The squaws offered no resistance. Every one I saw dead was scalped. I saw one squaw cut open with an unborn child . . . lying by her side. . . . I saw the body of White Antelope [the oldest of the chiefs] with the privates cut off, and I heard a soldier say he was going to make a tobacco pouch out of them. I saw one squaw whose privates had been cut out. . . . I saw a little girl about five years of age who had been hid in the sand; two soldiers discovered her, drew their pistols and shot her, and they pulled her out of the sand by the arm. I saw quite a number of infants in arms killed with their mothers.[18]

Extreme desensitization even leads to perpetrators' perverse enjoyment of, and sadistic pleasure in, their excesses of extraordinary evil. In December 1937, the Japanese army swept into the ancient city of Nanking, then the capital of China, and systematically raped, tortured, and murdered more than 300,000 Chinese civilians. In *The Rape of Nanking*, Iris Chang claims that according to eyewitness reports, some of the Japanese perpetrators showed clear evidence of enjoying the grisly excesses of their work —killing contests, torture, and rape.[19] Honda Katsuichi, a Japanese investigative journalist, has supported Chang's claim in a more recent publication.[20] Paul van Vuuren, a security policemen during the 1980s under South Africa's apartheid regime, chillingly admits of his extraordinarily evil excesses: "It was exciting days, those years. At times I could not wait to do it. They say to kill is like sleeping with a woman. It's true."[21]

Staub relates a telling testimony of a U.S. veteran recalling his initiation as a skyborne killer in Vietnam, flouting the Geneva conventions of war: "Flying over a group of civilians in a helicopter, he was ordered to fire at them, an order he did not obey. The helicopter circled over the area and again he was ordered to fire, which again he did not do. The officer in charge then threatened him with court-martial, which led him to fire the next time around. He vomited, felt profoundly distressed. The veteran reported that in a fairly short time firing at civilians became like an experience at a target-shooting gallery, and he began to enjoy it."[22]

While such accounts do not prove that the act of killing itself is pleasant, they do certainly reveal the shockingly callous attitude toward extraordinary evil that can be fostered by professional socialization—including escalating commitments, ritual conduct, and repression of conscience—into a culture of cruelty.

Binding Factors of the Group

In analyzing his experiments on obedience to authority, Milgram emphasized the importance of binding factors, or cementing mechanisms, that endow a hierarchy of authority with at least minimal stability. Such binding factors constitute the social authority of a group and hold the individual tightly to a rigid definition of the situation, closing off the freedom of movement to focus on features of the situation other than its authority structure. In short, *binding factors of the group* refers to the pressures—the group dynamics—that work to keep people within an evildoing organization or hierarchy. Through these binding factors, the agentive role in extraordinary evil is obscured and minimized. Specifically, three mechanisms, often institutionalized in military or paramilitary organizations, serve to help perpetrators disregard or distort the effects of their acts of extraordinary evil: (1) diffusion of responsibility, (2) deindividuation, and (3) conformity to peer pressure.

1. Diffusion of Responsibility

On March 15, 1921, Soghomon Tehlirian, a young Armenian refugee who had seen his family murdered and his town destroyed, assassinated Talaat Pasha, one of the architects of the Armenian genocide. Tehlirian was put on trial, only to be acquitted when the jury heard the anguished testimony of several eyewitnesses. One of the eyewitnesses testified: "I asked the captain [of the local police] if he had any regrets. I asked him whether or not he felt responsible to answer to God, to mankind, and to what we call civilization. The captain replied that he felt no responsibility whatsoever. He was only obeying orders given to him from Constantinople. He indicated that he was only a captain and had been ordered to kill everyone because a 'Holy War' had been declared. When the massacre was over with, he told me he said a prayer and absolved his soul."[23]

The captain's ability to sidestep his personal responsibility for his role in the atrocities is an example of *diffusion of responsibility*. When people act alone, it is obvious who made the decisions and who is to blame. In large and complex groups, however, responsibility can sometimes be divided up into such small parts and pieces that no one seems to be to blame even if there are extraordinarily evil results. Even when one person acts, they may regard their own actions as being done for the group, so that other members of the group share the responsibility.

The concept of diffusion of responsibility was first introduced in social psychology as an explanation for lack of bystander intervention in emergencies. The seminal work in this area by social psychologists John Darley and Bibb Latane was stirred by the murder of Kitty Genovese in Queens, New York, on March 13, 1964. For nearly forty-five minutes, Genovese was beaten, stabbed, and raped by an assailant. Two times the sound of bystanders' voices and the sudden glow of their bedroom lights interrupted the assailant and frightened him off. Each time, however, he returned to continue his assault. All told, no fewer than thirty-eight respectable, law-abiding citizens saw or heard what was going on, but no one came to Genovese's aid or even called the police. Only one witness called the police after the woman was dead.

Why such cold-hearted apathy? Darley and Latane proposed that the mere fact that there were so many observers made each of them feel that someone else would probably act—in other words, their individual responsibility was diffused among other members of the observing group. In a host of controlled laboratory studies, Darley and Latane found that lone bystanders would often come forward to help a victim, whereas bystanders who believed they were part of a large group would not. When more than one person can help in an emergency situation, we often assume that someone else *will* or *should* help—so we back off and avoid getting involved. In this case, there is danger, not safety, in numbers.[24]

The concept of diffusion of responsibility also can be applied to extraordinary evil. In an organization committed to the sanctioning of inhumanity, no one person feels the pressure to say that such actions are wrong. There is a routinization of bureaucratic subroutines in which responsibility for evil is divided among members of the group. The larger the group, the less responsible any individual person feels. This makes it possible for many perpetrators to claim a specious personal exception—"I, personally, did not kill anybody"—for their involvement in extraordinary evil.

In addition to group size, however, diffusion of responsibility also is accomplished by the segmentation and fragmentation of the killing tasks. Such division of labor, in addition to making the killing process more efficient and effective, allows perpetrators to reduce their identification with the consequences of their extraordinary evil. Once activities are routinized into detached subfunctions, perpetrators shift their attention from the morality of what they are doing to the operational details and efficiency of their specific job. They are then able to see themselves totally as performers of a role — as participants *in*, not originators *of*, evil. In short, it is easier for perpetrators to avoid the implications of their extraordinary evil since they are focusing on the *details* of their job rather than on its *meaning*.

In most mass killing and genocide, for example, care is taken to separate as widely as possible the architects of genocide from the people who actually carry out the murders. The existence of a massive bureaucratic organization, with thousands of people doing thousands of jobs, diminishes the responsibility of any one person. As Baumeister describes the Nazi killing system:

> The death of one person was the result of dozens of individual actions by different people, no one of whom felt anything more than a slight responsibility for the lethal outcome. Each person could say something like "I just drove the train, I didn't kill anybody." Even the one who did administer the poison gas knew it was hardly his fault. The people had been selected, brought here, stripped naked, and lined up in the bogus showers for death, without any doing of his. His own role was that of a technician, and his responsibility was a mere formality.[25]

Similarly, Darley writes:

> When death, like cars or chairs, is produced on assembly lines, each individual eventually concentrates on the microrequirements of his or her part in the process; the eventual outcome is rarely thought of. A group of police in a city round up the Jews and take them to a stadium. Later an army contingent takes them to the boxcars. A railroad worker throws the switches that bring the train to one or another subdestination on the way to the concentration camp. The fact of the eventual deaths is so remote that no participant finds it salient. Each person doing a subtask does so in a routinized way; it is only the final assembly of those subtasks that is horrible, and no individual "sees" that final solution.[26]

Lifton also points to the bureaucratic diffusion of responsibility in his analysis of Nazi doctors:

> The structure served to diffuse individual responsibility. In the entire sequence — from the reporting of cases by midwives or doctors, to the supervision of such reporting by institutional heads, to expert opinions rendered by central consultants, to coordination of the marked forms by Health Ministry officials, to the appearance of the child at the Reich Committee institution for killing — there was at no point a sense of personal responsibility for, or even involvement in, the murder

of another human being. Each participant could feel like no more than a small cog in a vast, officially sanctioned, medical machine.[27]

The bureaucratic division of labor also creates an ethos in which refusing to kill would only alienate — in a condemnatory fashion — one's friends and colleagues and, in the end, not deter in the least bit the killing operations. The bureaucracy and the killing continue unabated; the organization becomes impermeable to the wishes of the individuals within it. The diffusion of responsibility inherent in bureaucratic organizations built on a division of labor increases the confidence that the evil actions are good because surely an entire group could not be making a major moral blunder. In short, there is a depersonalized regression from individual morality to an organizational morass of nonresponsibility. (We also should note, however, that while routinization characterizes many cases of mass killing and genocide, it is not relevant to all. There was not, for instance, much routinization or segmentation of tasks in the ethnic cleansing perpetrated by the Bosnian Serbs or in the massacre of the Tutsis by the Hutu majority in Rwanda.)

Finally, a bureaucratic division of labor also leads to the displacement of responsibility. People will behave in ways they typically renounce if a legitimate authority accepts responsibility for the effects of their behavior. Under displaced responsibility, they view their actions as stemming from the dictates of authority. They do not feel personally responsible as the actual agent of their actions and, as a result, are spared overwhelming, self-condemning guilt. Even in cases where the hierarchy of authority does not explicitly convey the displacement of responsibility, professional socialization lays out the implicit framework by which perpetrators can sanction their evil behavior.

That said, we should note that if perpetrators displaced *all* responsibility for their evil behavior, they would perform their duties only when told to do so. The fact that many perpetrators work dutifully to be good at their evildoing suggests that not all perpetrators displace all of the responsibility for their extraordinarily evil behavior. Many of them retain enough responsibility to be "good" functionaries who are not simply mindless extensions of others higher on the organizational hierarchy. In this way, retaining guilt — rather than displacing it — is an endorsement of their essential goodness. It is precisely this emotion that makes them feel more "human" and enables them to return to ordinary society afterward. Guiltless killers are immoral. Paradoxically, perpetrators may maintain their ability to commit extraordinary evil by retaining some portion of moral responsibility—and corresponding guilt—for their atrocities.

2. Deindividuation

The segmented activities of bureaucratic organizations provide a cloak of deindividuation that facilitates the commission of extraordinary evil. *Deindividuation* is a social psychological concept introduced half a century ago. It refers to a state of relative anonymity in which a person cannot be identified as a particular individual but only as a group member. The concept usually includes a decreased focus on personal identity, loss of contact with general social norms, and the submergence of the individual in situation-specific group norms. These are conditions that confer anonymity and increase the likelihood of extraordinary evil as people partially lose awareness of themselves as individuals and cease to evaluate their own actions thoughtfully. Such evil behavior is only antinormative in respect to general social norms; it may be fully normative in respect to situation-specific group norms.

In the social psychological literature, experiments have generally found that people show an increased tendency toward aggressive behavior in deindividuated conditions (though a few studies suggest that deindividuated acts can also be prosocial). A classic study conducted in the late 1960s by Zimbardo deindividuated college women by shrouding them in oversized lab coats and hoods and placing them in groups of four in a dark room. In contrast, other women were "individuated" by wearing large, prominent name tags with normal clothes and taking part in the experiment in a bright room. Zimbardo found that the deindividuated women delivered longer shocks than the individuated women when given an opportunity to aggress against a victim. Moreover, although individuated women administered fewer shocks to an undeserving victim than to a deserving victim, deindividuated women did not discriminate between the two types of victims.[28]

A real-world analogue to Zimbardo's deindividuation research came from the 1973 work of Robert I. Watson Jr., a Harvard anthropologist. Watson hypothesized that groups that changed their appearance before going to war (for example, painting their faces or bodies, wearing masks, cutting hair) would be more aggressive against their victims—more likely to kill, torture, or mutilate them—than would groups that did not change their appearance. The results of his extensive research clearly reveal that there is a significant relationship between the process of deindividuation and aggression in warfare. Of those cultures that were reported to go through some deindividuating process before entering into battle, 80 percent were coded as extremely aggressive in warfare. Of the thirteen cultures that killed, tortured, and mutilated their victims, 92 percent had previously changed their appearance.[29] In a similar vein, social psychologist Brian Mullen content-analyzed newspaper accounts of sixty lynchings committed in the United States between 1899 and 1946 and found that the more people there were in the mob, the greater the savagery and viciousness with which they killed their victims.[30]

Why are deindividuation and aggression so closely connected? The most common explanation is that a deindividuated individual is less aware of personal standards and less concerned with self-evaluation or evaluations by others than is an individual in a non-deindividuated state. In other words, the threshold for evil acts is lowered because sanctions—either imposed from within or without—cannot be easily implemented in such conditions. This loss of self-awareness may lead to a breakdown of such internalized controls as shame, guilt, or fear and result in increased levels of aggression—particularly in organizations devoted to the commission of extraordinary evil.

Deindividuation is especially relevant to episodes of mass killing and genocide where the perpetrators are members of a military or paramilitary organization, all dressed in similar uniforms and seldom personally identified. We should note, however, that organizational affiliations—though important—are not absolutely necessary for deindividuation to be an operative factor in the commission of extraordinary evil. Being submerged in a crowd, disguised or masked, or covered by darkness can confer deindividuation even on those who are not state functionaries acting under orders.

At times, deindividuation may not even be significantly operative in explaining the perpetration of extraordinary evil. In Bosnia and Rwanda, for instance, many of the atrocities were inflicted on neighbors by other neighbors, and even by one's own close relatives. In a recent provocative book, Jan T. Gross, professor of politics and European studies at New York University, chronicled the destruction of the Jewish community in Jedwabne, Poland. On July 10, 1941, 1,600 Jewish men, women, and children—all but seven of the town's Jews—were murdered. The prevailing historical belief had been that the massacre was carried out, or at least compelled, by the newly occupying German army. However, Gross meticulously pieces together eyewitness accounts and other evidence to show that

Jedwabne's Jews were beaten, drowned, gutted, and burned alive not by faceless, deindividuated Nazis but by neighbors whose features and names they knew well and with whom they had previously enjoyed neighborly and cordial relations. As Gross concludes: "In Jedwabne ordinary Poles slaughtered the Jews. . . . And what the Jews saw, to their horror and, I dare say, incomprehension, were familiar faces. Not anonymous men in uniform, cogs in a war machine, agents carrying out orders, but their own neighbors, who chose to kill and were engaged in a bloody pogrom—willing executioners."[31]

3. Conformity to Peer Pressure

Inherent in any group setting is an explicit or implicit dynamic of *conformity to peer pressure*. One form of conformity to peer pressure is what social psychologists call "normative social influence." Normative social influence is operative when we conform so that we will be liked and accepted by other people. Conformity for normative reasons occurs in those situations where we do what other people are doing because we do not want be ridiculed, punished, or rejected by our peers. In short, the influence of our peers leads us to conform in order to be liked and accepted by them—especially in groups that are highly cohesive.

Military science is replete with assertions that the cohesive bonds soldiers form with one another in military and paramilitary organizations are often stronger than the bonds they will form with anyone else at any other point in their lifetimes. Among people who are bonded together so intensely, there is a powerful dynamic of conformity to peer pressure—or "mutual surveillance"—in which the individual cares so deeply about his comrades and what they think of him that he would rather die than let them down.

Browning's analysis of Reserve Police Battalion 101 reveals the powerful dynamic of conformity to peer pressure. Recall that 80 to 90 percent of the men followed orders to kill Jews, though almost all of them—at least initially—were horrified and disgusted by what they were doing. To adopt overtly nonconformist behavior—to refuse to kill—was simply beyond most of the men. Why? Browning suggests that nonconforming ultimately meant refusing one's share of an unpleasant collective obligation. The battalion still had to kill even if some individuals chose not to. "Those who did not shoot," Browning writes, "risked isolation, rejection, and ostracism—a very uncomfortable prospect within the framework of a tight-knit unit stationed abroad among a hostile population, so that the individual had virtually nowhere else to turn for support and social contact."[32]

Moreover, acceptance by the group was so important that nonshooters went out of their way to make sure that their refusal was not seen as a form of moral reproach of their peers. Nonshooters pleaded not that they were "too moral" or "too good" but rather that they were "too weak" to kill. This preserved acceptance by the group not only by avoiding a challenge to the esteem of one's peers but also by legitimizing and affirming the killers' "toughness" and "courage" as a superior quality. In the end, though, the difference between being "weak" and being a "coward" was not great. Only the very exceptional nonshooter could remain indifferent to the persistent ridicule from his comrades and could live with the taunts of "weakling" and the fact that he was considered to be "no man" by his peers. While some still tried to find behaviors of compromise—bringing Jews to the shooting site but firing and intentionally missing—most nervous nonshooters eventually became practiced killers.

The following testimony from an SS-Scharführer (sergeant) and Kriminal-Assistant from the General-Gouvernement reveals the power of conformity to peer pressure in a highly cohesive group: "The reason I did not say to Leideritz that I could not take part in these things [mass executions] was that I was afraid that Leideritz and others would think I was a coward. I was worried that I would be affected adversely in some way in the future if I allowed myself to be seen as being too weak. I did not want Leideritz or other people to get the impression that I was not as hard as an SS-Mann ought to have been."[33]

Normative social influence (that is, other people as a source of acceptance) is complemented by a second form of conformity to peer pressure—"informational social influence" (that is, other people as a source of information). Conformity for informational reasons occurs in those situations where we do what other people are doing not simply because we want to be accepted by them but because we are using them as a source of information. Informational social influence is operative when we have a need to know what is "right" in a given social context. In many situations, we are initially uncertain about what to think or how to act. We simply do not know enough to make good or accurate choices. As a result of our uncertainty, we believe that others' interpretation of the situation is more correct than ours. Asking them what they think, or watching what they do, helps us more appropriately define the situation. By using others—especially those we perceive as experts—as a source of information, we are able to ascertain the norms that should guide our thoughts and behaviors.

This account of a new Aufseherin, a female guard at Ravensbruck, clearly illustrates informational social influence:

> The beginners usually appeared frightened upon first contact with the camp, and it took some time to attain the level of cruelty and debauchery of their seniors. Some of us made a rather grim little game of measuring the time it took for a new Aufseherin to win her stripes. One little Aufseherin, twenty years old, who was at first so ignorant of proper camp "manners" that she said "excuse me" when walking in front of a prisoner, needed exactly four days to adopt the requisite manner, although it was totally new for her. (This little one no doubt had some special gifts in the "arts" we are dealing with here.) As for the others, a week or two, a month at the most, was an average orientation period.[34]

In summary, conformity to peer pressure helps initiate and sustain perpetrators' involvement in extraordinary evil. It is difficult for anyone who is bonded by links of mutual affection and interdependence to break away and openly refuse to participation in what the group is doing, even if it is perpetrating extraordinary evil.

Merger of Role and Person

To this point, our emphasis on professional socialization and the binding factors of the group in a culture of cruelty may imply that, once removed from such a culture, perpetrators can cease to become evil people. In other words, the outcome of sustained socialization in a culture of cruelty is only a temporary one. But we should be careful about this assumption. Could it be that as we work our way into a culture of cruelty, the culture of cruelty also works its way into us?

Chapter 6 introduced the counterintuitive reality that ego-organization links work not only by our egos driving us to specific organizations but also the other way—organizations shaping the egos of the people who join them. That is, the process of brutalization can lead to a merger of role and person in which our external behaviors and roles can transform who we are—our attitudes, our perceptions of ourselves and of others, our ego needs, and so on. So here, rather than ego needs shaping behavior, we have a case where behaviors shape ego needs. Rather than joining an organization because it fulfills our needs, it is the organization itself that shapes our needs. This perspective tells us how evildoing organizations can change the people in them over time. A person may be quite ordinary in the beginning phase of a scenario of destructive obedience, only to ultimately become quite extraordinary as a consequence—not a cause—of participation in extraordinary evil.

Social psychology has clearly established the principle that one's external behaviors and roles can become internalized in one's psychological framework. In other words, when one performs the behaviors appropriate for a given role, there is a merger of role and person in which one often acquires the attitudes, beliefs, values, and morals consonant with that role and its behaviors. As we play the role assigned to us, our fundamental self can be altered. For example, professional actors and actresses often testify to becoming so absorbed in a role that it leads to fundamental internal alterations—sometimes rather troubling ones.

The classic social psychological experiment examining the influence of external behaviors and roles on internal psychological frameworks is the Stanford Prison Experiment (SPE) conducted by Zimbardo, Craig Haney, Curt Banks, Dave Jaffe, and Carlo Prescott in August 1971 (interestingly, Zimbardo attended James Monroe High School in the Bronx with Stanley Milgram in the late 1940s).[35] Recent prison uprisings—particularly the death of George Jackson at San Quentin and the deadly rebellion and retribution at Attica—had piqued Zimbardo's interest in what it means psychologically to be a prisoner or a prison guard. Why were prisoners so disposed toward violence? Why were prison guards so brutal? For many, the answers seemed obvious: Prisoners are violent because they are antisocial criminals who have little regard for other people. Guards are brutal because only brutal people want to become guards. Zimbardo and his colleagues, however, suspected that the immediate social context of prison life—its roles, rules, and norms—might transform the character of some of the people within it.

Under very realistic circumstances, twenty-one male undergraduates—each to be paid fifteen dollars a day—were randomly assigned to play the role of a prisoner or prison guard for a two-week study of prison life. Neither group was given any instructions on how to behave. Each of the subjects had been through an interview process after which they were selected as the most stable mentally and physically, the most mature, and the least likely to commit antisocial acts. In Haney's words, the selected subjects were "abnormally normal."[36] Random assignment, the sine qua non of experimental research, meant that, at the outset, the two groups should have been reasonably alike with respect to prior personality characteristics and experience with aggression.

On the first day of the simulation, ten of the students were "arrested" at their homes by real officers from the local police department on suspicion of burglary or armed robbery. At the mock prison in a basement corridor of the psychology building at Stanford, the prisoners were stripped, deloused, and given loose-fitting gowns with a number that appeared on the front and back of the gown. Guards, too, wore uniforms, along with dark, silver-reflecting sunglasses (adopted from the movie *Cool Hand Luke*), and carried billy clubs to reinforce their roles. In a general group orientation, guards were told that their job was to observe the behavior of the prisoners and maintain order—without inflicting physical punishment. For the prisoners, the simulation continued twenty-four hours a day, but the guards could return to their normal lives when their three-man, eight-hour shifts ended (though some volunteered to work overtime with no additional pay).

Several of the mock prisoners and guards very quickly started to act like their counterparts in the real world. Many of the prisoners became increasingly resigned, ineffectual, apathetic, submissive, and depressed. Three had to be released in the first four days because they had such acute situational traumatic reactions as hysterical crying, confusion in thinking, and severe depression. Another was released after he broke out in a full body rash following the rejection of his appeal for parole by a mock parole board. Just to get out of prison, all but three of the remaining prisoners were willing to forfeit all the money they had earned for participating. When told they had been "denied parole," however, the prisoners docilely returned to their cells.

Despite their knowledge that they might just as easily have been randomly assigned as prisoners, about a third of the eleven guards took on cruel, callous, sadistic, dominating, authoritarian, tyrannical, coercive, and aggressive roles. These guards became extremely hostile, arbitrary, and inventive in their forms of degradation and humiliation, and they appeared to thoroughly enjoy the power they wielded when they put on the guard uniform. "Most dramatic and distressing to us," Zimbardo continued, "was the observation of the ease with which sadistic behavior could be elicited in individuals who were not 'sadistic types.'"[37] This daily escalation of brutality, this moral drift, demoralized the mock prisoners to such an extent that the study—planned to last two weeks—was aborted after only six days.

The SPE demonstrated the evil that ordinary people can be readily induced into doing to other ordinary people within the context of socially approved roles, rules, and norms, a legitimizing ideology, and institutional support that transcends individual agency. It also demonstrated that the egregious brutality of some perpetrators does not automatically indicate an *inherent*, preexisting brutality; not everyone playing a brutal role has to have sadistic traits of character. Rather, brutality can be a consequence, not only a cause, of being in a duly certified and legitimized social hierarchy committed to extraordinary evil. In other words, the nature of the tasks of extraordinary evil may have been sufficient to produce that brutality even if the perpetrators were not initially sadists. It was a vicious social arrangement, and not the preexisting viciousness of the participants, that led to the cruel behaviors exhibited by the guards.

Zimbardo's research also reminds us that situations interact with dispositions to produce behavior. Not all of the guards in the Stanford prison experiment were equally aggressive. Two actually emerged as "good guards" and tried to help the prisoners when they could—though stopping far short of publicly resisting the aggressive guards. A middle group of guards were average, tough but fair, and did nothing excessively good or evil. Had the simulation continued, perhaps all would have eventually behaved aggressively. Regardless, even in a situation that called for a set of specific behaviors, individual dispositions played some role in determining how and whether an individual behaved aggressively. As a matter of fact, it was the subjects themselves who created the reality of their roles and therefore defined the power that the social context of the prison exerted over them.

How analogous is the behavior of Zimbardo's guards to perpetrators of mass killing and genocide? Browning notes that compared to his research (see chapter 3), "Zimbardo's spectrum of guard behavior bears an uncanny resemblance to the groupings that emerged within Reserve Police Battalion 101."[38] In Browning's sample, there was a nucleus of increasingly enthusiastic killers who volunteered for the firing squads and "Jew hunts." There was a larger group of policeman who performed as shooters and ghetto clearers when assigned but who did not actively seek out opportunities to kill. Some of this middle group even refrained from killing, contrary to standing orders, when no one was monitoring their actions. Finally, there was a small group (less than 20 percent) of outright refusers and evaders parallel to the "good guards" in the SPE.

At the beginning of the SPE, there were no differences between those randomly assigned to guard and prisoner roles. In less than a week, however, there were almost no similarities among them; they had become totally different creatures. Why do our external behaviors and roles so dramatically affect our internal psychological framework?

Primarily because we tend toward integration between the external and internal. In other words, we are troubled by inconsistencies between *what* we do and *who* we think we are. We are motivated to alleviate these inconsistencies to preserve the integrity of the self. Sometimes there are ready external justifications that help reduce the discomfort we are experiencing—for example, obedience to orders. Indeed, external justifications are the cover most often made by perpetrators in their own defense. In truth, however, such external justifications are often absent, difficult to discern, or not viable as a long-term adaptation necessary to sustain one's continued participation in extraordinary evil. So we must turn to other options to alleviate the inconsistencies between what we do and who we think we are. Those who continue in roles not congruent with their personality often have a psychological tendency to adjust their underlying beliefs and values to what is consistent with their roles. In a malicious cycle, these alterations in the internal psychological frameworks produce further changes in behavior that lead to more profound alterations in the psychological framework. In short, evil acts not only reflect the self; they shape the self.

The guards and prisoners of the SPE engaged in external role-dictated behaviors that were inconsistent with who they were. To restore psychic equilibrium, they altered their internal psychological frameworks to match their role-dictated behaviors. In other words, the role-given superiority of the guards rebounded in the submissiveness of the prisoners, which then tempted the guards into further displays of their powers, which were then duly reflected in more self-humiliation on the part of the prisoners. As Zimbardo states, "The majority had indeed become prisoners or guards, no longer able to clearly differentiate between role playing and self. There were dramatic changes in virtually every aspect of their behavior, thinking and feeling."[39] Kurt Lewin, founder of modern social psychology and a refugee from Nazi Germany, even recognized this phenomenon as early as 1943: "While it is correct that [a] change of values will finally lead to a change of social conduct, it is equally correct that changes of action patterns and of actual group life will change cultural values. This indirect change of cultural values probably reaches deeper and is more permanent than direct changes of values by propaganda. There is no need to point out how thoroughly Hitler has understood this fact."[40]

We should also recognize, however, that coerced behavior is rarely internalized. In other words, the impact on attitude change will be minimal if we perceive a clear, external source of our behavior. The less coercion is used in our initial compliance, the more we will continue to see our engagement in the activity as part of ourselves. Even if initially there is some external pressure, it often becomes difficult to experience regular participation in evildoing as alien to who we are. It is difficult to maintain inner resistance while outwardly conforming to and participating in an evildoing system. We may easily draw the conclusion that our attitudes are consistent with the attitudinal implications of our ongoing behaviors.

It is tempting to believe that the rigid hierarchical structure inherent in the Nazi movement provided the sole justification, exclusively external and coercive, for the perpetrators' behaviors. Indeed, this is the claim made by Holocaust perpetrators in their own defense. The previous discussion, however, reveals that the process (often voluntary) of engaging in escalating commitments can lead to fundamental alterations in the perpetrators' internal psychological frameworks. These alterations would then provide the internal justification necessary to sustain their evildoing.

In the Holocaust, initial voluntary compliance was reflected in one's joining of, or nonopposition to, the Nazi movement. This was buttressed by obeying Nazi laws, reading Nazi newspapers, attending Nazi rallies, voting for Nazis in plebiscites, taking an oath to Adolf Hitler—in short, performing Nazi behaviors publicly. As persons engaged in actions, either of commission or omission, in support of the movement, they changed and became ready for greater efforts. Later acts of atrocity, required by insertion in the hierarchy structure, built on the initial voluntary compliance. In Staub's words: "Initial acts that cause limited harm result in psychological changes that make further destructive actions possible."[41] Richard Grunberger relates a similar viewpoint: "The 'German greeting' was a powerful conditioning device. Having once decided to intone it as an outward token of conformity, many experienced discomfort at the contradiction between their words and their feelings. Prevented from saying what they believed, they tried to establish their psychic equilibrium by consciously making themselves believe what they said."[42]

Relevant here is the distinction between three processes of social influence—compliance, identification, and internalization—outlined by social psychologist Herbert C. Kelman and sociologist V. Lee Hamilton.[43] Kelman and Hamilton maintain that in *compliance*, one obeys authority, doing what one perceives that others want done, in order to receive a positive response from the authority. In compliance, people perform a behavior not because they agree with it but because its expression is necessary to producing a desired social effect. Compliant behavior has little to do with one's internal beliefs; it occurs only when closely observed by the authority. Such nominal compliance reflects an orientation to social rules, a set of behavioral requirements.

In *identification*, one copies behavior that seems to go with a particular role. Though one may gradually come to believe in the copied behavior, the behavior is acted out only when one is playing the role. Identification represents more than mere compliance designed to placate an authority but less than private acceptance of new stable, internal beliefs in the person's own value structure. Behaviors adopted through identification remain tied to a continuing relationship with the authority and are stable only as long as the person operates in a social environment that is relatively unchanging. Identification reflects an orientation to a particular social role, not just a set of behavior requirements.

Finally, in *internalization*, one accepts authority because it is congruent with one's value system. Social influence is accepted because the requested behavior meets with our personal values, beliefs, and worldview. In contrast to compliance and identification, internalized behavior is independent of an external source or a set of social-role expectations from which it was originally derived. Internalized behaviors are part and parcel of a personal value system. Internalization reflects an orientation to social values that the individual personally shares.

Compliance, identification, and internalization encourage one to obey legitimate authority under most circumstances. The value of identifying the different responses to social influence is that they enable us to hear the several voices with which a perpetrator may be speaking when he or she says, "I was just following orders." We should note, however, that these three responses are characterized as ideal types, or reifications, in order to clarify their qualitative differences. In truth, they rarely appear in pure, isolated form in real-life situations. They are not mutually exclusive; two or more may be operating simultaneously or alternately and in differing degrees in different contexts for different individuals. At a general level, we can say that the merger of an extraordinarily evil role and an ordinary person involves transitioning from compliance, through identification, to internalization—although elements of compliance and identification may persist or reappear throughout the process.

Moreover, as I argued in chapter 4, the internalized alterations resulting from a merger of the role and person are normally permanent. As a consequence, perpetrators should have an increased readiness to participate in extraordinary evil again if the "right" immediate social context is re-created. Some, such as Lifton, want to maintain that perpetrators can cease to become evil people once their life returns to ordinary pursuits—even without confronting the extraordinary evil they committed. From what we know about the merger of role and person, however, there is ample reason to suspect that the usual outcome of *sustained* socialization in a culture of cruelty is a permanent one.

In professionally trained military personnel, for instance, we see clear evidence of the way in which killing destroys parts of the perpetrators' humanity. The following is a testimony from an army commando: "As time passed I felt better and better. I fell in love with the idea [of killing]. I felt like a king. Strong. The best. . . . After I was discharged I realized that I actually needed all of this tension. . . . Two things began to penetrate my soul that weren't in me before my military service. First of all, I started to lie. Until this day I can't stop lying. The additional impact was on my behavior which turned violent. Before military service I wouldn't raise a hand to a person, and my service made violence my second nature."[44] It is reasonable to assume that the impact of committing extraordinary evil *outside* the context of traditionally defined military roles (that is, against unarmed civilians) leaves an even greater mark on perpetrators. In the words of Erich Fromm: "If man does evil he becomes more evil. Thus, Pharaoh's heart 'hardens' because he keeps on doing evil; it hardens to a point where no more change or repentance is possible."[45]

In summary, the merger of role and person has tremendous capacity for internalizing evil and shaping later evil behaviors. Most of us easily slip into the roles society offers us. A person who becomes invested in the logic and practices of an evildoing organization becomes owned by it. In a self-perpetuating cycle of evildoing, our behaviors and attitudes feed on each other as this altered psychological framework produces further changes in behavior that lead to more profound alterations in our psychological framework.

Conclusion

The notion that there are only good and evil people is a dispositional explanation based on traits and other inner personal characteristics. This chapter focused on an alternative explanation of evil behavior as a product of situational influences that channel action in particular directions. In this analysis, people tend to do evil because of where they are, not who they are.

The focus here is on the fact that the huge predominance of extraordinary evil committed in the world is, in some sense, a societal product in which a complex and sustained series of social forces enable ordinary people to commit extraordinary evil. In that process, the perpetrators are themselves fundamentally changed and become capable of autonomously and knowledgably committing extraordinary evil. In short, forces of the immediate social context, cultures of cruelty, make active and actual the latent evil in all of us. As Darley states, "Being 'processed through a killing machine' can create an 'evil individual.'"[46]

The primary lesson we take from our analysis of cultures of cruelty is that ordinary people can be immersed in "total situations" or "total institutional environments" that can transform who they are in ways that challenge our sense of the stability and consistency of individual personality, character, and morality. The unsettling truth is that any deed that perpetrators of extraordinary evil have ever done, however atrocious, is possible for any of us to do—under particular situational pressures.

This recognition does not excuse extraordinary evil. Perpetrators cannot be absolved by the notion that others in the same situation might have done as they did. For even among them, some refused to kill and others stopped killing. We cannot, and should not, displace responsibility to the situation rather than the person. But recognizing the power of the situation does democratize extraordinary evil rather than demonizing it. It puts the blame of extraordinary evil where it should be—squarely on ordinary people like you and me.

Why are we so resistant to recognizing the power of the immediate social context in enabling extraordinary human evil? In part, our resistance reflects a general cognitive tendency for dispositional thinking. This tendency is so pervasive that it has its own name—the fundamental attribution error (FAE). We commit the FAE when we overemphasize dispositional influences while simultaneously underemphasizing situational ones—in other words, when we attribute behavior to the internal dispositions of an individual rather than recognize that it stems from situational pressure; when we think people do what they do because of the kind of people they are, not because of the situation they are in.

Beyond a cognitive bias, though, we are resistant to situational explanations because it is more absolving to attribute extraordinary evil to the dispositional flaws of others. In so doing, we are lulled into finding comfort in our own inability for such extraordinary evil. In addition, dispositional explanations soothe our relationship to the various social problems that we observe in the world around us. We are reassured that we are not responsible for the evil social or institutional frameworks to which others succumb by nature of their weak dispositions.

We should remember, however, the caution expressed in both this chapter and the previous one: most human behavior is an interaction of dispositional and situational influences. This brings us to a central question: what is the nature of their interaction in understanding how ordinary people commit extraordinary evil? One answer is to see the immediate social context as leaving individuals' margins of discretion within which perpetrators can exercise freedom of choice in how they carry out the functions of their roles. These margins are expanded when people have a high degree of moral and social intelligence. They are restricted, however, when situations become "total" and powerful.

Fromm concludes with an insightful summary of the interactional approach between persons and situations:

> Man is inclined to regress *and* to move forward; this is another way of saying he is inclined to good *and* to evil. If both inclinations are still in some balance he is free to choose, provided that he can make use of awareness and that he can make an effort. He is free to choose between alternatives which in themselves are determined by the total situation in which he finds himself. If, however, his heart has hardened to such a degree that there is no longer a balance of inclinations he is no longer free to choose. In the chain of events that lead to the loss of freedom the last decision is usually one in which man can no longer choose freely; at the first decision he may be free to choose that which leads to the good, provided he is aware of the significance of his first decision.[47]

In summary, a culture of cruelty—buttressed by professional socialization, binding factors of the group, and the merger of role and person—envelops perpetrators in a social context that encourages and rewards extraordinary evil. It reminds us that the normal reaction to an abnormal situation is abnormal behavior; indeed, normal behavior would be an abnormal reaction to an abnormal situation. We must borrow the perspective of the perpetrators and view their extraordinary evil not as the work of "lunatics" but as actions with a clear and justified purpose—so defined by a culture of cruelty. Such cultures of cruelty lay the groundwork for the final component of our explanatory model—the psychological and sociological construction of victims as the "other."

The Church of Ntamara

THE HISTORICAL RECORDS indicate that Rwanda's first inhabitants were the Twa, hunters and gatherers related to cave-dwelling pygmies. They were followed from the south by the agriculturalist Hutu, with Bantu features including woolly hair, broad noses, dark skin, and full lips. During the sixteenth century, the Tutsi—very slender and tall, straight-nosed, and light brown in complexion—arrived from the north, perhaps from Ethiopia, in a migration that appears to have been gradual and mostly peaceful. Throughout their history, the three groups spoke the same language, shared the same territory, followed the same traditions, and even acknowledged the same king (the Mwami). Over the years, however, the Tutsi cattle ranchers emerged as an aristocratic elite, the Hutu farmers as commoners, and the Twa as potters and entertainers who were generally held in low regard by the other groups.

When German explorers first entered the country in 1894, Rwanda—"the land of a thousand hills"—was a growing and expansive empire. Only a few neighboring peoples were as strong or stronger than Rwanda. It also is true that precolonial Rwanda was one of the most centralized and rigidly stratified societies in the Great Lakes region of east central Africa. In this vertically structured society, Hutu peasants were, for all practical purposes, now on the lowest rung of the ladder, socially, economically, and politically (given the Twa's diminishing numbers). Though Hutus represented about 85 percent of a total population estimated at 2 million at the turn of the twentieth century, power, status, and wealth were generally in the hands of the Tutsi—a minority accounting for a bit less than 15 percent of the population.[1] Rather than ethnic categories, the early conceptions of "Hutu" and "Tutsi" conveyed class status, since power and prestige in Rwanda depended on possession of cattle.

Inequality was inscribed in the differential treatment accorded to each group and, as a result, the potential for conflict certainly existed between

Hutus and Tutsi. For most of their history, however, the two groups coexisted relatively peacefully. Generally, this can be credited to the stability of Rwandan society as maintained by the patrimonial and sacred power of their dynasty of kings. That stability would be shaken by the advent of European rule. Rwanda first was annexed to become part of German East Africa in 1897. After World War I, Belgium became Rwanda's colonial ruler, first as a League of Nations mandate and, later, after World War II, as a United Nations Trust territory.

The processes of social change introduced by the colonial state had far-reaching implications for the polarization of Hutus and Tutsi. The class descriptors of Hutu and Tutsi, having become progressively less reliable templates, were reshaped and mythologized as ethnic identities. The Belgians, in particular, were devoted to the idea of a racialized Tutsi superiority and imposed a system of apartheid on Rwanda in which Hutus were denied all privileges. Beginning in 1933, it was required that each individual carry an identity card specifying his or her ethnic background; this was necessary because extensive rates of intermarriage had greatly diminished the once noticeable physical differences among the groups. In short, the norms and texture that held traditional Rwandan society together were destroyed by distant and indirect colonial rule that gave unrelenting support to oppressive Tutsi governance and sharpened, to a dangerous degree, the Hutu-Tutsi fault line.

For a variety of reasons, Belgian policies in Rwanda underwent a radical shift in the mid-1950s as a sustained effort was made to extend opportunities to an increasing number of Hutus. This radical policy shift provoked immediate resistance from Tutsi power holders as well as countervailing pressure from disenfranchised Hutus for expansive social reform. In the social revolution of 1959–1962, with substantial backing from the Catholic Church and the Belgian authorities, the Tutsi monarchy was overthrown, and power was seized by a de facto republican regime under Hutu rule. This led an estimated 200,000 Tutsi men, women, and children to flee; the majority found asylum in Uganda, Burundi, and Zaire. By the time Belgium withdrew from Rwanda in 1962, the country had become an equally polarized mirror image of its prior self—a Hutu-dominated republic with the Tutsi minority effectively excluded from participating in the political life of the country.

On October 1, 1990, a Tutsi-dominated paramilitary organization, the Rwandese Patriotic Front (RPF), invaded northeastern Rwanda from Uganda, declaring war on President Juvenal Habyarimana's Hutu ruling party. Most of these "refugee-warriors" were sons of Uganda-based Tutsi refugees of the 1959-1962 social revolution. Hutu politicians in Rwanda, recalling the 1972 genocide in Burundi in which 100,000 to 150,000 Hutus were killed by an all-Tutsi army (in retaliation for a failed Hutu insurgency that caused thousands of deaths among innocent Tutsi civilians), feared similar atrocities if the RPF came to power. These fears were inflated by the 1993 assassination of the newly elected Hutu president of Burundi, and several other key people in the government, by factions of the all-Tutsi Burundi army.

As panic-stricken Hutus from Burundi began to seek refuge in Rwanda, battle lines were drawn to counter the political threats — both external and internal — to Habyarimana's Hutu ruling party. Thousands of Hutu paramilitary militias, most drawn from the unemployed youth of the capital (Kigali), were recruited and trained to become ground-level operatives. By the end of 1993, these so-called *interhamwe* (those who stand together) claimed a total membership of 50,000. The final stick in this tinderbox of violence came when Habyarimana's plane was shot down on April 6, 1994, on return from a regional peace summit in Dar es Salaam. By blaming the assassination on the RPF, Hutu extremists (who in reality were most likely responsible for the attack) had the final rationale needed to justify their genocide of the Tutsi population in Rwanda.

A clique of Hutu leaders from the military high command immediately seized power and implemented a systematic plan of annihilation throughout Rwanda. The killing of political opposition leaders — both Tutsis and moderate Hutus — began moments after the crash, on the basis of preestablished lists with instructions on how to find the victims. Some 20,000 people were killed in Kigali in the three weeks following Habyarimana's death. The violence quickly spread from the capital city to the countryside. For days and weeks, in one village after another, hundreds and thousands of Tutsi civilians (and civilians who looked like Tutsi) were murdered. In a number of areas, many ordinary citizens joined in the killing, either willingly or under coercion by the militias. A report by the Physicians for Human Rights describes the range of extraordinary evil: "The *interhamwe* used the following methods of killing: machetes, massues (clubs studded with nails), small axes, knives, grenades, guns, fragmentation grenades, beatings to death, amputations with exsanguination, buried alive, drowned, or raped and killed later. Many victims had both their Achilles tendons cut with machetes as they ran away, to immobilize them so that they could be finished off later."[2]

In Rwanda—the most Christianized country in Africa, where at least 65 percent of the population were Catholics and 15 percent were Protestants—the worst massacres occurred in churches and mission compounds where Tutsis had sought refuge. Human rights groups even charge that some church leaders from various denominations used their authority to encourage the massacres and join in the killing. Among many others, the churches of Ntamara, Nyarabuye, and the Centre Christus in Kigali became the scenes of incredible atrocities. The following is excerpted from the testimony of a fifteen-year-old schoolgirl, Josianne Mukeshimana, who had fled for protection to the church of Ntamara:

The day after the President died, houses started burning in our commune. Refugees began streaming in from other areas. We panicked as we saw *interhamwe* following people everywhere. The second day we left home and went to look for protection in the church of Ntamara. But we were not to find any protection in the church.

About five days after we had been there, there was an attack against the church. When we saw them coming, we closed the doors. They broke the doors down and tore down some of the bricks in the back wall. They threw a few grenades through the holes where the bricks had been. But most people who died were killed by machetes. When they came in, they were obviously furious that we had closed the doors. So they really macheted the refugees. The attackers were *interhamwe* but they were not from our sector. They were ordinary villagers from somewhere else. They surrounded the church to knock down anyone who escaped.

In a fury those inside really desecrated the church, destroying the statues. They told us: "We are destroying your church!" People could not leave. But it was intolerable to remain in one's position as the macheting continued. So like the mad, people ran up and down inside the church. All around you, people were being killed and wounded.

Eventually I decided to drop down among the dead. I raised my head slightly; an *interhamwe* hurled a brick at me. It hit me just on top of my eye. My face became covered with blood which was useful in making them think I was even more dead. I tried to stop breathing so they would really believe that I was dead. The macheting continued all round me.

Once they thought most people were dead, they paid more attention to looting the dead. Most of them left. But one of them was not satisfied with his loot. He remained in the church. . . . He came to search my pockets and discovered that I was alive. He threatened to kill me unless I paid him. I said I had no money. He took my watch. In the meantime the other attackers were calling out to him, warning him that he might be killed if he delayed any longer. He left.[3]

Thousands of abandoned machetes collect at the border of Rwanda and Tanzania, where Hutu refugees fleeing Rwanda were allowed across the border on the condition that they leave behind their weapons (1994). Photo by David and Peter Turnley/CORBIS.

The assault on the Tutsi ended when Kigali fell to the RPF on July 4, 1994. All told, at least 800,000 people (possibly as many as 1 million) were killed in just a hundred days in the spring and early summer of 1994 in Rwanda. Three hundred and thirty-three and a third murders an hour—or five and a half lives terminated every minute. That represents a rate of death nearly three times the rate of Jewish dead during the Holocaust. Of these, the vast majority belonged to the Tutsi minority, but more than 50,000 Hutus identified with opposition parties also were slaughtered.

In October 1994, a Commission of Experts set up by the UN Security Council concluded that the "concerted, planned, systematic and methodical" acts of "mass extermination perpetrated by Hutu elements against the Tutsi group" in Rwanda "constitute genocide." This report marked the first time, since the passage of the Genocide Convention in 1948, that the United Nations had officially identified an instance of genocide.

Tragically, Rwanda—a tiny country where the group subjected to genocide must live side by side with the killers—remains caught in the grip of an unbroken cycle of fear, mistrust, and death. Between 50,000 and 60,000 Hutus have been killed in retaliation by Tutsi. One and a half million to 2 million Hutu refugees live in camps, the largest ones in Zaire, very near the Rwandan border. Many of these camps are run by the former army and the *interhamwe*, who use them as launching pads for guerrilla raids on Tutsi and army installations inside Rwanda and Burundi. In retaliation, government soldiers engage in deadly search-and-destroy operations against the rebels and those they suspect—rightly or wrongly—of supporting them. In 1996–1997, it was estimated that between 50,000 and 100,000 Hutu refugees from Rwanda and Burundi had been killed by the Tutsi army from Rwanda.

As of this writing, about 125,000 Rwandans are in prison awaiting trial on genocide-related charges. While many of those are undoubtedly guilty, some were arrested on, at best, circumstantial evidence in the early days following the end of the genocide. Rwandan courts have been holding mass trials to relieve these overcrowded prisons, where many of the suspects continue to be held for years without charges. The October 2001 election of nearly 260,000 new judges to sit on *gacaca* panels, or traditional people's courts, was hoped to expedite the country's backlog of genocide cases.

The UN's International Criminal Tribunal for Rwanda, based in Arusha, Tanzania, is holding its own trial of the top genocide leaders from Rwanda. Since its inception in 1995, over seventy suspects have been indicted, of whom more than fifty have been arrested and transferred to the tribunal's custody. Of those so far apprehended, the trials of nine have been completed, resulting in eight convictions and one acquittal. Those convicted include Jean Kambanda, the prime minister of the Rwandan government during the genocide, who was the first head of state to be indicted and subsequently convicted for genocide. The tribunal is expected to complete its work no later than 2008.

Today, the destiny of Rwanda is once again entrusted to Tutsi hands. Struggling to promote reconciliation, the Tutsi-dominated transitional government unveiled a new flag, national anthem, and coat-of-arms at a gathering of national reconciliation in Kigali on the last day of 2001. The new flag has a golden sun with twenty-four rays on a field of green, yellow, and blue. President Paul Kagame said the colors stood for prosperity, wealth, peace, and happiness. The new national anthem, which refers to the country's 8.3 million people simply as Rwandans, was composed by a group of jailed Hutus awaiting trial on charges of genocide. The transitional government is supposed to lead the country until 2003, when parliamentary and presidential elections are tentatively scheduled to be held.[4]

8

Who Is the "Other"?

Social Death of the Victims

Nothing belongs to us any more; they have taken away our clothes, our
shoes, even our hair; if we speak, they will not listen to us, and if they
listen, they will not understand. They will even take away our name:
and if we want to keep it, we will have to find in ourselves the strength
to do so, to manage somehow so that behind the name something of
us, of us as we were, still remains.

Primo Levi, *Survival in Auschwitz*

LT. COL. DAVE GROSSMAN, in his *On Killing: The Psychological Cost of
Learning to Kill in War and Society*, examines the killing process at different points along the distance spectrum—from maximum range to hand-
to-hand combat. He argues that maximum-range killing—defined as a
range at which the killer is unable to perceive his individual victims without using some form of mechanical assistance—carries with it a group absolution, mechanical distance, and physical distance that facilitates killing.
In his research, he has "not found one single instance of individuals who
have refused to kill the enemy under these circumstances [maximum
range], nor . . . a single instance of psychiatric trauma associated with this
type of killing."[1] As the range between perpetrator and victim decreases,
however, killing becomes increasingly difficult—becoming most difficult
in edged-weapons and hand-to-hand combat range.

Grossman's work makes clear the inverse relationship between distance
and killing—killing is made easier as the distance between perpetrators
and their victims increases. This exact relationship also was observed in follow-up studies on Milgram's original obedience to authority experiment.
We should understand, though, that distance is not simply a physical construct; it is a moral and psychological construct as well. In this way, range
also is defined by the perpetrators' perception of the victims. Face-to-face

killing is enabled when the victims already have already died a "social death" in the eyes of the perpetrators. In his provocative research on comparative slavery, Harvard sociologist Orlando Patterson introduced the concept of social death to describe the slave condition. Three features add up to the social death of slavery—subjection or personal domination, excommunication from the legitimate social or moral community, and relegation to a perpetual state of dishonor.[2] Historian Marion Kaplan later applied the concept of social death to Jews in Nazi Germany: "Well before the physical death of German Jews, the German 'racial community'—the man and woman on the street, the real 'ordinary Germans'—made Jews suffer social death every day. This social death was the prerequisite for deportation and genocide."[3]

The social death of victims may come after the extraordinary evil, or it may lead to it. Most times, it makes sense to argue that the social death of victims precedes their physical death. At times, though, one could argue that the social death of victims is a *consequence* of their physical death. For instance, in Cambodia, the Khmer Rouge may have viewed Lon Nol's supporters as guilty of treason or corruption, but they were not inhuman in their eyes. The same may be said of the Cultural Revolution in China and the purges in the Soviet Union. In each case, however, the social death of victims—as a justification mechanism—came quickly after the killings began.

This brings us to the fourth, and final, component of our explanatory model of how ordinary people commit extraordinary evil: perpetrators' definition of the target of their atrocities, or who the victims have been made out to be in the eyes of the perpetrators. Often, the common ground between perpetrators and victims in a mass killing or genocide is obliterated by social and legal sanctions. It is the development of moral sanctions, or exclusions, however, that result in the social death of the victims. Sociologist Helen Fein affirms the importance of this in contending that a necessary, though not sufficient, condition for genocide is the definition of the victim as outside the perpetrator's universe of moral obligation: "A church holding out the possibility of conversion to all must assume a common humanity, and therefore may not sanction unlimited violence. But a doctrine that assumes people do not belong to a common species knows no limits inhibiting the magnitude of permissible crime."[4] There are three mechanisms central to understanding the social death of the victims, or the legitimization of the "other" as the enemy, in cases of mass killing and genocide: us-them thinking, dehumanization of the victims, and blaming the victims (see figure 5).

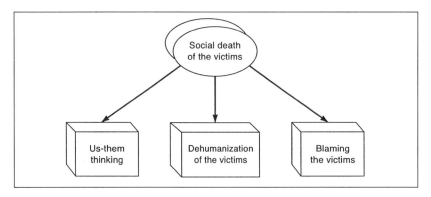

Figure 5. Who Is the "Other"?

Us-Them Thinking

In the summer of 1954, twenty-two normal, well-adjusted, eleven-year-old boys—with no significant preexisting cultural, physical, or status differences among them—participated in a three-week study conducted by social psychologist Muzafer Sherif and his colleagues at a campsite in Robbers' Cave in Oklahoma. On arrival, the boys were randomly assigned to one of two groups. Each group stayed in its own cabin; the cabins were located quite a distance apart in order to reduce contact between the two groups as well as encourage bonding and cohesiveness within each group. It took about a week for each group to give themselves an identity, a leader, and a culture. One group took the name Rattlers, and the other became the Eagles. The researchers then set up a series of competitive activities in which the two groups were pitted against each other. In addition, the researchers contrived other realistic situations to further intensify the conflict. Most were "zero-sum" situations—one group's gain was always the other group's loss. Rather quickly, strong feelings of conflict and tension were aroused between the two groups. The hostility escalated so much that the two groups could not even enjoy a benign noncompetitive activity, such as watching a movie, without it degenerating into name-calling, food-throwing, and fighting.[5]

The Robbers' Cave experiment reminds us that whenever groups form, their members sense the existence of boundaries that divide them from other groups—even when there is no blood relation, common history, or prior similarity. Once the boundaries are established, comparisons with other groups follow. Generally, these comparisons are favorable to our group and hostile to outsiders: Us versus Them. Insiders versus Outsiders. The

Tribe versus the Enemy. How is it that we so quickly and easily form groups, differentiate our group from others, favor those in our own group, and even swiftly mobilize to aggress against those in another group?

Social psychologists believe this process of *us-them thinking* begins with social categorizations. Social categorizations are cognitive tools that segment, classify, and order our social environment. They are the handles with which we approach interpersonal relations; they enable us to assign people to broad social categories. These social categories can include groups (for example, blacks, women, homosexuals), roles (mothers, sons), and occupations (teachers, maids, ministers). The more conspicuous a group, role, or occupation, the more likely we are to categorize. With little cognitive effort, we immediately notice whether a stranger fits the essential characteristics, or "essence," of a particular social category and place them into that category.

Social categorization simplifies an incredibly complex world by filtering the amount of data we must actively process. Not only do social categorizations systematize our social world; they also create and define our place in it. Social categorization is the nature of how the human mind works. It is an inescapable feature of human existence. It is the behavioral manifestation of the universal psychological tendencies of ethnocentrism and xenophobia that we introduced in chapter 5. Though the *content* of social categories may differ, the *process* of social categorization is universal and pervasive across humankind. It is as natural to our minds as breathing is to our lungs.

The most significant legacy of social categorization lies in its influence on our perception of who we are and whose we are. Social psychologists often speak about these perceptions in terms of "in-group" and "out-group." The in-group is any group to which we belong or with which we identify. In-groups can range from small, face-to-face groupings of family and friends to large social categories such as race, ethnicity, gender, or religion. Out-groups are any groups to which we do not belong or with which we do not identify. Over time, as Pat Shipman writes, "we have shifted the identity of those for whom we will fight. It is no longer simply kinfolk or immediate neighbors; it is vast groups like 'those who proclaim themselves citizens of this thing we call a nation' or 'those who follow the practices of this holy man.'"[6] Using social categorization in assigning people to in-groups and out-groups has four important effects: assumed similarity, out-group homogeneity, accentuation, and in-group bias.

First, there is the *assumed similarity effect*, in which we perceive other in-group members as more similar to us than to out-group members. We solidify this perception by exaggerating the similarities within our own group. Even when we have been randomly, or arbitrarily, assigned to a group, we assume that other in-group members are especially similar to us on a surprisingly wide range of thoughts, feelings, and behaviors.

Defining what the in-group is requires defining what it is not, as well. The second consequence of assigning people to groups, defining what the in-group is not, is the *out-group homogeneity effect*. This is our tendency to see members of the out-group as all alike. So, as cognitive misers, if we know something about one out-group member, we are likely to feel that we know something about all of them. Similarly, since we assume that out-group members are highly similar, or essentially interchangeable, we can use our handy social group stereotype to quickly interpret an individual out-group member's behavior. They are, after all, all alike. Why waste our cognitive energy on attending to potentially distinctive information about a specific individual in the out-group?

We amplify our assumed similarity of in-group members and homogeneity of out-group members by drawing ever starker lines between "us" and "them." We draw these lines by exaggerating the differences between our group and the out-group. This exaggeration of out-group differentness, termed the *accentuation effect*, leaves us biased toward information that enhances the differences between social categories and less attentive to information about similarities between members of different social categories.

So we have different perceptions of "us" and "them." We think in-group members are similar to us and out-group members are all alike, and we overestimate the differences between "us" and "them." What is the danger in these distortions? They are not done out of malice. Rather, they reflect a cognitive perceptual bias that should be evaluatively neutral. Unfortunately, however, experience and research have demonstrated that such categorization is seldom neutral. We generally like people we think are similar to us and dislike those we perceive as different. Thus, the mere act of dividing people into groups inevitably sets up a bias in group members in favor of the in-group and against the out-group. We evaluate in-group members more positively, credit them more for their successes, hold them less accountable for their failures or negative actions, reward them more, expect more favorable treatment from them, and find them more persuasive than out-group members. Such in-group favoritism has been demonstrated across a wide range of groups, ages, contexts, and tasks. This fourth consequence of assigning people into groups, labeled the *in-group bias*, has the most profound implications for understanding the social death of victims.

The in-group bias has been most clearly articulated in the research program of a British social psychologist, Henri Tajfel, and his colleagues.[7] In Tajfel's "minimal group" experiments, complete strangers were divided into groups using the most arbitrary or trivial criteria imaginable. In one experiment, for example, groups were formed on the basis of a coin toss. In others, they were formed on the basis of musical preferences, estimates of the number of dots on a screen, or random assignment of an arbitrary label. In the most famous series of studies, participants were asked to express their opinions about indistinguishable abstract paintings by artists they had never heard of and were then randomly assigned to a group that preferred either the "Paul Klee style" or the "Wassily Kandinsky style."

Similar to the Robbers' Cave experiment, the participants in these minimal groups were strangers prior to the experiment. Likewise, the groups were formed using random criteria. In direct contrast to the Robbers' Cave experiment, however, the individuals in Tajfel's minimal groups remained anonymous to each other. They had no contact or interaction with each other during the experiment. There were no pleasurable interactions with other in-group members, nor were there any unpleasurable interactions with out-group members. Finally, the minimal groups were not competing for a prize or scarce resources. There were no selfish gains to be made.

Despite the stark "minimalness" of these groups, however, individuals still showed bias, discrimination, and a competitive orientation in favor of the in-group and against the out-group. They rated members of their own group as more pleasant and better workers. They liked the members of their own group better. They allocated more money or other resources to those who shared their label. Though in-group favoritism need not be always mirrored by a negative bias against the out-group, the sequence does often follow. In one experiment, for example, in-group members voted to give themselves only two dollars instead of three dollars if it meant that out-group members got one dollar instead of four. They voted to take less money rather than let the out-group members make more money. They sacrificed absolute gain for a relative advantage. In other words, in-group members were more interested in beating the out-group than in gaining as much as possible for their own group.

In short, complete strangers arbitrarily assigned to groups, having no interaction or conflict with one another, and not competing against another group behaved as if those who shared their meaningless label were their dearest friends or closest relatives. Such findings have been replicated more than twenty times in several different countries using a wide range of experimental participants. In Tajfel's words: "The mere perception of belonging to two distinct groups—that is, social categorization per se—is sufficient to trigger intergroup discrimination favoring the in-group. In other words, the mere awareness of the presence of an out-group is sufficient to provoke intergroup competitive or discriminatory responses on the part of the in-group."[8]

Social psychologists were jolted by Tajfel's original findings. Before these experiments, most social psychologists assumed that social exclusion was the result of existing prejudice and hostility that developed over time in the course of active intergroup relations. Social exclusion produced by mere categorization into separate groups, in the absence of any previous history of intergroup contact or conflict, simply did not fit our understanding of intergroup behavior. Even Tajfel himself only began with minimal groups to create a kind of baseline condition in which no group effects would occur. His intention was then to systematically introduce additional group-forming properties until discrimination did occur. He never anticipated that bias and discrimination would emerge from meanings that the participants themselves imposed on the minimal groups.

Tajfel's unexpected findings led to a flurry of research questions. Why does the mere act of placing people into groups lead to in-group bias? What is the motivational explanation for this cognitive phenomenon? Does in-group bias stem from a liking for our own group, a dislike for the out-group, or both?

On the basis of his research program with minimal groups, Tajfel believes that the major underlying motive for in-group bias is self-esteem. In his social identity theory, one tool used by individuals to enhance their self-esteem is identification with specific social groups. By allowing the in-group to become an extension of ourselves, we open another avenue to enhance our self-esteem. For self-esteem to be enhanced, however, the individual must see their group as superior to other groups. In-group bias, rooted in the assumed similarity and out-group homogeneity effects and amplified by the accentuation effect, is the cognitive mechanism that makes it possible for us to see our group as superior to other groups. Thus, according to Tajfel, our natural tendency for in-group favoritism stems from a basic motivational need to enhance our self-esteem. Intergroup comparisons indirectly contribute to individual self-esteem. In summary, the mere perception of belonging to a group is sufficient to trigger preferential treatment of in-group members.

Contrary to some depictions of us-them thinking, discrimination *for* in-groups and discrimination *against* out-groups are not necessarily two sides of the same coin. In other words, they are not always reciprocally related. Out-groups can be viewed with indifference, sympathy, even admiration, as long as their distinctiveness from the in-group is maintained. In this way, discrimination can be motivated solely by in-group preference for those that we acknowledge to be "us," in the absence of hostile thoughts, feelings, or behaviors toward out-groups of "them."

As social psychologist Marilynn Brewer points out, however, "there is a fine line between the absence of trust and the presence of active distrust, or between noncooperation and overt competition."[9] In-group favoritism, even in the absence of overt antagonism toward out-groups, is not benign. There are a number of ways in which the effects of social categorization set the stage for conflict and hate. As Brewer summarizes, "The very factors that make in-group attachment and allegiance important to individuals also provide a fertile ground for antagonism and distrust of those outside the in-group boundaries. The need to justify in-group values in the form of moral superiority to others, sensitivity to threat, the anticipation of interdependence under conditions of distrust, social comparison processes, and power politics all conspire to connect in-group identification and loyalty to disdain and overt hostility toward out-groups."[10] Us-them thinking is a dualistic and dichotomous form of thinking that takes over when our vital interests are involved. Instead of judging other people across a broad spectrum ranging from good to bad, we make extreme categorical judgments based on the polar opposites of "good us" versus "bad them." Our cause is sacred; theirs is evil. We are righteous; they are wicked. We are innocent; they are guilty. We are the victims; they are the victimizers. It is rarely *our* enemy or *an* enemy, but *the* enemy—a usage of the definite article that hints of something fixed and immutable, abstract and evil.

In summary, social categorization, and its role in us-them thinking, does not lead us to hate all out-groups. Social exclusion, let alone mass killing and genocide, is not an inevitable consequence of social categorization. Social categorization does remind us, however, that, once identified with a group, we find it easy to exaggerate differences between our group and others, enhancing in-group cooperation and effectiveness, and—frequently—intensifying antagonism with other groups. Combined with other components of the explanatory model, social categorization helps us understand how the suggestive message of us against them can be ratcheted up to the categorically compelling kill or be killed.

Dehumanization of Victims

A story in the *New York Times* that appeared on the last day of 1994 describes an incident in which a Bosnian Serb, armed with an automatic weapon, knocked on the door of a Muslim neighbor and ordered her outside. The Muslim woman proclaimed, "Visovic, you know me, you know my husband. . . . How can you do this to me?" Visovic replied: "That time is over. I no longer know you." Whereupon he ordered her to crawl along the street as he kicked her repeatedly.[11]

How do we no longer know the other? How do we make the other not there? Erik Erikson, the famous developmental psychologist, advanced the concept of "pseudospeciation" to refer to the extreme lines that we draw between "us" and "them." He wrote:

> Originally, pseudospeciation was meant to refer to the fact that mankind, while one species, has divided itself through its history—territorially, culturally, politically—into various groups that permit their members, at decisive times, to consider themselves, more or less consciously and explicitly, the only truly human species, and *all* others (and especially *some* others) as less than human. . . . Some of these pseudospecies, indeed, have mythologized for themselves a place and a moment in the very center of the universe, where and when an especially provident diety caused it to be created superior to, or at least unique among, all others. . . . What renders this "natural" process a potential malignancy of universal dimensions is the fact that in times of threat and upheaval the idea of being the foremost species tends to be reinforced by a fanatic fear and hate of other pseudospecies. The feeling that those others must be annihilated or kept "in their places" by warfare or conquest or the force of harsh custom can become a periodical and reciprocal obsession of man.[12]

Elsewhere, he summarized pseudospeciation as the process whereby "people lose the sense of being one species and try to make other kinds of people into a different and mortally dangerous species, one that doesn't count, one that isn't human. . . . You can kill them without feeling that you have killed your own kind."[13]

In social psychology, Erikson's concept of pseudospeciation is more commonly understood as the *dehumanization of victims*. In a classic experiment, Albert Bandura and his colleagues used a group of college students to help train another group of students from a nearby college. The supervisory team was given the power to punish the other group of problem solvers with varying intensities of electric shock for deficient performances. Just as the study was about to begin, the supervisory team overheard an assistant characterize the other group in either humanized ("The subjects from the other school are here; they seem nice"), dehumanized ("The subjects from the other school are here; they seem like animals"), or neutral ("The subjects from the other school are here") terms. Supervisors were influenced only by those brief descriptions—there was no actual interaction between the groups. Results revealed that dehumanized individuals were "shocked" at a significantly higher rate and level than those who had been humanized or were in the neutral condition. This pattern was even more pronounced when dehumanization was coupled with diffusion of responsibility in a collective condition.[14]

In cases of mass killing and genocide, the dehumanization of victims involves categorizing a group as inhuman either by using categories of subhuman creatures (that is, animals) or by using categories of negatively evaluated unhuman creatures (such as demons and monsters). Dehumanization is most likely when the target group can be readily identified as a separate category of people belonging to a distinct racial, ethnic, religious, or political group that the perpetrators regard as inferior or threatening. These isolated subgroups are stigmatized as alien and memories of their past misdeeds, real or imaginary, are activated by the dominant political or social group.

Kelman and Hamilton state that dehumanization includes dual deprivations. The first is depriving victims of their *identity* by defining them entirely by a category to which they belong. The second deprivation is excluding this category from the *community* of the human family. Once exclusion from the human family is obtained, exclusion from the moral universe of obligation easily follows.[15] As we saw in chapter 6, regarding victims as outside our universe of moral obligation and, therefore, not deserving of compassionate treatment removes normal moral restraints against aggression. The body of a dehumanized victim possesses no meaning. It is waste, and its removal is a matter of sanitation. There is no moral or empathic context through which the perpetrator can relate to the victim.

For example, the groundwork for the moral exclusion of Jewish victims was laid in the centuries preceding the Holocaust: Jews were regarded as aliens who were on the remote fringes of Christian Europe's universe of moral obligation. The historical stigmatization and exclusion of the Jews meant that the traditions, habits, images, and vocabularies for extreme dehumanization were already well established. The centuries-old image of the vile and diabolical Jew was woven into the fabric of German, and European, culture. The deluge of racist and antisemitic propaganda ribboning throughout Germany society during the rise of Nazism was thus profoundly effective in placing, and keeping, the Jews entirely outside the realm of moral obligation for perpetrators.

Regarding victims as outside our moral universe of obligation impacts how we view and describe them. Perpetrators often disparage their victims, thus helping to justify their hurtful behavior. A common form of disparagement is the use of language to redefine the victims so they will be seen as warranting the aggression. The surreal gentility of the euphemistic labeling of evil actions central to the moral disengagement of the perpetrators is complemented by a barbarity of language that dehumanizes the victims. As Haig Bosmajian, a professor of communication studies, states: "The distance between the linguistic dehumanization of a people and their actual suppression and extermination is not great."[16]

Military organizations make extensive use of linguistic dehumanization in their preparations for war. An American sergeant who fought with the First Marine Division in Vietnam said, "It wasn't like they were humans. We were conditioned to believe that this was for the good of the nation, the good of our country, and anything we did was okay. And when you shot someone you didn't think you were shooting at a human. They were a gook or a Commie and it was okay."[17] Similarly, mass killing and genocide are replete with examples of the linguistic dehumanization of victims. In the Holocaust, for instance, the Nazis redefined Jews as "bacilli," "parasites," "vermin," "demons," "syphilis," "cancer," "excrement," "filth," "tuberculosis," and "plague." In the camps, male inmates were never to be called "men" but *Haftlinge* (prisoners), and when they ate the verb used to describe it was *fressen*, the word for animals eating. Statisticians and public health authorities frequently would list corpses not as *corpses* but as *Figuren* (figures or pieces), mere things, or even rags. Similarly, in a memo of June 5, 1942, labeled "Secret Reich Business," victims in gas vans at Chelmno are variously referred to as "the load," "number of pieces," and "the merchandise."[18] As a final, but no means exhaustive, example, a Gestapo official once told a member of the Warsaw Jewish Council: "You are no human, you are no dog, you are a Jew."[19]

Perpetrators so consistently dehumanize their victims that the words themselves become substitutes for perceiving human beings. Before the

Japanese performed medical experiments on human prisoners in World War II, they named them *maruta*—logs of wood. The Greek torturers studied by Janice Gibson and Mika Haritos-Fatouros (see chapter 7) referred to their victims as "worms." The Hutu extremists called the Tutsi *inyenzi*, meaning "cockroaches" or "insects." Interestingly, a synonym for cockroach in Polish is *prusak*, meaning "Prussian," and the German equivalent is *Russe*, meaning "Russian." Such dehumanization often leads to an escalation of the brutality of the extraordinary evil.

Linguistic dehumanization of victims also was revealed in "body count" estimates that became a sign of killing prowess and a door to promising rewards based on productivity rates. This is a quantitative process of dehumanization in which victims become mere statistics—bodies to be counted and numbers to be entered into reports. Reduced to data, dehumanized victims lose their moral standing and become objects requiring disposal. This sense of dehumanization appears in a remark scribbled on the pages of an anonymous diary found in Auschwitz: "We're not human beings anymore, nor have we become animals; we are just some strange psychophysical product 'made in Germany.'"[20] To even speak of "6 million Jews" killed is a dangerous abstraction that obscures the victims' standings as individuals with distinct aspirations, desires, strengths, and weaknesses.

In her work with children and grandchildren of grandparents who identified with National Socialism or were actually implicated in the Nazi crimes themselves, Gabriele Rosenthal even maintains that linguistic dehumanization is part of the intergenerational dialogue in these families. She found that in the life stories passed from generation to generation in families with a Nazi past, Jews are recalled as people with identities, or at least with professions, and, perhaps, even a name, in the early years of the Third Reich. In later years, however, and especially after the November pogrom of 1938, Jews disappear more and more from these life stories. Typical of these recollections is an indirect way of speaking about "them" in the third person—for example, "and then suddenly *they* were gone." This is a linguistic dehumanization of the victims, continuing through present-day life stories, that makes the Jews identityless and nameless as individuals and as a collective.[21]

Linguistic dehumanization is complemented by physical machinations that make the victims seem less than human. These degrading, often ritualistic, processes remake the individual self in the institutional image of something less than a full person. What do these processes look like? Victims held as prisoners are often kept hungry and helpless. Starvation, along with reducing the economic burden of the victims to the perpetrators, removes the individual from the social world by fixating their attention on their internal state. They are often forced to scavenge through the garbage for food, steal food from others, or turn informant to receive food—all actions that result in dehumanization. Victims also are often forced to live in filth and urinate and defecate on themselves. They become emaciated figures of total misery, lice-infested, soiled, and wrapped in rags, furthering their dehumanization in the eyes of the perpetrators. The assignment, even the tattooing, of numbers on some victims is yet another physical, tangible, and readily identifiable representation of their dehumanization.

Such realities not only reduced the will of the victims but also destroyed their identity and sense of dignity in the eyes of the perpetrators, making it easier for perpetrators to inflict extraordinary evil. In other words, perpetrators are reinforced in their perception of the victims as less than human by observing—and causing—their very victimization. Social psychologist John Sabini explains: "We are ordinarily unaware of the degree to which our being treated as civilized, decent, autonomous, moral agents depends on our ability to look and act like such agents. To the degree that we make it impossible for other people to look and act that way, we make it easy to treat them as less than human."[22] In short, when victims cannot present a worthy self, it becomes exceedingly difficult to exert a direct and powerful demand for moral and humane treatment.

Finally, the dehumanization of victims is reinforced by propaganda that visualizes the victims as representations of all that is bad in the world. The myriad complexities of the victim group are masked under a singular evil image. A U.S. Army film made during World War II characterized Japanese soldiers as "alike as photoprints from the same negative." Similarly, the acts of September 11 were rationalized by the terrorists' depiction of all Americans as the purveyors of all that is wrong in the world. The universal evil image of the enemy is reinforced in posters, cartoons, and magazine illustrations depicting the enemy as a crazed killer, sadistic torturer, greedy conspirator, rapist, barbarian, gorilla, saber-toothed monster, reptile, rat, insect, or demonic enemy of God, or even as death. In contrast, one's own group is seen as the embodiment of all that is good—exceptionally moral and decent, specially chosen by God or destiny, intelligent and strong.

Why is the dehumanization of victims important to their social death? First—similar to the distancing effects deriving from the division of labor, bureaucratization, or technology—dehumanization of victims ensures a degree of psychological distance between the perpetrator and their acts of evildoing. The dehumanized victim is no longer perceived as a feeling, thinking, or acting person, and consequently, extraordinary evil can be released from its restraints. In *A Rumor of War*, Philip Caputo writes of the need that such distance fills for killers: "There was nothing on him, no photographs, no letters, or identification. That would disappoint the boys at intelligence, but it was fine with me. I wanted this boy to remain anonymous. I wanted to think of him not as a dead human being with a name, age, and family, but as a dead enemy. That made everything easier."[23]

Second, the dehumanization of victims justifies or rationalizes extraordinary evil. Since victims are often depicted as highly threatening, extreme measures are justified in order to avert the potential danger they represent. In this way, the dehumanization of victims even implies that they *deserve* extreme treatment. As a result, the perpetrator no longer empathically considers the effects of his actions, however atrocious. As Bandura put it, "People seldom condemn punitive conduct—in fact, they create justifications for it—when they are directing their aggression at persons who have been divested of their humanness."[24]

In closing, we should remember that for all the potency that dehumanization of victims brings to the commission of extraordinary evil, Milgram's research demonstrates that it is *not* necessary to have a dehumanized victim in order to demonstrate destructive obedience to authority. Indeed, Milgram's confederate subject was incredibly humanized—"a forty-seven-year-old accountant, trained for the role; he was of Irish-American descent and most observers found him mild-mannered and likable"[25]—and participants certainly had reason to empathize with him. He was a pleasant man, in the same general category as the participants, and it was only by chance that he was playing the role of the victim. Had he been dehumanized in any of the ways discussed above, however, we can certainly expect that the disturbing level of obedience seen in Milgram's laboratory would have been even *more* pronounced. As Milgram admits: "In all likelihood, our subjects would have experienced greater ease in shocking the victim, had he been convincingly portrayed as a brutal criminal or pervert."[26]

Blaming the Victims

Social categorization and the dehumanization of victims not only recategorize victims into a subhuman grouping; they also carry an understanding that victims deserve or even require their victimization. The social death of victims feeds on itself and is driven by our brain's remarkable capacity to seek, and find, explanation in the events surrounding us, our actions, and the behaviors of people with whom we interact. Social psychology has a rich history of studying our ways of finding explanation. This history shows that, in general, we tend to grant ourselves the benefit of the doubt in explaining our own behaviors but are much harsher in explaining other people's behaviors.

Our harshest explanations are reserved for finding meaning in why people suffer. We recognize that victims can be grouped in two broad categories—those who deserve their suffering and those who do not deserve their suffering. We know that bad things do happen to good people. To a large degree, it is not a just world. But we do not want to relinquish our illusion of a world that is fair and just. We must hold on to that notion, however misguided, so that we have the courage to go out into the world and to send our children out into the world. Our need to believe in a just world often overwhelms our recognition that bad things can happen to good people. As a result, we assume that victims deserve, and can be blamed for, their fates. Indeed, we show a hardy cognitive tendency to search for ways to blame individuals for their own victimization. On the whole, the general tendency to blame the victim for her own suffering is a central truth about human experience.

This concept of *blaming the victims* was captured in a phrase, "the just-world phenomenon," originally coined by social psychologist Melvin Lerner.[27] Lerner has described the just-world phenomenon as the tendency of people to believe that the world is just and that therefore people get what they deserve and deserve what they get. In other words, victims have earned their suffering by their actions or character. Thus, the devaluation of victims and their suffering allows us to retain a sense that we are just people living in a just world—a world where people get what they deserve.

Two other psychologists, Zick Rubin and Letitia Anne Peplau, developed the Just-World Scale (JWS) to calculate the strength of an individual's belief in a just world.[28] When the JWS was first developed, Rubin and Peplau tested it in relation to the 1971 national draft lottery of nineteen-year-olds. While most people responding to the survey expressed sympathy for the "losers" (those who were inducted), those who scored high on the JWS resented the "losers" more than the "winners." It was as if their strong belief in a just world necessitated a need to blame the "losers" for their own misfortune—even though the lottery selections were completely random. Subsequent research with the JWS demonstrated that people believe in a just world with different degrees of conviction: that is, some may hold a strong belief in a just world, while others may hold such a belief less strongly.

A belief in a just world also is found in controlled laboratory settings. Lerner and others, for example, have had two people work equally hard on the same task. By the flip of a coin, however, one received a sizable reward and the other received nothing. Later, observers were asked to reconstruct what had happened. In general, the observers convinced themselves that the unlucky person who had lost the coin flip must have worked less hard. The observers knew that the coin flip was the sole determinant of rewards. In their reconstruction of the events, however, their minds drove them to find a reason for the inequitable distribution of rewards. A random coin flip was not sufficient; the observers reinterpreted events to lay blame on the victim's inferior work habits.

In another experiment conducted by Lerner and Carolyn Simmons, seventy-two female undergraduates watched a peer receive what they believed to be severe and painful electric shocks when she gave wrong answers to questions. Some observers were told that they could stop the shocks after the first ten-minute session. Others were told that they had no control over the experiment and were led to believe that their peer was going to suffer more shocks in a second session. Those students who thought that they controlled the fate of the victim described her in much more positive terms than those who thought they had no influence. Only a minority of the students blamed the experimenter. Lerner and Simmons concluded that those who believed the suffering was unstoppable denigrated the victim so that they could justify what they had seen.[29]

Similarly, many of the subjects in Milgram's obedience to authority study blamed the victim for volunteering for the experiment—even though, in their perception, they might well have been sitting in his chair themselves if they had drawn the other piece of paper. Milgram wrote: "Such comments as: 'He was so stupid and stubborn he deserved to get shocked,' were common. Once having acted against the victim, it seems to be necessary for many persons to view him as an unworthy individual, whose punishment was made inevitable by his own deficiencies of intellect and character."[30] In another series of experiments, psychologists Timothy Brock and Arnold Buss confirmed that subjects' perceptions of the individual to whom they gave shocks altered in ways that justified their morally ambiguous actions; they derogated the victim, implying a justification of the victim's suffering. In both cases, blaming the victim reduced perpetrators' own sense of guilt and allowed them to maintain their belief in a just world.[31]

The tendency to blame persons for their own victimization has significant implications outside the experimental laboratory. Strong belief in a just world is associated with rigid application of social rules and belief in the importance of convention, as opposed to empathy and concern with human welfare. How do we explain, for instance, the plight of the poor and homeless? Those who display a strong belief in a just world are most likely to blame the poor and homeless for their own suffering. Similarly, some find it more comfortable to believe that battered spouses must have provoked their beatings; that sick people are responsible for their illness; that persons involved in a traffic accident must have been driving carelessly; that victims of theft surely brought it on themselves by not taking adequate security precautions.

We often see the same pattern of blame attribution directed at victims of mass killing and genocide by both perpetrators and bystanders. During the Turkish genocide of the Armenians, for instance, the German government—the only nation in a position to exert influence on Turkey—never intervened to halt the killing. While many factors coalesced to explain their passivity, at least some of it can be understood as just-world thinking. An article in the *Frankfurter Zeitung* on October 9, 1915, betrays part of the German attitude toward the Armenian victims: "The Armenian . . . enjoys, through his higher intellect and superior commercial ability, a constant business advantage in trade, tax-forming, banking, and commission-agency over the heavy-footed Turk, and so accumulates money in his pocket, while the Turk grows poor. That is why the Armenian is the best-hated man in the East—in many cases not unjustly, though a generalization would be unfair."[32]

Rosenthal's extensive interviews with three generations of non-Jewish Germans tellingly reveal the ways in which perpetrators blamed Jews for their own destruction in the Holocaust. One perpetrator, for instance, blamed the Holocaust on big international capitalists, who he claimed were mostly Jews and for whom Hitler was just a puppet. Another perpetrator's recollection depicted mass murder as if the Jews themselves had carried it out: "And of course epidemics came and many, many people died—many Jews died there. We never burned them, they went and killed themselves there 'cause they had nothing to eat."[33] Rosenthal's contrastive comparison of life stories and family histories indicated that the deeper family members of the first generation were implicated in Nazi crimes, the more directly and openly they tried to exonerate themselves by assigning the guilt to the Jews.

Similarly, Lars Rensmann of the Freie Universität Berlin records the following, somewhat paranoid, testimony of a former member of the Nazi SA and SS: "Well, the Jews are not innocent in this entire development. . . . The Jews, very experienced in money business, seized the whole financial sphere, then they went into the administration, even Berlin's head of the police was a Jew. The Prussian government . . . there were Jews everywhere. My personal experiences, for I went to school with many Jews . . . these people were known that they cheated on people. . . . They have cheated on people, then they also lent them money, then there was the harvest on the fields, that was already impounded, the Jew already controlled that."[34]

One of the most direct examples of the lengths to which perpetrators will go to develop a context of blame attribution directed at the victims comes from Jan Gross's account of the slaughter of the Jews of Jedwabne, Poland (see chapter 7). Julian Sokolowski recalls: "I remember that when Jews were chased [toward the barn], citizen Sobuta gave his stick to the rabbi and ordered him to put his hat on it and scream, 'War is because of us, war is for us.' All this crowd of Jews on the way toward the barn outside town was screaming, 'War is because of us, war is for us.' "[35] This crowd of Jews, numbering as many as fifteen hundred, was eventually burned alive in the barn. Several other eyewitness accounts offer the same description of this episode.

At other times, Rosenthal relates, blaming the Jews was often expressed indirectly in rhetorical questions such as: "Time and again I wonder what it is about the Jews that they've been persecuted for centuries?" Similarly, Henry Dicks reports an instance when the British forced a group of German civilians to march through a nearby concentration camp in the days just after the war. One of the civilians was overheard to remark, "What terrible criminals these prisoners must have been to get such punishment."[36]

At still other times, blaming the victim focuses less on what they have allegedly done and more on what they have allegedly not done. Here, there is a focus on the victims' passivity that may partly be a result of just-world thinking. In this case, the thinking goes, the victims bring their fate on themselves not by deserving it but by not fighting back. During the genocide of the Armenians, for instance, victims were instructed to render themselves to the Turkish commissariats on a given day and at a given time. Once there, they were loaded onto trucks, driven into the desert, and shot. Others soon learned about the procedure, yet they kept coming. A similar lack of resistance was true of the Hutus in Burundi. Hannah Arendt was the first notable scholar to suggest that victims of the Holocaust contributed to their own demise. She claimed that far fewer than 6 million Jews would have died if Jewish leaders had not collaborated to various degrees with Nazis like Eichmann.[37] Others wondered whether it all might have been different if the victims had been unwilling to move, so that they had had to be bodily dragged from their houses, shouting and screaming.

While it can be argued that such questions underestimate the power of situational constraints as well as discount the reality of victim resistance (now well documented in the case of the Holocaust), they do nevertheless suggest how the absence of resistance may confirm perpetrators' beliefs of their victims' inferiority. Franz Stangl, commandant of Treblinka, spoke to this directly: "They were so weak; they allowed everything to happen—to be done to them. They were people with whom there was no common ground, no possibility of communication—that is how contempt is born. I could never understand how they could just give in as they did."[38]

The reach of the just-world phenomenon is further evidenced by the fact that even victims often go to great lengths to blame themselves for their own victimization. Some rape victims, for example, see their victimization as stemming from some inappropriate behaviors (for example, hitchhiking or leaving the apartment window unlocked). Similarly, victims of robbery may blame themselves for being too passive, careless, or trusting. A Holocaust survivor I once spoke with lamented: "Every day, I still try to understand what I, or what the Jewish people, did to deserve such a fate." The fact that many victims of arbitrary suffering find meaning by pointing the finger at themselves attests to our overwhelming urge to see the world as a fair and just place—of necessity implying that victims deserve their fate.

In short, a solid body of research evidence attests to the tendency of perpetrators, bystanders, and even victims to see the world as just. For perpetrators, this tendency is invaluable in our striking propensity to devalue victims and their suffering. We will rearrange our perception of people and events so that it seems everyone is getting what they deserve. Victims must be suffering because they have done "something," because they somehow are inferior or dangerous or evil, or because a higher cause is being served. The belief that the world is a just place leads us to accept the suffering of others more easily, even of people we ourselves have harmed.

Why is the just-world phenomenon such a prevailing cognitive tendency? Why are we so driven to see the world as a fair and just place, one where people get what they deserve and deserve what they get? The most obvious answer is socialization. Certainly, some of this tendency stems from early childhood, where we are taught that good is rewarded and evil punished. The end of nearly every Hollywood movie continues to teach us that hard work and virtue ultimately pay dividends.

But is socialization the only answer? Like many "obvious" answers, it is only partially correct. Socialization may explain what reinforces the just-world phenomenon, but it doesn't tell us "why." Why is it so important for us to see the world in this way? What motivates our inclination to blame victims for their own suffering? Why is it so much easier to blame than to understand or confess?

A major motivational source of the just-world phenomenon lies in its use as a self-protective device. Seeing others hurting, wanting, or suffering is terrifying because it reminds us of our fragile existence. The best way to protect us from this fear is to convince ourselves that the victim must have done something to bring it on himself. In our minds, we remain safe—and in control of our world—because we would always behave more cautiously or wisely than other victims have. By implicating the victims in their own destruction, we are protected from the painful recognition that the world is not a fair or just place. If victims are to blame for their fate, then there is no reason for the perpetrators to feel guilty. The moral foundation of much evildoing rests on the principle that because of their damaging behaviors, certain individuals or target groups forfeit their rights to humane treatment and can be harmed without guilt or remorse.

In addition to its protective function, blaming the victim may even have an enhancing function, particularly for perpetrators' self-esteem. Grossman writes: "He [perpetrator] *must* deny the guilt within him, and he *must* assure himself that the world is not mad, that his victims are less than animals, that they are evil vermin, and that what his nation and his leaders have told him to do is right. He *must* believe that not only is this atrocity right, but it is proof that he is morally, socially, and culturally superior to those whom he has killed. It is the ultimate act of denial of their humanity. It is the ultimate act of affirmation of his superiority."[39]

Often it becomes easier to blame the victim when we are frustrated and the cause of our frustration is too intimidating or vague to confront directly. In those cases, we may redirect, or displace, our hostility to convenient target groups—that is, scapegoats. Scapegoats are used as a focus for our hostilities, no matter how unwarranted or displaced this aggression may be. C. I. Hovland and R. Sears posited this redirection of hostility as a contributory factor to the number of lynchings of blacks in the U.S. South between 1882 and 1930. During that time, there was a tendency for more lynchings to occur in years when the price of cotton was lower and, presumably, economic frustration was higher.[40] As Ervin Staub states: "Blaming others, scapegoating, diminishes our own responsibility. By pointing to a cause of the problems, it offers understanding that, although false, has great psychological usefulness. It promises a solution to problems by action against the scapegoat."[41] In so doing, scapegoating gives perpetrators the illusion of understanding and control that arises from identifying the "cause" of one's problem.

In short, the just-world phenomenon allows us to be indifferent to extraordinary evil. The indifference is not because we are without concern for good but, rather, because we see no evil. The suffering of victims is just and deserved. Interventions are not warranted. This is yet another reminder that mere exposure to suffering does not automatically lead to compassion.

Conclusion

Sam Keen begins his *Faces of the Enemy: Reflections of the Hostile Imagination* (1986) with the following poem:

Start with an empty canvas
Sketch in broad outline the forms of men, women, and children.
Dip into the unconscious well of your own
disowned darkness
with a wide brush and
stain the strangers with the sinister hue
of the shadow.
Trace onto the face of the enemy the greed,
hatred, carelessness you dare not claim as
your own.
Obscure the sweet individuality of each face.
Erase all hints of the myriad loves, hopes,
fears that play through the kaleidoscope of every finite heart.
Twist the smile until it forms the downward
arc of cruelty.
Strip flesh from bone until only the
abstract skeleton of death remains.
Exaggerate each feature until man is
metamorphosized into beast, vermin, insect.
Fill in the background with malignant
figures from ancient nightmares—devils,
demons, myrmidons of evil.

When your icon of the enemy is complete
you will be able to kill without guilt,
slaughter without shame.
The thing you destroy will have become
merely an enemy of God, an impediment
to the sacred dialectic of history.[42]

Keen's powerful poem illustrates well the role that us-them thinking, dehumanization of victims, and blaming the victims play in the social death of the victims. Us-them thinking reveals that the psychological burden of extraordinary evil is eased by the fact that it is performed, in part, in the pursuit of one's own self-esteem. The psychological primacy in us-them thinking is on "us." In other words, the process of in-group formation and attachment take precedence over attitudes toward out-groups.

There is a point, however, at which dividing people into in-group and out-group members produces human estrangement that fosters a second mechanism of social death—dehumanization of the victims—and a line is crossed that more easily enables "us" to perpetrate extraordinary evil against "them." In the words of Richard Wrangham and Dale Peterson, "Taken to an extreme, in-group-out-group bias effectively dehumanizes Them, which means that moral law does not apply to Them and that therefore even ordinary and very moral people can do the most appalling things with a clear conscience."[43]

The ease with which perpetrators can depersonalize victims, particularly when there is a tremendous power differential between the two groups, is paralleled by the ease with which perpetrators can rationalize harming their victims. Despite their role in proving the contrary, perpetrators maintain their belief in a just and fair world by implicating the victims in their own victimization. In so doing, they protect themselves from any implication that people anywhere in the world—including them—could fall victim to unfair treatment.

Where is the hope? What are the implications of this four-stage explanatory model? And how can we, as a society and as individuals, cultivate the moral sensibilities that will check the forces that lead to the commission of extraordinary evil? These questions are the focus of part III of this book.

The "Safe Area" of Srebrenica

U NDER MARSHAL TITO, the former communist republic of Yugo-
slavia was a multiethnic state of six component republics or regions
—Bosnia, Croatia, Macedonia, Montenegro, Serbia, and Slovenia. When
Tito died in 1980, however, he left a Yugoslavia too decentralized for any
ethnic group to dominate. Into this vacuum stepped Serbia's Slobodan
Milosevic and his ultranationalistic campaign to make "Greater Serbia" the
new postcommunist Yugoslavia. This led to the secession of Slovenia and
Croatia in 1991, triggering ethnic fighting between Croats, Muslims, and
Serbs in those countries. The residents of Bosnia, Macedonia, and Montenegro faced the choice of whether to stay in what remained of Serb-dom-
inated Yugoslavia. The Montenegrins, closely related to the Serbs and less
economically developed, decided to stay. The Macedonians left and, while
presently struggling with an increase in ethnic intolerance, have managed
independence relatively peacefully.

In 1992, the Bosnian government, supported by Muslims and Croats,
also voted for secession. The United States and European Union recognized
the newly independent state of Bosnia-Herzegovina in April 1992. But the
Bosnian Serbs (about one-third of the population) refused to accept the
mostly Muslim Bosnian government. Milosevic immediately armed local
Bosnian Serbs and began a wider war—a land grab masquerading as an
age-old ethnic conflict.

Unfortunately for Milosevic, too many members of rival ethnic communities remained in the seized territories. As a result, the more territories
the Bosnian Serbs seized, the more difficult the territories became to occupy
and administer. To achieve his ideal of an ethnically homogeneous state,
Milosevic turned to ethnic cleansing—that is, the use of violence and deportations to remove any trace of the other ethnic communities who had
previously cohabited with Serbs in the coveted territories.

In Bosnia, the internal Serbian minority, allied with the Serbian/Yugoslav army, waged war against Muslims. In the name of ethnic cleansing, they created conditions of comprehensive oppression; systematically raped, tortured, and murdered civilians; appropriated and pillaged civilian property; used detainees as human shields on front lines and in minefields; and threw Muslims into concentration camps. In 1993, emboldened by Milosevic's campaign of terror against the Muslims and his support for a Greater Croatia, the Croats entered the war against their former Muslim allies, using many of the same methods of ethnic cleansing as the Serbs.

War in the region would not end until November 1995. It would stand as the most violent event Europe had experienced since World War II. For years, major world powers chose to characterize the Balkan conflict as a civil war built on an ancient ethnic feud. In that understanding, ethnic cleansing was just a by-product of war. In reality, however, ethnic cleansing was always the foremost goal of the war, not an unintended consequence.

Srebrenica is a traditional Muslim town tucked away in a steep-sloped valley in eastern Bosnia, about forty-five miles northeast of Sarajevo and right beside the Serbian border. By spring 1993, Srebrenica contained an estimated 30,000 refugees, mostly Bosnian Muslims fleeing past Serb assaults. Bosnian Serb forces, wanting to make the hills along their border a pure Serb heartland, initiated a sustained and vicious attack on Srebrenica. On April 16, 1993, the Security Council of the United Nations passed Resolution 819, demanding that all parties treat Srebrenica as a "safe area" and that the Bosnian Serbs cease their attacks and withdraw.

With no foreign government willing to reverse the Serbian military gains in the surrounding areas, Srebrenica was kept artificially alive for another two years as a small, isolated, "safe area." On July 6, 1995, the Serbs again began an assault on Srebrenica. Despite the presence of UN troops, Bosnian Serbs at Srebrenica perpetrated the single worst war crime since the end of World War II. While the world stood by and watched, Serb forces advanced into the "safe area" and rounded up tens of thousands of refugees. Some 23,000 Muslim women and children were separated from the men and deported. The women were "reassured" that everyone would be bussed out and safely reunited. Zumra Shekhomerovic lived in downtown Srebrenica with her husband, son, and daughter for twenty-seven years. She describes the separation:

> From the direction of Bratunac, towards Srebrenica, trucks full of people came and they were going to Srebrenica, and they said that we *balije* [derogatory

word for Muslim] are leaving and that this is not for us anymore. They are going to live there now, and they were not the people who had lived there before. These people were strangers. When we came down and came to the slaughterhouse, then we saw, from some 10–15 meters in front of us, [that] they started separating. They were separating boys from 12 years of age and old men to 77 years of age.

When our turn came, two of our neighbors were separated in front of us. They separated many from my family, and [people] from my area, I know many of those by name and surname, those that were separated. And now it was our turn. We came, as we were approaching, there was a checkpoint, and at the checkpoint stood armed Chetniks [Serbs]. And [one] said to my husband, as we were coming from above, "You come this way" and to me, " You go on!"

For me to go on, while he stopped for a moment. While we were standing in the queue, he was very worried about me, as my health is a bit fragile. He told me not to worry, that everything will be all right. It was so hot, he was worried I would faint.

His hand was on my shoulder, trembling. . . . Somewhere deep inside me it still trembles. . . . It seems to me that every moment I feel it here on my left shoulder and that hot whisper of his that was reaching my ear as he told me not to worry, that everything will be all right. [He said] to tell, when I come to Tuzla [Bosnia], to tell my son that he sends his warmest regards and to tell him to listen to me. And when I talk to my daughter, who is in Slovenia, by phone to tell her that her daddy has been missing her very much and that he cannot wait until the moment he will see her. . . . But he never lived to see that moment. These were his last words. They separated him and I stayed mute, I could not talk. . . . How I walked to the trucks, believe me, I don't know. I don't know how I climbed the truck or came by [the] truck. I don't know what I stood on to climb up [onto the truck]. I passed, and he stayed with his black jacket which he held in his hand. I could see him for another 10 yards while the truck went around the transporter, and afterwards another truck parked in the way. I never saw him again and don't know what happened to him. I regret so much that I did not say, "Don't take him," that I didn't scream or shout for help. Maybe it would be easier to live now. I just left silently, and could not speak, while my tears were flowing like a river and still do today, believe me.[1]

Her children survived, but her husband was never to be seen again. Over the next several days, the Serb forces executed between 5,000 and 8,000 unarmed Muslim men and boys (some as young as ten years of age)— soldiers and civilians alike—on football fields, in gymnasiums, and in abandoned factories and warehouses. The bodies of the victims were then bulldozed into mass graves.

A very few eyewitnesses to these massacres survived, often by pretending to be dead and lying still under bodies until they could escape. The following is excerpted from the account of fifty-two-year-old Hakija Huseinovic. He was one of a group of men herded into an agricultural warehouse into which Serbs opened fire:

> When it got dark, the shooting stopped. There was a lot of screaming, shouting, people were crying out for help in the warehouse. Many were wounded. As I lay down, the right-hand side of my body got soaked in blood. I couldn't stand it any longer, so I got up from the blood and pulled a dead body underneath me to lie on top of it. When dawn started breaking, [my neighbor] Zulfo Salilovic got up to urinate and have a drink of water. I tugged at his coat and told him, "Stay down," and he said, "I can't hold it any longer." A machine-gun burst cut him in half and he fell down. I covered myself with two dead bodies and stayed underneath for twenty-four hours. . . . Afterwards, a truck and a mechanical shovel appeared. They started tearing down the side of the warehouse facing the road, then they started loading. They loaded until nightfall. The shovel came very close. I was thinking, "This is the end for me. All that fear has been in vain," but you have to keep hoping whilst you're still alive. And then I heard someone say, "Park the shovel, wash the tarmac, and cover the dead bodies with hay. It's enough for today."[2]

Later that night, Huseinovic managed to escape, together with another man. Seventeen-year-old Nezad Avdic was with another group of Muslim men taken to a school complex in Karakaj near Zvornik. He described the events at the site of his intended execution:

> When the trucks stopped, we immediately heard shooting outside. . . . The Chetniks told us to get out, five at a time. I was in the middle of the group, and the men in front didn't want to get out. They were terrified, they started pulling back. But we had no choice, and when it was my turn to get out with five others, I saw dead bodies everywhere. . . . They ordered us to lie down, and as I threw myself on the ground, I heard gunfire. I was hit in my right arm and three bullets went through the right side of my torso. I don't recall whether or not I fell on the ground unconscious. But I remember being frightened, thinking it would soon be all over. While lying there I heard others screaming and moaning. . . . The man next to me was moaning, and one of the Chetniks ordered the others to check and see what bodies were still warm. "Put a bullet through all the heads, even if they're cold." Another Chetnik replied, "Fuck their mothers! They're all dead!" Only one Chetnik came over to the pile and shot the man next to me, and I felt stones hitting the upper part of my right arm. He continued his job until he was done.[3]

Later, Avdic and another man managed to escape and make it to Bosnian territory—two of only five survivors from the Karakaj massacre.

Ademovic Fatima, a survivor of the massacre at Srebrenica, watches the initial appearance of former Yugoslav president Slobodan Milosevic before the International Criminal Tribunal for the former Yugoslavia in the Hague (July 3, 2001). Photo by Reuters NewMedia Inc./CORBIS.

To date, more than 4,000 bodies have been found in mass graves near Srebrenica. As of this writing, the discovery and exhumation of mass graves continues. In September 2001, a mass grave containing dismembered body parts stacked in 162 sacks was discovered near the Bosnian Serb town of Zvornik, just a few miles from Srebrenica. The site may contain the remains of as many as 250 people.

All parties—Serbs, Croats, and Muslims—committed some verifiable atrocities in the conflict. Observers generally agree, however, that Bosnian Serbs bear responsibility for the overwhelming preponderance of war crimes. Their victims were mostly Muslims, but also Croats. In an exhaustive report to the United Nations, a special commission of experts, chaired by Cherif Bassiouni of DePaul University in Chicago, concluded that 90 percent of the crimes committed in Bosnia-Herzegovina were the responsibility of Serb extremists, 6 percent by Croat extremists, and 4 percent by Muslim extremists. Most significant, the Bosnian Serbs were the only party that systematically attempted to eliminate all traces of other ethnic groups from their territory.

In response, in 1993, the United Nations formed the International

Criminal Tribunal for the former Yugoslavia (ICTY) in the Hague. The ICTY was charged with the prosecution of persons responsible for serious violations of international humanitarian law committed in the territory of the former Yugoslavia since 1991. In March 2000, General Radislav Krstic, a Bosnian Serb, stood trial before the ICTY for his role in atrocities committed by soldiers under his command at Srebrenica. In early August 2001, Krstic was sentenced for forty-six years after being found guilty on eight counts—two of genocide, five of crimes against humanity, and one of violations of the laws or customs of war. Krstic's superiors—Serb leader Radovan Karadzic and his military chief, General Ratko Mladic (personally present at the slaughter in Srebrenica)—also were indicted for genocide at Srebrenica. Unfortunately, many Bosnian Serb war crime suspects still enjoy strong popular support, and both men are believed free and at large in Serb-controlled territory.

In a trial that began on February 12, 2002, Slobodan Milosevic was indicted by the ICTY on charges of genocide and crimes against humanity in Kosovo, Croatia, and Bosnia and Herzegovina. As of this writing, Milosevic's trial in the Hague continues. The UN's chief war crimes prosecutor, Carla del Ponte, believes that the work of the ICTY will not be completed before 2010.[4]

III

WHAT HAVE WE LEARNED AND WHY DOES IT MATTER?

9

Conclusion

Can We Be Delivered from Extraordinary Evil?

> Without evil goodness would not be possible either. . . . Without the
> forever-lurking inclination to selfishness and discord, there can be no
> ethical ideal and practice.
>
> Eliezer Berkovits, *God, Man, and History*

IS THERE ANY HOPE THAT the twentieth-century's "Age of Genocide" will be supplanted by an increase in cooperative, caring, nonviolent relations between countries and the people in them? Unfortunately, most futurists and scholars in genocide studies think not. Current trends suggest that there will be escalating conditions of extreme hardship, even disaster, in many parts of the world throughout the twenty-first century. These trends include a combination of environmental damage, loss of agricultural lands, dwindling of food and fuel resources, and a doubling of population to between 8.5 and 9.5 billion by 2025. Disconcertingly, the most volatile areas of social instability, mainly in the Third World, are the very places where much of the genocide since 1945 already has taken place.

How well have the lessons of the past century been learned by the international community? Unfortunately, the harsh reality is that most states lack the political will to enlarge their definition of national interest to include the prevention, stopping, or punishing of genocide and mass killing. In the words of journalist William Shawcross, "We want more to be put right, but we are prepared to sacrifice less."[1] Political leaders typically recoil when faced with the reality that intervention cannot always be cost- or risk-free. When states do intervene, the determinants of "national interest" are more often money and practical politics, rather than moral outrage or humanitarian concern. To overcome the problem of political will, it is necessary that each of us—in a concerted, organized fashion—call out for action and make clear our belief that preventing, stopping, and punishing genocide and mass killing is indeed in all of our national interests.

Once a new political will is established, however, it remains futile unless the potential to act effectively is present. No single nation, even one as powerful as America, can or should shoulder the burden of ensuring international peace and security for all people. Generally, individual states lack both the resources and the authority to take action in every situation of mass killing and genocide. Indeed, the forces of globalization and international cooperation are redefining the notion of state sovereignty. As a result, countries throughout the world turn to the United Nations, the only universal-membership organization mandated to ensure international peace and human rights.

What can we expect the UN to do? In terms of *prevention*, the UN can call for the continued development of early warning systems that identify and monitor societies likely to resort to mass killing and genocide. The UN, along with other international organizations, can support social and political transformation in instable societies—particularly the promotion of stable democracies. The socialization effects observed in countries where there is a restraint on power by the participation of middle and lower classes in the determination of power holders and policy making are striking. In addition, the right of humanitarian pressure and intervention, including those from nongovernmental organizations, can be recognized and encouraged.

Focusing additional efforts on healing, forgiveness, and reconciliation after mass killing or genocide also can facilitate prevention. Ervin Staub is one of many scholars who believe that past victimization is among the cultural characteristics that contribute to the likelihood of violence by groups against others. Victims of group violence suffer numerous aftereffects, one of which is a tremendous sense of vulnerability in the world. When new conflicts arise with other groups, this sense that others are dangerous and not to be trusted may lead victims of past violence to feel the need to strike out in order to defend themselves. Healing from the trauma of mass killing and genocide therefore becomes extremely important to the prevention of recurring group violence. In Staub's words: "When the two groups, the perpetrators and the victims, continue to live together . . . you cannot progress very far without some kind of reconciliation beginning between the two groups, because healing implies some sense of security."[2] Staub is applying his principles of reconciliation in Rwanda, and early results indicate that, relative to a control group, the treatment group shows a higher level of "conditional forgiveness"—a willingness to forgive the perpetrating group, conditional on acknowledgment of what they have done.

Central to *stopping* mass killing and genocide, the UN can mandate the creation of a permanent, standing international force that can be rapidly deployed—in days or weeks, not months—against repressive regimes that threaten, or are perpetrating, killing of targeted victim groups. At present, the UN lacks a strong and effective military force capable of rapid response to situations of developing violence. Once in place, this may also necessitate a reform of UN decision-making structures so that deployment of military (or civilian) missions cannot be blocked by just one of the five permanent members (China, France, Great Britain, Russia, and the United States) of the Security Council.

Finally, in terms of *punishment*, international law can be strengthened, with particular emphasis on creating a standing, permanent tribunal to judge those accused of crimes against humanity. On July 17, 1998, at the United Nations diplomatic conference in Rome, a treaty was adopted for the creation of a permanent International Criminal Court (ICC) to investigate and bring to justice individuals who commit the most serious violations of international humanitarian law—war crimes, crimes against humanity (including terrorist attacks), and genocide. Unlike the International Court of Justice in the Hague, in which only states can bring suits against one another, the ICC will have the capacity to try individuals. The ICC will *not* supersede or interfere with functioning national judicial systems. It will be able to take action only in situations where national courts are either unwilling or unable to investigate or prosecute alleged criminals.

The ICC will enter into force once 60 states have ratified the Rome Treaty. As of this writing, 56 have ratified and 139 states have signed the Rome Treaty. President Clinton pledged the United States as a signatory on the day of the December 31, 2000, deadline established in the treaty. In so doing, he acknowledged continuing concerns about significant flaws in the treaty while also committing the United States to ongoing involvement in making the ICC an instrument of impartial and effective justice in the years to come. Clinton's signing of the treaty drew immediate and fierce opposition from conservatives—most notably Sen. Jesse Helms (R-N.C.), chairman of the Senate Foreign Relations Committee. "Today's action is a blatant action by a lame-duck president to tie the hands of his successor," said Helms, who feared the "international kangaroo court" would leave U.S. service personnel subject to unwarranted prosecution.[3]

On July 19, 2001, forty-four members of the U.S. House of Representatives sent a letter imploring President Bush to "remain engaged" and "actively participate" in discussions regarding the ICC. The following day, ten senators sent a similar plea to Secretary of State Colin Powell, stating that "whatever concerns the United States has with the Court, they can be best addressed by vigorously asserting U.S. negotiating rights as a signatory to the Treaty." On August 1, Sen. Christopher Dodd (D-Conn.) and Rep. William D. Delahunt (D-Mass.) joined with Rep. Amo Houghton (R-N.Y.) and Rep. Tom Lantos (D-Calif.) to introduce legislation that supports continued U.S. engagement with the ICC negotiations and cooperation with the court to try war criminals. On September 26, Helms countered with the proposed American Servicemembers' Protection Act (ASPA). If adopted, the ASPA would permanently prohibit all U.S. cooperation with the ICC, severely limit military assistance to most countries that ratify the treaty, and authorize the president to use "all means necessary and appropriate" to free individuals held on behalf of or by the ICC. On December 7, Helms offered the ASPA as an amendment to the Department of Defense appropriations bill for fiscal year 2002. On December 20, however, the House and Senate conference committee stripped the bill of the Helms amendment and deferred to a previous amendment by Rep. Henry Hyde (R-Ill.) that restricts the use of U.S. funds to support or negotiate the ICC during fiscal year 2002 only.

While most observers believe the ICC will come into existence by the end of 2002, so far the Bush administration has delayed the release of its policy on the ICC—though a letter of September 25, 2001, ominously indicated its support for some version of the ASPA. It is even possible that the policy review may recommend the unprecedented and controversial step of nullifying the United States' signature of the Rome treaty. Such actions, and lack of action, have prompted considerable concern that our noninvolvement will undermine our international human rights objectives and may lead to a court that is antagonistic to the United States.[4]

Given the myriad uncertainties surrounding these issues, a more complete understanding of how ordinary people come to take part in extraordinary evil may be our best hope in lowering the death toll from our seemingly inevitable litany of genocide and mass killing. If we fail to learn, or to act on what we have learned, we forfeit our power to alter ourselves and, eventually, heal the world.

What Have We Learned?

I developed this explanatory model so that we will have a clearer understanding of how extraordinary evil is produced and, thus, be in a better position to cut off that evil. Education has substantial humanizing effects and, when applied, can be an effective antidote to our collective inhumanity. Ultimately, being aware of our own capacity for extraordinary evil— and the dispositional, situational, and social influences that foster it—is the best safeguard we can have against future genocide.

Now that we have outlined the disease, is there a remedy? What have we learned about how ordinary people commit extraordinary evil which we can then apply to the prevention of mass killing and genocide? The explanatory model, which uses the three components *actor, context of the action,* and *definition of the target,* can sensitize us to the forces that shape our responses to authority and, in so doing, help us cultivate the moral sensibilities that can curb our capacity for extraordinary evil.

Actor

The dispositions and personalities of perpetrators *do* matter. There is certainly something about *who* the perpetrators are that must be taken into account in understanding how ordinary people commit extraordinary evil. The model outlined two sets of dispositional influences most relevant to understanding perpetrators of extraordinary evil.

Chapter 5 examined the universal dispositional nature of human nature —*our ancestral shadow*. We recognized that we cannot underestimate the impact of *what* we are on *who* we are. We cannot ignore our evolutionary heritage in our attempt to understand how ordinary people commit extraordinary evil. Building on our innate, evolution-produced tendencies for ethnocentrism, xenophobia, and the desire for social dominance, we found that extraordinary evil is readily available in our human potential. The nature of our human nature endows us with psychological mechanisms that leave us all *capable* of extraordinary evil when activated by appropriate cues.

While it is not reasonable to hope for dramatic or quick evolution of who we are, we should remember that the dark side of our human nature is not inevitable. We can, and should, identify those elements of our human nature that can most usefully serve cooperative and peaceful goals, and build on them. There are certainly innate tendencies for cooperative, caring, nonviolent relations that enhanced our ancestors' survival and reproductive success in a world of limited resources. Such prosocial tendencies would have been favored by natural selection and would still be retained, at some level, as long-term adaptations. We can foster cultural practices and resources that activate these adaptations and produce mutually beneficial outcomes for formerly antagonistic groups. As biologist Lyall Watson concludes, "The roots of war lie deep in nature, it seems, but then so too do the roots of peace."[5]

Understanding the universal dispositional nature of human nature, however, tells us only that we all are *capable* of extraordinary evil. It does not explain why only *some* of us actually perpetrate extraordinary evil and, in fact, why the great majority of us never do. To explain why some people do perpetrate extraordinary evil but most do not requires sharpening our focus to the more particular dispositional influences that mold the *identities of the perpetrators*.

In chapter 6, we focused on three such dispositional influences: cultural belief systems, moral disengagement, and rational self-interest. These influences remind us that all cultures, communities, and family systems leave their fingerprints on the members within them. The belief systems in which we have been marinated, and to which we adhere, impact our moral engagement or disengagement with the "other." While respecting the diversity of belief systems through the world, we can—and should—identify the socialization practices that transfer control and responsibility from the individual to an external influence or authority, particularly those practices that facilitate a moral disengagement from a specified target group. While cultures and social institutions themselves may not be evil, we must acknowledge that they can—in myriad ways—create the preconditions or enhance the potential for the generation of extraordinary evil. German political philosopher Eric Voegelin reminds us of the importance of the restraining effects of society when he writes of "the simple man, who is a decent man as long as the society as a whole is in order but who then goes wild, without knowing what he is doing, when disorder arises somewhere and the society is no longer holding together."[6]

Certain socialization practices also influence how each of us defines rational self-interest. On a professional level, we must recognize that the choices and compromises we make in our own self-interest, though often small and localized, may have dangerous cumulative consequences we cannot predict. On a personal level, some socialization practices can encourage a restricted understanding that defines self-interest only in terms of myself and the people closest to me. Others can encourage a broader understanding that defines self-interest in a more global way—recognizing that evil perpetrated against anyone is evil perpetrated against everyone.

Context of the Action

The universal and particular dispositional influences that mold the actors do not occur in a vacuum. Their influence must be considered relative to the context of the actors' action. The focus here is on the fact that the huge predominance of extraordinary evil committed in the world is, in some sense, a societal product in which a complex and sustained series of social forces enable ordinary people to commit extraordinary evil.

In chapter 7, we examined features of the immediate social context— *a culture of cruelty*—that help perpetrators initiate, sustain, and cope with their extraordinary evil. In particular, we focused on three momentum-inducing features of a culture of cruelty most relevant to understanding how ordinary people commit extraordinary evil: professional socialization, binding factors of the group, and the merger of role and person.

If, as I argued, extraordinary evil is facilitated by a culture of cruelty, then the diminution of extraordinary evil may be partially done at the organizational level. We have created an understanding of how cultures of cruelty can purposively move—or even accidentally lurch—toward causing extraordinary evil. We now need to develop a set of interventions designed to prevent the development of a culture of cruelty in military and paramilitary organizations. These should include a review of the professional socialization involved in such organizations (with particular focus on the role of ritual conduct in the repression of conscience), suggestions to moderate the binding factors of the group that obscure and minimize the agentive role in extraordinary evil, and a renewed understanding of the ways in which evildoing organizations transform the people within them.

Definition of the Target

Finally, in chapter 8 we looked at the definition of the target, the psychological and sociological construction of victims as the "other." I argued that the *social death of the victims* involves an exclusion that removes them from the perpetrators' universe of moral obligation. This ostracism is built on the backs of three cognitive mechanisms: us-them thinking, dehumanization of the victims, and blaming the victims.

Fortunately, social psychologists have developed specific strategies to combat intergroup biases stemming from these cognitive mechanisms. These can involve structuring intergroup contact to produce more individualized perceptions of the members of the other group, fostering personalized interactions between members of the different groups, engaging in activities to achieve common goals, or redefining group boundaries to create more inclusive, superordinate representations of the groups.

Recall the Robbers' Cave experiment from chapter 8. When we left them, the Rattlers and Eagles were two rival groups with hostile attitudes and negative images of each other. Muzafer Sherif and his colleagues then were faced with a daunting task of conflict reduction—that is, a removal of the intergroup biases they had created. As we saw, simply bringing the two groups together in neutral situations only increased the hostility. It was only by introducing tasks of mutual interdependence (for example, both groups cooperating to solve the breakdown of the water supply system to the camp) that Sherif was able to restore harmony between the two groups. In other words, group membership was redefined along the boundaries of an interdependent, or superordinate, group. "They" came to be included into "us." By the end of the three-week camp, friendships had formed across group lines, and intergroup hostility had reduced significantly.[7] Sherif's results also have been replicated in experiments among 150 groups of executives from industrial organizations.[8] Taken as a whole, such research demonstrates that anytime we can alter who is a "we" and who is a "they," we can undermine a contributing force to the social death of victims.

Humanizing, decategorizing, or personalizing others all create a powerful self-restraining effect. It is difficult to mistreat a person who has an actual identity, with flesh and blood and family, without suffering a significant level of personal distress and self-condemnation. Milgram's research showed that obedience decreased as the physical distance between the teacher and learner decreased, testifying to the power of personalization to counteract cruel conduct and to promote a strong sense of social obligation. Craig Haney also has advocated the power of personalization to capital defense attorneys, who must bring the "defendant to life" so that the jury will want to let him or her live.[9] Albert Bandura's summary of the power of personalization is apt: "The joys and suffering of those with whom one identifies are more vicariously arousing than are those of strangers or of individuals who have been divested of human qualities."[10]

The power of personalization is exactly why—as a collective and as individuals—we must resist the tendency, however comfortable, to become isolationist after the attacks of September 11. We must persist in our pursuit of a greater "us." To not do so is to fall willing prey to our evolutionarily primed tendencies of ethnocentrism and xenophobia. Central to this pursuit are educational and societal programs that broaden our boundaries and experiences of the "other." As Maxine Greene writes: "It is through and by means of education . . . that individuals can be provoked to reach beyond themselves. . . . It is through and by means of education that they may become empowered to think about what they are doing, to become mindful, to share meanings, to conceptualize, to make varied sense of their lived worlds. It is through education that preferences may be released, languages learned, intelligences developed, perspectives opened, possibilities disclosed."[11]

A Final Note on Responsibility

To resist the compelling forces that shape our responses to authority requires a rare degree of individual strength—psychological, moral, and physical. Regardless, we do know that some people *do* resist, and it is in that reality that we both take hope and reserve the right of condemnation for those who perpetrate extraordinary evil. Here, in the final chapter, I again reassert an argument I made in the opening chapter and in the introduction to the model: to offer a psychological explanation for the atrocities committed by perpetrators is not to forgive, justify, or condone their behaviors. There are no "perpetratorless" mass killings or genocides. Perpetrators are not just the hapless victims of human nature or their social context. At each step of the explanatory model, there are many opportunities for choice. Sometimes the choosing may take place without awareness or conscious deliberation. At other times, it is a matter of very focused and deliberate decision making. Regardless, the perpetrators, in willfully failing to exercise their moral judgment, retain full moral and legal accountability for the atrocities they committed. No explanatory model will ever take that away.

What Do We Still Need to Learn?

I have a colleague who, when preparing to introduce a new proposal or plan, is fond of saying, "Only the whale that surfaces gets harpooned." Certainly, this explanatory model—representing an understanding of how ordinary people commit extraordinary evil—will receive its fair share of criticism and revision. In a way, though, that is exactly why I developed the model. In my research, I have found that the fascination of the question of how ordinary people commit extraordinary evil pales in comparison to the frustration of incomplete, inadequate, and incoherent explanations that dot the academic landscape. To be sure, some good work has been done. To be equally sure, though, many of the explanatory efforts, as we saw in part I of the book, have emphasized the particular instead of the whole—uninterpreted fact instead of fundamental principle. The model, and this book, is an attempt to synthesize and systematize the diversity of explanations into one coherent whole—or whale. Now that the whale has surfaced, future research should sharpen and clarify where necessary. At this point, I envision three specific directions for future research.

First, scholars in genocide studies now need to take the model and test its applicability to a broader range of cases of perpetrator behavior than those I have included in this book. This model was based on primary source material collated by a host of historians, political scientists, psychologists, and sociologists. The substantial majority of this material was related to one particular instance of genocide—the Holocaust. As I pointed out earlier, however, the opening of archives throughout Eastern Europe; the emergence of primary source materials from Cambodia, Rwanda, and the former Yugoslavia; and the cultivation of oral collections from victims and perpetrators of extraordinary evil around the world continue to yield even more documentation against which this model can be compared. This model, and other competing explanations, could and should be subjected to continuing primary research from the broadest possible range of cases of mass killing and genocide; otherwise we might forever generalize only on the basis of the Holocaust-related biographies and case studies we have at our present disposal.

Is the model a valid and reliable fit for the diversity of perpetrator behavior across human history? Is it sensitive to the vast array of cultural differences that characterize perpetrators of mass killing and genocide throughout the world? While retaining a professionally appropriate skepticism about the reliability of perpetrator testimony (particularly the fact that such testimony may be biased toward "ordinariness" and "banality"), can we even break the conspiracy of silence that surrounds most former perpetrators throughout the world and discover where *they* believe the model does or does not fit their own experiences?

As just one particularly intriguing example, we need to determine the specific applicability of the model to female perpetrators of mass killing and genocide. Most analyses of women in military or paramilitary actions have emphasized their complicity in supporting husbands, sons, and brothers; working in factories making weapons of destruction; or standing silently by as witnesses to the atrocities committed in their lands or on foreign shores. Contemporary research, however, reveals an increasing and extensive documentation of females involved in extraordinary evil—either in defined military roles or as bureaucratic or brutal genocidal killers.[12]

Second, we need to clarify the relative importance of each of the components in the model in explaining how ordinary people commit extraordinary evil. The intensity of each component is uneven. Some are more powerful than others. Specifically, which components are more central, or more psychologically primary, than others? Which are most important, which are less important, and which are relatively trivial? Recognizing that the components of the model are not, in reality, as easily separable as they appear on paper, where are the discernible areas of overlap that may be clarified to sharpen the model's explanatory capability?

Do certain pieces of the model correlate more to the initial willingness of ordinary people to commit extraordinary evil while other pieces correlate more to perpetrators' sustained involvement in extraordinary evil? Which components act jointly, and which are unlikely, by themselves, to lead ordinary people to commit extraordinary evil? What, if anything, do we lose by reducing the complex phenomenon of extraordinary evil to discrete, component elements?

Third, and finally, future research needs to discover what practical applications the model has for inhibiting ordinary people from committing extraordinary evil. The model falls far short if it cannot lead us to some better strategies to prevent the evil and promote the good where the dramas of our lives unfold. The lesson that ordinary people commit extraordinary evil should not be compartmentalized only as "bad news"—a disturbing, unsettling, disquieting truth about the human condition. The lesson does contain potentially "good news" as well: the commission of extraordinary evil is no longer a mystery. By understanding how ordinary people commit extraordinary evil, we gain insight into how such evil can be lessened. When we understand the ordinariness of extraordinary evil, we will be less surprised by evil, less likely to be unwitting contributors to evil, and better equipped to forestall evil.

In short, now that we have begun to understand how extraordinary evil is done, we can begin to understand how to diminish it. Just as ordinary people can commit extraordinary evil, ordinary people can also subvert extraordinary evil. The work done on the prevention of extraordinary evil presents a rich field with newly emerging theories, but relatively little research. Much more research, from a wide range of academic disciplines and in both laboratory and real-life settings, is needed to educate us about how to make the world of our children a safer place.

These three suggestions are obviously only a sampling of the directions future research may take. One of the measures of the usefulness of any theoretical construct, including this explanatory model, is the "fertility criterion"—that is, the degree to which it stimulates future research. I hope and expect that this model will be the beginning—not the end—of much fruitful research. If this beginning succeeds in increasing our powers of explanation, prediction, and control over extraordinary evil, then the model will have served its purpose.

Why Does It Matter?

It is arrogant to believe that any study of extraordinary human evil can offer closure. As I write this last page, I certainly cannot say to myself with any measure of absolute and unequivocal certainty, "Well, I fully understand now how ordinary people commit extraordinary evil." While the model offered here gives us a framework within which to continue our investigations, it certainly raises as many questions as it gives definitive answers. It is a point of departure rather than a point of arrival—the end of a beginning rather than the beginning of an end. Given that, I am committed to remain open to new information or a different take on the problem of extraordinary human evil.

As the tragedy of September 11 reminded us, it is equally arrogant to believe that we sit anywhere near the beginning of a world in which extraordinary human evil—resulting either from state-directed terrorism or terrorism from below—is dissipating. As conventional and unconventional warfare escalate across the world, our hope for an increase in cooperative, caring, nonviolent relations continues to fade away. We are left with the humbling and painful recognition that the persistence of inhumanity in human affairs is incontrovertible. It is hard to argue that we can do something beyond merely make the world a little less horrible. This is a humbling recognition, but—in this case—humility will serve us well. It is only in accepting the limits of who we are that we have a legitimate chance to structure a society in which the exercise of human evil is lessened. It is important to understand the conditions under which we can be transformed into killing machines. The more we know, and the more open we are to seeing ourselves as we are, the better we can control ourselves. Civility, after all, is a chosen state, not a natural condition. If we can understand more accurately how ordinary people come to commit extraordinary evil, there is at least a faint glimmer of hope that we all may, ultimately, be delivered from extraordinary evil.

> Long is the way and hard, that out of hell leads up to light.
>
> John Milton, *Paradise Lost*

NOTES

Preface

1. The account of Sadri and Mihrie Sikaqi comes from a special section titled "Crisis in Kosovo" in the June 16, 1999, edition of the *Washington Post*, p. A28.

2. Cited in Lance Morrow, "Evil," *Time* (June 10, 1991), p. 52.

3. See A. Westing, "War as a Human Endeavour," *Journal of Peace Research* 3 (1982). The data on war-related deaths is drawn from William Eckhardt's "War-Related Deaths since 3000 B.C.," *Bulletin of Peace Proposals* (December 1991).

4. Michael P. Ghiglieri, *The Dark Side of Man: Tracing the Origins of Male Violence* (Reading, Mass.: Perseus, 1999), p. 162.

5. Associated Press, "Third of Nations Mired in Conflict," December 30, 1999.

6. The distinction between terrorism "from below" and state-directed terrorism comes from the groundbreaking work in this area by Walter Laqueur. See particularly his *Terrorism* (Boston: Little, Brown, 1977).

7. The estimate of 60 million victims of mass killing and genocide comes from Smith's "Human Destructiveness and Politics" in Isidor Wallimann and Michael N. Dobkowski, eds., *Genocide and the Modern Age: Etiology and Case Studies of Mass Death* (Syracuse, N.Y.: Syracuse University Press, 2000), p. 21.

8. James Waller, *Face to Face: The Changing State of Racism across America* (New York: Perseus, 1998); *Prejudice across America* (Jackson: University Press of Mississippi, 2000).

Introduction

1. Much of the material on the Mauthausen camp is drawn from Gordon J. Horwitz, *In the Shadow of Death: Living outside the Gates of Mauthausen* (New York: Free Press, 1990), and Evelyn Le Chene, *Mauthausen: The History of a Death Camp* (London: Methuen, 1971). Also helpful were a brief chapter on Mauthausen in Jon Bridgman, *The End of the Holocaust: The Liberation of the Camps* (Portland, Ore.: Areopagitica Press, 1990); Gordon J. Horwitz's "Places Far Away, Places Very Near: Mauthausen, the Camps of the Shoah, and the Bystanders," in Michael Berenbaum and Abraham J. Peck, *The Holocaust and History: The Known, the Unknown, the Disputed, and the Reexamined* (Bloomington: Indiana University Press, 1998), pp. 409–420; and Robert H. Abzug's *Inside the Vicious Heart: Americans and the Liberation of Nazi Concentration Camps* (New York: Oxford University Press, 1985). The quote is taken from Horwitz, *In the Shadow of Death,* p. 23.

2. Cited in Bridgman, *The End of the Holocaust*, p. 90.

3. Ibid., p. 92.

Chapter 1

1. Saul Friedlander's call for psychological explanations is most clear in his "Trauma, Memory, and Transference," in Geoffrey H. Hartman, ed., *Holocaust Remembrance: The Shapes of Memory* (Oxford: Basil Blackwell, 1994), pp. 252–263. For more on Friedlander's work, see his *Nazi Germany and the Jews*, vol. 1: *The Years of Persecution, 1933–1939* (New York: HarperCollins, 1997).

2. Kurt H. Wolff, "For a Sociology of Evil," *Journal of Social Issues* 25 (1969), pp. 111–125; quote is on p. 111.

3. See H. Newton Malony, "The Question of Evil in Psychology," *Catalyst* 24 (March 1998).

4. "Perspectives on Evil and Violence," *Personality and Social Psychology Review* 3 (1999).

5. Quoted in chapter 46 of *The Leviathan* (1660), taken around October 2001 from http://www.orst.edu/instruct/phl302/texts/hobbes/leviathan-k.html.

6. Quoted in Stephen Miller, "A Note on the Banality of Evil," *WQ: Wilson Quarterly* 21 (Autumn 1998), p. 55.

7. See Daniel Jonah Goldhagen, *Hitler's Willing Executioners: Ordinary Germans and the Holocaust* (New York: Alfred A. Knopf, 1996), pp. 166–168.

8. The 75,000 to 150,000 estimate comes from David Norman Smith, "The Psycho-Cultural Roots of Genocide: Legitimacy and Crisis in Rwanda," *American Psychologist* 53 (July 1998), pp. 743–753. For a higher estimate, see Philip Gourevitch, *We Wish to Inform You That Tomorrow We Will Be Killed with Our Families: Stories from Rwanda* (New York: Farrar, Straus and Giroux, 1998), p. 244.

9. Bruno Bettelheim's quote comes from his review of Lifton's *The Nazi Doctors* in the *New York Times Book Review* (October 5, 1986), p. 62.

10. Bernhard Schlink, *The Reader* (New York: Vintage Books, 1995), p. 157.

11. Arthur G. Miller, Anne K. Gordon, and Amy M. Buddie, "Accounting for Evil and Cruelty: Is to Explain to Condone?," *Personality and Social Psychology Review* 3 (1999), pp. 254–268; quote is on p. 265.

12. Christopher R. Browning, *Ordinary Men: Reserve Police Battalion 101 and the Final Solution in Poland* (New York: HarperCollins, 1992), p. xx.

13. Roy F. Baumeister, *Evil: Inside Human Cruelty and Violence* (New York: W. H. Freeman and Company, 1997), p. 387.

14. Inga Clendinnen, *Reading the Holocaust* (New York: Cambridge University Press, 1999), p. 4.

15. Richard L. Rubenstein's quote is taken from his review of "The Nuremberg Mind" in *Psychology Today* (July 1976), p. 84.

"Nits Make Lice"

1. See Ward Churchill, *A Little Matter of Genocide: Holocaust and Denial in the Americas, 1492 to the Present* (San Francisco: City Lights Books, 1997), pp. 85–88, and James Wilson, *The Earth Shall Weep: A History of Native America* (New York: Grove Press, 1998), p. 34.

2. Churchill, *A Little Matter of Genocide*, p. 97.

3. Quotes compiled from Churchill, *A Little Matter of Genocide*, pp. 228–238; Stan Hoig, *The Sand Creek Massacre* (Norman: University of Oklahoma Press, 1961); and Dee Brown, *Bury My Heart at Wounded Knee: An Indian History of the American West* (New York: Henry Holt, 1970), chap. 4.

4. International Work Group for Indigenous Affairs, *IWGIA Yearbook 1987: Indigenous Peoples and Development* (Copenhagen, Denmark: International Work Group for Indigenous Affairs, 1988), p. 1.

Chapter 2

1. Gustave Le Bon, *The Crowd: A Study of the Popular Mind*, 2d ed. (1895; reprint, Dunwoody, Ga.: Norman S. Berg, 1968), p. 12. The best discussion of the Le Bon–Freud theories of crowd psychology is in a book by the eminent French social psychologist Serge Moscovici: *The Age of the Crowd: A Historical Treatise on Mass Psychology* (New York: Cambridge University Press, 1985).

2. Le Bon, *The Crowd*, pp. 5–6.

3. Reinhold Niebuhr, *Moral Man and Immoral Society: A Study in Ethics and Politics* (New York: Charles Scribner's Sons, 1932), p. ix.

4. Reinhold Niebuhr, *The Nature and Destiny of Man*, 2 vols. (New York: Charles Scribner's Sons, 1943), p. 35.

5. M. Scott Peck, *People of the Lie: The Hope for Healing Human Evil* (New York: Simon and Schuster, 1983), p. 218.

6. Dave Grossman, *On Killing: The Psychological Cost of Learning to Kill in War and Society* (Boston: Little, Brown, 1995), p. 152.

7. Richard Gregg, *The Power of Nonviolence*, 2d rev. ed. (Canton, Maine: Greanleaf Books, 1960), p. 118.

8. See Clark R. McCauley and Mary E. Segal, "Social Psychology of Terrorist Groups," in Clyde Hendrick, ed., *Group Processes and Intergroup Relations: Review of Personality and Social Psychology* (Newbury Park, Calif.: Sage Publications, 1987), pp. 231–256.

9. Robert Zajonc, "Massacres: Mass Murder in the Name of Moral Imperatives" (unpublished manuscript, 2000), p. 24.

10. Henry V. Dicks, "Personality Traits and National Socialist Ideology: A War-Time Study of German Prisoners of War," *Human Relations* 3 (1950), pp. 111–154; quote is from p. 112.

11. Goldhagen, *Hitler's Willing Executioners*, p. 167.

12. Christopher R. Browning, "Review Essay: Daniel Goldhagen's Willing Executioners," *History and Memory* 8 (1996), pp. 88–108; quote is from p. 99.

13. Ron Rosenbaum, *Explaining Hitler: The Search for the Origins of His Evil* (New York: Random House, 1998), p. 350.

14. Goldhagen, *Hitler's Willing Executioners*, p. 9.

15. Marion A. Kaplan, *Between Dignity and Despair: Jewish Life in Nazi Germany* (New York: Oxford University Press, 1998), p. 12.

16. Arnd Kruger, "'Once the Olympics Are Through, We'll Beat Up the Jew': German Jewish Sport, 1898–1938, and the Anti-Semitic Discourse," *Journal of Sport History* 26 (1999), pp. 353–375.

17. William Brustein, *The Logic of Evil: The Social Origins of the Nazi Party, 1925–1933* (New Haven, Conn.: Yale University Press, 1996).

18. Ibid., pp. 59–60.

19. David Bankier, *Germans and the Final Solution: Public Opinion under Nazism* (New York: Oxford University Press), pp. 151–152.

20. Ian Kershaw, "The Persecution of the Jews and German Public Opinion in the Third Reich," *Leo Baeck Institute Year Book* 26 (1981), pp. 281, 288.

21. Cited in Omer Bartov, "The Last German," *New Republic* (December 28, 1998), p. 38.

22. Ibid., p. 40.

23. Victor Klemperer, *Ich will Zeugnis ablegen bis zum letzten: Tagebuecher, 1933–1945* (Berlin: Aufbau-Verlag GmbH, 1995), p. 406.

24. Goldhagen, *Hitler's Willing Executioners*, p. 32.

25. Henry Friedlander, *The Origins of Nazi Genocide: From Euthanasia to the Final Solution* (Chapel Hill: University of North Carolina Press, 1995), p. 295.

26. Christopher R. Browning, lecture presented at Northwestern University, Evanston, Ill., for the Holocaust Educational Foundation, June 26, 1996.

27. Charny's quote comes from Israel W. Charny and Chanan Rapaport, *How Can We Commit the Unthinkable? Genocide: The Human Cancer* (Boulder, Colo.: Westview Press, 1982), p. 160.

28. Browning, "Review Essay," p. 102.

Dovey's Story

1. The leading scholar on the Armenian genocide is Vahakn Dadrian. Of his many works, I recommend his "The Naim-Andonian Documents in the World War I Destruction of the Ottoman Armenians: The Anatomy of a Genocide," *International Journal of Middle East Studies* 18 (1986), pp. 311–360, and his definitive book, *The History of the Armenian Genocide: Ethnic Conflict from the Balkans to Anatolia to the Caucasus* (Providence, R.I.: Berghahn Books, 1995). Also highly relevant is the eyewitness account of the U.S. ambassador to Turkey, Henry Morganthau's *Ambassador Morganthau's Story* (Plandome, N.Y.: New

Age Publishers, 1975), as well as Gerard J. Libaridian's "The Ultimate Repression: The Genocide of the Armenians, 1915–1917," in Walliman and Dobkowski, *Genocide and the Modern Age*, pp. 203–235.

2. Peter Balakian's PEN Albrand Award–winning memoir, from which this selection is excerpted, is *Black Dog of Fate: A Memoir* (New York: Basic Books, 1997), pp. 214–217.

3. For more information about the continuing Turkish denial, I recommend Dadrian's *The Key Elements in the Turkish Denial of the Armenian Genocide: A Case Study of Destruction and Falsification* (Cambridge, Mass.: Zoryan Institute, 1999) and Roger Smith, Eric Markusen, and Robert Jay Lifton's "Professional Ethics and the Denial of the Armenian Genocide," *Holocaust and Genocide Studies* 9 (Spring 1995), pp. 1–22.

Chapter 3

1. Michael R. Marrus, *The Nuremberg War Crimes Trial, 1945–1946: A Documentary History* (Boston: Bedford/St. Martin's, 1997), p. 1.

2. Joseph E. Persico, *Nuremberg: Infamy on Trial* (New York: Penguin Books, 1994), p. 439.

3. Douglas M. Kelley, *22 Cells in Nuremberg: A Psychiatrist Examines the Nazi War Criminals* (New York: MacFadden Books, 1947), p. 127.

4. Quoted in Louise E. Hoffman, "American Psychologists and Wartime Research on Germany, 1941–1945," *American Psychologist* 47 (1992), p. 269.

5. Dicks, "Personality Traits," pp. 113–114.

6. Douglas M. Kelley, "Preliminary Studies of the Rorschach Records of the Nazi War Criminals," *Rorschach Research Exchange* 10 (1946), pp. 45–48; quote is on p. 47.

7. Ibid.

8. "No Geniuses," *New Yorker* (June 1, 1946), p. 6.

9. G. M. Gilbert, "Hermann Goering, Amiable Psychopath," *Journal of Abnormal and Social Psychology* 43 (1948), pp. 211–229; quote is on p. 217.

10. G. M. Gilbert, "The Mentality of SS Murderous Robots," *Yad Vashem Studies* 5 (1963), pp. 35–41; quote is on p. 36.

11. Ibid., p. 40.

12. See Eric A. Zillmer, Molly Harrower, Barry A. Ritzler, and Robert P. Archer, *The Quest for the Nazi Personality: A Psychological Investigation of Nazi War Criminals* (Hillsdale, N.J.: Lawrence Erlbaum, 1995), chap. 4.

13. Molly Harrower, "Were Hitler's Henchmen Mad?," *Psychology Today* (July 1976), pp. 76–80; quote is on p. 76.

14. Molly Harrower, "Rorschach Records of the Nazi War Criminals: An Experimental Study after 30 Years," *Journal of Personality Assessment* 40 (1976), pp. 341–351; quote is on p. 342.

15. Florence R. Miale and Michael Selzer, *The Nuremberg Mind: The Psychology of the Nazi Leaders* (New York: New York Times Book Company, 1975), p. 286.

16. Ibid., p. 287.

17. Harrower, "Were Hitler's Henchmen Mad?," p. 76.

18. Harrower, "Rorschach Records," p. 350.

19. Harrower, "Were Hitler's Henchmen Mad?," p. 80.

20. Scott O. Lilienfeld, James M. Wood, and Howard N. Garb, "The Scientific Status of Projective Techniques," *Psychological Science in the Public Interest* 1 (November 2000), p. 38. Their critical review of one specific projective technique, the Rorschach, is mirrored on a more general level by the American Psychological Association's suggested model graduate assessment curriculum for the twenty-first century—a curriculum that excludes training in projective techniques.

21. Zillmer et al., *Nazi Personality*, p. 194.

22. Heinz Hohne, *The Order of the Death's Head: The Story of Hitler's SS* (New York: Ballantine, 1971), p. 405.

23. Similarly, potential recruits into terrorist organizations who seem to be merely seeking danger and excitement are not encouraged. See McCauley and Segal, "Social Psychology of Terrorist Groups."

24. Hohne, *The Order of the Death's Head*, p. 405.

25. Hilberg, *The Destruction of the European Jews, Revised and Definitive Edition,* 3 vols. (New York: Holmes and Meier, 1985), 3:1011.

26. Browning, *Ordinary Men*, p. 165.

27. Quoted in Neil J. Kressel, *Mass Hate: The Global Rise of Genocide and Terror* (New York: Plenum Press, 1996), p. 117.

28. Browning, *Ordinary Men*, p. 69.

29. For additional information on Perpetration-Induced Traumatic Stress (PITS), see Rachel MacNair, "Psychological Reverberations for the Killers: Preliminary Historical Evidence for Perpetration-Induced Traumatic Stress," *Journal of Genocide Research* 3 (2001), pp. 273–282.

30. American Psychiatric Association, *Diagnostic and Statistical Manual of Mental Disorders*, 4th ed., text revision (Washington, D.C.: American Psychiatric Association, 2000), p. 685.

31. Lingens's testimony is quoted in Bernd Naumann's *Auschwitz: A Report on the Proceedings against Robert Karl Ludwig Mulka and Others before the Court at Frankfurt* (London: Pall Mall Press, 1966), p. 91.

32. The first section of the Kren and Rappoport quote is taken from their *The Holocaust and the Crisis of Human Behavior*, rev. ed. (New York: Holmes and Meier, 1994), p. 76. The second section of the quote, beginning with "Our judgement," is taken from the 1980 edition of the same book, p. 70.

33. Dirk Welmoed de Mildt, *In the Name of the People: Perpetrators of Genocide in the Reflection of Their Post-War Prosecution in West Germany* (London: Martinus Nijhoff, 1996), p. 14.

34. Dicks, "Personality Traits," pp. 137–138.

35. Elsewhere, Gilbert seemed to waver on his broad stamp of pathology among the Nuremberg defendants. He concluded that half of the defendants were suffering "no gross pathology." In other words, they were normal—albeit suffering from this deviate personality type. Another 25 percent, in his opinion, were diagnosed as suffering from relatively minor disorders such as emotional instability, dependency, inadequacy, or aggressiveness. Finally, a mere three prisoners were given more serious labels like "schizoid personality" or "paranoid neurosis." See his *Psychology of Dictatorship: Based on an Examination of the Leaders of Nazi Germany* (New York: Ronald Press, 1950).

36. Kelley, *22 Cells in Nuremberg*, p. 171.

37. Zillmer et al., *Nazi Personality*, p. 99.

38. Ibid., p. 119.

39. Ibid., p. 181.

40. *The Authoritarian Personality* (New York: Harper and Row, 1950) is Adorno, Frenkel-Brunswik, Levinson, and Sanford's classic work. The authors' respective contributions to the volume cannot be measured by the order of authorship because it was decided to list the contributors alphabetically. Later, Levinson and Sanford edited an abridged edition of the same title (New York: W. W. Norton, 1982).

41. As Franz Samelson points out in his "Authoritarianism from Berlin to Berkeley: On Social Psychology and History," *Journal of Social Issues* 42 (1986), pp. 191–208, Adorno et al. did briefly respond to the response set issue in the original work (see pp. 161, 280). It should be noted, however, that these were very epigrammatic one- or two-sentence responses that were only tied indirectly to the *F* scale and clearly did not anticipate the furor of methodological criticism that would follow.

42. See Jos D. Meloen, "The F Scale as a Predictor of Fascism: An Overview of 40 Years of Authoritarianism Research," in William F. Stone, Gerda Lederer, and Richard Christie, eds., *Strength and Weakness: The Authoritarian Personality Today* (New York: Springer-Verlag, 1993), pp. 47–69.

43. See Bob Altemeyer, *Right-Wing Authoritarianism* (Winnipeg: University of Manitoba Press, 1981) and *Enemies of Freedom: Understanding Right-Wing Authoritarianism* (San Francisco: Jossey-Bass, 1988).

44. See Gerda Lederer, "Authoritarianism in German Adolescents: Trends and Cross-Cultural Comparisons," in Stone et al., *Strength and Weakness*, pp. 182–198.

45. Kressel, *Mass Hate*, p. 229.

46. Unpublished doctoral dissertation cited in Zillmer et al., *Nazi Personality*, pp. 95–96.

47. John M. Steiner, "The SS Yesterday and Today: A Sociopsychological View," in J. E. Dimsdale, ed., *Survivors, Victims, and Perpetrators: Essays on the Nazi Holocaust* (Washington, D.C.: Hemisphere, 1980), p. 431.

48. Ervin Staub, *The Roots of Evil: The Origins of Genocide and Other Group Violence* (New York: Cambridge University Press, 1989), p. 134.

49. George C. Browder, *Hitler's Enforcers: The Gestapo and the SS Security Service in the Nazi Revolution* (New York: Oxford University Press, 1996), p. 168.

50. Ibid.

51. Browning, *Ordinary Men*, p. 169.

52. Ibid., p. 189.

53. Bauman's quote is from his *Modernity and the Holocaust* (Ithaca, N.Y.: Cornell University Press, 1989), p. 166.

The Massacre at Babi Yar

1. For further reading about the activities of the Einsatzgruppen, I recommend chap. 7 in Hilberg, *The Destruction of the European Jews*, vol. 1. An abridged version of the same work can be found in his one-volume student edition of the same name, also published by Holmes and Meier (1985). The *Historical Atlas of the Holocaust*, published by the United States Holocaust Memorial Museum (New York: Macmillan, 1996), includes several helpful maps on

the invasion of the Soviet Union and the murderous activities of the Einsatzgruppen (pp. 50-53).

2. The quote from the report to the chief of the Security Police and Security Service in Berlin was taken from Yitzhak Arad, Shmuel Krakowski, and Shmuel Spector's *The Einsatzgruppen Reports* (New York: Holocaust Library, 1989), p. 168, Operational Situation Report USSR No. 101.

3. The two eyewitness accounts, archived in the Central Agency for the State Administrations of Justice (Zentrale Stelle der Landesjustizverwaltungen) in Ludwigsburg, are excerpted from Ernst Klee, Willi Dressen, and Volker Riess, eds., *"The Good Old Days": The Holocaust as Seen by Its Perpetrators and Bystanders* (1988; reprint, New York: Free Press, 1991), pp. 63–67.

Chapter 4

1. One of the more intriguing sources on Arendt's life, and the controversy over *Eichmann in Jerusalem* (*Eichmann in Jerusalem: A Report on the Banality of Evil* [New York: Viking Press, 1963]), is Elisabeth Young-Bruehl's *Hannah Arendt: For Love of the World* (New Haven, Conn.: Yale University Press, 1982). Also recommended is Bernard J. Bergen's *The Banality of Evil: Hannah Arendt and "The Final Solution"* (Lanham, Md.: Rowman and Littlefield, 1998). Finally, a book by Elzbieta Ettinger (a survivor of the Warsaw ghetto), *Hannah Arendt/Martin Heidegger* (New Haven, Conn.: Yale University Press, 1995), explores one of the gossipy curiosities of Arendt's life—her passionate and secret love affair in the 1920s with the influential philosopher, and later prominent Nazi, Martin Heidegger.

2. Arendt, *Eichmann in Jerusalem*, p. 25.

3. Ibid., p. 287.

4. Ibid., p. 252.

5. See Elisabeth Young-Bruehl, "From the Pariah's Point of View: Reflections on Hannah Arendt's Life and Work," in Melvyn Hill, ed., *Hannah Arendt: The Recovery of the Public World* (New York: St. Martin's Press, 1979), p. 17.

6. Peter Novick, *The Holocaust in American Life* (New York: Houghton Mifflin, 1999), p. 135.

7. Arendt, *Eichmann in Jerusalem*, p. 25.

8. Ibid., p. 276.

9. Stephen Miller, "A Note on the Banality of Evil," *WQ: The Wilson Quarterly* 12 (Autumn 1998), pp. 54-59.

10. Raul Hilberg, *The Politics of Memory: The Journey of a Holocaust Historian* (Chicago: Ivan R. Dee, 1996), p. 150.

11. Norman Podhoretz, "Hannah Arendt on Eichmann: A Study in the Perversity of Brilliance," *Commentary* (1963), p. 206.

12. de Mildt, *In the Name of the People*, p. 311.

13. Michael Geyer, foreword to Hamburg Institute for Social Research, ed., *The German Army and Genocide: Crimes against War Prisoners, Jews, and Other Civilians, 1939–1944* (New York: New Press, 1999), p. 9.

14. Quoted in Stephen Miller, "A Note on the Banality of Evil," p. 55.

15. The original publication of Milgram's experiments on obedience to authority ap-

peared in a 1963 issue of the *Journal of Abnormal and Social Psychology* with the innocuous title "Behavioral Study of Obedience" ("Behavioral Study of Obedience," *Journal of Abnormal and Social Psychology* 67 [1963], pp. 371–378). Also helpful is his "The Compulsion to Do Evil: Obedience to Criminal Orders," *Patterns of Prejudice* 1 (1967), pp. 3–7. The complete and most authoritative account of Milgram's series of studies on obedience to authority can be found in his book *Obedience to Authority: An Experimental View* (New York: Harper and Row, 1974). There also are several notable journals and books devoted exclusively to the legacy of the Milgram experiments. Among the ones I consulted are "Perspectives on Obedience to Authority: The Legacy of the Milgram Experiments," *Journal of Social Issues* 51 (Fall 1995); Arthur G. Miller, *The Obedience Experiments: A Case Study of Controversy in the Social Sciences* (New York: Praeger, 1986); and Thomas Blass, ed., *Obedience to Authority: Current Perspectives on the Milgram Paradigm* (Mahweh, N.J.: Lawrence Erlbaum, 2000).

16. Milgram, "Behavioral Study of Obedience," p. 377.

17. The study on Munich citizens was David M. Mantell's "The Potential for Violence in Germany," *Journal of Social Issues* 27 (1971), pp. 101–112. As another example of the cross-cultural applicability of Milgram's findings, see Israel W. Charny and Daphna Fromer's fascinating description of some similar studies with Jewish Israelis, "The Readiness of Health Profession Students to Comply with a Hypothetical Program of Forced Migration of a Minority Population," *American Journal of Orthopsychiatry* 60 (1990), pp. 486–495.

18. See Andrew M. Colman, "Crowd Psychology in South African Murder Trials," *American Psychologist* 46 (October 1991), pp. 1071–1079.

19. Milgram, *Obedience to Authority*, p. 175. The Chicago fire Milgram was referencing actually took place in 1871, not 1898.

20. Ibid., p. 6.

21. Ibid., p. 175.

22. Ibid., p. 133.

23. Ibid., pp. 145–146.

24. Ibid., p. 143.

25. David M. Mantell and R. Panzarella, "Obedience and Responsibility," *British Journal of Social and Clinical Psychology* 15 (1976), p. 242.

26. Robert Jay Lifton, *The Nazi Doctors: Medical Killing and the Psychology of Genocide* (New York: Basic Books, 1986), p. 17; italicized material from Adolf Hitler, *Mein Kampf* (Boston: Houghton Mifflin, 1943), pp. 397–398.

27. For a comprehensive treatment of the Nazi biomedical and euthanasia programs, see Friedlander, *The Origins of Nazi Genocide*.

28. Lifton, *The Nazi Doctors*, p. 419.

29. Ibid., p. 423.

30. Ibid., p. 5.

31. Ibid., p. 418.

32. Ibid., p. 211.

33. Ibid., p. 424.

34. Ibid., p. 447.

35. Robert Jay Lifton and Eric Markusen, *The Genocidal Mentality: Nazi Holocaust and Nuclear Threat* (New York: Basic Books, 1990), p. 228.

36. Ervin Staub, *The Roots of Evil* (New York: Cambridge University Press, 1989), pp. 146–147.

37. Personal communication cited in John M. Darley, "Social Organization for the Production of Evil," *Psychological Inquiry* 3 (1992), pp. 199–218; quote is from p. 210. It should be noted, however, that elsewhere Lifton seems to imply a bit less compartmentalization, and a bit more permanence, as a result of evildoing. "I believe that once a man performs evil acts, he is changed as a man" (Lifton, "Reflections on Genocide," *Psychohistory Review* 14 [1986], pp. 39–54; quote is on p. 51).

38. Lifton, *The Nazi Doctors*, p. 458.

39. Darley, "Social Organization," p. 210.

40. Steiner, "The SS Yesterday and Today," p. 441.

41. Friedlander, *The Origins of Nazi Genocide*, p. 217.

42. Lifton, *The Nazi Doctors*, p. 420.

43. Berel Lang, *Act and Idea in the Nazi Genocide* (Chicago: University of Chicago Press, 1990), p. 53.

The Invasion of Dili

1. Etelvina Correia's testimony is taken from James Dunn, "Genocide in East Timor," in Samuel Totten, William S. Parsons, and Israel W. Charny, *Century of Genocide: Eyewitness Accounts and Critical Views* (New York: Garland Publishing, 1997), pp. 284–285.

2. Zito Soares's testimony is excerpted from TimorNet, an Internet page maintained by the University of Coimbra, Portugal, and devoted to information on East Timor (http://www.uc.pt/timor/stc2.htm). Soares was interviewed by Joao Keating and Isabel Bolas; I accessed the site on June 19, 2000.

3. Cited in Israel W. Charny, *Encyclopedia of Genocide*, 2 vols. (Santa Barbara, Calif.: ABC-CLIO, 1999), 1:193.

4. While the saga of East Timor continues, accessible introductions to the conflict can be found in Dunn, "Genocide in East Timor," pp. 264–290, and Frank Chalk and Kurt Jonassohn, *The History and Sociology of Genocide: Analyses and Case Studies* (New Haven, Conn.: Yale University Press, 1990), pp. 408–411, 451. The best overall account of East Timor's history is John G. Taylor, *East Timor: The Price of Freedom* (New York: Zed Books, 1999).

Chapter 5

1. Erich Fromm, *The Heart of Man: Its Genius for Good and Evil* (New York: Harper and Row, 1964), p. 123.

2. Quoted at http://www.rjgeib.com/thoughts/glad/glad.html, accessed December 2000.

3. See Franklin H. Littell's review of *Ordinary Men* in *Holocaust and Genocide Studies* 7 (1993), p. 123.

4. Quoted in Carl N. Degler, *In Search of Human Nature: The Decline and Revival of Darwinism in American Social Thought* (New York: Oxford University Press, 1991), p. 7.

5. Quoted in Henry Plotkin, *Evolution in Mind: An Introduction to Evolutionary Psychology* (Cambridge: Harvard University Press, 1998), p. 38.

6. William James, *The Principles of Psychology*, 2 vols. (Cambridge: Harvard University Press, 1981), p. 1004.

7. Sigmund Freud, *Civilization and Its Discontents* (1930; reprint, New York: Dover, 1994), p. 46.

8. Ibid.

9. Quoted in Ilham Dilman, *Freud and Human Nature* (London: Basil Blackwell, 1983), p. 130.

10. Freud, *Civilization and Its Discontents*, p. 49.

11. Quoted in Hans Schwarz, *Evil: A Historical and Theological Perspective* (Minneapolis: Fortress Press, 1995), p. 18.

12. John B. Watson, *Behaviorism* (New York: W. W. Norton, 1924), pp. 103–104.

13. See John Tooby and Leda Cosmides, "The Psychological Foundations of Culture," in Jerome H. Barkow, Leda Cosmides, and John Tooby, *The Adapted Mind: Evolutionary Psychology and the Generation of Culture* (New York: Oxford University Press, 1992), pp. 23–49.

14. Degler, *In Search of Human Nature*, p. 349.

15. Cited on p. 74 of Kari Konkola and Glenn Sunshine, "Theology and Evolutionary Psychology: A Historical Perspective on a Very Old Problem," *Skeptic* 7 (1999), pp. 74–80.

16. Philip Yancey, "Dark Nature," *Books and Culture* (March/April 1998), p. 10.

17. See Leda Cosmides and John Tooby, *Evolutionary Psychology: A Primer* (available at http://www.psych.ucsb.edu/research/cep/primer.html, 1997).

18. David M. Buss, Martie G. Haselton, Todd K. Shackelford, April L. Bleske, and Jerome C. Wakefield, "Adaptations, Exaptations, and Spandrels," *American Psychologist* 53 (1998), pp. 533–548; quote is from p. 539.

19. Cosmides and Tooby, *Evolutionary Psychology*, p. 6.

20. Ibid., p. 12.

21. Ibid. It should be noted that Tooby and Cosmides recognize there is no single EEA that captures the nearly 2-million-year period of the geological epoch known as the Pleistocene. Rather, they use "EEA" to refer to "a statistical composite of the adaptation-relevant properties of the ancestral environments encountered by members of ancestral populations, weighted by their frequency and their fitness consequences" (Tooby and Cosmides, "The Past Explains the Present: Adaptations and the Structure of Ancestral Environments," *Ethology and Sociobiology* 11 [1990], pp. 375–424; quote is on p. 386).

22. Elliott Sober and David Sloan Wilson, *Unto Others: The Evolution and Psychology of Unselfish Behavior* (Cambridge: Harvard University Press, 1998), p. 194.

23. Plotkin, *Evolution in Mind*, p. 229.

24. Ibid., p. 230.

25. Sober and Wilson, *Unto Others*, p. 9.

26. Steven Pinker, *How the Mind Works* (New York: W. W. Norton, 1997), p. 51.

27. Donald E. Brown, *Human Universals* (Philadelphia: Temple University Press, 1991), pp. 138–139.

28. W. G. Sumner, *Folkways* (New York: Ginn, 1906), pp. 12–13.

29. R. A. Hinde, "Patriotism: Is Kin Selection Both Necessary and Sufficient?," *Politics and the Life Sciences* 8 (1989), pp. 58–61; quote is on p. 60.

30. See Jacques-Philippe Leyens, Paola M. Paladino, Ramon Vaes, Jeroen Rodriguez-

Torres, Stephanie Demoulin, Armando Rodriguez-Perez, and Ruth Gaunt, "The Emotional Side of Prejudice: The Attribution of Secondary Emotions to Ingroups and Outgroups," *Personality and Social Psychology Bulletin* 4 (2000), pp. 186–197.

31. Quoted in Marilynn B. Brewer and Norman Miller, *Intergroup Relations* (Pacific Grove, Calif.: Brooks/Cole, 1996), pp. 47–48.

32. See Matt Ridley, *The Origins of Virtue: Human Instincts and the Evolution of Cooperation* (New York: Viking Penguin, 1997).

33. See Martin Daly and Margo Wilson, *Homicide* (New York: Aldine, 1988).

34. Ghiglieri, *The Dark Side of Man*, p. 211.

35. Steven J. C. Gaulin and Donald H. McBurney, *Psychology: An Evolutionary Approach* (Upper Saddle River, N.J.: Prentice Hall, 2001), p. 339.

36. These findings are discussed at length in A. M. Sluckin and P. K. Smith, "Two Approaches to the Concept of Dominance in Preschool Children," *Child Development* 48 (1977), pp. 917–923; Bruce J. Ellis, "The Evolution of Sexual Attraction: Evaluative Mechanisms in Women," in Barkow et al., *The Adapted Mind*, pp. 267–288; and J. S. Gillis, *Too Tall, Too Small* (Champaign, Ill.: Institute for Personality and Ability Testing, 1982).

37. See Konrad Lorenz, *On Aggression* (New York: Harcourt, Brace and World, 1963).

38. Richard Wrangham and Dale Peterson, *Demonic Males: Apes and the Origins of Human Violence* (Boston: Houghton Mifflin Company, 1996).

39. Ibid., p. 23.

40. Ibid., p. 63.

41. See, for instance, Hilary Rose and Steven Rose, *Alas, Poor Darwin: Arguments against Evolutionary Psychology* (New York: Harmony Books, 2000).

42. Stephen Jay Gould, "Exaptation: A Crucial Tool for Evolutionary Psychology," *Journal of Social Issues* 47 (1991), pp. 43–65.

43. See George Williams, *Adaptation and Natural Selection* (Princeton, N.J.: Princeton University Press, 1966).

44. Daniel C. Dennett, *Darwin's Dangerous Idea: Evolution and the Meanings of Life* (New York: Touchstone, 1995), pp. 80–83.

45. Rose and Rose, *Alas, Poor Darwin*, p. 299.

46. Gould, *Ever Since Darwin*, cited in Philip Appleman, ed., *Darwin* (New York: W. W. Norton, 2001), p. 415.

47. For additional information on the controversial work of the Charles Darwin Research Institute, see http://www.charlesdarwinresearch.org. I accessed the site in January 2001.

48. Edward Hagen, "The Evolutionary Psychology FAQ," Web site maintained by the Center for Evolutionary Psychology at the University of California, Santa Barbara, pp. 13–14 in printed version that I obtained on April 20, 2001, from the following URL: http://www.anth.ucsb.edu/projects/human/evpsychfaq.html.

49. James Q. Wilson, *The Moral Sense* (New York: Free Press, 1993), p. 251.

50. Pinker, *How the Mind Works*, p. 54.

51. Cited in ibid.

52. Ridley, *The Origins of Virtue*, cited in Appleman, *Darwin*, p. 522.

53. Konkola and Sunshine, "Theology and Evolutionary Psychology," p. 79.

54. Gourevitch, *We Wish to Inform You*, p. 239.

The Tonle Sap Massacre

1. A recent accessible review of the temples of Angkor can be found in Douglas Preston's "The Temples of Angkor: Still Under Attack," *National Geographic* 198 (August 2000), pp. 82–103. The definitive work on the genocide in Cambodia is Ben Kiernan's *The Pol Pot Regime: Race, Power, and Genocide in Cambodia under the Khmer Rouge, 1975–1979* (New Haven, Conn.: Yale University Press, 1996). As founder of the Cambodian Genocide Program at Yale University, Kiernan is one of the world's foremost authorities on Cambodia. See also Kiernan's chapter, "The Cambodian Genocide, 1975–1979," in Totten et al., *Century of Genocide*, pp. 334–371, and the chapter titled "Cambodia" in Chalk and Jonassohn, *The History and Sociology of Genocide*, pp. 398–407.

2. Ronnie Yimsut's testimony is excerpted from "From Sideshow to Genocide: Stories of the Cambodian Holocaust," an Internet page maintained by Andy Carvin (http://edweb. gsn.org/sideshow/stories/ronnieyimsut.html). I accessed the site on July 18, 2000. Two particularly poignant published memoirs are Loung Ung's *First They Killed My Father: A Daughter of Cambodia Remembers* (New York: HarperCollins, 2000) and Chanrithy Him's *When Broken Glass Floats: Growing Up under the Khmer Rouge* (New York: W. W. Norton, 2000).

Chapter 6

1. Christopher R. Browning, "Human Nature, Culture, and the Holocaust," *Chronicle of Higher Education* (October 18, 1996), p. A72.

2. Thomas Blass, "Understanding Behavior in the Milgram Obedience Experiment: The Role of Personality, Situations, and Their Interactions," *Journal of Personality and Social Psychology* 60 (1991), pp. 398–413; the quote is from p. 405.

3. Quoted in Hilberg, "The Nature of the Process," in J. E. Dimsdale, ed., *Survivors, Victims, and Perpetrators: Essays on the Nazi Holocaust* (Washington, D.C.: Hemisphere, 1980), p. 35.

4. Staub, *The Roots of Evil*, p. 75.

5. See David Norman Smith, "The Psychocultural Roots of Genocide."

6. Jochen von Lang (editor) in collaboration with Claus Sibyll, *Eichmann Interrogated: Transcripts from the Archives of the Israeli Police* (New York: Farrar, Straus & Giroux, 1983), pp. 291, 11, 159.

7. Gourevitch, *We Wish to Inform You*, p. 23.

8. Staub, *The Roots of Evil*, p. 50.

9. Staub, "The Roots of Evil," p. 183.

10. Robert J. Sternberg, "A Duplex Theory of Hate and Its Development and Its Application to Massacres and Genocide" (unpublished manuscript, 2001), p. 13.

11. See Felicia Pratto, Jim Sidanius, Lisa M. Stallworth, and Bertram F. Malle, "Social Dominance Orientation: A Personality Variable Predicting Social and Political Attitudes," *Journal of Personality and Social Psychology* 67 (1994), pp. 741–763, and Katherine J. Reynolds, John C. Turner, S. Alexander Haslam, and Michelle K. Ryan, "The Role of Personality and Group Factors in Explaining Prejudice," *Journal of Experimental Social Psychology* 37 (2001), pp. 427–434.

12. See Albert Bandura, "Moral Disengagement in the Perpetration of Inhumanities,"

Personality and Social Psychology Review 3 (1999), pp. 193–209, and "Exercise of Human Agency through Collective Efficacy," *Current Directions in Psychological Science* 9 (June 2000), pp. 75–78.

13. Gourevitch, *We Wish to Inform You*, p. 18.

14. Zajonc, "Massacres," p. 36.

15. Quoted in ibid., pp. 18, 27.

16. Bandura, "Moral Disengagement," p. 195.

17. See Hilberg, "The Nature of the Process," pp. 24–35.

18. Quoted in Michael Burleigh, *Ethics and Extermination: Reflections on Nazi Genocide* (New York: Cambridge University Press, 1997), p. 105.

19. Bandura, "Moral Disengagement," p. 195.

20. Ibid., p. 196.

21. Friedlander, "The T4 Killers," in Berenbaum and Peck, *The Holocaust and History*, p. 246.

22. Weinberg, "The Allies and the Holocaust," in Berenbaum and Peck, *The Holocaust and History*, pp. 488–489.

23. Klee et al., *"The Good Old Days,"* p. 78.

24. John Keegan, *A History of Warfare* (New York: Vintage Books, 1994).

25. See Browder, *Hitler's Enforcers*, pp. 170–174.

26. Baumeister, *Evil*, p. 25.

27. Roy F. Baumeister, Brad J. Bushman, and W. Keith Campbell, "Self-Esteem, Narcissism, and Aggression: Does Violence Result from Low Self-Esteem or from Threatened Egotism?," *Current Directions in Psychological Science* 9 (2000), pp. 26–29; quote is from p. 26.

28. Roy F. Baumeister, Laura Smart, and Joseph M. Boden, "Relation of Threatened Egotism to Violence and Aggression: The Dark Side of High Self-Esteem," *Psychological Review* 103 (1996), pp. 5–33; quote is from p. 24.

29. Ibid., p. 8.

30. Browder, *Hitler's Enforcers*, p. 171.

31. Evelin Gerda Lindner, "Were Ordinary Germans Hitler's 'Willing Executioners'?," *Idea: A Journal of Social Issues* 5 (December 11, 2000).

32. See Craig Haney, "Violence and the Capital Jury: Mechanisms of Moral Disengagement and the Impulse to Condemn to Death," *Stanford Law Review* 49 (1997), pp. 1447–1486.

Death of a Guatemalan Village

1. For more historical and demographic information on Guatemala, see Lillian Comas-Diaz, M. Brinton Lykes, and Renato D. Alarcon, "Ethnic Conflict and the Psychology of Liberation in Guatemala, Peru, and Puerto Rico," *American Psychologist* 53 (July 1998), pp. 778–792; T. Barry, *Inside Guatemala* (Albuquerque, N.M.: Inter-Hemispheric Education Resource Center, 1992); and Samuel Totten, "Genocide in Guatemala," in Charny, *Encyclopedia of Genocide*, 1:281–284.

For years, the United States trained numerous Guatemalan military leaders at its School of the Americas in Fort Benning, Georgia. Many of these leaders were active in the genocidal activities carried out by the Guatemalan government. For additional reading, see Jack Nelson-Pallmeyer, *School of Assassins: The Case for Closing the School of the Americas and for Fundamentally Changing U.S. Foreign Policy* (Maryknoll, N.Y.: Orbis Books, 1997).

2. Quoted at http://www.leftwatch.com/964, accessed October 19, 2000.

3. Excerpted from Victor Montejo, *Testimony: Death of a Guatemalan Village* (Willimantic, Conn.: Curbstone Press, 1987), pp. 81–86. See also Montejo's *Voices from Exile: Violence and Survival in Modern Maya History* (Norman: University of Oklahoma Press, 1999). Another compelling testimony, though mired in recent controversy about its authenticity, is Rigoberta Menchu, *I, Rigoberta Menchu, an Indian Woman of Guatemala* (London: Verso Editions, 1984).

4. See, for instance, Jeremy Nelson, "Documents Reveal Extent of U.S. Complicity in Guatemala's Repression," *Central America/Mexico Report* 20 (July 2000), available at http://www.rtfcam.org/report/volume_20/No_3/article_3.htm, accessed February 1, 2001.

Chapter 7

1. Philip G. Zimbardo, "Pathology of Imprisonment," *Society* 6 (1972), pp. 4, 6, 8; quote is on p. 6.

2. Milgram, "Some Conditions of Obedience and Disobedience," reprinted in Milgram, *The Individual in a Social World: Essays and Experiments* (Reading, Mass.: Addison-Wesley, 1977), p. 118.

3. Fred E. Katz, *Ordinary People and Extraordinary Evil: A Report on the Beguilings of Evil* (Albany: State University of New York, 1993), p. 31.

4. See, for instance, Arthur L. Beaman, C. M. Cole, M. Preston, Bonnel A. Klentz, and Nancy M. Steblay, "Fifteen Years of Foot-in-the-Door Research: A Meta-Analysis," *Personality and Social Psychology Bulletin* 9 (1983), pp. 181–196; John E. Hunter and Michael Burgoon, "Sequential-Request Persuasive Strategies: Meta-Analysis of Foot-in-the-Door and Door-in-the-Face," *Human Communication Research* 10 (1984), pp. 461–488.

5. Staub, *The Roots of Evil*, p. 17.

6. Lifton, *The Nazi Doctors*, p. 426.

7. Darley, "Social Organization," p. 208.

8. See Janice T. Gibson and Mika Haritos-Fatouros, "The Education of a Torturer," *Psychology Today* 20 (1986), pp. 50–58, and Mika Haritos-Fatouros, "The Official Torturer: A Learning Model for Obedience to the Authority of Violence," *Journal of Applied Social Psychology* 18 (1988), pp. 1107–1120.

9. Clendinnen, *Reading the Holocaust*, p. 141.

10. Ibid., p. 142.

11. Sereny cited in T. Des Pres, *The Survivor: An Anatomy of Life in the Death Camps* (New York: Pocket Books, 1977), p. 67.

12. David E. Stannard, *American Holocaust: Columbus and the Conquest of the New World* (New York: Oxford University Press, 1992), p. xi; from Major Scott Anthony, Report on the Conduct of the War, 38th Congress, 2d sess. (1865), p. 27.

13. Hilberg, "The Nature of the Process," p. 23.

14. Gourevitch, *We Wish to Inform You*, p. 24.

15. Browning, *Ordinary Men*, p. 161.

16. Lifton, *The Nazi Doctors*, p. 195; Kremer quote taken from Katz, *Ordinary People and Extraordinary Evil*, p. 52.

17. Rudolf Hoess, *Commandant of Auschwitz: The Autobiography of Rudolf Hoess*, trans. C. FitzGibbon (London: Weidenfeld and Nicolson, 1959), p. 163.

18. Quoted in Dee Brown, *Bury My Heart at Wounded Knee*, p. 90.

19. Iris Chang, *The Rape of Nanking: The Forgotten Holocaust of World War II* (New York: BasicBooks, 1997).

20. Honda Katsuichi, *The Nanjing Massacre: A Japanese Journalist Confronts Japan's National Shame* (New York: M. E. Sharpe, 1999).

21. Jacques Pauw, "Inside the Mind of Torture: The Story of Apartheid's Electrician," *Covert Action Quarterly* (Winter 1998), p. 22.

22. Staub, *The Roots of Evil*, p. 134.

23. Balakian, *Black Dog of Fate*, p. 256.

24. See the classic study by John M. Darley and Bibb Latane, "Bystander Intervention in Emergencies: Diffusion of Responsibility," *Journal of Personality and Social Psychology* 8 (1968), pp. 377–383.

25. Baumeister, *Evil*, p. 325.

26. Darley, "Social Organization," p. 210.

27. Lifton, *The Nazi Doctors*, p. 55.

28. Philip G. Zimbardo, "The Human Choice: Individuation, Reason, and Order vs. Deindividuation, Impulse, and Chaos," in W. J. Arnold and D. Levine, eds., *Nebraska Symposium on Motivation* (Lincoln: University of Nebraska Press, 1969), pp. 237–307.

29. Robert I. Watson Jr., "Investigation into Deindividuation Using a Cross-Cultural Survey Technique," *Journal of Personality and Social Psychology* 25 (1973), pp. 342–345.

30. Brian Mullen, "Atrocity as a Function of Lynch Mob Composition: A Self-Attention Perspective," *Personality and Social Psychology Bulletin* 12 (1986), pp. 187–197.

31. Jan T. Gross, *Neighbors: The Destruction of the Jewish Community in Jedwabne, Poland* (Princeton, N.J.: Princeton University Press, 2001), pp. 120–121.

32. Browning, *Ordinary Men*, p. 185.

33. Klee et al., *"The Good Old Days,"* p. 78.

34. Germaine Tillion, *Ravensbruck* (Garden City, N.J.: Anchor Books, 1975), p. 69.

35. Philip G. Zimbardo, "Pathology of Imprisonment"; Craig Haney, Curtis Banks, and Philip G. Zimbardo, "Interpersonal Dynamics in a Simulated Prison," *International Journal of Criminology and Penology* 1 (1983), pp. 69–97; see also the following URL: http://www.zimbardo.com/prisonexp.

36. Philip G. Zimbardo, Christina Maslach, and Craig Haney, "Reflections on the Stanford Prison Experiment," in Blass, *Obedience to Authority*, p. 225.

37. Quoted in Browning, *Ordinary Men*, p. 168.

38. Ibid.

39. Zimbardo, "Pathology of Imprisonment," p. 4.

40. Kurt Lewin, "Cultural Reconstruction," *Journal of Abnormal and Social Psychology* 38 (1943), pp. 166–173, reprinted in Kurt Lewin, *Resolving Social Conflicts: Selected Papers on Group Dynamics*, ed. Gertrud Weiss Lewin (New York: Harper and Row, 1948), p. 38.

41. Staub, *The Roots of Evil*, p. 17.

42. Richard Grunberger, *The 12-Year Reich: A Social History of Nazi Germany, 1933–1945* (New York: Holt, Rinehart and Winston, 1971), p. 27.

43. See Herbert C. Kelman and V. Lee Hamilton, *Crimes of Obedience: Toward a Social Psychology of Authority and Responsibility* (New Haven, Conn.: Yale University Press, 1989).

44. Quoted in Charny, *Encyclopedia of Genocide*, 2:479.

45. Fromm, *The Heart of Man*, p. 20.

46. Darley, "Social Organization," p. 210.

47. Fromm, *The Heart of Man*, p. 149.

The Church of Ntamara

1. The Twa would come to account for less than 1 percent of Rwanda's population by the time of the genocide.

2. Physicians for Human Rights, *Rwanda 1994: A Report of the Genocide* (London: Physicians for Human Rights, 1994), p. 11.

3. Quoted in Rakiya Omaar, *Rwanda: Death, Despair and Defiance* (London: African Rights, 1994), pp. 488–489.

4. For additional reading, I recommend Kressel, *Mass Hate*, chap. 4; Gourevitch, *We Wish to Inform You*; David Norman Smith, "The Psychocultural Roots of Genocide"; Gerard Prunier, *The Rwanda Crisis: History of a Genocide* (New York: Columbia University Press, 1995); Alain Destexhe, *Rwanda and Genocide in the Twentieth Century* (New York: New York University Press, 1994); Fergal Keane, *Season of Blood: A Rwandan Journey* (New York: Viking, 1995); Barrie Collins, *Obedience in Rwanda: A Critical Question* (Sheffield, U.K.: Sheffield Hallam University Press, 1998); Howard Adelman and Astri Suhrke, eds., *The Path of a Genocide: The Rwanda Crisis from Uganda to Zaire* (New Brunswick, N.Y.: Transaction Publishers, 1999); and Rene Lemarchand, "The Rwanda Genocide," in Totten et al., *Century of Genocide*.

Chapter 8

1. Grossman, *On Killing*, p. 108. Grossman illustrates his general point with specific examples from the cases of individuals who dropped the atomic bombs on Hiroshima and Nagasaki. Contrary to popular myth, he argues, these individuals evidenced no indications of psychological problems stemming from their involvement in the maximum-range killing of thousands upon thousands of Japanese civilian victims.

2. Orlando Patterson, *Slavery and Social Death: A Comparative Study* (Cambridge: Harvard University Press, 1990).

3. Marion A. Kaplan, *Between Dignity and Despair*, p. 5.

4. Helen Fein, *Accounting for Genocide* (New York: Free Press, 1979), p. 30.

5. M. Sherif, O. J. Harvey, B. J. White, W. R. Hood, and C. Sherif, *Intergroup Conflict and Cooperation: The Robbers' Cave Experiment* (Norman: Oklahoma Book Exchange, 1961).

6. Pat Shipman, "On the Nature of Violence," *American Scientist* 89 (November–December, 2001), p. 489.

7. See Henri Tajfel and John C. Turner, "An Integrative Theory of Intergroup Conflict," in W. Austin and S. Worchel, eds., *The Social Psychology of Intergroup Relations* (Monterey, Calif.: Brooks/Cole, 1979).

8. Ibid., p. 38.

9. Marilynn B. Brewer, "The Psychology of Prejudice: Ingroup Love or Outgroup Hate?," *Journal of Social Issues* 55 (1999), p. 435.

10. Ibid., p. 442.

11. Cited in Kai Erikson, "On Pseudospeciation and Social Speciation," in Charles B. Strozier and Michael Flynn, eds., *Genocide, War, and Human Survival* (Lanham, Md.: Rowman and Littlefield), p. 57.

12. Ibid., pp. 51–52.

13. Elizabeth Hall, "A Conversation with Erik Erikson," *Psychology Today* (June 1983), p. 30.

14. Albert Bandura, B. Underwood, and M. E. Fromson, "Disinhibition of Aggression through Diffusion of Responsibility and Dehumanization of Victims," *Journal of Research in Personality* 9 (1975), pp. 253–269.

15. Kelman and Hamilton, *Crimes of Obedience*, pp. 19–20.

16. Haig A. Bosmajian, *The Language of Oppression* (Lanham, Md.: University Press of America, 1983), p. 29.

17. Quoted in Joanna Bourke, *An Intimate History of Killing: Face-to-Face Killing in Twentieth-Century Warfare* (New York: Basic Books, 1999), p. 193.

18. Claude Lanzmann, *Shoah: The Complete Text of the Acclaimed Holocaust Film* (New York: Da Capo Press, 1985), pp. 92–93.

19. Quoted in Yehuda Bauer, *The Holocaust in Historical Perspective* (Seattle: University of Washington Press, 1978), p. 8.

20. Quoted in Harold Kaplan, *Conscience and Memory: Meditations in a Museum of the Holocaust* (Chicago: University of Chicago Press, 1994), p. 130.

21. See Gabriele Rosenthal, *The Holocaust in Three Generations: Families of Victims and Perpetrators of the Nazi Regime* (Washington, D.C.: Cassell, 1998).

22. John Sabini, *Social Psychology*, 2d ed. (New York: W. W. Norton, 1995), p. 58.

23. Quoted in Sam Keen, *Faces of the Enemy: Reflections of the Hostile Imagination* (San Francisco: Harper and Row, 1986), p. 26.

24. Quoted in Haney, "Violence and the Capital Jury," p. 1451.

25. Milgram, *Obedience to Authority*, p. 16.

26. Milgram, "The Compulsion to Do Evil," p. 7.

27. See Melvin J. Lerner, *The Belief in a Just World: A Fundamental Decision* (New York: Plenum Press, 1980).

28. Zick Rubin and Letitia Anne Peplau, "Who Believes in a Just World?," *Journal of Social Issues* 31 (1975), pp. 65–89.

29. Melvin J. Lerner and Carolyn Simmons, "Observer's Reaction to the 'Innocent Victim': Compassion or Rejection," *Journal of Personality and Social Psychology* 4 (1966), pp. 203–210.

30. Milgram, "The Compulsion to Do Evil," p. 7.

31. Timothy C. Brock and Arnold H. Buss, "Dissonance, Aggression, and the Evaluation of Pain," *Journal of Abnormal and Social Psychology* 65 (1962), pp. 197–202.

32. Quoted in Staub, *The Roots of Evil*, p. 186.

33. Rosenthal, *The Holocaust in Three Generations*, p. 243.

34. Lars Rensmann, "Belated Narratives: New Testimonies of Average Perpetrators and Bystanders in the Context of Contemporary Post-Holocaust Germany," paper presented at

the Twenty-Ninth Annual Scholar's Conference on the Holocaust and the Churches (Garden City, N.Y., 1999), p. 10.

35. Gross, *Neighbors*, pp. 98–99, 233.

36. Rosenthal, *The Holocaust in Three Generations*, p. 244; quoted in Henry V. Dicks, *Licensed Mass Murder: A Socio-Psychological Study of Some SS Killers* (New York: Basic Books, 1972), p. 262.

37. See Arendt, *Eichmann in Jerusalem*.

38. Quoted in Gitta Sereny, *Into That Darkness: An Examination of Conscience* (New York: Random House, 1982), pp. 232–233.

39. Grossman, *On Killing*, pp. 209–210.

40. C. I. Hovland and R. Sears, "Minor Studies in Aggression: 6. Correlation of Lynchings with Economic Indices," *Journal of Psychology* 9 (1940), pp. 301–310.

41. Staub, *The Roots of Evil*, p. 17.

42. Keen, *Faces of the Enemy*, p. 9.

43. Wrangham and Peterson, *Demonic Males*, p. 196.

The "Safe Area" of Srebrenica

1. The testimony of Zumra Shekhomerovic is taken from the documentary film *Srebrenica: A Cry from the Grave*. The testimony can be accessed on-line at http://www.pbs.org/wnet/cryfromthegrave/eyewitnesses/eyewitness.html; I accessed the site July 19, 2001.

2. The account of Huseinovic is excerpted from Jan Willem Honig and Norbert Both, *Srebrenica: Record of a War Crime* (New York: Penguin, 1996), p. 56.

3. Ibid., p. 62.

4. For additional reading, I recommend Steven L. Burg, "Genocide in Bosnia-Herzegovina?," in Totten et al., *Century of Genocide*; Roger Cohen, *Hearts Grown Brutal: Sagas of Sarajevo* (New York: Random House, 1998); Chuck Sudetic, *Blood and Vengeance: One Family's Story of the War in Bosnia* (New York: Penguin, 1998); the documentary film, *Srebrenica: A Cry from the Grave*, directed and produced by Leslie Woodhead, an Antelope Films production for BBC2's Storyville in association with Thirteen/WNET for PBS (information on-line at http://www.pbs.org/wnet/cryfromthegrave/); David Rohde, *Endgame: The Betrayal and Fall of Srebrenica, Europe's Worst Massacre since World War II* (New York: Farrar, Straus and Giroux, 1997); Florence Hartmann, "Bosnia," in Roy Gutman and David Rieff, eds., *Crimes of War: What the Public Should Know* (New York: W. W. Norton, 1999), pp. 50–56; Kressel, *Mass Hate*, chap. 2; William Shawcross, *Deliver Us from Evil: Peacekeepers, Warlords, and a World of Endless Conflict* (New York: Simon and Schuster, 2000), chap. 6; Honig and Both, *Record of a War Crime*. Information on the Srebrenica Justice Campaign can be found at http://ds.dial.pipex.com/srebrenica.justice/.

Chapter 9

1. Shawcross, *Deliver Us from Evil*, p. 411.

2. Jill D. Kester, "Success and Surprises in the Application of Psychological Science: From Eyewitness Testimony to Post-Genocide Healing," *American Psychological Society Observer* 14 (July/August 2001), p. 11.

3. Cited at http://ww.wfa.org/issues/wicc/helmsrel.html, accessed September 13, 2001.

4. For additional information about the International Criminal Court, see the URLs http://www.iccnow.org and http://www.un.org/law/icc/index.html.

5. Lyall Watson, *Dark Nature: A Natural History of Evil* (New York: HarperPerennial, 1995), p. 140.

6. Eric Voegelin, *Hitler and the Germans* (Columbia: University of Missouri Press, 1999), p. 105.

7. Sherif et al., *The Robbers' Cave Experiment.*

8. R. R. Blake and J. S. Mouton, "From Theory to Practice in Interface Problem Solving," in S. Worchel and W. Austin, eds., *Psychology of Intergroup Relations* (Chicago: Nelson-Hall, 1986), pp. 67–82.

9. See Haney, "Violence and the Capital Jury."

10. Bandura, "Moral Disengagement," p. 200.

11. Quoted in William S. Parsons and Samuel Totten, "Teaching and Learning about Genocide: Questions of Content, Rationale, and Methodology," *Social Education* (February 1991), p. 85.

12. While old-school militarists maintain that female combatants disrupt the concept of war as a masculine activity, political scientist Jean Bethke Elshtain of the University of Chicago has shown that throughout history women have also been militant in wartime. In the first century B.C.E., Plutarch described barbarians "whose fierce women charged with swords and axes, and fell upon their opponents uttering a hideous outcry. . . . When summoned to surrender, they killed their children, slaughtered one another, or hanged themselves to trees" (*Women and War* [New York: Basic Books, 1987], p. 197). In World War II, more than 1 million Soviet women served in combat as snipers, machine gunners, artillery women, tank women, and bombers. Since the 1970s, there has been an increased proportion, and acceptance, of women in the military across the world. As Gwynne Dyer summarizes: "Women have almost always fought side by side with men in guerrilla or revolutionary wars, and there isn't any evidence they are significantly worse at killing people" (quoted in Grossman, *On Killing*, p. xii).

More recently, the role of female perpetrators as bureaucratic or brutal genocidal killers has become more extensively documented. For instance, Bronwyn Rebekah McFarland-Icke of the University of Maryland's European Division has recently analyzed the role of German psychiatric nurses—many of whom were women—who directly or indirectly participated in the Nazis' program of medicalized killing (see her *Nurses in Nazi Germany: Moral Choice in History*, Princeton, N.J.: Princeton University Press, 1999). We also know that there are records of 3,950 women concentration camp guards in the archives of Ravensbruck. Ravensbruck, a concentration camp about one hundred kilometers north of Berlin, served as the training center for many, but not all, female guards, suggesting that the actual number was much higher. Women guards worked at camps with female prisoners, where they had direct supervision of women inmates.

While women—comprising about 10 percent of concentration camp staff—never were placed in administrative control of a concentration camp, but always served under male authority, they did possess the same power over life and death as their male counterparts. They murdered as easily; their sadism was no less. They felt little noticeable compassion for "fellow" women prisoners. They carried out a wide range of violent abuse of prisoners. There are few survivor recollections of SS women guards being "soft" or more "lenient" than their male colleagues. The evidence of their atrocities is in the memoir literature, in trial records, and in the records maintained by the camp administrators.

Women as perpetrators of extraordinary evil are not limited to the Holocaust. During Pol Pot's genocidal reign, many Khmer Rouge women committed the same atrocities as men. Most recently, in August 1999, Pauline Nyiramasuhuko, the former Rwandan minister for family and women's affairs, became the first woman to be indicted by the United Nations Tribunal on charges of genocide, complicity in genocide, conspiracy to commit genocide, crimes against humanity, and serious violations of the Geneva Conventions. She was accused of identifying, kidnapping, and killing members of the Tutsi population. Her original indictment was later amended to include six additional counts, one of which accused her of being responsible for rape "as part of a widespread and systematic attack against a civilian population on political, ethnic and racial grounds."

To this point, detailed analyses of female perpetrators have been restricted, in part, because of the assumptions we often bring to the investigation. Susannah Heschel of the Department of Religion of Dartmouth College points out that, since the immediate postwar era, the portrayal of women concentration camp guards has been demonized or eroticized. She writes: "Both memoirs and the press generally describe women guards as more cruel than men, not because of the nature of the atrocities they committed, but because of the pleasures, usually erotic, they allegedly enjoyed while tormenting prisoners. In addition, in both memoirs and the press, women's acts of cruelty either collide with their physical beauty or express their physical ugliness. Whatever the case, women's cruelty is presented with a sense of surprise, transgressing gender expectation" ("Feminist Theory and the Perpetrators," paper presented at the Lessons and Legacies Conference [Chicago: Northwestern University, 2000], p. 4). In contrast, Heschel argues, male perpetrators have continued to belong to humanity and be recognized as normal, ordinary men, albeit criminal. Almost universally, men's cruelty is discussed without reference to their gender.

Such disparate gender images present significant methodological problems. There may well be some significant gender differences in how ordinary females commit extraordinary evil. For example, there is some reason to expect that conformity to peer pressure may not carry the same weight for female perpetrators as it does for males. As another example, revisiting Milgram's experiments, we see that, compared to men, women share a strikingly similar proclivity for obedience to authority. As a matter of fact, compared to male subjects in the initial experiment, the exact same percentage of female subjects (65 percent) exhibited full compliance. The mean maximum shock level, though, was significantly lower for females. Where no males defied the experimenter before the 300-volt level, 25 percent of females had done so by that same level.

The challenge for future research is to transcend our gender expectations that women are basically innocent by nature, so that their acts of cruelty are viewed as deviant and abnormal, and approach their perpetration of extraordinary evil the same way we have men— as ordinary people influenced by dispositional, situational, and environmental factors. Only when we stop stereotyping the assumed extraordinariness of female perpetrators can we determine the applicability of this model to female perpetrators of extraordinary evil.

SELECTED BIBLIOGRAPHY

*Works marked with an asterisk are not directly cited in this book, but I recommend them for additional reading.

Altemeyer, Bob. *The Authoritarian Specter*. Cambridge: Harvard University Press, 1996.
———.*Enemies of Freedom: Understanding Right-Wing Authoritarianism*. San Francisco: Jossey-Bass, 1988.
Appleman, Philip, ed. *Darwin*. New York: W. W. Norton, 2001.
Arendt, Hannah. *Eichmann in Jerusalem: A Report on the Banality of Evil*. New York: Viking Press, 1963.
*Ashmore, Richard D., Lee Jussim, and David Wilder, eds. *Social Identity, Intergroup Conflict, and Conflict Reduction*. New York: Oxford University Press, 2001.
Balakian, Peter. *Black Dog of Fate: A Memoir*. New York: Basic Books, 1997.
Bandura, Albert. "Moral Disengagement in the Perpetration of Inhumanities." *Personality and Social Psychology Review 3* (1999), pp. 193–209.
Barkow, Jerome H., Leda Cosmides, and John Tooby. *The Adapted Mind: Evolutionary Psychology and the Generation of Culture*. New York: Oxford University Press, 1992.
*Bar-On, Dan. *Legacy of Silence: Encounters with Children of the Third Reich*. Cambridge: Harvard University Press, 1989.
*Bauer, Yehuda. *Rethinking the Holocaust*. New Haven, Conn.: Yale University Press, 2001.
Baumeister, Roy F. *Evil: Inside Human Cruelty and Violence*. New York: W. H. Freeman and Company, 1997.
Baumeister, Roy F., Brad J. Bushman, and W. Keith Campbell. "Self-Esteem, Narcissism, and Aggression: Does Violence Result from Low Self-Esteem or from Threatened Egotism?" *Current Directions in Psychological Science 9* (2000), pp. 26–29.

Baumeister, Roy F., Laura Smart, and Joseph M. Boden. "Relation of Threatened Egotism to Violence and Aggression: The Dark Side of High Self-Esteem." *Psychological Review* 103 (1996), pp. 5–33.

*Beck, Aaron T. *Prisoners of Hate: The Cognitive Basis of Anger, Hostility, and Violence.* New York: HarperCollins, 1999.

*Benz, Wolfgang. *The Holocaust: A German Historian Examines the Genocide.* New York: Columbia University Press, 1999.

Berenbaum, Michael, and Abraham J. Peck. *The Holocaust and History: The Known, the Unknown, the Disputed, and the Reexamined.* Bloomington: Indiana University Press, 1998.

Blass, Thomas, ed. *Obedience to Authority: Current Perspectives on the Milgram Paradigm.* Mahweh, N.J.: Lawrence Erlbaum, 2000.

Blass, Thomas. "Understanding Behavior in the Milgram Obedience Experiment: The Role of Personality, Situations, and Their Interactions." *Journal of Personality and Social Psychology* 60 (1991), pp. 398–413.

Bourke, Joanna. *An Intimate History of Killing: Face-to-Face Killing in Twentieth-Century Warfare.* New York: Basic Books, 1999.

Bridgman, Jon. *The End of the Holocaust: The Liberation of the Camps.* Portland, Ore.: Areopagitica Press, 1990.

Browder, George C. *Hitler's Enforcers: The Gestapo and the SS Security Service in the Nazi Revolution.* New York: Oxford University Press, 1996.

Brown, Dee. *Bury My Heart at Wounded Knee: An Indian History of the American West.* New York: Henry Holt, 1970.

Brown, Donald E. *Human Universals.* Philadelphia: Temple University Press, 1991.

Browning, Christopher R. *Ordinary Men: Reserve Police Battalion 101 and the Final Solution in Poland.* New York: HarperCollins, 1992.

———. "Review Essay: Daniel Goldhagen's Willing Executioners." *History and Memory* 8 (1996), pp. 88–108.

Brustein, William. *The Logic of Evil: The Social Origins of the Nazi Party, 1925–1933.* New Haven, Conn.: Yale University Press, 1996.

Burleigh, Michael. *Ethics and Extermination: Reflections on Nazi Genocide.* New York: Cambridge University Press, 1997.

*Burleigh, Michael, and Wolfgang Wippermann. *The Racial State: Germany, 1933–1945.* New York: Cambridge University Press, 1991.

Buss, David M., Martie G. Haselton, Todd K. Shackelford, April L. Bleske, and Jerome C. Wakefield. "Adaptations, Exaptations, and Spandrels." *American Psychologist* 53 (1998), pp. 533–548.

Chalk, Frank, and Kurt Jonassohn. *The History and Sociology of Genocide: Analyses and Case Studies.* New Haven, Conn.: Yale University Press, 1990.

Charny, Israel W. *Encyclopedia of Genocide.* 2 vols. Santa Barbara, Calif.: ABC-CLIO, 1999.

*———. "Genocide and Mass Destruction: Doing Harm to Others as a Missing Dimension in Psychopathology." *Psychiatry* 49 (1986), pp. 144–157.

*Charny, Israel W., and Chanan Rapaport. *How Can We Commit the Unthinkable? Genocide: The Human Cancer.* Boulder, Colo.: Westview Press, 1982.

Churchill, Ward. *A Little Matter of Genocide: Holocaust and Denial in the Americas, 1492 to the Present.* San Francisco: City Lights Books, 1997.

Clendinnen, Inga. *Reading the Holocaust*. New York: Cambridge University Press, 1999.

*Conroy, John. *Unspeakable Acts, Ordinary People: The Dynamics of Torture*. New York: Alfred A. Knopf, 2000.

Cosmides, Leda, and John Tooby. *Evolutionary Psychology: A Primer*. Available at http:// www.psych.ucsb.edu/research/cep/primer.html, 1997.

Darley, John M. "Social Organization for the Production of Evil." *Psychological Inquiry* 3 (1992), pp. 199–218.

*Dawidowicz, Lucy S. *The War against the Jews, 1933–1945*. Originally published 1975. Reprint, New York: Bantam Books, 1986.

Degler, Carl N. *In Search of Human Nature: The Decline and Revival of Darwinism in American Social Thought*. New York: Oxford University Press, 1991.

Dennett, Daniel C. *Darwin's Dangerous Idea: Evolution and the Meanings of Life*. New York: Touchstone, 1995.

Dicks, Henry V. *Licensed Mass Murder: A Socio-Psychological Study of Some SS Killers*. New York: Basic Books, 1972.

———. "Personality Traits and National Socialist Ideology: A War-Time Study of German Prisoners of War." *Human Relations* 3 (1950), pp. 111–154.

Dimsdale, J. E., ed. *Survivors, Victims, and Perpetrators: Essays on the Nazi Holocaust*. Washington, D.C.: Hemisphere, 1980.

*Du Preez, Wilhelmus Petrus. *Genocide: The Psychology of Mass Murder*. London/New York: Boyars/Bowerdean, 1994.

Fein, Helen. *Accounting for Genocide*. New York: Free Press, 1979.

Friedlander, Henry. *The Origins of Nazi Genocide: From Euthanasia to the Final Solution*. Chapel Hill: University of North Carolina Press, 1995.

Fromm, Erich. *The Heart of Man: Its Genius for Good and Evil*. New York: Harper and Row, 1964.

Gaulin, Steven J. C., and Donald H. McBurney. *Psychology: An Evolutionary Approach*. Upper Saddle River, N.J.: Prentice Hall, 2001.

Geyer, Michael. Foreword to Hamburg Institute for Social Research, ed., *The German Army and Genocide: Crimes against War Prisoners, Jews, and Other Civilians, 1939–1944*. New York: New Press, 1999.

Ghiglieri, Michael P. *The Dark Side of Man: Tracing the Origins of Male Violence*. Reading, Mass.: Perseus, 1999.

Gibson, Janice T., and Mika Haritos-Fatouros. "The Education of a Torturer." *Psychology Today* 20 (1986), pp. 50–58.

Gilbert, G. M. "Hermann Goering, Amiable Psychopath." *Journal of Abnormal and Social Psychology* 43 (1948), pp. 211–229.

———. "The Mentality of SS Murderous Robots." *Yad Vashem Studies* 5 (1963), pp. 35–41.

*Glass, James M. *"Life Unworthy of Life": Racial Phobia and Mass Murder in Hitler's Germany*. New York: Basic Books, 1997.

Goldhagen, Daniel Jonah. *Hitler's Willing Executioners: Ordinary Germans and the Holocaust*. New York: Alfred A. Knopf, 1996.

Gourevitch, Philip. *We Wish to Inform You That Tomorrow We Will Be Killed with Our Families: Stories from Rwanda*. New York: Farrar, Straus and Giroux, 1998.

Gross, Jan T. *Neighbors: The Destruction of the Jewish Community in Jedwabne, Poland*. Princeton, N.J.: Princeton University Press, 2001.

Grossman, Dave. *On Killing: The Psychological Cost of Learning to Kill in War and Society.* Boston: Little, Brown and Company, 1995.

Gutman, Roy, and David Rieff, eds. *Crimes of War: What the Public Should Know.* New York: W. W. Norton, 1999.

Haney, Craig. "Violence and the Capital Jury: Mechanisms of Moral Disengagement and the Impulse to Condemn to Death." *Stanford Law Review* 49 (1997), pp. 1447–1486.

Haritos-Fatouros, M. "The Official Torturer: A Learning Model for Obedience to the Authority of Violence." *Journal of Applied Social Psychology* 18 (1988), pp. 1107–1120.

Harrower, Molly. "Rorschach Records of the Nazi War Criminals: An Experimental Study after 30 Years." *Journal of Personality Assessment* 40 (1976), pp. 341–351.

———. "Were Hitler's Henchmen Mad?" *Psychology Today* (July 1976), pp. 76–80.

Hilberg, Raul. *The Politics of Memory: The Journey of a Holocaust Historian.* Chicago: Ivan R. Dee, 1996.

———. *The Destruction of the European Jews, Revised and Definitive Edition.* 3 vols. New York: Holmes and Meier, 1985.

Hinde, R. A. "Patriotism: Is Kin Selection Both Necessary and Sufficient?" *Politics and the Life Sciences* 8 (1989), pp. 58–61.

Hohne, Heinz. *The Order of the Death's Head: The Story of Hitler's SS.* New York: Ballantine, 1971.

Horowitz, Donald L. *The Deadly Ethnic Riot.* Berkeley: University of California Press, 2001.

Horwitz, Gordon J. *In the Shadow of Death: Living outside the Gates of Mauthausen.* New York: Free Press, 1990.

*Jacobs, Alan. "Aspects of Survival: Triumph over Death and Onliness." *Transactional Analysis Journal* 21 (1991), pp. 4–11.

*Johnson, Eric A. *Nazi Terror: Gestapo, Jews, and Ordinary Germans.* New York: Basic Books, 1999.

Kaplan, Marion A. *Between Dignity and Despair: Jewish Life in Nazi Germany.* New York: Oxford University Press, 1998.

Katz, Fred E. *Ordinary People and Extraordinary Evil: A Report on the Beguilings of Evil.* Albany: State University of New York, 1993.

Keen, Sam. *Faces of the Enemy: Reflections of the Hostile Imagination.* San Francisco: Harper and Row, 1986.

Kelley, Douglas M. "Preliminary Studies of the Rorschach Records of the Nazi War Criminals." *Rorschach Research Exchange* 10 (1946), pp. 45–48.

———. *22 Cells in Nuremberg: A Psychiatrist Examines the Nazi War Criminals.* New York: MacFadden Books, 1947.

Kelman, Herbert C., and V. Lee Hamilton. *Crimes of Obedience: Toward a Social Psychology of Authority and Responsibility.* New Haven, Conn.: Yale University Press, 1989.

Klee, Ernst, Willi Dressen, and Volker Riess, eds. *"The Good Old Days": The Holocaust as Seen by Its Perpetrators and Bystanders.* Originally published 1988. Reprint, New York: Free Press, 1991.

Konkola, Kari, and Glenn Sunshine. "Theology and Evolutionary Psychology: A Historical Perspective on a Very Old Problem." *Skeptic* 7 (1999), pp. 74–80.

Kressel, Neil J. *Mass Hate: The Global Rise of Genocide and Terror.* New York: Plenum Press, 1996.

Kruger, Arnd. "'Once the Olympics Are Through, We'll Beat Up the Jew': German Jewish

Sport, 1898–1938, and the Anti-Semitic Discourse." *Journal of Sport History* 26 (1999), pp. 353–375.

Le Bon, Gustave. *The Crowd: A Study of the Popular Mind*. 2d ed. Originally published in 1895. Reprint, Dunwoody, Ga.: Norman S. Berg, 1968.

Le Chene, Evelyn. *Mauthausen: The History of a Death Camp*. London: Methuen, 1971.

Levi, Primo. *The Drowned and the Saved*. London: Michael Joseph, 1986.

Lifton, Robert Jay. *The Nazi Doctors: Medical Killing and the Psychology of Genocide*. New York: Basic Books, 1986.

———. "Reflections on Genocide." *Psychohistory Review* 14 (1986), pp. 39–54.

Lifton, Robert Jay, and Eric Markusen. *The Genocidal Mentality: Nazi Holocaust and Nuclear Threat*. New York: Basic Books, 1990.

*Mann, Michael. "Were the Perpetrators of Genocide 'Ordinary Men' or 'Real Nazis'? Results from Fifteen Hundred Biographies." *Holocaust and Genocide Studies* 14 (2000), pp. 331–366.

*Marrus, Michael R. *The Holocaust in History*. New York: Penguin, 1987.

———. *The Nuremberg War Crimes Trial, 1945–1946: A Documentary History*. Boston: Bedford/St. Martin's, 1997.

*Matthaus, Jurgen. "What about the 'Ordinary Men'?: The German Order Police and the Holocaust in the Occupied Soviet Union." *Holocaust and Genocide Studies* 10 (1996), pp. 134–150.

McCauley, Clark R., and Mary E. Segal. "Social Psychology of Terrorist Groups." In *Group Processes and Intergroup Relations: Review of Personality and Social Psychology*, ed. Clyde Hendrick, pp. 231–256. Newbury Park, Calif.: Sage Publications, 1987.

Miale, F. R., and M. Selzer. *The Nuremberg Mind: The Psychology of the Nazi Leaders*. New York: New York Times Book Company, 1975.

de Mildt, Dirk Welmoed. *In the Name of the People: Perpetrators of Genocide in the Reflection of Their Post-War Prosecution in West Germany*. London: Martinus Nijhoff, 1996.

Milgram, Stanley. "Behavioral Study of Obedience." *Journal of Abnormal and Social Psychology* 67 (1963), pp. 371–378.

———. "The Compulsion to Do Evil: Obedience to Criminal Orders." *Patterns of Prejudice* 1 (1967), pp. 3–7.

———. *Obedience to Authority: An Experimental View*. New York: Harper and Row, 1974.

Miller, Arthur G., Anne K. Gordon, and Amy M. Buddie. "Accounting for Evil and Cruelty: Is to Explain to Condone?" *Personality and Social Psychology Review* 3 (1999), pp. 254–268.

Niebuhr, Reinhold. *Moral Man and Immoral Society: A Study in Ethics and Politics*. New York: Charles Scribner's Sons, 1932.

Novick, Peter. *The Holocaust in American Life*. New York: Houghton Mifflin, 1999.

*Opotow, S. "Moral Exclusion and Injustice: An Introduction." *Journal of Social Issues* 46 (1990), pp. 173–182.

*Palmer, Jack A., and Linda K. Palmer. *Evolutionary Psychology: The Ultimate Origins of Human Behavior*. Boston: Allyn and Bacon, 2002.

Peck, M. Scott. *People of the Lie: The Hope for Healing Human Evil*. New York: Simon and Schuster, 1983.

Persico, Joseph E. *Nuremberg: Infamy on Trial*. New York: Penguin Books, 1994.

Pinker, Steven. *How the Mind Works*. New York: W. W. Norton, 1997.

Plotkin, Henry. *Evolution in Mind: An Introduction to Evolutionary Psychology*. Cambridge: Harvard University Press, 1998.

*Posner, Gerald L. *Hitler's Children: Sons and Daughters of Third Reich Leaders Speak Out about Themselves and Their Fathers*. New York: Random House, 1991.

Pratto, Felicia, Jim Sidanius, Lisa M. Stallworth, and Bertram F. Malle. "Social Dominance Orientation: A Personality Variable Predicting Social and Political Attitudes." *Journal of Personality and Social Psychology* 67 (1994), pp. 741–763.

Rose, Hilary, and Steven Rose. *Alas, Poor Darwin: Arguments against Evolutionary Psychology*. New York: Harmony Books, 2000.

Rosenbaum, Ron. *Explaining Hitler: The Search for the Origins of His Evil*. New York: Random House, 1998.

Rosenthal, Gabriele. *The Holocaust in Three Generations: Families of Victims and Perpetrators of the Nazi Regime*. Washington, D.C.: Cassell, 1998.

*Ross, Marc Howard. "The Role of Evolution in Ethnocentric Conflict and Its Management." *Journal of Social Issues* 47 (1991), pp. 167–185.

Shawcross, William. *Deliver Us from Evil: Peacekeepers, Warlords, and a World of Endless Conflict*. New York: Simon and Schuster, 2000.

Sherif, M., O. J. Harvey, B. J. White, W. R. Hood, and C. Sherif. *Intergroup Conflict and Cooperation: The Robbers' Cave Experiment*. Norman: Oklahoma Book Exchange, 1961.

*Sichrovsky, Peter. *Born Guilty: Children of Nazi Families*. Trans. Jean Steinberg. New York: Basic Books, 1988.

Smith, David Norman. "The Psychocultural Roots of Genocide: Legitimacy and Crisis in Rwanda." *American Psychologist* 53 (July 1998), pp. 743–753.

Sober, Elliott, and David Sloan Wilson. *Unto Others: The Evolution and Psychology of Unselfish Behavior*. Cambridge: Harvard University Press, 1998.

*Sofsky, Wolfgang. *The Order of Terror: The Concentration Camp*. Trans. William Templer. Princeton, N.J.: Princeton University Press, 1999.

Staub, Ervin. *The Roots of Evil: The Origins of Genocide and Other Group Violence*. New York: Cambridge University Press, 1989.

———. "The Roots of Evil: Social Conditions, Culture, Personality, and Basic Human Needs." *Personality and Social Psychology Review* 3 (1999), pp. 179–192.

Steiner, John M. "The SS Yesterday and Today: A Sociopsychological View." In *Survivors, Victims, and Perpetrators: Essays on the Nazi Holocaust*, ed. J. E. Dimsdale, pp. 405–456. Washington, D.C.: Hemisphere, 1980.

Sternberg, Robert J. "A Duplex Theory of Hate and Its Development and Its Application to Massacres and Genocide." Unpublished manuscript, 2001.

Stone, William F., Gerda Lederer, and Richard Christie, eds. *Strength and Weakness: The Authoritarian Personality Today*. New York: Springer-Verlag, 1993.

Tooby, John, and Leda Cosmides. "The Past Explains the Present: Adaptations and the Structure of Ancestral Environments." *Ethology and Sociobiology* 11 (1990), pp. 375–424.

Totten, Samuel, William S. Parsons, and Israel W. Charny. *Century of Genocide: Eyewitness Accounts and Critical Views*. New York: Garland Publishing, 1997.

*Waller, James E. "Ordinary People, Extraordinary Evil: Understanding the Institutional Frameworks of Evildoing." *Proteus* 12 (1995), pp. 12–16.

*———. "Perpetrators of the Holocaust: Divided and Unitary Self Conceptions of Evil doing." *Holocaust and Genocide Studies* 10 (1996), pp. 11–33.

Wallimann, Isidor, and Michael N. Dobkowski, eds. *Genocide and the Modern Age: Etiology and Case Studies of Mass Death.* Syracuse, N.Y.: Syracuse University Press, 2000.

Watson, Lyall. *Dark Nature: A Natural History of Evil.* New York: HarperPerennial, 1995.

*Weiss, John. *Ideology of Death.* Chicago: Ivan R. Dee, 1996.

Wilson, James. *The Earth Shall Weep: A History of Native America.* New York: Grove Press, 1998.

Wilson, James Q. *The Moral Sense.* New York: Free Press, 1993.

Wolff, Kurt H. "For a Sociology of Evil." *Journal of Social Issues* 25 (1969), pp. 111–125.

Wrangham, Richard, and Dale Peterson. *Demonic Males: Apes and the Origins of Human Violence.* Boston: Houghton Mifflin Company, 1996.

Zajonc, R. B. "Massacres: Mass Murder in the Name of Moral Imperatives." Unpublished manuscript, 2000.

Zillmer, Eric A., Molly Harrower, Barry A. Ritzler, and Robert P. Archer. *The Quest for the Nazi Personality: A Psychological Investigation of Nazi War Criminals.* Hillsdale, N.J.: Lawrence Erlbaum, 1995.

Zimbardo, Philip G. "Pathology of Imprisonment." *Society* 6 (1972), pp. 4, 6, 8.

INDEX

Abdul-Hamid, II, Sultan, 50
accentuation effect, 240
adaptations, 146
adaptive problems, 147
Adorno, Theodor, 76
aggression
    and self-esteem, 193–194
agentic state, 108–111
Aktion Reinhard, 99, 100
Altemeyer, Bob, 81–82
American Military Tribunal, 92
American Servicemembers' Protection Act
    (ASPA), 270
Amnesty International, 128
ancestral shadow, 19, 134, 153, 271
Antisocial Personality Disorder (APD), 69–70
Archer, Robert P., 65
Arendt, Hannah, 94–102, 121, 253
Armenia, genocide in, 50–54, 252
assumed similarity effect, 239
Augustine, Saint, 137
authoritarian personality, 76–86
    and its applicability to perpetrators of ex-
        traordinary evil, 83–86
    measurement of, 79
    personality dimensions of, 78–79
    waning of interest in, 80–81
authoritarian sleepers, 84
authority orientation, 180–182
    definition of, 180
Avdic, Nezad, 261

Babi Yar, 88–93
Balakian, Peter, 51
banality of evil
    Arendt's conception of, 96–98
    reaction to, 98–99, 101–102
Bandura, Albert, 185–190, 244, 249, 274
Bankier, David, 42
Banks, Curt, 221
Bassiouni, Cherif, 262
Bauman, Zygmunt, 87
Baumeister, Roy, 17, 193, 214
Behaviorism (Watson), 143
Belo, Carlos Filipe Ximenes, 127
Bent, Robert, 25
Berkovits, Eliezer, 267
Bettelheim, Bruno, 15
Beveridge, Sen. Albert J., 187
binding factors of the group, 20, 134, 212–220
    definition of, 212
*Black Dog of Fate: An American Son Uncovers His
    Armenian Past* (Balakian), 51
blaming the victims, 20, 134, 237, 238, 249–
    256
Blass, Thomas, 178, 181
Blobel, Paul, 92
Bonner, Raymond, 69
Bormann, Martin, 56
Bosmajian, Haig, 246
Bosnia, 191, 215, 217
    "ethnic cleansing" in, 189
Brewer, Marilynn, 243

Brock, Timothy, 251
Browder, George C., 84, 193, 195
Brown, Donald, 154
Browning, Christopher
   critique of Goldhagen, 45, 46, 49
   on understanding perpetrators, 16, 177
   Reserve Police Battalion 101, 68–69, 86, 87,
     118–119, 183, 209, 218, 223
Brustein, William, 41–42
Bultmann, Rudolf, 94
Bush, President George, 270
Buss, Arnold, 251
Buss, David, 146

Calley, Lt. William, 106
Cambodia, 191, 237
   genocide in, 169–174
Cambodian Genocide Program (Yale Univer-
   sity), 170
Caputo, Philip, 249
Chang, Iris, 211
Charny, Israel, 48
Chivington, Col. John Milton, 24
Churchill, Ward, 23
Civilization and Its Discontents (Freud), 141
Clendinnen, Inga, 17, 207
Clinton, President Bill, 269
collective potentiation, 36
Coming of Age in Samoa (Mead), 143
conformity to peer pressure, 218–220
Connor, Lt. James, 25
contrast effect, 189
Correia, Etelvina, 125
Cosmides, Leda, 145, 148, 149, 152
Crowd: A Study of the Popular Mind, The (Le Bon),
   30
cultural belief systems, 20, 134, 178–185
culture of cruelty, 20, 134, 203–204, 273
   definition of, 203

Dadrian, Vahakn, 284 n. 1, 285 n. 3
Daly, Martin, 155
Darley, John, 119, 206, 228
   research on bystander intervention, 213–214
Darwin, Charles, 139–141, 150
Deadly Ethnic Riot, The (Horowitz), 34
de Mildt, Dick, 71, 94, 119, 120, 121
   research on German postwar trials, 99–100
Degler, Carl, 144
dehumanization of the victims, 20, 134, 237–
   238, 244–249
deindividuation, 216–218
Delahunt, Rep. William D., 270
Dennett, Daniel, 162, 165
Descartes, René, 138
Descent of Man, The (Darwin), 139
desire for social dominance, 19, 134, 156–160
   as related to physical traits, 157
*Diagnostic and Statistical Manual of Mental Disor-
   ders* (*DSM-IV-TR*), 69, 70, 114
Dicks, Henry V., 36, 58, 72, 253

diffusion of responsibility, 212–216
Dili, invasion of, 124–129
dissociation, 114
divided self, 121
Djemal Pasha, 50, 55
Dobrodeljane, Kosovo, ix
Dodd, Christopher, 270
Donitz, Karl, 57
doubling, 113–120
   characteristics of, 115
   critique of, 116–120
Dyer, Gwynne, 300 n. 12

East Timor, 124–129
ego-organizational links, 193, 195–196
Eichmann, Adolf, 61, 95, 181, 210, 254
*Eichmann in Jerusalem: A Report on the Banality
   of Evil* (Arendt), 96
Einsatzgruppen, 88
   activities of, 88–93
   trials of, 92–93
Einstein, Albert, 136
eliminationist antisemitism
   as central motive for the Holocaust, 38–39
   critique of, 39–48
   definition of, 37
   uniqueness of, 37–38
Elshtain, Jean Bethke, 300 n. 12
Enver Pasha, 50, 55
Environment of Evolutionary Adaptedness
   (EEA), 148
Epstein, Leslie, 102
Erikson, Erik, 76, 244
escalating commitments, 205–207
ethnocentrism, 19, 134, 153–156
   definition of, 154
euphemistic labeling of evil actions, 188–
   189
Euthanasia Aktion, 99
evil
   human, 12
   natural, 12
   nature of, 10–13
   nature of extraordinary human evil, 13–15
   understanding, 15–18
evolutionary psychology (EP)
   applied to understanding extraordinary
     human evil, 149–160
   critique of, 160–166
   definition of, 144–145
exaptations, 161
Exner's Comprehensive System (CS), 65–66
exonerating comparisons, 189–190
external, controlling influences on one's life,
   178–180
   religious belief systems, 179–180
extraordinary human evil, 13–15

F scale, 79–81
*Faces of the Enemy: Reflections of the Hostile Imagi-
   nation* (Keen), 256

Face to Face: The Changing State of Racism across America (Waller), xiii
Fatima, Ademovic, 262
Fein, Helen, 237
female perpetrators, 276–277, 300–301 n. 12
Forgas, J. P., 155
Frankl, Viktor, 71
Frenkel-Brunswik, Else, 76
Freud, Sigmund
    and concept of instincts, 141–142
    on group psychology, 30–31
Friedlander, Henry, 46, 120, 191
Friedlander, Saul, 9
Fromm, Erich, 76, 137, 227, 229
fundamental attribution error (FAE), 228

Garcia, Romeo Lucas, 200
Gaulin, Steven, 156
genocide
    definition of, xi
    prevention of, 268–269
    punishment of, 269–270
    stopping of, 269
Genovese, Kitty, 213
German Army and Genocide: Crimes against War Prisoners, Jews, and Other Civilians, 1941– 1944 (Institute for Social Research, Hamburg), 100–101, 121
German Turner organization, 40–41
Geyer, Michael, 101
Ghiglieri, Michael, x, 156
Gibson, Janice, 206, 247
Gilbert, Gustave, 59–64, 73, 74
Glass, James M., 37
Godi, 159
Goebbels, Joseph, 56
Goldhagen, Daniel Jonah, 183
    and the influence of an extraordinary ideology, 36–39
    critique of, 39–48
Gombe National Park, 159
Goodall, Jane, 159
Göring, Hermann, 56, 61
Gould, Stephen Jay, 161, 163
Gourevitch, Philip, 182, 186
greedy reductionism, 162
Greene, Maxine, 275
Gregg, Richard, 33
Gross, Jan T., 217, 253
Grossman, Lt. Col. David, 33, 34, 236, 255
group polarization, 35
Group Psychology and Analysis of the Ego (Freud), 30
group selection
    arguments for, 151–152
    Darwin's view of, 150
    definition of, 150
Grunberger, Richard, 225
Guatemala
    massacres in, 197–201
Guatemala's Commission for Historical Clarification, 200

Habyarimana, Juvenal, 231
Hagen, Edward, 164–165
Hamilton, V. Lee, 225, 245
Haney, Craig, 196, 221, 274
Haritos-Fatouros, Mika, 206, 247
Harrower, Molly, 62–63, 64, 65
hate
    burning, 184
    Sternberg's ideology of, 184
    three components of, 184
Heidegger, Martin, 94
Helms, Sen. Jesse, 269–270
Heschel, Susannah, 301 n. 12
Hess, Rudolf, 36, 56–57, 210
Heydrich, Reinhard, 4, 56
Hilberg, Raul, 67–68, 99, 189
    on moral justification by perpetrators, 188
    on repression of conscience by perpetrators, 208
Himmler, Heinrich, 7, 56
Hinde, R. A., 155
History of Warfare, A (Keegan), 192
Hitler, Adolf, 3, 44, 56, 188, 224, 225
    and authorization of the T4 project, 112
    and external, controlling influences, 179
    as a dummy or puppet, 38, 252
Hitler's Willing Executioners: Ordinary Germans and the Holocaust (Goldhagen), 36–48
Hobbes, Thomas, 11, 137, 142
Hofer, Fritz, 89
Hohne, Heinz, 67
Holocaust
    activities of Einsatzgruppen in, 88–93
    and Mauthausen, 3–8
    and the Nuremberg Trials, 55–57
    as caused by eliminationist antisemitism, 36–39
    as exemplar of extraordinary human evil, 22
    number of perpetrators in, 14
Horowitz, Donald L., 34
Horwitz, Gordon J., 3
Houghton, Rep. Amo, 270
Hovland, C. I., 255
human nature
    definition of, 136–138
    in modern social science, 138–144
    and its influence on extraordinary human evil, 149–160, 166–168
hunter-gatherer ancestors, 147–149
Huseinovic, Hakija, 261
Hyde, Rep. Henry, 270

identities of the perpetrators, 20, 134, 176–177, 272
ideological commitment, 182–185
Ignatyev, Count Nikolai Pavlovich, 41
Indian Wars, 24
informational social influence, 219–220
in-group bias, 241–244
instinct
    as defined by Darwin, 140

instinct *(coninued)*
    as defined by Freud, 141–142
    as defined by James, 140–141
    as opposed by behaviorism, 142–143
interhamwe, 232–233
International Congress of the World Federation
    of Mental Health, 62
International Criminal Court (ICC), 269–270
International Criminal Tribunal for the former
    Yugoslavia (ICTY), 262–263
International Military Tribunal (IMT), 56
International Work Group for Indigenous Af-
    fairs, 28

Jaffe, Dave, 221
James, William, 113, 140
Jaspers, Karl, 94
Jedwabne, Poland, 217, 253
Just-World Scale (JWS), 250–251

Kagame, Paul, 235
Kaplan, Marion A., 40, 237
Karadzic, Radovan, 263
Karakaj massacre, 261
Katsuichi, Honda, 211
Katz, Fred, 203
Keegan, John, 192
Keen, Sam, 256
Kelley, Douglas M., 59–63, 73
Kelman, Herbert C., 225, 245
Kerry, Sen. John, 174
Kershaw, Ian, 42
Khmer Rouge, 169–170, 174, 182
Kiernan, Ben, 170
Klemperer, Victor, 43–44
Konkola, Kari, 167
Kremer, Johann Paul, 209–210
Kren, George M., 71
Kressel, Neil, 82
Krstic, Radislav, 263
Kruger, Arnd, 40–41
Krupp, Gustav, 56

Laden, Osama bin, xi
Lang, Berel, 122
Lantos, Rep. Tom, 270
Latane, Bibb, 213
Le Bon, Gustav, 29–30, 34
Lederer, Gerda, 81
Lemkin, Raphael, xi
Lerner, Melvin, 250, 251
Levi, Primo, 46, 236
Levinson, Daniel, 76
Lewin, Kurt, 224
Ley, Robert, 56, 58
Lifton, Robert Jay, 121, 122, 206, 209, 227
    concept of doubling, 113–116
    critique of doubling, 116–120
    diffusion of responsibility in Nazi doctors,
      214–215
Lindner, Evelin Gerda, 196

Lingens, Ella, 70
Littell, Franklin, 138
Lorenz, Konrad, 144, 158–159

"mad Nazi" thesis, 55–71
manifest destiny, 187
Mantell, David Mark, 110–111
Markusen, Erik, 118
Marrus, Michael R., 56
Maslow, Abraham, 76
mass killing, xi
Matama, Hillali, 159
Mauthausen, 3–8
McBurney, Donald, 156
McCauley, Clark, 35
McFarland-Icke, Bronwyn Rebekah, 300 n. 12
Mead, Margaret, 143
Mein Kampf (Hitler), 38, 84, 185
Meloen, Jos D., 81
Menchu, Rigoberta, 200
merger of role and person, 20, 134, 220–227
Merton, Thomas, 55
Miale, Florence R., 63–64
Milgram, Stanley, 10, 121, 122, 209, 221, 236,
    249, 251, 274
    agentic state, 108–111
    binding factors of the group, 212
    critique of the agentic state, 110–111
    limitations of "obedience to authority" exper-
      iments in explaining extraordinary evil,
      107–108
    "obedience to authority" experiments,
      102–111
    on a situationist perspective, 203
    subsequent "obedience to authority" studies,
      105–106
Miller, Arthur G., 16
Miller, Stephen, 98
Milosevic, Slobodan, 258, 262, 263
minimal group experiments, 241–243
Mladic, Ratko, 263
model of extraordinary human evil
    and its applicability to female perpetrators,
      276–277, 300–301 n. 12
    directions for future research, 275–278
    overview of, 133–135
Montejo, Victor, 198
Montt, Efrain Rios, 198, 200
moral disengagement, 20, 134, 185–190
moral justification, 186–188
Moral Man and Immoral Society (Niebuhr), 31–32
Morris, Desmond, 144
Mrugamba, Edmond, 167
Mukeshimana, Josianne, 233
Mullen, Brian, 217
Murray, Henry, 57
My Lai massacre, 32, 106

Naked Ape, The (Morris), 144
National Defense Council Foundation, xi
naturalistic fallacy, 165–166

natural selection, theory of
　role in designing universal reasoning circuits,
　　146–147
　three ingredients of, 139
Nazi Doctors: Medical Killing and the Psychology of Genocide, The (Lifton), 113
"Nazi personality," search for the, 72–87
Niebuhr, Reinhold, 31–32, 33, 34
Nol, Gen. Lon, 169
normative social influence, 218–219
Novick, Peter, 97
Ntamara, massacre at, 230–235
Nuremberg Diary (Gilbert), 61
Nuremberg Mind: The Psychology of Nazi Leaders, The (Miale and Selzer), 63
Nuremberg Trials, 55–57
Nyilinkwaya, Theodore, 209
Nyiramasuhuko, Pauline, 301 n. 12

obedience to authority
　experiments by Milgram, 102–111
　experiments' limitations in explaining
　　extraordinary evil, 107–108
　and subsequent studies, 105–106
On Aggression (Lorenz), 144, 159
On Killing: The Psychological Cost of Learning to Kill in War and Society (Grossman), 33, 236
On the Origin of Species by Means of Natural Selection (Darwin), 139
Operation Barbarossa, 88
out-group homogeneity effect, 240

pan-adaptationism, 161
Panzarella, Robert, 110–111
Patterson, Orlando, 237
Peck, M. Scott, 32, 34
People of the Lie: The Hope for Healing Human Evil (Peck), 32
Peplau, Letitia Anne, 250
Perpetration-Induced Traumatic Stress (PITS), 286 n. 29
Persico, Joseph E., 57
Personality and Social Psychology Review, 11
personality disorder, 69
personal self-interest, 193–196
personal shadow, 113–114
Peterson, Dale, 159, 160, 257
Physicians for Human Rights, 232
Pinker, Steven, 152, 165, 166
Plotkin, Henry, 151
Podhoretz, Norman, 99
Pol Pot, 169, 174, 182
Portillo, President Alfonso, 201
Powell, Secretary of State Colin, 270
power of personalization, 274–275
Pratto, Felicia, 185
Prejudice across America (Waller), xiii
Prescott, Carlo, 221
Principles of Psychology (James), 140
professional socialization, 20, 134, 203–211
pseudospeciation, 244

Psychological Foundations of the Wehrmacht (Dicks), 72
Psychology of Dictatorship: Based on an Examination of the Leaders of Nazi Germany (Gilbert), 61
psychopathology and extraordinary human evil, 55–71

Radio Télévision Libre des Mille Collines (RTLMC), 184–185
Ramos-Horta, Jose, 127
Rank, Otto, 113
Rape of Nanking, The (Chang), 211
Rappoport, Leon, 71
Rasch, Otto, 93
rational self-interest, 20, 134, 176–177, 190–196
Reader, The (Schlink), 15
Reich, Wilhelm, 76
Rensmann, Lars, 253
repression of conscience, 208–211
Resnick, Mark N., 83
Revolutionary Front for East Timor Independence (FRETILIN), 124–125
Ridley, Matt, 155, 166
Right-Wing Authoritarianism (RWA), 82
ritual conduct, 207–208
Ritzler, Barry A., 65
Robber's Cave experiment, 238, 241, 274
Rorschach, Hermann, 59
Rorschach technique, 59–60
Rose, Steven, 162
Rosenbaum, Ron, 38
Rosenthal, Gabriele, 247, 252, 253
Rubenstein, Richard L., 19
Rubin, Zick, 250
Rumor of War, A (Caputo), 249
Rushton, J. Philippe, 164
Rwanda, 184, 186, 191, 215, 217
　authoritarian tradition in, 181–182
　"bush clearing" in, 189
　genocide in, 230–235
　number of perpetrators in, 14
Rwandese Patriotic Front (RPF), 231

Sabini, John, 248
Salilovic, Zulfo, 261
Sand Creek massacre, 24–26, 27, 211
Sanford, Nevitt, 76
Santa Cruz massacre, 126–127, 128
scapegoating, 255–256
Schlemmer, Eva, 43
Schlink, Bernhard, 15
Sears, R., 255
self-esteem
　as motive for in-group bias, 242–243
　and its relationship with aggression, 193–194
Segal, Mary, 35
Selzer, Michael, 63
Sereny, Gitta, 207
Shawcross, William, 267

Shekhomerovic, Zumra, 259
Sherif, Muzafer, 238, 274
Shipman, Pat, 239
Sidanius, Jim, 185
Sierra Leone, 191
Simmons, Carolyn, 251
Skinner, B. F., 143
Smith, David Norman, 181
Smith, John, 26
Soares, Zito, 126
Sober, Elliott, 151, 152
social categorization, 239, 242, 243
Social Darwinism, 164
social death, 237
    of slavery, 237
    of the victims, 20, 134, 238, 257, 273
social dominance orientation (SDO), 185
social identity theory, 242–243
social influence
    three processes of, 225–226
Sokolowski, Julian, 253
Solzhenitsyn, Alexander, 175
Sontag, Susan, 12
spandrels, 161
Specter of Creeping Exculpation, 165
Srebrenica massacre, 258–263
Stagner, Ross, 76
Standard Social Science Model (SSSM), 143–144
Stanford Prison Experiment (SPE), 221–224
Stangl, Franz, 207, 254
Stannard, David, 207
Staub, Ervin, 84, 118, 194, 211, 225
    authority orientation, 180–182
    ideology, definition of, 183
    on escalating commitments, 205–206
    on scapegoating, 256
    research on reconciliation after genocide,
        268–269
Steinbeck, John, 138
Steiner, John M., 83, 119
Sternberg, Robert, 184
Stoppard, Tom, 202
Study of Instinct (Tinbergen), 144
Sudan, xii
Sumner, W. G., 154
Sunshine, Glenn, 167

T4, 112–113
Taino, 23
Tajfel, Henri, 155, 241–243
Talaat Bey, 50, 55, 212
Tehlirian, Soghomon, 212
threatened egotism, 193–194

Timorese Democratic Union (UDT), 124–125
Tinbergen, Nikolaus, 144
Tito, Marshal, 258
Tonle Sap massacre, 169–174
Tooby, John, 145, 148, 149, 152
22 Cells in Nuremberg: A Psychiatrist Examines the
    Nazi War Criminals (Kelley), 61

ultra-Darwinian, 161–162
unitary self, 121–123
United Nation's International Criminal Tribunal
    for Rwanda, 235, 301
Universal People, 154
universal reasoning circuits, 145–146, 153
us-them thinking, 20, 134, 237, 238–244

van Vuuren, Paul, 211
Vietnam, 190
Voegelin, Eric, 272

Watson, John B., 142–143
Watson, Lyall, 154, 272
Watson, Robert, 216
Wechsler-Bellevue Intelligence Test, 59
Weinberg, Gerhard, 192
Werner, Kurt, 91
Wiesel, Elie, x
Wiesenthal, Simon, 5
Williams, George, 161
Wilson, David Sloan, 151, 152
Wilson, James, 165
Wilson, Margo, 155
Wolff, Kurt, 11
Wolterstorff, Nicholas, 9
Wrangham, Richard, 159, 160, 257
Wrinkle in Time, A (L'Engle), 18

xenophobia, 19, 134, 153–156
    definition of, 155

yetzer ha-ra, 138
yetzer ha-tov, 138
Yimsut, Ronnie, 170–174
Young-Bruehl, Elisabeth, 97

Zajonc, Robert, 35–36, 187
Ziereis, Franz, 5–8, 36, 49
Zillmer, Eric A., 65, 73, 86
Zimbardo, Philip, 10
    and deindividuation, 216
    on a situationist perspective, 203
    Stanford Prison Experiment (SPE), 221–224
Zvornik, Bosnia, 262